Anna Jameson, Anna Jameson

Legends Of The Monastic Orders

As Represented In The Fine Arts

Anna Jameson, Anna Jameson

Legends Of The Monastic Orders
As Represented In The Fine Arts

ISBN/EAN: 9783741100604

Manufactured in Europe, USA, Canada, Australia, Japa

Cover: Foto ©Thomas Meinert / pixelio.de

Manufactured and distributed by brebook publishing software
(www.brebook.com)

Anna Jameson, Anna Jameson

Legends Of The Monastic Orders

Legends

OF

The Monastic Orders

AS REPRESENTED IN THE FINE ARTS.

FORMING THE SECOND SERIES OF SACRED AND LEGENDARY ART

BY MRS. JAMESON.

NEW EDITION.

LONDON:

LONGMANS, GREEN, AND CO.

AND NEW YORK: 15 EAST 16th STREET.

1890.

Ballantyne Press
BALLANTYNE, HANSON AND CO.
EDINBURGH AND LONDON

CONTENTS.

———⟡———

ST. BENEDICT AND THE EARLY BENEDICTINES IN ITALY, FRANCE, SPAIN, AND FLANDERS.

THE BENEDICTINES IN ENGLAND AND IN GERMANY.

THE REFORMED BENEDICTINES.

ORDERS DERIVED FROM THE AUGUSTINE RULE.

THE MENDICANT ORDERS.

THE JESUITS.

THE ORDER OF THE VISITATION OF ST. MARY.

LIST OF ILLUSTRATIONS.

Woodcuts.

Etchings.

PREFACE.

———◇———

In PRESENTING to the public this Second Series of SACRED AND LEGENDARY ART, I can but refer to the Preface and general Introduction prefixed to the First Series for an explanation of the purpose of the work *as a whole*, and the motives from which it was first undertaken.

I spoke of it there as, at best, only an attempt to do what has not hitherto been done—to interpret, as far as I could in a limited space, and with very imperfect knowledge, those works of Art which the churches and galleries of the Continent, and our own rich collections, have rendered familiar to us as objects of taste, while they have remained unappreciated as subjects of thought ;—to show that, while we have been satisfied to regard sacred pictures merely as decorations, valued more for the names appended to them than for their own sakes, we have not sufficiently considered them as books—as poems—as having a vitality of their own for good and for evil, and that thus we have shut out a vast source of delight and improvement, which lay in the way of many, even the most uninstructed in the technicalities of Art.

This was the object I had in view—knowing that, doing my best, I could do no more nor better than make the first step in a new direction. No one can feel more strongly than myself the deficiencies of the First Series of this work. That it has met with great and unhoped-for success, is no evidence of its merit; but rather a proof that it did, opportunely, supply a want, which, as I had felt myself, I thought others might feel also.

For the gentle and generous tone of criticism towards that work—
public and private—I am deeply grateful. But, in this Second
Series, I shall require even more especially the candour and forbear-
ance of the reader.

To speak of the religious pictures painted for the monastic communities, and to avoid altogether any allusion to disputed points of faith,
of history, of character, has been impossible. It was said of the First
Series, by an authority for which I have a high respect, that I had
'spoiled my book by not making it *Roman Catholic.*' But I am
not a Roman Catholic; how, therefore, could I honestly write in the
tone of thought, feeling, conviction, natural and becoming in one of
that faith? I have had to tread what all will allow to be difficult and
dangerous ground. How was this to be done safely, and without
offence, easily given in these days? Not, surely, by swerving to the
right or to the left;—not by the affectation of candour;—not by
leaving wholly aside aspects of character and morals which this
department of the Fine Arts, the representations of monastic life,
necessarily place before us. There was only one way in which the
task undertaken could be achieved in a right spirit—by going
straight forward, according to the best lights I had, and saying what
appeared to me the truth, as far as my subject required it; and my
subject—let me repeat it here—is artistic and æsthetic, not religious.
This is too much of egotism, but it has become necessary to avoid
ambiguity. I will only add that, as from the beginning to the end of
this book there is not one word false to my own faith—my own feeling
—so I truly hope there is not one word which can give offence to the
earnest and devout reader of any persuasion:—if there be, I am sorry;
—what can I say more?

The arrangement is that which naturally offered itself; but, in
classing the personages under the various Orders, I have not pedan-
tically adhered to this system: it will be found that I have departed
from it occasionally, where the subjects fell into groups, or were to
be found in the same pictures. Much has been omitted, and omitted
with regret, to keep the volume within those portable dimensions on

which its utility and its *readability* depended. If it be asked on what principle the selection has been made, it would be difficult to reply. I have just followed out the course of my own thoughts—my own associations. If I have succeeded in carrying my readers with me, there needs no excuse : they can pursue the path into which I have led them, to far wider knowledge and higher results. But if so far they find it difficult or tedious to accompany me, what excuse would avail ?

Here, as in the former series, the difficulty of compression has been the greatest of all my difficulties ; it was hard sometimes, when in the full career of reflection or fancy, to pull up, turn short round, and retrace my steps, lest I should be carried beyond the limits absolutely fixed by the nature and object of the work. There was great temptation to load the text with notes of reference to authorities, or notes of comment where such authorities were disputed and contradictory ; but I found it would only encumber, not elucidate, the matter in hand. The authorities consulted are those enumerated in the Preface to the First Series, with the addition of separate and authentic biographies of the most remarkable persons. To Mr. Maitland's Essays on the Dark Ages ; to Sir James Stephen's Essays in Ecclesiastical Biography ; and to Lord Lindsay's beautiful work on Christian Art, I have been largely indebted, and have great pleasure in thus acknowledging my obligations.

Of the illustrations—both woodcuts and etchings—I will say nothing, for they are to be considered merely as sketches—helps to the memory and the fancy. To illustrate the book as it ought to be illustrated, would have involved an expense which would have rendered it inaccessible to the general reader, and thus defeated its purpose. It would not be difficult for those interested in the subject to collect a little portfolio of engravings after the pictures referred to, which, placed in the same order, would be, as a series, most interesting and suggestive in itself, as well as illustrative of the pages which follow.

NOTE TO THE SECOND EDITION.

In PREPARING the Second Edition for the press, the authoress has availed herself of the opportunity to correct the work carefully throughout; to insert much additional matter and several new legends, as well as many new illustrations, which will be found to increase materially any value or interest the book may possess as a volume of reference.

86

Introduction.

I.

IN the first series of this work, I reviewed the scriptural personages and the poetical and traditional saints of the early ages of the Church, as represented in Art.

I endeavoured to show that these have, and ought to have, for us a deep, a lasting, a universal interest; that even where the impersonation has been, through ignorance or incapacity, most imperfect and inadequate, it is still consecrated through its original purpose, and through its relation to what we hold to be most sacred, most venerable, most beautiful, and most gracious, on earth or in heaven. Therefore the Angels still hover before us with shining, wind-swift wings, as links between the terrestrial and the celestial; therefore the Evangelists and Apostles are still enthroned as the depositaries of truth; the Fathers and Confessors of the Church still stand robed in authority as dispensers of a diviner wisdom; the Martyrs, palm-sceptred, show us what once was suffered, and could again be suffered, for truth and righteousness' sake; the glorified penitents still hold out a blessed hope to those who, in sinning, have loved much; the Virgin Patronesses

b

still represent to us the Christian ideal of womanhood in its purity
and its power. The image might be defective, but to our forefathers
it became gracious and sanctified through the suggestion, at least,
of all they could conceive of holiest, brightest, and best; the lesson
conveyed, either by direct example or pictured parable, was always
intelligible, and, in the hands of great and sincere artists, irresistibly
impressive and attractive. To us, therefore, in these later times, such
representations are worthy of reverent study for the sake of their own
beauty, or for the sake of the spirit of love and faith in which they
were created.

Can the same be said of the monastic personages, and the legends
relating to them, as we find them portrayed in sculpture and painting? I think not. It appears to me that, here, the pleasure and the
interest are of a more mingled nature, good and ill together. At the
very outset we are shocked by what seems a violation of the first
principles of Art. Monachism is not the consecration of the beautiful, even in idea; it is the apotheosis of deformity and suffering.
What can be more unpromising, as subjects for the artist, than the
religious Orders of the Middle Ages, where the first thing demanded
has been the absence of beauty and the absence of colour? Ascetic
faces, attenuated forms, dingy dark draperies, the mean, the squalid,
the repulsive, the absolutely painful,—these seem most uncongenial
materials, out of which to evolve the poetic, the graceful, and the
elevating! True, this has been done, and done in some cases
so effectually, that we meet constantly with those whose per-
ceptions have become confused, whose taste is in danger of being
vitiated through the conventional associations awakened by the
present passion for what is called Mediæval Art. But with all our
just admiration and sympathy for greatness achieved through the
inspiration of faith and feeling in spite of imperfect means and
imperfect knowledge, let us not confound things which, in their very
essence, are incompatible. Pain is pain; ugliness is ugliness; the
quaint is not the graceful. Therefore, dear friends, be not deceived!
—every long-limbed, long-eyed, long-draped saint is not 'a Giotto;'
nor every meagre simpering nun, or woe-begone monk, 'a Beato
Angelico.'

And again : the effigies of the monastic personages do not only fail,
and necessarily fail, in beauty ;—they have a deeper fault. Generally speaking, the moral effect of such pictures upon the mass of the
people was not, at any time, of a healthy kind. The subjects were

not selected to convey a precept, or to touch the heart; the aim
was not to set forth the virtue of the good man as an example; but
to glorify the community to which he belonged, and to exalt the
saints of the respective Orders as monks, not as men. Even where,
as men, they shine most attractively, the holy example conveyed in
the representation is neutralised through a species of assumption
in the purpose of the work, a vainglorious and exclusive spirit,
which has certainly interfered with, and diminished, the religious
impression. Sometimes, where the sentiment which the painter
brought to his task was truly pious, we still feel that the glory of
his community was the object at heart; and that the exaltation of
his own patriarch, whether that were St. Benedict, St. Francis, or
St. Dominick, had become to him an act of devotion. I have
observed that many who have resided long in Catholic countries are
apt to see, in the monastic pictures, only this selfish, palpable
purpose; and, associating such representations with the depravation
of the priestly character, the tyranny of rulers, and the ignorance of
the people, regard them either as mere objects of virtù, where the
artist is rare and the workmanship beautiful,—or as objects of
disgust and ridicule, where they have not this fancied value in the
eyes of the connoisseur.

The want of physical beauty, the alloy of what is earthly and self-
seeking in the moral effect,—these are surely important drawbacks
in estimating the value of the monastic pictures considered as religious
Art. If they can still charm us, still attract and rivet attention, still
excite to elevated feeling, it is owing to sources of interest which I
will now endeavour to point out.

In the first place, then, Monachism in Art, taken in a large sense,
is historically interesting, as the expression of a most important era
of human culture. We are outliving the gross prejudices which once
represented the life of the cloister as being from first to last a life of
laziness and imposture; we know that, but for the monks, the light
of liberty, and literature, and science, had been for ever extinguished;
and that, for six centuries, there existed for the thoughtful, the
gentle, the inquiring, the devout spirit, no peace, no security, no
home but the cloister. There, Learning trimmed her lamp; there
Contemplation 'pruned her wings;' there the traditions of Art, preserved from age to age by lonely, studious men, kept alive, in form
and colour, the idea of a beauty beyond that of earth—of a might
beyond that of the spear and the shield,—of a Divine sympathy with

suffering humanity. To this we may add another and a stronger
claim on our respect and moral sympathies. The protection and the
better education given to women in these early communities; the
venerable and distinguished rank assigned to them when, as governesses of their Order, they became in a manner dignitaries of the
Church; the introduction of their beautiful and saintly effigies,
clothed with all the insignia of sanctity and authority, into the decoration of places of worship and books of devotion,—did more, perhaps,
for the general cause of womanhood than all the boasted institutions of
chivalry.

This period is represented to us in the Benedictine pictures or
effigies. Those executed for the Cistercians, the Vallombrosians, the
Camaldolesi (or by them, for these communities produced some of the
most excelling of the early artists), are especially characterised by an
air of settled peace, of abstract quietude—something fixed in the
attitude and features, recalling the conventual life as described by
St. Bernard.[1] There is an example at hand in the assemblage of
Saints by Taddeo Gaddi, now in our National Gallery. The old
mosaics, and the most ancient Gothic sculpture, exhibit still more
strongly this pervading sentiment of a calm, peaceful, passionless life;
sometimes even in the female figures, grave, even to sternness, but
oftener elevated, even to grandeur.

Then followed a period when the seclusion of the cloister-life ceased
to be necessary, and ceased to do good. The strong line of demar-
cation between the active and the contemplative life, between life in
the world and life out of the world, could no longer be safely drawn.
The seventh century after the death of St. Benedict saw the breaking
forth of a spirit which left the deepest, the most ineffaceable, impression on the arts and the culture of succeeding times; and some

---

[1] *Bonum est nos hic esse, quia homo vivit purius, cadit rarius, surgit volocius,
incedit cautius, quiescit securius, moritur felicius, purgatur citius, præmiatur
copiosius.*' ('Good is it for us to dwell here, where man lives more purely; falls
more rarely; rises more quickly; treads more cautiously; rests more securely; dies
more happily; is absolved more easily; and rewarded more plenteously.')
This sentence was usually inscribed on some conspicuous part of the Cistercian
houses. Wordsworth, from whom I take the quotation, has thus paraphrased it :—

> ' Here man more purely lives; less oft doth fall;
> More promptly rises; walks with nicer tread;
> More safely rests; dies happier; is freed
> Earlier from cleansing fires; and gains withal
> A brighter crown.'

of the grandest productions of human genius, in painting, sculpture, and architecture, signalised the rise of the Mendicant Orders.

To understand fully the character of these productions, it is necessary to comprehend something of the causes and results of that state of spiritual excitement, that frenzy of devotion, which seized on Christian Europe during the period I allude to. It seems to me, that in this movement of the thirteenth century there was something analogous to the times through which we of this present generation have lived. There had been nearly a hundred years of desolating wars. The Crusades had upheaved society from its depths, as a storm upheaves the ocean, and changed the condition of men and nations. Whole provinces were left with half their population; whole districts remained uncultivated; whole families, and those the highest in the land, were extinguished, and the homes of their retainers and vassals left desolate. Scarce a hearth in Christendom beside which there wept not some childless, husbandless, hopeless woman. A generation sprang up, physically predisposed to a sort of morbid exaltation, and powerfully acted on by the revelation of a hitherto unseen, unfelt world of woe. In the words of Scripture, 'men could not stop their ears from hearing of blood, nor shut their eyes from seeing of evil.' There was a deep, almost universal, feeling of the pressure and the burden of sorrow; an awakening of the conscience to wrong; a blind, anxious groping for the right; a sense that what had hitherto sufficed to humanity would suffice no longer. But, in the uneasy ferment of men's minds, religious fear took the place of religious hope, and the religious sympathies and aspirations assumed in their excess a disordered and exaggerated form. The world was divided between those who sought to comfort the afflictions, and those who aspired to expiate the sins, of humanity. To this period we refer the worship of Mary Magdalene, the passion for pilgrimages, for penances, for martyrdom; for self-immolation to some object or for some cause lying beyond *self*. An infusion of Orientalism into Western Christianity added a most peculiar tinge to the religious enthusiasm of the time, a sentiment which survived in the palpable forms of Art long after the cause had passed away. Pilgrims returning from the Holy Land, warriors redeemed from captivity among the Arabs and Saracens, brought back wild wonders, new superstitions, a more dreamy dread of the ever-present invisible,—enlarging in the minds of men the horizon of the possible, without enlarging that of experience. With more abundant food for the fancy, with a larger sphere of action, they remained ignorant and wretched. As one, whose dungeon-walls have been thrown down by an earthquake in the dead of night, gropes and stumbles amid the ruins, and knows not, till the dawn comes, how to estimate his own freedom, how to use his recovered powers,—thus it was with the people. But what was dark misery and bewilderment in the weak and ignorant, assumed in the more highly endowed a higher form; and to St. Francis and his Order we owe what has been happily called the Mystic school in poetry and painting: that school which so strangely combined the spiritual with the sensual, and the beautiful with the terrible, and the tender with the inexorable ; which first found utterance in the works of Dante and of the ancient painters of Tuscany and Umbria. It has been disputed often, whether the suggestions of Dante influenced Giotto, or the creations of Giotto inspired Dante : but the true influence and inspiration were around both, and dominant over both, when the two greatest men of their age united to celebrate a religion of retribution and suffering ; to solemnise the espousals of sanctity with poverty— with the self-abnegation which despises all things, rather than with the love that pardons and the hope that rejoices; and which, in closing 'the gates of pleasure,' would have shut the gates of mercy on mankind.[1] We still recognise in the Franciscan pictures, those at least which reflect the ascetism of the early itinerant preachers and their haggard enthusiasm, something strangely uncouth and dervish-like. Men scourging themselves, haunted by demons, prostrate in prayer, uplifted in ecstatic visions, replaced in devotional pictures the dry, formal, but dignified figures of an earlier time. For the calmly meditative life of the Benedictine pictures, we have the expression of a life which panted, trembled, and aspired ; a life of spiritual contest, of rapture, or of agony. This is the life which is reflected to us in the pictures painted for those religious brotherhoods which sprang up between 1200 and 1300, and drew together and concentrated, in a common feeling, or for a common purpose, the fervid energies of kindred minds.

If the three great divisions of the regular Ecclesiastics seem to have had each a distinct vocation, there was at least one vocation

[1] For the espousals of St. Francis with Poverty, 'the Dame to whom none openeth pleasure's gate,' as represented by Giotto, see p. 255 ; and Dante *Par.* c. xi.

common to all. The Benedictine monks instituted schools of learning; the Augustines built noble cathedrals; the Mendicant Orders founded hospitals; *all* became patrons of the fine arts, on such a scale of munificence that the protection of the most renowned princes has been mean and insignificant in comparison. Yet, in their relation to Art, this splendid patronage was the least of their merits. The earliest artists of the Middle Ages were the monks of the Benedictine Orders. In their convents were preserved from age to age the traditional treatment of sacred subjects, and that pure unworldly sentiment which in later times was ill exchanged for the learning of schools and the competition of academies; and as they were the only depositaries of chemical and medical knowledge, and the only compounders of drugs, we owe to them also the discovery and preparation of some of the finest colours, and the invention or the improvement of the implements used in painting;— for the monks not only prepared their own colours, but when they employed secular painters in decorating their convents, the materials furnished from their own laboratories were consequently of the best and most durable kind. [1] As architects, as glass painters, as mosaic workers, as carvers in wood and metal, they were the precursors of all that has since been achieved in Christian Art; and if so few of these admirable and gifted men are known to us individually and by name, it is because they worked for the honour of God and their community, not for profit, nor for reputation.

Theophilus the Monk, whose most curious and important treatise on the fine arts and chemistry was written in the twelfth century and lately republished in France and in England, was a Benedictine. Friar Bacon was a Franciscan, and Friar Albert-le-Grand (Albertus Magnus) a Dominican. It is on record that the knowledge of physics attained by these two remarkable men exposed them to the charge of magic. Shakspeare, 'who saw the thing that hath been as the thing that is,' introduces Friar Laurence as issuing from his cell at dawn of day to gather simples and herbs, and moralising on their properties. The portrait is drawn throughout with such wonderful and instinctive truth, it is as if one of the old friars of the fourteenth century had sat for it. [2]

---

[1] Materials for a History of Oil Painting, by Sir Charles Eastlake, p. 6.

[2] 'The good friar of this play,' says Mr. Knight, in his Notes to Romeo and Juliet, 'in his kindliness, his learning, and his inclination to mix with and

In reference to the monastic artists, it is worth observing that the Benedictines are distinguished by the title Don or Dom (*Dominus*), peculiar, I believe, to the ecclesiastics of this Order: as Don Lorenzo Monaco, who painted the beautiful Annunciation in the Florence Gallery;[1] Don Giulio Clovio, the famous miniatore of the sixteenth century. The painters of the Mendicant Orders have the prefix of Fra or Frate, as Fra Giacopo da Turrita, a celebrated mosaic worker in the thirteenth century; Fra Antonio da Negroponte, who painted that supremely beautiful and dignified Madonna in the Frari at Venice; —both Franciscans: Fra Filippo Lippi, the Carmelite; Fra Beato Angelico da Fiesole, and Fra Bartolomeo (styled, *par excellence*, Il Frate, *the* Friar),—both Dominicans.

Thus much for the historical and artistic interest of the monastic representations taken generally. Considered separately, some of these pictures have even a deeper interest.

The founders of the various religious communities were all re-markable men, and some of them were more,—they were wonderful men; men of genius, of deep insight into human nature, of deter-mined will, of large sympathies, of high aspirations,—poets who did not write poems but acted them; all differing from each other in character, as their various communities differed from each other in aim and purpose. As a matter of course, in all works of art dedicated by those communities, the effigies of their patriarchs and founders claim a distinguished place. Thus we have in the monastic pictures a series of biographies of the most interesting and instructive kind. It will be said that this is biography *idealised*. Idealised certainly, but not falsified;—not, I think, nearly so falsified as in books. After having studied the written lives of St. Benedict, St. Bernard, St. Francis, St. Clara, St. Dominick, and others, to enable me to understand the pictures which relate to them, I found it was the pictures which enabled me better to understand their lives and characters. I speak, of course, of good pictures, painted by earnest and conscientious artists, where traditional or characteristic resemblance has been attended to. The monkish pictures of the later schools are in general as ignorantly false in character as they are degraded in taste and style.

perhaps control, the affairs of the world, is no unapt representation of one of the distinguished Order of St. Francis in its best days.'

[1] *Vide* Sacred and Legendary Art, vol. i. p. 86.

I have spoken of the want of beauty in the early pictures of monastic subjects; but though the figures of the ascetic saints are not in themselves beautiful, the pictures in which they occur are sometimes of the highest conceivable beauty, either through the effect of suggestive and harmonious combination, or the most striking and significant contrasts. For instance, a group which meets us at every turn is the combination of the dark-robed, sad-visaged, self-denying monk, with the lovely benign Madonna and the godlike innocence of her Child. Sometimes the votary kneels, adoring in effigy the divine Maternity, the glorification of those soft affections which, though removed far from him in his seclusion, are brought near to him, and at once revealed and consecrated through the power of Art. Sometimes the sainted recluse stands with an air of dignity by the throne of the Virgin-mother; sometimes the introduction of angels scattering flowers, or hymning music, for the solace of the haggard hermit, forms most striking and poetical contrasts.

And, again, the grouping in some of the monastic pictures is not merely beautiful, it is often in the highest degree significant. It has struck me that such pictures are not sufficiently considered like books, as having a sort of vitality of meaning; only, like books, before we can read them we must understand the language in which they are written. I have given a number of instances in the course of this volume. I will add another which has just occurred to me. In the Pitti Palace there is an 'Annunciation of the Virgin,' in which St. Philip Benozzi, who lived in the fourteenth century, stands by in his ample black robes, listening to the angelic salutation. We are struck, not by the anachronism—where the subject is not treated as an event, but as a mystery, there can be no anachronism, as I have elsewhere shown,—but we are embarrassed by what appears a manifest incongruity; and such it is on the walls of a palace: in its original place the whole composition was full of propriety, and through its associations, became harmonised into poetry. It was painted for the Order of the Servi, in honour of their chief saint, Filippo Benozzi; it was suspended in their church at Florence, dedicated to the Annunciation of the Blessed Virgin (the famous Annunziata). The Order was founded in especial honour of the Virgin, and, by a rule of the original institute, all their devotions began with the words of the angel Gabriel, 'Ave Maria!' Thus we have the explanation at once; and the dark-robed, listening monk in the background becomes an object of intelligent interest to those who understand the import and the original purpose of this fine picture.

I will give another example: we often meet with pictures of St. Dominick holding the keys of St. Peter, or receiving them from the apostle. The allusion is to a custom of the papal court, which has prevailed since the days of Innocent III. The important and confidential office of Master of the Sacred Palace was given to St. Dominick in 1218, and has ever since been held by a member of the Dominican Order. The pictured allegory is thus the record of an historical fact, and commemorates one of the chief honours of the community.

II.

The representations of Monastic Saints may be classed, like other sacred and legendary subjects, as either *devotional* or *historical*.

The Devotional pictures exhibit the saint as an object of reverence, either in his relation to God or his relation to man; they set forth his *sanctity* or his *charity*.

In those effigies which express his sanctity, he stands with his proper habit and attribute, either alone or beside the throne of the Virgin; or he is in the attitude of prayer, kneeling before the Madonna and Child; or he is uplifted on clouds, with outstretched arms; or he is visited by angels; or he beholds the glory of Paradise; or the most blessed of Mothers places in his arms her Divine Infant; or the Saviour receives him into joy eternal. In all such pictures, the purpose is to exalt the human into the divine. The principle of Monachism which pervades the early legends of St. Anthony and others of the saintly hermits, that which made sanctity consist in the absolute renunciation of all natural feelings and affections, we find reproduced in the later monastic representations, sometimes in a painful form:—

> They who, through wilful disesteem of life,
> Affront the eye of Solitude, shall find
> That her mild nature can be terrible.

And *terrible* it certainly appears to us in some of these pictures, where the solitude is haunted by demons, or defiled by temptations, or agonised by rueful penance, or visited by awful and preternatural apparitions of the crucified Redeemer. In the later pictures of the female saints of the various Orders,—those, for instance, of St. Catherine of Siena, St. Theresa, St. Maria Maddalena de' Pazzi, and others,—the representation becomes offensive, as well as painful and pathetic. I recollect such a picture in the Corsini Palace, which I cannot recall without horror, and dare not attempt to describe. The gross materialism of certain views of Christianity, not confined to the Roman Catholics, strikes us in pictures more than in words; yet surely it is the same thing.

On the other hand, there is a view of the sanctity of solitude placed before us in the earlier monastic pictures, which is soothing and attractive far beyond the power of words. How beautiful that soft settled calm, which seems to have descended on the features, as on the souls, of those who have kept themselves unspotted from the world! How dear to the fatigued or wounded spirit that blessed portraiture of stillness with communion, of seclusion with sympathy, which breathes from such pictures! Who, at some moments, has not felt their unspeakable charm?—felt, when the weight of existence pressed on the fevered nerves and weary heart, the need of some refuge from life on this side of death, and all the real, or at least the possible, sanctity of solitude?

But again: where the saint has been canonised for works of charity, which exalted him in his human relation, it is common in the devotional effigies to express this, not by some special act, but in a poetical and general manner. He stands looking up to heaven, with a mendicant or a sick man prostrate at his feet; or he is giving alms to Christ in the likeness of a beggar; or he is holding aloft the crucifix, or the standard, as a preacher to the poor. Such pictures are often of exceeding beauty; and the sentiment conveyed,—'Be Phil. iii. 17 followers together of me, and mark them which walk so as ye have us for an ensample,' would be irresistible were it not for that frequent alloy of pride and emulation, in the purpose of the picture, of which I have spoken.

Such figures as those of St. Theresa interceding for souls in purgatory, and St. Dominick doing penance for the sins of others, express, at once, the sanctity and the charity of the saint.

The Historical subjects are those which exhibit some event or action in the life of the saint, generally expressing the virtues for which he was canonised; consequently, they may be regarded as the attestation, in a dramatic form, either of his sanctity or his charity.

Thus we have in the first class his miracles performed either before or after death, and these miracles are almost invariably copied from those of our Saviour. The dead are raised, the blind see, the dumb speak, the sick are restored, food is multiplied ; the saint walks through fire or over water, stills the tempest, or expels evil spirits. When these wonders are not copied literally from the Gospels, they are generally allegorical ; as where roses spring from the blood of St. Francis, or fall from the lips of St. Angelo ; or where St. Francis preaches to the birds, or St. Antony of Padua to the fishes ; or where the same saint discovers the miser's heart buried in his treasure-chest—' where his treasure is, there shall his heart be also.' Or they are parables for the purpose of setting forth some particular or disputed dogma of the Church, as the mule kneeling before the Host when carried by St. Antony, or the Saviour administering in person or by an angel the consecrated wafer to St. Bonaventura. Or they are obvious inventions to extol the glory of some particular saint, and, through him, the popularity and interests of the community to which he belonged : such is the whole story of St. Diego d'Alcalà.

Martyrdoms, of course, come under this designation, but among the monastic saints there are few who suffered death for their faith. The death of St. Peter the Dominican, called the Martyr (persecutor at once and victim), was an assassination rather than a martyrdom : it is, however, the most important among these representations, and, in the hands of Titian, in the highest degree tragic and striking.

Less frequent in the churches, but more interesting, are those dramatic and historical pictures which place the saint before us in his relation to humanity ; as where he is distributing alms, or ministering to the sick, or redeeming slaves and prisoners, or preaching to the poor. Pictures of St. Elizabeth of Hungary tending the sick boy in the hospital ; of St. Charles Borromeo walking amid the plague-stricken wretches, bearing the sacrament in his hand ; of St. Antony of Padua rebuking the tyrant Eccellino ; of St. Vincent de Paul carrying home the foundlings ; of St. Catherine of Siena converting the robbers ; and innumerable others,—belong to this class.

III.

In arranging according to their dignity the saints of the different Orders, the Founders would claim, of course, the first place; after them follow the Martyrs, if any; then the Royal Saints who wear the habit; lastly, the Canonised Saints of both sexes, taking rank according to their celebrity and popularity.

St. Benedict is the general patriarch of all the Benedictine communities, who, next to him, venerate their separate founders:

St. Romualdo, founder of the Camaldolesi;

St. John Gualberto—of the Vallombrosians;

St. Bruno—of the Carthusians;

St. Bernard—of the Cistercians.

St. Augustine of Hippo, one of the four great Latin Doctors, is considered as the general patriarch of the Augustines, and of all the communities founded on his Rule; each venerating besides, as separate head or founder,—

St. Philip Benozzi—of the Servi;

St. Peter Nolasco—of the Order of Mercy;

St. Bridget of Sweden—of the Brigittines.

The Augustine Canons also regard as their patriarch and patron St. Joseph, the husband of the Virgin.

St. Francis is the general patriarch of the Franciscans, Capuchins, Observants, Conventuals, Minimes, and all other Orders derived from his Rule.

St. Dominick founded the Dominicans, or Preaching Friars.

St. Albert of Vercelli is generally considered as the founder of the Carmelites, who, however, claim as their patriarch Elijah the Prophet.

St. Jerome is claimed as patriarch by the Jeronymites; and St. Ignatius Loyola was the founder of Jesuitism.

In those grand sacred subjects which exhibit a congregation of saints, as the Paradiso, the Last Judgment, and the Coronation of the Virgin, the founders of the different Orders are usually conspicuous. I will give an example of such a poetical assemblage of the various Orders, because it is especially interesting for the profoundly significant treatment; because it is important as a *chef-d'œuvre* of one of the greatest of the early artists, Angelico da Fiesole; and because, having been recently engraved by Mr. George Scharf for the Arundel Society, it is likely to be in the hands of many, and convenient for immediate reference.

The picture to which I allude is the fresco of the Crucifixion painted on the wall of the Chapter House of St. Mark at Florence. To understand how profoundly every part of this grand composition has been meditated and worked out, we must bear in mind that it was painted in a convent dedicated to St. Mark, in the city of Florence, in the days of the first and greatest of the Medici, Cosmo and Lorenzo, and that it was the work of a Dominican friar, for the glory of the Dominican Order.

In the centre of the picture is the Redeemer crucified between the two thieves. At the foot of the cross is the usual group of the Virgin fainting in the arms of St. John the Evangelist, Mary Magdalene, and another Mary. To the right of this group, and the left of the spectator, is seen St. Mark, as patron of the convent, kneeling and holding his Gospel ; behind him stands St. John the Baptist, as protector of the city of Florence. Beyond are the three martyrs, St. Laurence, St. Cosmo, and St. Damian, patrons of the Medici family. The two former, as patrons of Cosmo and Lorenzo de Medici, look up to the Saviour with devotion ; St. Damian turns away and hides his face. On the left of the cross we have the group of the founders of the various Orders. First, St. Dominick, kneeling with hands outspread, gazes up at the Crucified ; behind him St. Augustine and St. Albert the Carmelite, mitred and robed as bishops ; in front kneels St. Jerome as a Jeronymite hermit, the cardinal's hat at his feet ; behind him kneels St. Francis ; behind St. Francis stand two venerable figures, St. Benedict and St. Romualdo ; and in front of them kneels St. Bernard, with his book ; and, still more in front, St. John Gualberto, in the attitude in which he looked up at the crucifix when he spared his brother's murderer. Beyond this group of monks Angelico has introduced two of the famous friars of his own community : St. Peter Martyr kneels in front, and behind him stands St. Thomas Aquinas ; the two, thus placed together, represent the *sanctity* and the *learning* of the Dominican Order, and close this sublime and wonderful composition. Thus considered, we may read it like a sacred poem, and every separate figure is a study of character. I hardly know anything in painting finer than the pathetic beauty of the head of the penitent thief, and the mingled fervour and intellectual refinement in the head of St. Bernard.

It will be remarked that, in this group of patriarchs, ' *Capi e Fonda-tori de' religiosi*,' St. Bruno, the famous founder of the Carthusians, is omitted. At the time the fresco was painted, about 1440, St. Bruno was not canonised.

We have portraits of distinguished members of the various commu-nities who were never canonised, but these do not properly belong to sacred Art. The decree of beatification did not confer the privilege of being invoked as intercessor and portrayed in the churches ; it was merely a declaration that the personage distinguished for holiness of life had been received into bliss, and thence received the title of *Beato*, Blessed. The bull of canonisation was a much more solemn ordin-ance, and conferred a species of divinity : it was the apotheosis of a being supposed to have been endowed while on earth with privileges above humanity, with miraculous powers, and regarded with such favour by Christ, whom he had imitated on earth, that his prayers and intercessions before the throne of grace might avail for those whom he had left in the world. To obtain the canonisation of one of their members became with each community an object of ambition. The popes frequently used their prerogative in favour of an Order to which they had belonged, or which they regarded with particular interest. Sometimes the favour was obtained through the intercession of crowned heads.

In the monastic pictures it is most especially necessary to ascertain the date of the canonisation in order to settle the identity of the personage. I will give an example. There is in the Dresden Gallery a remarkably fine devotional picture, by Garofalo, representing St. Peter and St. George standing, and a little behind them, in the centre, a saint in a white habit, seated with a pen and an open book in his hand, looking up to the Madonna in glory. This figure is called in the catalogue *St. Bruno*. Now there can be no doubt that it is St. Bernard, and not St. Bruno ; for, in the first place, the habit has not the proper form of the Carthusian habit,—there is no scapulary united by the band at the sides ; secondly, it was St. Bernard, not St. Bruno, who wrote the praises of the Virgin ; and, thirdly, the whole question is set at rest by the fact that St. Bruno was not canonised till the beginning of the seventeenth century, consequently could not appear between St. Peter and St. George in a picture painted in the beginning of the sixteenth.

The colour and form of the habit are also of great importance in ascertaining the name of the personage ; but though, at a single glance, we distinguish the black Benedictine monk from the white Cistercian, and the grey or brown tunic of the Franciscan from the white tunic and black mantle of the Dominican, it is not always easy to discriminate further. St. Benedict, for instance, sometimes wears the black, and sometimes the white, habit; and the colour will decide whether the picture was painted for the *Monaci Neri*, or for the Reformed Benedictines. I have explained this at length in the legend of the saint, and will only point to the picture by Francia in our National Gallery as an example of St. Benedict in the *white* habit.

Grey was the original colour of the Franciscan habit. The Reformed Franciscans introduced the dark-brown tunic : the girdle, of a twisted hempen cord, remains the peculiar distinction of the habit at all times.

The black habit is worn by the Augustines, the Servi, the Oratorians, and the Jesuits.

The white habit is worn by the Cistercians, the Camaldolesi, the Port-Royalists, the Trappistes, the Trinitarians.

Black over white, by the Dominicans.

White over black, by the Premonstratensians and the Carmelites.

The tonsure, the shaven crown, has been from very early times one of the distinguishing signs of the priesthood. To shave the head was anciently an expression of penitence and mourning, and was thence adopted by the primitive hermits in the solitudes of Egypt. The form of the tonsure was settled by the Synod of Toledo in 633; and the circle of short hair left round the head has since been styled the *clerical crown* (corona clericalis). The Carthusians alone of the Monkish Orders shaved the whole head, in sign of greater austerity.

I do not know what is the specific rule of the different Orders with regard to beards; but in pictures we find long beards worn only by the early Benedictines, the Hermits, and the Capuchins.

But when, with some attention, we have settled the Order, it requires some further examination to discriminate the personage. This is determined by some particular attribute, or by some characteristic treatment; by the relative position of the figures; or by the locality for which the picture was painted,—all of which have to be critically considered. Some saints, as St. Francis, St. Catherine of Siena, St. Elizabeth of Hungary, are easily and at once discriminated;

others, after a long study of characteristics and probabilities, leave us at a loss.

And first with regard to the distinctive emblems and attributes. They are the same already enumerated and explained, in the first series of this work, as of general application in the sacred and legendary subjects; but in the monastic pictures they have sometimes a particular significance, which I shall endeavour to point out.

The GLORY expresses the canonised saint: it ought not to be given to a *Beato*. In some instances, where the figure of the saint has been painted before the date of the canonisation, the glory has been added afterwards; in the later schools of the sixteenth and seventeenth centuries it is omitted.

The DRAGON or the DEMON at the feet of the saint is a common attribute, and bears the common meaning,—that of sin and the world overcome: but sometimes the Demon or Demons, chained to a rock behind, or led captive, signify heresy vanquished; as in pictures of St. Bernard, the great polemic of the Middle Ages.

The HIND or STAG, as the general emblem of solitude, is frequent; but it has a special meaning in the legends of St. Giles and St. Felix de Valois.

WILD BEASTS, such as bears, wolves, &c., at the feet of a saint, originally signified that he had cleared a wilderness, or founded a convent in a solitude. When the original signification was forgotten, some legend was invented or suggested to account for it.

The CRUCIFIX held in the hand signified a preacher; in this sense it is given to St. Francis, St. Dominick, St. Peter Martyr, St. John Capistrano, St. Francis Xavier, St. Vincent Ferrier. Merely as a symbol of penance and devout faith it is given to St. Francis, St. Margaret of Cortona, St. Theresa. It has a special significance in the pictures of St. John Gualberto and St. Catherine of Siena.

The LILY, as the emblem of purity and chastity, is common to hundreds of saints, male and female; it is, however, especially characteristic of St. Clara, St. Antony of Padua, St. Dominick, and St. Catherine of Siena; and also of those young saints who made early vows of celibacy, as St. Casimir, St. Stanislas, St. Aloysius of Gonzaga. The crucifix twined with the lily, common in late pictures, signifies devotion and purity of heart: it is given particularly to St. Nicholas of Tolentino. But the lily being also the symbol of the Virgin, and consecrated to her, is placed near those saints who were

d

distinguished by their devotion to the Mother of the Redeemer, as in pictures of St. Bernard.

The INFANT CHRIST placed in the arms of a saint is a common allegory or legend, but comparatively modern, and a favourite subject of the later schools of art. I believe it to be derived from the legend of St. Antony of Padua, of whom it is related that the radiant figure of Christ descended and stood on the open book of the Gospel while preaching to the people. The pictures of the Madonna and Child, that universal subject in all religious edifices, may, in heated imaginations, have given rise to those visions so common in the lives of the monastic saints, where the Virgin-Mother, bending from her throne, or attended by a train of angels, resigns her Divine Infant to the outspread eager arms of the kneeling recluse. Such representations we have of St. Catherine of Siena, St. Theresa, St. Catherine of Bologna, and indeed of all the nun-saints; also of St. Francis, St. Antony of Padua, St. Felix of Cantalicio, and others; never of St. Dominick, nor, that I remember, of St. Clara. They strike me sometimes as very pathetic.

The STANDARD with the CROSS is the general symbol of Christianity triumphant, and is given to the early preachers and missionaries. But it is also given to the royal and warrior saints connected with the different Orders, as St. Oswald, St. Wenceslaus, St. Henry, St. Leopold.

The FLAMING HEART is the rather vulgar and commonplace emblem of Divine love. I have never met with it in any of the very early pictures, expect those of St. Augustine. The heart crowned with thorns is given to St. Francis de Sales; impressed with the name of Christ, the I H S, it is given to the Jesuit saints, to St. Theresa, to St. Bridget of Sweden, and to St. Maria Maddalena de' Pazzi. It has a particular meaning in the legend of St. Catherine of Siena.

The CROWN OF THORNS, placed on the head or in the hand of a saint, is a modern emblem, and expresses suffering for Christ's sake. It has a more special meaning in the pictures of St. Francis, who is considered by his followers as a type of the Redeemer; and also in the legends of St. Louis of France, of St. Catherine of Siena, and St. Rosa di Lima.

The PALM, as the meed of martyrdom, is proper to a few only of the monastic saints. St. Placidus, the disciple of St. Benedict, is the earliest monastic martyr; St. Boniface and St. Thomas à Becket were also Benedictines. St. Albert and St. Angelo were Carmelites, and St. Peter Martyr a Dominican;—these, I believe, are the only monkish martyrs who are conspicuous and individualised in works of Art. The only nun-martyr is St Flavia, the sister of St. Placidus.

We find, also, pictures and prints commemorating the five Franciscans martyred at Morocco; a long procession of about a hundred Dominican martyr-missionaries; and the Jesuit martyrs of Japan: but they are not individually named, nor have they, I believe, been regularly canonised.

But the palm is also occasionally given to several saints who have not suffered a violent death, but have been conspicuous for their victory over pain and temptation; for instance, to St. Francis and St. Catherine of Siena.

The LAMB, as an attribute, is proper to St. Francis, both as the symbol of meekness and with an especial meaning for which I must refer to the legend.

The FISH, the ancient Christian symbol of baptism, is proper to some of the old missionaries and primitive bishops who converted the heathen; but the original meaning being lost or forgotten, a legend has been invented by way of interpretation, as in the stories of St. Ulrich of Augsburg and St. Benno of Meissen.

The CROWN, placed near the saint, or at his feet, signifies that he was of royal birth, or had resigned a kingdom to enter a monastery. Those royal saints who retained the sovereign power till their death wear the crown; and the sainted queens and princesses frequently wear the diadem over the veil.

A SERAPH is sometimes introduced as an ornament, or hovering near, to distinguish the saints of the Seraphic Order; as in a figure of St. Bonaventura (p. 327).

The STIGMATA, the wounds of Christ impressed on the hands, feet, and side, are, as an attribute, proper to St. Francis and St. Catherine of Siena; improperly given also to St. Maria Maddalena de' Pazzi, and related of several other saints whom I have not met with in pictures.

A SUN on the breast expresses the light of Wisdom, in figures of St. Thomas Aquinas. It is carried in the hand of St. Bernardino of Siena in the form of a tablet, and within the radiant circle are the letters I H S. This is the proper attribute of that famous Franciscan, and is explained in his legend. The *Mont de Piété* is given to him in some pictures, as in the small Franciscan predella, attributed to Raphael, in Lord Ward's collection; but it is, I am assured by a high authority, the proper attribute of Fra Bernardino da Feltre (who was never canonised), and given by mistake to St. Bernardino of Siena.

The STAR, over the head or on the breast, is given to St. Dominick (black and white habit), and St. Nicholas of Tolentino (black habit); and seems to express a divine attestation of peculiar sanctity, the idea being borrowed from the star in the East. The five stars given to St. John Nepomuck have a special significance, which is explained by his story.

A BOOK in the hand of a saint is, in a general way, the Scriptures or the Gospel. It is given in this sense to preachers and missionaries. It has, however, a special meaning in pictures of St. Boniface. Books in the hand or at the feet of St. Bernard, St. Thomas Aquinas, Cardinal Bonaventura, St. Theresa, accompanied by the pen or inkhorn, express the character of author or writer, and the books are often lettered with the titles of their works.

The DOVE, as the scriptural emblem of the Holy Spirit, and expressing direct inspiration, is also given as an attribute to the same saints; but in the effigies of St. Scholastica, the sister of St. Benedict, it has a special meaning.

The OPEN BOOK in the hands of a founder, often indicates the written Rule of the Order, and sometimes the first words of the Rule are inscribed on the page.

The SCOURGE indicates self-inflicted penance, and is given in this sense to St. Dominick (who was famous for scourging himself), and St. Margaret of Cortona.

WALKING over the SEA or over rivers is a miracle attributed to so many saints, that it becomes necessary to distinguish them. St. Raymond the Dominican, and St. Francis de Paula the Capuchin, cross the sea on a cloak. St. Peter of Alcantara, a Franciscan, walks over the water. St. Hyacinth, the Dominican, walks over the river Dniester when swollen to a torrent, and is always distinguished by the image of the Virgin in his hand. St. Sebald, in a German print, crosses the Danube on his cloak. In devotional figures of these saints the miracle is often represented as an attribute in the background.

ROSES are sometimes an allusion to the name of the saint; St. Rosalia of Palermo, St. Rosa di Viterbo (Franciscan), St. Rosa di Lima (Dominican), all wear the crown of roses, or it is presented by an angel. But roses in the lap or the hand of St. Elizabeth, are an attribute taken from her beautiful legend.

The CARDINAL'S HAT is proper to St. Bonaventura, and he is the only monkish saint to whom it belongs; he is distinguished from St. Jerome, the other Cardinal-saint, by the Franciscan girdle, and the absence of the long beard.[1]

The MITRE and PASTORAL STAFF are borne by abbots as well as bishops: the pastoral staff only, without the mitre, by abbesses.

SLAVES with their chains broken, BEGGARS, CHILDREN, LEPERS, at the feet of a saint, express his beneficence; and in the ancient devotional figures these are sometimes of diminutive size, showing that they are merely emblems to signify charity, and not any particular act of charity.

Other attributes in use in the monastic representations, and *peculiar* to certain saints (as the kneeling mule in pictures of St. Antony of Padua), will be explained in their respective legends.[2]

To understand and to sympathise with the importance attached to almsgiving, and the prominence given to this particular aspect of charity in the old pictures, we must recall a social condition very different from our own; a period when there were no poor-laws; when the laws for the protection of the lower classes were imperfect and perpetually violated; when for the wretched there was absolutely no resource but in private beneficence. In those days a man began his religious vocation by a literal and practical application of the text in Scripture, 'Sell all thou hast, and distribute to the poor.' The laws against debtors were then very severe, and the proximity of the Moors on one side, and the Turks on the other, rendered slavery a familiar thing. In all the maritime and commercial cities of Italy and Spain, brotherhoods existed for the manumission of slaves and debtors. Charitable confraternities performed then, and in Italy perform now, many duties left to our police, or which we think we fulfil in paying our poor-rates. These duties of charity shine in the monastic pictures, and were conspicuous on the walls of churches, I am persuaded to good purpose. Among the most interesting of the

---

[1] In the German 'Christliche Ikonographie,' and other books of the kind, the cardinal's hat is mentioned as an attribute of St. Francis Borgia, the Jesuit. He was not a cardinal: if the cardinal's hat be introduced into his effigies (of which I do not remember an instance), it must signify that he rejected that dignity when offered to him.

[2] A very useful book, as a companion to churches and picture galleries, is the little manual, 'Emblems of Saints,' compiled by the Rev. F. C. Husenbeth.

canonised saints whose stories I have related in reference to Art, are the founders of the charitable brotherhoods; and among the most beautiful and celebrated pictures, were those painted for these communities; for instance, for the *Misericordia* in Italy, the various *Scuole* at Venice, the *Merced* and the *Caritad* in Spain, and for the numerous hospitals for the sick, the houseless travellers, the poor, and the penitent women (*Donne Convertite*). All these institutions were adorned with pictures, and in the oratories and chapels appended to them the altarpiece generally set forth some beneficent saint,— St. Roch, or St. Charles Borromeo, the patrons of the plague-stricken; or St. Cosmo and St. Damian, the saintly apothecaries; or St. Leonard, the protector of captives and debtors; or that friend of the wretched, St Juan de Dios, or the benign St Elizabeth;— either standing before us as objects of devout reverence, or kneeling at the feet of the Madonna and her Son, and commending to the Divine mercy 'all such as are anyways afflicted in mind, body, or estate.'

The pictures, too, which were suspended in churches as votive memorials of benefits received, are often very touching. I recollect such a picture in the Gallery at Vienna. A youth about fifteen, in the character of Tobias, is led by the hand of his guardian angel Raphael; and on the other side is St. Leonard, the patron of captives, holding his broken fetters: Christ the Redeemer appears above; and below, in a corner, kneels an elderly man, his eyes fixed on the youth. The arrangement of this group leaves us no doubt of its purpose; it was the votive offering of a father, whose son had escaped, or had been redeemed, from captivity. The picture is very beautiful, and either by Andrea del Sarto or one of his school.[2] If we could discover where it had been originally placed, we might discover the facts and the personages to which it alludes; but even on the walls of a gallery we recognise its pathetic significance: we read it as a poem —as a hymn of thanksgiving.

When we consider the deep interest which is attached to pictures and other works of Art in their connection with history and character, we have reason to regret that in the catalogues of galleries and col-

---

[1] For some account of the objects of these *Scuole*, see 'Sacred and Legendary Art,' p. 168, second edition.

[2] The two figures of St. Raphael and Tobias, without the others, are in a small picture in the Pitti Palace: the peculiar dress and physiognomy of the youth give to the picture the look of a portrait; the reason of this is understood in the complete group.

lections, the name of the church, chapel, or confraternity whence the picture was purchased, or where it was originally placed, has been so seldom mentioned. The locality for which a picture was painted will often determine the names of the personages introduced, and show us why they were introduced, and why they held this or that position relatively to each other. A saint who is the subordinate figure in one place is the superior figure in another; and there was always a reason, a meaning, in the arrangement of a group, even when it appears, at first sight, most capricious and unaccountable. What a lively, living, really religious interest is given to one of these sacred groups when we know the locality or the community for which it was executed; and how it becomes enriched as a production of mind, when it speaks to the mind through a thousand associations, will be felt, I think, after reading the legends which follow.

IV.

Those who have thought on works of Art with this reference to their meaning and intention should be able, on looking round a church or any other religious edifice, to decide at once to what community it belongs, and to understand the relation which the pictures bear to each other and to the locality in which they are placed. This is a very interesting point, and leads me to say a few words of some of the most important of these edifices and the memorials of Art and artists which they contain.

There is a Latin distich which well expresses the different localities and sites affected by the chief Monastic Orders,—

> Bernardus vales, colles Benedictus amabat,
> Oppida Franciscus, magnas Ignatius urbes ;

and we shall find almost uniformly the chief foundations of the Benedictines on hills or mountains, those of the Cistercians in fertile valleys by running streams, those of the Franciscans in provincial towns, and those of the Jesuits in capital cities.

To begin with the Benedictines; the Order produced the earliest painters and architects in Europe, and their monasteries and churches are among the earliest and most important monuments of art in our own and other countries. The term *Abbey* applies particularly to the foundations of this Order.

In looking round one of the Benedictine edifices, we shall find of course St. Benedict as patriarch, his sister St. Scholastica, and the other principal saints of his Order enumerated in the introduction to his legend. We shall also find the apostle Paul frequently and conspicuously introduced into pictures painted for this community. He is their patron saint and protector, and their Rule was framed in accordance with his precepts.

The parent monastery of Monte Cassino was founded by St. Benedict on the spot where stood a temple of Apollo. The grand masses of the conventual buildings now crown the summit of a mountain, rising above the town of San Germano; the river Rapido, called, farther on, the Garigliano, flows through the valley at its base. The *Hospice*, or house for the reception and entertainment of strangers and travellers, stands lower down. The splendid church and cloisters are filled with works of Art,—the series of statues in marble of the most illustrious members and benefactors of the community being perhaps the most remarkable; but the monastery having been restored, almost rebuilt, in the seventeenth century, most of the pictures belong to the modern schools.

More interesting for the antiquity of its decorations is Subiaco, formerly the mountain cave in which St. Benedict at the age of sixteen hid himself from the world. The *Sacro Speco*, or sacred cavern, is now a church; the natural rocks forming the walls in some parts, are covered with ancient frescoes, the works of Concioli, painted in 1219, before the time of Cimabue, and most important in the history of early Italian Art. About a mile from the *Sacro Speco* is the monastery of Santa Scholastica, once famous for its library, and still interesting as the spot where the first printing-press in Italy was set up;—as the first printing-press in England was worked in the cloisters of the Benedictine Abbey of Westminster.

San Paolo-fuor-le-Mure at Rome belongs to the Benedictines.

For the San Severino at Naples, Antonio lo Zingaro painted the series of pictures of the life of St. Benedict which I have described at p. 18.

For the Benedictine convent of San Sisto, at Piacenza, Raphael painted his Madonna di San Sisto, now at Dresden. The monks have been sorely chidden for parting with their unequalled treasure; but that they knew how to value it is proved by the price they set on it, 60,000 florins (about £6500 English money), probably the largest sum which up to that time had ever been given for a single picture, and which, be it observed, was paid by a petty German prince, Augustus, Elector of Saxony. With this sum the Benedictines repaired their church and convent, which were falling into ruin.

For the monks of Grotta Ferrata, Domenichino painted the life of San Nilo. The cloisters of San Michele in Bosco were painted by all the best painters of the later Bologna school (Ludovico Caracci and his pupils) in emulation of each other. These once admirable and celebrated frescoes, executed between 1600 and 1630, are now more ruined than the frescoes at Subiaco, painted four centuries earlier.

The San Giustina at Padua is one of the oldest and most celebrated of the Benedictine foundations. The church having been rebuilt between 1502 and 1549 by contributions collected throughout Europe by the monks of the community, all the best artists, from 1550 to 1640, were employed in its decorations. Much more valuable than any of these late works, though good of their kind and date, are the paintings in the old cloisters by a very rare and admirable master, Bernardo Parentino, who died in the habit of an Augustine friar about 1500.

In France the most celebrated of the Benedictine houses were the abbeys of St. Maur, Marmoutier, and Fontevrauld, all ruined or desecrated during the first French Revolution, and their splendid libraries and works of Art destroyed or dispersed.

In Germany one of the greatest of the Benedictine communities was that of Bamberg.

With regard to the Reformed Benedictines, the monasteries of Vallombrosa and Camaldoli in Tuscany produced some of the most interesting of the early monastic artists. The pictures in our National Gallery by Taddeo Gaddi were painted for the Camaldolesi. Perugino painted for the Vallombrosians the grandest of his altarpieces, the Assumption now in the Florence Academy with the saints of Vallombrosa ranged below. Ghirlandajo and Andrea del Sarto painted for these Orders some of their finest works,—for instance, the frescoes of the Sassetti Chapel in the Trinità, and the Cenacolo in the San Salvi.

Of the Carthusian monasteries, the parent institution is the Chartreuse at Grenoble. The *Certosa di Pavia* remains unap-

e

proached for its richness and beauty, and is filled with the works
of the finest of the Lombard sculptors and painters,—Luini, Borgog-
none, Fossano, Solari, Cristoforo Romano, Amadeo, and others beyond
number.

The Certosa at Rome, built by Michael Angelo out of the ruins of
the Baths of Diocletian, is filled with pictures by the later artists.
Zurbaran and Carducho painted for the Carthusians of Spain ; and Le
Sueur painted for the Carthusians of Paris his finest work—the life of
St. Bruno, now in the Louvre.

In the churches and abbeys of the Cistercians we shall generally
find St. Bernard a prominent figure, and the companion of the patriarch
St. Benedict. In consequence of his particular devotion to the Virgin,
the Cistercian churches are generally dedicated in her name ; and
St. Bernard visited by the Virgin, or presenting his books to her, are
favourite subjects.

In our own country, the cathedrals of Canterbury, Westminster,
Winchester, Durham, Eli, Peterborough, Bath, Gloucester, Chester,
Rochester, were Benedictine. St. Albans, which took precedence of
all the others, Croyland, Glastonbury, Malmsbury, Malvern, Tewkes-
bury, and hundreds of others, lie in ruins, except that here and there
the beautiful abbey-churches have been suffered to remain, and have
become parish churches.

The Olivetans, a congregation of Reformed Benedictines, produced
some celebrated artists. Lanzi mentions three lay-brothers of this
Order, all of Verona, who excelled in the beautiul inlaid work called
Tarsia or *Intarsiatura.* The monastery at Monte Oliveto near Siena,
the beautiful Church of San Lorenzo at Cremona, and S. Maria in
Organo at Verona, belong to this Order.

In the churches of the Augustines we shall generally find St.
Augustine and his mother, Monica, as principal personages. The
Apostles, and stories from their lives and ministry ; St. Joseph the
husband, and Joachim and Anna the parents, of the Virgin, are also
conspicuous ; and the saints, martyrs, and bishops of the earliest ages,
as St. Sebastian, St. Nicholas, St. Laurence, St. Mary Magdalene,
though common to all the Orders, figure especially in their pictures.
In the convents of the Augustine Hermits we frequently find the
pattern and primitive hermits, St. Anthony and St. Paul, and others
whose legends are given in the first series of this work. The principal saints who belonged to the different branches of this great Order,
many of them canonised for their charities, of course find a place in

their churches; as St. Thomas of Villanueva, St. Lorenzo Giustiniani: but their great saint is St. Nicholas of Tolentino.

The churches of the Agostini in Italy most remarkable for works of Art are—the Sant' Agostino at Rome, for which Raphael painted his prophet Isaiah; the Sant' Agostino at Pavia, which contains the shrine of the patron saint, marvellous for its beauty, and *peopled* with exquisite statuettes; the Eremitani at Padua, and the San Lorenzo at Florence, both rich in early works of Art. Churches dedicated to St. Laurence, St. Sebastian, St. Mary Magdalene, St. Antonio Abbate, generally belong to the Augustines.

Most of the great cathedral churches along the Rhine—Cologne, Mayence, Strasburg—belonged to this Order; in our own country, the cathedrals of Oxford, Lincoln, Salisbury, Lichfield, Carlisle, Hereford; and York Minster and Beverley Minster, though founded by the Benedictines, afterwards belonged to the Augustines.

The most celebrated edifices of the Franciscans are, first, the parent convent and church at Assisi, in the decoration of which the greatest artists of Italy, for a space of three hundred years, were successively employed.

Some of the finest pictures of the Perugino school were executed for this Order. Raphael painted his Madonna di Foligno for the Ara-Celi at Rome. In the same church Pinturicchio painted the chapel of St. Bernardino. The Santa-Croce at Florence is a treasury of early Florentine Art,—of the frescoes of Giotto, Taddeo, and Angelo Gaddi, and Giottino, and the sculptures of Luca della Robbia and Benedetto da Maiano. Titian rests in the Frari at Venice; but round this noble church I looked in vain for any pictures especially commemorating the Franciscan worthies.

The St. Antonio-di-Padova is rich with most precious monuments of Art, with the bronzes of Donatello and Andrea Riccio; the marbles of the Lombardi, Sansovino, Sammichele; and pictures and frescoes of all the great painters of Upper Italy, from the earliest Paduan masters, Avanzi, Zevio, and Andrea Mantegna, down to Campagnola.

When Murillo returned from Madrid to his native Seville, poor and unknown, the Franciscans were the first to patronise him. They had resolved to devote a sum of money, which had been collected by one of the begging brothers, upon a series of pictures for their small cloister: for the eleven pictures required, they could give only the sum in their possession—a trifling remuneration for an artist of established name; but Murillo was glad to undertake the commission, and thus laid the foundation of his future fame. He afterwards, when at the height of his reputation, painted for another Franciscan community (the Capuchins of Seville) twenty of his finest pictures.

The Dominicans have a splendid reputation as artists and patrons of Art. The principal church of the Order is the San Domenico at Bologna, in which is the shrine of the patriarch. The Dominicans employed Niccolò Pisano to build their church as well as to execute this wonderful shrine. The church has, however, been rebuilt in a modern style, and is now chiefly remarkable for the works of the Caracci school.

The most interesting, the most important, and the largest of all the Dominican edifices, is the Santa Maria-sopra-Minerva, at Rome. Here sleeps that gentlest of painters, Angelico da Fiesole, among the brethren of his Order. Around him are commemorated a host of popes and cardinals : among them Leo X., Cardinal Howard, Cardinal Bembo, and Durandus. The whole church is filled with most interesting pictures and memorials of the Dominican saints and worthies, particularly the chapels of St. Thomas Aquinas and St. Catherine of Siena. To the right of the choir stands Michael Angelo's statue of Our Saviour.

Not less interesting is the principal church of the Dominicans at Florence, the Santa Maria Novella. In this church is the famous chapel *Dei Spagnuoli*, painted by Taddeo Gaddi and Simone Memmi ; and the chapel of the Strozzi, painted by Andrea Orcagna. In the cloisters is a series of fifty-six pictures of the lives of Dominican saints, St. Thomas Aquinas, San Pietro Martire, St. Vincent Ferrier, and others, painted by Santi di Tito and Cigoli. In this church is preserved the Virgin and Child by Cimabue, which excited such admiration at the time, and such delight and wonder among the people, that the quarter of the town through which it was carried to its destination was styled for ages afterwards, and is even to this day, the Borgo Allegri.

In the same city is the convent of St. Mark, where Angelico and Fra Bartolomeo lived and worked, and have left some of their finest productions.

In the San Domenico at Siena are some of the finest productions of that remarkable school of Art,—the famous Madonna by Guido da

Siena which preceded that of Cimabue, and the admirable frescoes by Razzi.

The churches of San Sabino and San Giovanni-e-Paolo at Rome, and the San Giovanni-e-Paolo at Venice, belong to this Order. For the last-named church Titian painted his San Pietro Martire.

For the Dominicans of S. Maria alle Grazie at Milan, Leonardo da Vinci painted his Last Supper. Other interesting churches of this Order are Sant' Eustorgio at Milan, Sant' Anastasia at Verona, and Santa Catarina at Pisa.

It is worthy of remark that the churches built by the Dominicans generally consist of a nave only, without aisles, that when preaching to the people, their chief vocation, they might be heard from every part of the church. This form of their churches showed off their pictures to great advantage.[1]

Among the churches of the Carmelites, I may mention as the most interesting the Carmini at Florence, in which Masaccio, Masolino, and Filippino Lippi painted, in emulation of each other, the frescoes of the Brancacci Chapel, the most important works of the fifteenth century.

In this convent worked that dissolute but accomplished friar, Fra Filippo Lippi.

I must say one word of the Jeronimites, who are scarcely alluded to in the succeeding pages, because I do not find one of their Order who, as a canonised saint, has been a subject of Art. They claim as their patriarch St. Jerome, whose effigy, with the stories from his life, is always conspicuous in their churches. Stories of the Nativity and of Bethlehem (where St. Jerome planted his first monastery), and of a certain holy bishop of Lyons, St. Just (San Giusto), who left his diocese and turned hermit in the deserts of Egypt about the end of the fourth century, are also to be found there.

The Jeronimites were remarkable for the splendour of some of their edifices : in Spain, the Escurial belonged to them ; the monastery of San Just, to which Charles V. retired after his abdication, and the remarkable monastery of Belem (Bethlehem) in Portugal, also belonged to them. St. Sigismond, near Cremona, is perhaps the finest

---

[1] The S. Maria-sopra-Minerva, at Rome, is an exception.

in Italy. A community of this Order, the Jesuati, had a convent near Florence (the *San-Giusto*, now suppressed), in which the friars carried on an extensive manufactory of painted glass; and it is particularly recorded that they employed Perugino and other artists of celebrity to make designs, and that Perugino learned from them the art of preparing colours. Vasari has given us a most picturesque description of this convent, of the industry of the friars, of their laboratories, their furnaces, and their distilleries; of their beautiful well-ordered garden, where they cultivated herbs for medicinal purposes; and of the vines trained round their cloisters. This abode of peace, industry, and science, with its gardens and beautiful frescoes, was utterly destroyed by the Imperialist army in 1529.

The Jesuits employed Rubens and Vandyck to decorate their splendid church at Antwerp. The best pictures painted for this Order were by the late Flemish and Spanish artists.

Though the religious communities of Spain were most generous patrons of Art, and though some of the very finest pictures of the Valentian and Seville schools were those which commemorated the monastic saints; yet these subjects, considered as Sacred Art, do not appear to advantage in the Spanish pictures, for it was the monachism of the seventeenth century, and the Spanish painters rendered it from the life. In the representation of Spanish friars, Zurbaran perhaps excelled all others: his cowled Carthusians, with dark deep-set eyes and thin lips, his haggard Franciscans, his missionary fathers and inquisitors, convey the strongest idea of physical self-denial and the consciousness of spiritual power. Murillo, Juanes, and Alonzo Cano frequently give us vulgar heads, sublimated through the intense truth of expression; but, on the whole, we should seek in vain in the Spanish monastic pictures for the refined and contemplative grace and intellectual elevation of the early Italian painters.

Were it the purpose of my book to give a history of Monastic Art and Monastic Artists, I should have to extend these compressed notices into volumes; but it must be borne in mind that I have undertaken only to describe or to interpret briefly the lives and characters of those monastic personages who were subjects of Art,—thence subjects of thought to those who painted them, and sources of thought to those who behold them.

I cannot better conclude than in the appropriate words of an old monk, Wilhelm of Bamberg, who lived about eight hundred years ago :—' I offer this little work as long as I lived to the correction of those who are more learned : if I have done wrong in anything, I shall not be ashamed to receive their admonitions ; and if there be anything which they like, I shall not be slow to furnish more.'

83

Head of St. Benedict. (After Perugino.)

St. Benedict and the early Benedictines in Italy, France, Spain, and Flanders.

A.D. 529.

FIRST in point of time, and first in interest and importance, not merely in the history of art, but in the history of civilisation, we rank the Benedictine Order in all its branches.

The effigies of the saintly personages of this renowned and wide-spread Order occur in every period, and every form, and every school of art, from the earliest and rudest to the latest and worst,—from the 10th to the 18th century. To the reflecting mind they are surrounded with associations of the highest interest, and are suggestive of a thousand thoughts,—some painful and humiliating, such as wait on all the institutions

B

which spring out of the temporary conditions of society and
our imperfect human nature: yet predominant over these,
feelings of gratitude, sympathy, and admiration; if not in all
cases due to the individual represented, yet belonging of right
to that religious community, which under Providence became
the great instrument of civilisation in modern Europe.

Sacred and
Legend. Art,
vol. ii. 368.
I have alluded to the origin of Eastern monachism in the
life of St. Anthony.   There were monks in the West from the
days of Jerome.   The example and the rules of the oriental
anchorites and cenobites had spread over Greece, Italy, and
even into Gaul, in the fourth and fifth centuries; but the
cause of Christianity, instead of being served, was injured by
the gradual depravation of men, whose objects, at the best,
were, if I may so use the word, *spiritually* selfish, leading
them in those miserable times to work out their own safety
and salvation only;—men who for the most part were ignorant,
abject, often immoral, darkening the already dark superstitions
of the people by their gross inventions and fanatic absurdities.
Sometimes they wandered from place to place, levying contributions on the villagers by displaying pretended relics;
sometimes they were perched in a hollow tree or on the top of
a column, or housed, half-naked, in the recesses of a rock,
where they were fed and tended by the multitude, with whom
their laziness, their contempt for decency, and all the vagaries
of a crazed and heated fancy, passed for proofs of superior
sanctity.   Those who were gathered into communities, lived
on the lands which had been granted to them; and belonging
neither to the people nor to the regular clergy, responsible
to no external law, and checked by no internal discipline,
they led a useless and idle, often a miserable and perverted,
existence.   Such is the picture we have of monachism up to
the end of the fifth century.

Whether Benedict, in collecting out of such materials the
purer and better elements, subjugating such spirits to a far
stricter discipline, and supplying what was deficient in the
oriental monastic rule,—namely, the obligation to labour (not
merely for self-support, but as one of the duties towards God

and man),—contemplated the vast results which were to arise
from his institution, may well be doubted. We can none of
us measure the consequences of the least conscious of our acts;
nor did Benedict, probably, while legislating for a few monks,
anticipate the great destinies of his infant Order. Yet it is
clear that his views were not bounded by any narrow ideas of
expediency; and that while he could not wholly shake from his
mind the influences of the age in which he lived, it was not
the less a rarely gifted mind, large, enlightened, benevolent,
as well as enthusiastic,—the mind of a legislator, a reformer,
and a sage, as well as that of a Christian recluse.

The effigies of the Benedictines are interesting and suggestive
under three points of view:—

First, as the early missionaries of the north of Europe, who
carried the light of the Gospel into those wilds, of Britain,
Gaul, Saxony, and Belgium, where heathenism still solemnised impure and inhuman rites;—who with the Gospel
carried also peace and civilisation, and became the refuge of
the people, of the serfs, the slaves, the poor, the oppressed,
against the feudal tyrants and military spoilers of those barbarous times.

Secondly, as the sole depositaries of learning and the arts
through several centuries of ignorance; as the collectors and
transcribers of books, when a copy of the Bible was worth a
king's ransom. Before the invention of printing, every Benedictine abbey had its library and its *Scriptorium*, or writing-
chamber, where silent monks were employed from day to day,
from month to month, in making transcripts of valuable
works, particularly of the Scriptures: these were either sold
for the benefit of the convent, or bestowed as precious gifts,
which brought a blessing equally to those who gave and
those who received. Not only do we owe to them the multi-
plication and diffusion of copies of the Holy Scriptures: we
are indebted to them for the preservation of many classical
remains of inestimable value; for instance, of the whole or
the greater portion of the works of Pliny, Sallust, and Cicero.
They were the fathers of Gothic architecture; they were the

earliest illuminators and limners; and to crown their deservings under this head, the inventor of the gamut, and the first
who instituted a school of music, was a Benedictine monk,
Guido d'Arezzo.

Thirdly, as the first agriculturists who brought intellectual
resources, calculation, and science to bear on the cultivation of
the soil; to whom we owe experimental farming and gardening,
and the introduction of a variety of new vegetables, fruits, &c.
M. Guizot styles the Benedictines 'les défricheurs de l'Europe:'
wherever they carried the cross they carried also the plough. It
is true that there were among them many who preferred study
to manual labour; neither can it be denied that the 'shelter-
ing leisure' and 'sober plenty' of the Benedictine monasteries
sometimes ministered to indolence and insubordination, and
that the cultivation of their domains was often abandoned to
their farmers and vassals. 'But,' says Mr Maitland, 'it was,
and we ought most gratefully to acknowledge that it *is*, a most
happy thing for the world that they did not confine themselves
to the possession of such small estates as they could cultivate
with their own hands. The extraordinary benefit which they
conferred on society by colonising waste places—places chosen
because they were waste and solitary, and such as could be reclaimed only by the incessant labour of those who were willing
to work hard and live hard—lands often given because they
were not worth keeping—lands which for a long while left their
cultivators half-starved and dependent on the charity of those
who admired what we must too often call fanatical zeal,—even
the extraordinary benefit, I say, which they conferred on mankind by thus clearing and cultivating, was small in comparison
with the advantages derived from them by society, after they
had become large proprietors, landlords with more benevolence,
and farmers with more intelligence and capital, than any
others.'

Sir James Stephen thus sums up their highest claims upon
the gratitude of succeeding times: 'The greatness of the Benedictines did not, however, consist either in their agricultural
skill, their prodigies of architecture, or their priceless libraries,
but in their parentage of countless men and women illustrious

Maitland's
'Dark
Ages.'

Essays,
871.

for active piety, for wisdom in the government of mankind, for profound learning, and for that contemplative spirit, which discovers within the soul itself things beyond the limits of the perceptible creation.'

The annalists of the Benedictine Order proudly reckon up the worthies it has produced since its first foundation in 529; viz.—40 popes, 200 cardinals, 50 patriarchs, 1600 archbishops, 4600 bishops, and 3600 canonised saints. It is a more legitimate source of pride that ' by their Order were either laid or preserved the foundations of all the eminent schools of learning of modern Europe.' *Chronique de S. Benoît*

Thus, then, the Benedictines may be regarded as, in fact, the farmers, the thinkers and writers, the artists and the schoolmasters, of mediæval Europe ; and this brief imperfect sketch of their enlightened and enlightening influence, is given here merely as an introduction to the artistic treatment of characters and subjects connected with them. All the Benedictine worthies who figure in art are more or less interesting; as for the legendary stories and wonders by which their real history has been perplexed and disfigured, even these are not without value, as illustrative of the morals and manners of the times in which they were published and represented: while the vast area of civilisation over which these representations extend, and the curious traits of national and individual character exemplified in the variety of treatment, open to us, as we proceed, many sources of thoughtful sympathy with the past, and of speculation on the possible future.

The following is a list of the principal saints of the Benedictine Order whom I have found represented in works of art.

St. BENEDICT, patriarch and founder. In the religious edifices of the Benedictines, properly so called, which acknowledge the convent of Monte Cassino as the parent institution,— as for instance in St. Giustina at Padua, San Severo at Naples, Saint Maur and Marmoutier in France, San Michele-in-Bosco at Bologna, and all the Benedictine foundations in England, —St. Benedict is represented in the black habit; but when he figures as the Patriarch of the Reformed Orders who adopted the white habit—as the Camaldolesi, the Cistercians, the Carthusians—he is represented in the white habit, as in many pictures of the Tuscan school. This is a point to be kept in remembrance, or we shall be likely to confuse both names and characters.

The black habit is given to

St. Scholastica, the sister of St. Benedict, and to his immediate disciples, St. Maurus, St. Placidus, and St. Flavia;

To St. Boniface, the Apostle of Germany;

St. Bennet, Bishop of Durham;

St. Benedict of Anian;

St. Dunstan of Canterbury;

St. Walpurgis of Eichstadt;

St. Giles of Languedoc;

St. Ildefonso of Toledo;

St. Bavon of Ghent;

and in general to all the early Benedictines who lived previous to the institution of the Camaldolesi in 1020.

St. Romualdo and the monks of Camaldoli wear the white habit.

St. John Gualberto and the monks of Vallombrosa wear the pale grey, or ash-coloured habit. These occur in the foundations of their respective orders, and chiefly in Florentine art.

St. Peter of Clugny and the Cluniacs ought to wear the black habit.

St. Bernard of Clairvaux and the Cistercians wear the white habit, with variations of form which will be pointed out hereafter.

St. Bruno and the Carthusians also wear the white habit. It must be remembered that St. Bruno is not met with in any works of art before the sixteenth century, rarely before the seventeenth; while St. Bernard, who figures early as a canonised saint and as one of the great lights of the Catholic Church, occurs perpetually in Italian pictures, with his ample white robes, his pen, and his book; and not merely in the groups of his own Order, but in combination with St. Francis, St. Dominick, St. Thomas Aquinas, and other personages of remarkable authority and sanctity. There are a few instances in early German art of St. Bernard attired in the *black* Benedictine habit, which I shall notice in their proper place.

The Olivetani, a branch of the Benedictine Order founded by St. Bernardo Ptolomei, also wear the white habit.

Having thus introduced the Benedictine saints generally, we proceed to call them up individually, and bid them stand before us, each 'in his habit as he lived,' or as poetry has interpreted and art translated into form the memories and traditions of men. And first appears old Father Benedict—well named !—for surely he *was* BLESSED.

ST. BENEDICT.

Ital. San Benedetto. *Fr.* Saint Benoît. *Spa.* San Benito. Founder patriarch, and first abbot of the Order. March 21, 543.

HABIT AND ATTRIBUTES.—In the original rule of St. Benedict, the colour of the habit was not specified. He and his disciples wore black, as all the monks had done up to that time ; but in the pictures painted for the Reformed Benedictines, St. Benedict wears the white habit.

The proper and most usual attributes are, 1. The Rod for sprinkling holy water : 2. The Mitre and pastoral staff as abbot : 3. The Raven ; sometimes with a loaf of bread in its beak : 4. A pitcher or a broken glass, or cup containing wine : 5. A thorn-bush : 6. A broken sieve.

ST. BENEDICT was born of a noble family in the little town of Norcia, in the duchy of Spoleto, about the year 480. He was sent to Rome to study literature and science, and made so much progress as to give great hopes that he was destined to rise to distinction as a pleader ; but, while yet a boy, he appears to have been deeply disgusted by the profligate manners of the youths who were his fellow-students, and the evil example around him, instead of acting as an allurement, threw him into the opposite extreme. At this period the opinions of St. Jerome and St. Augustine, with regard to the efficacy of solitude and penance, were still prevalent throughout the West: young Benedict's horror of the vicious lives of those around him, together with the influence of that religious enthusiasm which was the spirit of the age, drove him into a hermitage at the boyish age of fifteen.

On leaving Rome, he was followed by his nurse, who had brought him up from infancy, and loved him with extreme tenderness. This good woman, doubtful, perhaps, whether her young charge was out of his wits or inspired, waited on his steps, tended him with a mother's care, begged for him, and prepared the small portion of food which she could prevail upon him to take. But while thus sustained and comforted, Benedict did not believe his penance entire or effective; he secretly fled from his nurse, and concealed himself among the rocks of Subiaco, a wilderness about forty miles from Rome. He met there a hermit, whose name was Romano, to whom he confided his pious aspirations; and then took refuge in a cavern (*il sagro Speco*), where he lived for three years unknown to his family and to the world, and supplied with food by the hermit—this food consisted merely of bread and water, which Romano abstracted from his own scanty fare.

In this solitary life, Benedict underwent many temptations, and he relates that on one occasion, the recollection of a beautiful woman whom he had seen at Rome, took such possession of his imagination as almost to overpower his virtue, so that he was on the point of rushing from his solitude to seek that face and form which haunted his morbid fancy and disturbed his dreams. He felt, however, or he believed, for such was the persuasion of the time, that this assault upon his constancy could only come from the enemy of mankind. In a crisis of these distracted desires, he rushed from his cave, and flung himself into a thicket of briars and nettles, in which he rolled himself until the blood flowed. Thereupon the fiends left him, and he was never again assailed by the same temptation. They show in the garden of the monastery at Subiaco the rose-bushes which have been propagated from the very briars consecrated by this poetical legend.

The fame of the young saint now extended through all the country around; the shepherds and the poor villagers brought their sick to his cavern to be healed; others begged his prayers; they contended with each other who should supply the humble portion of food which he required; and a neighbouring society of hermits sent to request that he would place himself at their head. He, knowing something of the morals and manners of this community, refused at first; and only yielded upon great persuasion, and in the hope that he might be able to reform the abuses which had been introduced into this monastery. But when there, the strictness of his life filled these perverted men with envy and alarm; and one of them attempted to poison him in a cup of wine. Benedict, on the cup being presented to him, blessed it as usual, making the sign of the cross; the cup instantly fell from the hands of the traitor, was broken, and its contents spilt on the ground. (This is a scene often represented in the Benedictine convents.) He, thereupon, rose up; and telling the monks that they must provide themselves with another superior, left them, and returned to his solitary cave at Subiaco, where, to use the strong expression of St. Gregory, *he dwelt with himself;* meaning thereby, that he did not allow his spirit to go beyond the bounds that he had assigned to it, keeping it always in presence of his conscience and his God.

But now Subiaco could no longer be styled a desert, for it was crowded with the huts and the cells of those whom the fame of his sanctity, his virtues, and his miracles, had gathered around him. At length, in order to introduce some kind of discipline and order in this community, he directed them to construct twelve monasteries, in each of which he placed twelve disciples with a superior over them. Many had come from Rome and from other cities; and, amongst others, came two Roman senators, Anicius and Tertullus, men of high rank, bringing to him their sons, Maurus and Placidus, with an earnest request that he would educate them in the way of salvation. Maurus was at this time a boy about eleven or twelve years old, and Placidus, a child not more than five.

c

Benedict took them under his peculiar care, and his community continued for several years to increase in number and celebrity, in brotherly charity and in holiness of life. But of course the enemy of mankind could not long endure a state of things so inimical to his power: he instigated a certain priest, whose name was Florentius, and who was enraged by seeing his disciples and followers attracted by the superior virtue and humility of St. Benedict, to endeavour to blacken his reputation, and even to attempt his life by means of a poisoned loaf; and this not availing, Florentius introduced into one of the monasteries seven young women, in order to corrupt the chastity of his monks. Benedict, whom we have always seen much more inclined to fly from evil than to resist it, departed from Subiaco; but scarcely had he left the place, when his disciple Maurus sent a messenger to tell him that his enemy Florentius had been crushed by the fall of a gallery of his house. Benedict, far from rejoicing, wept for the fate of his adversary, and imposed a severe penance on Maurus for an expression of triumph at the judgment that had overtaken their enemy.

Paganism was not yet so completely banished from Italy, but that there existed, in some of the solitary places, temples and priests and worshippers of the false gods. It happened (and the case is not without parallel in our own times) that while the bishops of Rome were occupied in extending the power of the church, and preaching Christianity in far distant nations, a nest of idolaters existed within a few miles of the capital of Christendom. In a consecrated grove, near the summit of Monte Cassino, stood a temple of Apollo, where the god, or, as he was then regarded, the demon, was still worshipped with unholy rites.

Benedict had heard of this abomination: he repaired therefore to the neighbourhood of Monte Cassino, he preached the kingdom of Christ to these deluded people, converted them by his eloquence and his miracles, and at length persuaded them to break the statue, throw down the altar, and burn up their consecrated grove. And on the spot he built two chapels, in honour of two saints whom he regarded as models, the one of the contemplative, the other of the active, religious life,—St. John the Baptist and St. Martin of Tours.

Sacred and Legend. Art, II. p. 350.

Then, higher up the summit of the mountain, he laid the foundation of that celebrated monastery which has since been regarded as the Parent Institution of his Order. Hence was promulgated the famous Rule which became, from that time forth, the general law of the monks of Western Europe, and which gave to monachism its definite form. The rule given to the cenobites of the East,—and which, according to an old tradition, had been revealed to St. Pachomius by an angel,—comprised the three vows of poverty, of chastity, and of obedience. To these Benedict added two other obligations; the first was manual labour,—those who entered his community were obliged to labour with their hands seven hours in the day: secondly, the vows were perpetual; but he ordained that these perpetual vows should be preceded by a noviciate of a year, during which the entire code was read repeatedly from beginning to end, and at the conclusion the reader said, in an emphatic voice, 'This is the law under which thou art to live and to strive for salvation: if thou canst observe it, enter; if thou canst not, go in peace,—thou art free.' But the vows once taken were irrevocable, and the punishment for breaking them was most severe. On the whole, however, and setting apart that which belonged to the superstition of the time, the Rule given by St. Benedict to his Order was humane, moderate, wise, and eminently Christian in spirit.

Towards the close of his long life Benedict was consoled for many troubles by the arrival of his sister Scholastica, who had already devoted herself to a religious life, and now took up her residence in a retired cell about a league and a half from his convent. Very little is known of Scholastica, except that she emulated her brother's piety and self-denial; and although it is not said that she took any vows, she is generally considered as the first Benedictine nun. When she followed her brother to Monte Cassino, she drew around her there a small community of pious women; but nothing more is recorded of her, except that he used to visit her once a year. On one occasion, when

they had been conversing together on spiritual matters till
rather late in the evening, Benedict rose to depart; his sister
entreated him to remain a little longer, but he refused : Scholastica then, bending her head over her clasped hands, prayed
that Heaven would interfere and render it impossible for her
brother to leave her.   Immediately there came on such a furious
tempest of rain, thunder, and lightning, that Benedict was
obliged to delay his departure for some hours.   As soon as the
storm had subsided, he took leave of his sister, and returned
to the monastery : it was a last meeting; St. Scholastica died
two days afterwards, and St. Benedict, as he was praying in his
cell, beheld the soul of his sister ascending to heaven in the
form of a dove.   This incident is often found in the pictures
painted for the Benedictine nuns.

It would take volumes to relate all the actions and miracles
of St. Benedict during the fourteen years that he presided over
the Convent of Monte Cassino.   In the year 540 he was visited
by Totila, king of the Goths, who cast himself prostrate at
his feet, and entreated his blessing.   Benedict reproved him
for the ravages and the cruelties that he had committed in
Italy, and it was remarked that thenceforward the ferocious
Goth showed more humanity than heretofore.

Shortly after the visit of Totila, Benedict died of a fever
with which he had been seized in attending the poor of the
neighbourhood.   On the sixth day of his illness, he ordered
his grave to be dug, stood for a while upon the edge of it
supported by his disciples, contemplating in silence the narrow
bed in which he was to be laid; then, desiring them to carry
him to the foot of the altar in the church, he received the last
sacraments, and expired, on the 21st of March 543.   Considering the great reputation and sanctity of life of this
extraordinary man, we cannot be surprised that he should have
been the subject of a thousand inventions.   The accomplished
ecclesiastics of his own Order who compiled the memoirs of
his life, reproach the legendary writers for admitting these
improbable stories; and remark with equal candour and good
sense, 'loin d'applaudir au faux zèle de ces écrivains, on doit
les condamner comme des personnes qui corrompent la vérité

Mabillon.

de l'histoire: et qui, au lieu de faire honneur au Saint, le déshonorent, en abusant de son nom pour débiter des fables et se jouer de la crédulité des simples.'

Even before his death, that is, before the year 543, institutions of the Order of St. Benedict were to be found in every part of Christian Europe. Of his two most famous disciples, the elder, St. Maurus, introduced the Rule into France and founded the monastery of Glanfeuil, since called St. Maure-sur-Loire; and so completely did this Rule supersede all others, that in the ninth century, when Charlemagne inquired whether in the different parts of his empire there existed other monks besides those of the Order of St. Benedict, none could be found. St. Maurus died in his convent of Glanfeuil.[1] St. Placidus was sent by his Superior into Sicily, where, according to the tradition, he was joined by his young sister Flavia and two of his brothers. But within a few years afterwards, and while Placidus himself was still in the bloom of youth, the convent near Messina, in which he dwelt, was attacked by certain pirates and barbarians. Placidus and his sister Flavia were dragged forth and massacred, with thirty of their companions, in front of the convent, on the 5th of October, about the year 540. It is fair to add that the martyrdom of St. Placidus and St. Flavia is considered by the later Benedictine writers as apocryphal.

Pictures of St. Benedict often perplex the observer, because, as I have already shown, he was frequently represented in early art wearing the *white* habit, whereas the original habit of his Order was *black*. Where he has the white habit, it is easy to confound him with St. Bernard, St. Bruno, or St.

[1] St. Maur was introduced into England, and held in great veneration by our Norman ancestors; I believe it is generally known that from this French saint is derived one of our greatest English surnames,—Seymaur or Seymour, from Saint-Maur; but I should regret a return to the French appellation. Saint-Maur is foreign, and interesting only as the name of a French monk: Seymour is English, and surrounded by all those historical associations which give the name its English claims to consideration, and its charm to English ears.

Romualdo; where he has the black habit, he may be mistaken for St. Antony. It is therefore necessary to attend particularly to some characteristic attributes which serve to distinguish him.

In all pictures painted for those Benedictine churches and edifices which depend on Monte Cassino and Subiaco, and in the single devotional effigies, St. Benedict wears the black habit

2   St. Benedict. (From an engraving by Wierx.)

with a hood; where he figures as patriarch of the Reformed Benedictines of Clairvaux, Citeaux, Camaldoli, or Vallombrosa, he wears the white habit. He is sometimes beardless, or with little beard; but more frequently he has a long white beard.

As abbot of Monte Cassino, he has sometimes the pastoral staff and mitre. He frequently carries an open book, on which are written the first words of his famous Rule, 'AUSCULTA, FILI, VERBA MAGISTRI.'

Like other saints who have resisted the attacks of the demon, he carries the asperge, or rod used to sprinkle holy water, here emblematical of the purity or holiness by which he conquered. The thorn-bush is an attribute which commemorates the means through which he conquered. A pitcher of wine in his hand, or a pitcher or a broken cup standing on his book, expresses the attempt to poison him in wine. The raven and a loaf of bread, with a serpent creeping from it, express the attempt to poison him in bread.

3   St. Benedict. (A. Mantegna.)

When he is grouped with his two disciples, St. Maurus and St. Placidus, they all wear the black habit; or St. Benedict appears as abbot, and the two disciples as deacons, wearing the rich dalmatica over the black tunic. St. Maurus has a book or a censer; St. Placidus bears his palm as martyr.

When a nun in a black habit is introduced into pictures of St. Benedict, or stands alone with a lily in her hand, and a dove at her feet or pressed to her bosom, it represents St. Scholastica. It is common to find in the Benedictine churches, especially in Italy, devotional figures of St. Benedict and St. Scholastica standing on each side of the altar.

When, in the Benedictine groups, a fourth saint is introduced, a female saint, young and beautiful, and with the

martyr palm and crown, it is probably, if not otherwise distinguished, St. Flavia, the martyred sister of St. Placidus.

Every one who has visited the Vatican will recollect the
three beautiful little heads by Perugino, styled in the catalogue
li tre Santi. In the centre is St. Benedict, with his black cowl
over his head and long parted beard, the book in one hand, and
the asperge in the other. On one side, St. Placidus, young, and
with a mild, candid expression, black habit and shaven crown,
bears his palm. On the other side is St. Flavia, crowned as
martyr, holding her palm, and gazing upward with a divine
expression. These exquisite little pictures were painted by
Perugino, for the sacristry of the church of the Benedictines

San Pietro dei Monaci neri.

at Perugia. There I afterwards saw the other pictures which
completed the series, and which are not less beautiful; St.
Scholastica and St. Maurus; St. Ercolano and St. Costanzo,
the patrons of Perugia; and Peter *the Venerable*, abbot of
Clugni.[1]

In a composition by Benedetto Montagna, engraved by himself and exceedingly rare, he has represented his patron saint
standing in the centre with his crozier and book. On the right
hand, St. Scholastica holding a book, and next to her, St. Giustina, the patroness of Padua, with a sword in her bosom, and
holding a palm. The engraving was executed at Padua, and
the name inscribed, otherwise I should have supposed this figure
to represent St. Flavia. On the other side of St. Benedict are
St. Maurus and St. Placidus.

Fl. Pitti Pal

By Paul Veronese : St. Benedict standing in the black habit
between St. Maurus and St. Placidus : lower down are five
Benedictine nuns, St. Scholastica being distinguished by her
dove; above, in a glory, is the marriage of St. Catherine. This
arrangement leaves no doubt that the picture was painted for a
convent of Benedictine nuns, '*Spose di Christo.*'

---

[1] Peter the Venerable, abbot of Clugni, was not canonised, but he was a *Beato*;
and I have met with him in one picture standing as companion to St. Benedict, but
unfortunately have no note of the place or the painter. He is very interesting for
his gentle spirit, as well as for his learning; and worthy of commemoration for
the asylum he afforded to Abelard when persecuted by St. Bernard, and for the
beautiful letter which he wrote to Heloise on the death of her husband.

There are one or two examples in which St. Benedict appears with St. Maurus and St. Placidus represented as children, wearing the albe and kneeling at his feet, or with censers in their hands.

These remarks apply chiefly to Italian art. In the early German school we find that the groups of Benedictine worthies vary according to the locality. In the place of St. Maurus, St. Placidus, St. Scholastica, we have, perhaps, St. Boniface, St. Cunibert, St. Willibald, St. Gertrude, or St. Ottilia. In the early memorials of English ecclesiastical art, the companions of St. Benedict are St. Gregory and St. Austin, of Canterbury, or St. Dunstan and St. Cuthbert. In the lives of these saints I shall have occasion to point out the motive and propriety of these variations; but here I will not anticipate.

Among the pictures of St. Benedict as Patriarch, should be mentioned those which represent him as seated on a throne; and around him a great number of figures, male and female, wearing the habits of the different Orders, religious and military, which were founded on his Rule. There is a grand picture of this subject in the Convent of San Martino near Palermo, by Novelli, the best of the late Sicilian painters.

Separate subjects from the life of St. Benedict, in general representing some of his most famous actions or miracles, are of course frequently found in the convents of his Order.

1. He stands on the step leading to the door of his convent at Monte Cassino; a man, kneeling at his feet, places a sick child before him, which is healed by the prayer of the saint; Louvre. as in a picture by Subleyras (where St. Benedict wears the Louvre. white habit); another by Silvestre; a third by Rubens; and Darmstadt Gal in a very fine Velasquez.

2. St. Benedict, in the monastery of Monte Cassino, gives Simone the Rule to his Order. Avanzi. Bologna Gal A D. 1370.

3. St. Benedict, when at Subiaco, is haunted by the recollection of a beautiful woman he had seen at Rome. He lies in Palma V. the midst of thorns; two angels in front scatter roses, while Milan. Brera. the tempting devil is gliding away behind.

D

Padua.
St. Giustina.
    4. St. Benedict receives St. Maurus and St. Placidus, who are presented by their respective fathers.

    5. St. Benedict, kneeling, with his hands outspread, and looking up with an expression of transport, sees, in a vision, his sister Scholastica, attended by two virgin martyrs (probably
Le Sueur.
Louvre.
St. Catherine and St. Agnes), and St. Peter and St. Paul. Here he wears the black habit with the cowl thrown back; the crozier and mitre, expressing his dignity as abbot, lie near him. This beautiful picture was painted for the convent of Marmoutier.

    6. The wicked monks attempt to poison St. Benedict. He is seated within the porch of a convent, a monk approaches and presents to him a cup of wine, another behind holds a
Fl. Acad.
pitcher, and turns away his head with a look of alarm: as in a predella by Andrea del Sarto. Here St. Benedict and the monks wear the white habit, the picture having been painted for the monastery of St. Salvi, near Florence, a branch of the Vallombrosian Order.

Flamingo.
St. Pietro dei
Monaci neri.
Perugia.
    7. The mission of St. Mauro and St. Placido: St. Benedict gives them his blessing before they depart, the one to France, the other to Sicily.

Bologna.
D. Canuti.
A.D. 1684.
    8. St. Benedict being near his end, stands looking down into his grave; he is sustained by two angels, and there are nine figures of monks and attendants.

    A complete history of the life and miracles of St. Benedict in a series of subjects executed in painting, sculpture, or stained glass, may still be found in many of the churches, chapels, and cloisters of the Benedictine convents. I will mention a few of the most celebrated.

Naples.
A. Solario.
    1. A series at Naples painted by Antonio Solario (called Lo Zingaro, *the Gipsy*), in the cloisters of the convent of San Severino. Here St. Benedict wears the *black* habit.

Florence.
Spinello.
    2. A series by Spinello Aretino, which covers the walls of the sacristy of San Miniato. Here, the convent being attached to the Vallombrosian Order, St. Benedict and his monks wear the *white* habit.

3. A series elaborately carved in wood, in forty-eight compartments, in the choir of the church of San Giorgio at Venice. By Albert de Brule. *(Venice. A. de Brule.)*

4. A series painted in fresco by Ludovico Caracci and his pupils, in the Benedictine convent of San Michele-in-Bosco; once famous as a school of art, now unhappily in a most ruined state, these magnificent cloisters having been converted into a horse-barrack by the French. *(The Caracci. Bologna.)*

5. A set of ten pictures by Philippe de Champagne: not very good. *(Musée. Brussels.)*

As the selection of subjects is nearly the same in all, I shall confine myself to the exact description of one complete series, which will assist the reader in the comprehension of any others he may meet with, and shall review that which is earliest in date, and in other respects the most remarkable. Perhaps it were best to begin with the story of the painter, one of those romances which enchant us in the histories of the early artists. It reminds us of the story of the Flemish blacksmith; but Antonio lo Zingaro sounds better, at least more musically, in a love tale, than Quinten Matsys—a name as quaint and hard as one of his own pictures. Antonio was either a gipsy by birth, or he followed the usual gipsy profession, that of a tinker or smith: he saw and loved the daughter of Col' Antonio dell' Fiore; the father refused his consent, but admiring the manly character and good looks of the handsome youth, he was heard to say, that if Antonio had been a painter he would have given him his daughter. On this hint Antonio left Naples; changed, as Lanzi says, his forge into an academy, his hammer into a pencil; placed himself for a few weeks under Lippo Dalmasio of Bologna; then, at Venice, studied the works of the Vivarini; at Florence those of the Bicci and Masaccio; at Rome those of Gentile da Fabriano; and returning to Naples in 1443, he claimed the love and the hand of the fair daughter of Col' Antonio. Shortly afterwards he painted for the Benedictines this life of their great founder, in the very convent which, according to tradition, had been endowed by Tertullus, the father of St. Placidus.

The series begins from the beginning, and all the stories represented may be found in the old legend.

1. Benedict, as a boy about seven or eight years old, journeys from Norcia to Rome. A mountain rising in the middle divides the picture into two parts : on one side is the city of Norcia, on the other a distant view of Rome. He is seen on horseback accompanied by his father Eutropius ; two servants armed with lances go before, and his nurse Cyrilla, mounted on a mule, follows behind.

2. On his flight from Rome, he arrives at Affide, and is received before the church of St. Peter by the men of the place. Behind him is seen his nurse Cyrilla, who has followed him from Rome.

3. Cyrilla, occupied in preparing food for her charge while he was busied in his devotions, borrowed from a neighbour a sieve or earthen vessel in which they clean the corn ; she broke it, and was in great distress, not having money wherewith to replace it. Benedict by a miracle repaired it. In this picture the youthful saint is represented at prayers in his chamber ; Cyrilla in front holds the broken sieve ; in the background is seen a church, and over the door the country people have hung the sieve, and are looking at it with admiration and amazement. The broken sieve is sometimes, but not often, introduced as an attribute in pictures of St. Benedict. To the left of this composition a beautiful woman is seen standing at a balcony smelling at a sprig of myrtle ; it is the portrait of the daughter of Col' Antonio : two doves billing upon the roof above, are supposed to allude to the recent marriage of the artist.

4. Benedict, in the wilderness of Subiaco, meets Romano. He puts on the dress of a hermit.

5. The cave at Subiaco, since famous as *lo sagro Speco;* Benedict seated within it intently reading ; beside him a basket tied to a string which communicates with a bell at the mouth of the cave. The demon is busy cutting the string. Various wild animals around express the solitude of the place.

6. Romano the hermit dies, and Benedict is left in his cave alone, with none to feed him or care for him ; but absorbed in his devotions, he is unmindful of the wants of nature. In the mean time, a certain priest had prepared himself a feast for Easter day, and on the eve, as he slept in his bed, an angel said to him, ' Thou hast prepared a feast for thyself while my servant on yonder mountain dies for food.' When the priest arose in the morning, he took the food that he had prepared for himself and went forth to seek the servant of God ; and after a long search, he found him towards the evening in his solitary cave, and he said unto him, ' Rise, brother, let us eat, for this is Easter day.' Benedict was surprised, for he had dwelt so long apart from men, that he knew not what day it was. The picture represents Benedict and the priest with food spread before them ; in the background is seen the priest asleep in his cell, and visited by the divine revelation.

Guido painted, in the cloisters of San Michele-in-Bosco, the peasants bringing their offerings to the cave of St. Benedict. From the beauty and graceful head-dress of one of the female figures, the Italians styled this picture *la Turbantina*. It has perished like the rest.

7. Benedict in his solitude is tempted by recollections and desires which disturb his devotions. On one side of the picture he is seated reading : he makes the sign of the cross to drive away a little black bird,—of course the demon in disguise,—which, hovering over his book, perpetually interrupts him by suggesting sinful thoughts. He flings down his book, tears off his garment, and throws himself down amidst the thorns and the nettles.

8. Benedict, being chosen superior of the monastery near Subiaco, endeavours in vain to reform the profligate monks. In return they attempt to poison him. A monk presents the cup of wine, five others stand behind with hypocritical faces. The saint raises his hand in benediction over the cup, which is seen to break.

'The seven women introduced into the monastery to tempt Benedict and his companions,' was painted by Ludovico Caracci in the series at Bologna, but is omitted in the series by Solario. Richardson.

9. The reception of the two children, St. Maurus and St. Placidus. This, in the Neapolitan series, is a rich and charming composition. The children are seen habited in magnificent dresses, and with glories round their heads. The two fathers, Anicius and Tertullus, present them. They are accompanied by a great retinue of servants on foot and on horseback, with hawks, dogs, &c. Lo Zingaro has introduced his own portrait at full length holding his pencils, and behind him his master, Lippo Dalmasio : the authenticity of these portraits gives additional value to the picture.

10. A certain monk in one of the dependent cells at Subiaco, was always inattentive to his religious duties, and, at the hour devoted to mental prayer, was seen to leave the choir and wander forth. Benedict, coming to reprove him, saw that he was led forth by a demon in the shape of a little black boy who pulled him by the robe (a personification of the demon of sloth) ; this demon, however, was visible to no other eyes but those of the saint, who, following the monk, touched him on the shoulder with his staff and exorcised the demon, who from that hour troubled the sinner no more.

11. Three monks come to complain to Benedict that three out of the twelve monasteries at Subiaco are in want of water. Benedict by his prayers procures an abundant fountain, which gushes forth and flows like a torrent down a mountain side. This subject is particularly striking in the frescoes by Spinello, in the church of San Mininto.

12. A Gothic peasant, employed in felling wood, lets the blade of his billhook fall into the lake. Benedict takes the handle of the billhook, puts it into the water, and the blade rises miraculously from the bottom, and unites to it. The disciple Maurus, behind, looks on with astonishment.

13. St. Placidus, while yet a child, in going to draw water, falls into the lake ; St. Benedict, who is praying in his cell, has a revelation of his danger, and sends Maurus in all haste to help him ; Maurus rushes to his assistance,

treading the water as if it had been dry land. (Benedict imputed this miracle to the ready obedience and unselfish zeal of Maurus, while his disciple, in his humility, insisted that he was miraculously sustained by the virtue and prayers of his superior.)

14. The wicked priest Florentius, being filled with jealousy and envy at the superior sanctity of Benedict, sent him a poisoned loaf. Benedict, aware of his treachery, threw the loaf upon the ground, and commanded a tame raven, which was domesticated in the convent, to carry it away and place it beyond the reach of any living creature. In the picture, the scene represents the refectory of the convent : on one side Benedict is receiving the poisoned loaf, on the other side the raven is seen flying through the window with it in his beak. In the background Florentius is seen crushed to death, by the walls of his house falling on him.

15. Benedict is seen preaching to the people near Monte Cassino. In the background, on the top of the hill, is the temple of Apollo, and Benedict flings down the idol.

16. He founds the monastery of Monte Cassino. The demon endeavours to retard the work, and seats himself on the top of a large stone required for the building, so that no human power avails to move it from its place. In the picture, several monks with long levers are endeavouring to move a

San Michele.   great stone : St. Benedict kneels in the foreground, and at his prayer the
Bologna.   demon takes to flight. (The composition of this subject, by Spada, is famous, and has been engraved.)

17. One of the monks who was assisting in the building of the monastery is crushed to death. He is brought to the feet of St. Benedict, who recalls him to life.

In digging the foundations of the monastery of Monte Cassino, they discover an idol of bronze, from which issues a supernatural fire which threatens to destroy the whole edifice. St. Benedict perceives at once that this is a delusion of the enemy, and at his prayer it disappears. This subject is not in the series by Lo Zingaro.

18. Totila, the king of the Goths, visits St. Benedict in his monastery. He is prostrate at the feet of the saint, while his warriors and his attendants are seen behind.[1]

---

[1] And Totila, king of the Goths, hearing that Benedict possessed the spirit of prophecy, and willing to prove him, attired Riggo, his armour-bearer, in his royal sandals, robes, and crown, and sent him, with three of his chief counts, Vuleni, Ruderi, and Bledi, to the monastery. Benedict witnessing his approach from a lofty place whereon he sat, called out to him, 'Put off, my son, those borrowed trappings : they are not thine own ;' and Totila, hearing of this, went to visit him ; and perceiving him from a distance seated, he presumed not to approach, but prostrated himself on the earth, and would not rise till, after having been thrice bidden to do so by Benedict, the servant of Christ deigned to raise him himself, and chid him for his misdeeds, and in a few words foretold all that was to befall him, the years of his reign, and the period of his death.—See *Lord Lindsay's Sketches of Christian Art.*

19. The sick child restored at the prayer of its parents; a frequent subject.

20. St. Benedict visits his sister Scholastica, and they spend the day in spiritual discourse and communion. 'And when the night approached, Scholastica besought her brother not to leave her; but he refused her request, saying that it was not right to remain all night from his convent. Thereupon Scholastica, who had a secret feeling that her end was approaching, and that she should never see him more, bent down her head upon her folded hands, and prayed to God for the power to persuade her brother; and behold, the heavens, which till that moment had been cloudless, were immediately overcast; and there arose such a tempest of thunder and lightning and rain, that it was impossible for Benedict and his attendant to leave the house, and he remained with his sister in prayer and holy converse till the morning.' (This subject also is omitted in the series by Lo Zingaro.)

21. Three days afterwards, St. Benedict, standing rapt in prayer, beheld the released soul of his sister, in the form of a dove, flying towards heaven.

The death of St. Scholastica has been painted by Luca Giordano.

22. St. Benedict dies at the foot of the altar. Two of his disciples behold at the same moment the selfsame vision; they see a path or a ladder extending upwards towards heaven strewed with silken draperies, and lamps on either side burning along it; and on the summit the Virgin and the Saviour in glory. And while they wondered, a voice said to them, 'What path is that?' and they said, 'We know not.' And the voice answering, again said, 'That is the path by which Benedict the Beloved of God is even now ascending to heaven.' So they knew that he was dead.

The following curious and picturesque legend seems to have been invented as a parable against idle and chattering nuns.

Two ladies of an illustrious family had joined the sisterhood of St. Scholastica. Though in other respects exemplary and faithful to their religious profession, they were much given to scandal and vain talk; which, being told to St. Benedict, it displeased him greatly; and he sent to them a message, that if they did not refrain their tongues and set a better example to the community he would excommunicate them. The nuns were at first alarmed and penitent, and promised amendment; but the habit was too strong for their good resolves; they continued their vain and idle talking, and, in the midst of their folly, they died. And being of great and noble lineage, they were buried in the church near the altar; and afterwards, on a certain day, as St. Benedict solemnised mass at that altar, and at the moment when the officiating deacon uttered the usual words, 'Let those who are excommunicated, and forbidden to partake, depart and leave us ; ' behold! the two nuns rose up from their graves, and in the sight of all the people, with faces drooping and averted, they glided out of the church.   And thus it happened every time that the mass was celebrated there, until St. Benedict, taking pity upon them, absolved them from their sins, and they rested in peace.

This most rich and picturesque subject, called by the Italians, ' *le Suore morte*,' was painted by Lucio Massari, in the series at Bologna.   Richardson mentions it with praise as equal to any of those by his master, Ludovico, or his competitor, Guido ; he calls it ' the dead nuns coming out of their tombs to hear mass.' The fresco has perished, and the engraving in Patina's work does not give a high idea of it as a composition.

Bologna.

Cloisters of
San Michele-
in-Bosco.

The above detailed description of a series of subjects from the life of St. Benedict will be found useful; for, in general, however varied in treatment, the selection of scenes and incidents has been nearly the same in every example I can recollect, and some of them may be found separately treated.

ST. ILDEFONSO.

Or St. Alphonso.   *Ger.* Der Heilige Ildelphons.   Archbishop and patron
saint of Toledo.   Jan. 23, 667.

THIS saint, famous in the Spanish hierarchy and hardly less famous in Spanish art, was a Benedictine and one of the earliest of the Order in Spain; he became archbishop of Toledo in 657, and died in 667.   He wrote a book in defence of the perpetual virginity of the Holy Virgin, which some heretics had questioned, and in consequence the Holy Virgin—could she do less?—regarded him with especial favour.   Once on a time, when St. Ildefonso was entering his cathedral at the head of a midnight procession, he perceived the high altar surrounded by a blaze of light.   He alone of all the clergy ventured to approach, and found the Virgin herself seated on his ivory episcopal throne, and surrounded by a multitude of angels chanting a solemn service from the psalter. He bowed to the ground before the heavenly vision, and the Virgin thus addressed him : ' Come hither, most faithful servant of God, and receive this robe which I have brought thee from the treasury of my Son.' Then he knelt before her, and she threw over him a chasuble or cassock of heavenly tissue, which was adjusted on his shoulders by the attendant angels. From that *Ford's Handbook.* night the ivory chair remained unoccupied and the celestial vestment unworn, until the days of the presumptuous archbishop Sisiberto, who died miserably in consequence of seating himself in the one, and attempting to array himself in the other.

This incident has been the subject of two magnificent pictures.

1. ' Murillo has represented the Virgin and two angels about *Madrid Gal. A.D. 267.* to invest the kneeling saint with the splendid chasuble; other angels stand or hover around and above; and behind the prelate there kneels, with less historical correctness, a venerable nun, holding in her hand a waxen taper. The Virgin and the angel on her left hand are lovely conceptions, and the richly embroidered chasuble is most brilliantly and carefully painted. The reputation of this picture has been extended by the excellent graver of Fernando Selma.' A good impression is in the *Stirling's Sp. Painters.* British Museum.

2. The second picture was painted by Rubens; it is an altar- *Vienna Imp. Gal.* piece with two wings; in the centre, the Virgin is seated on the episcopal throne attended by four angels, before her kneels St. Ildefonso, and receives from her hands the sacred vestment. On the right side kneels the archduke Albert, attended by his patron, St. Albert; and on the left wing, the archduchess-infanta, Clara Isabella Eugenia (daughter of Philip II.), who is attended by St. Clara.

The investiture of St. Ildefonso is a subject of frequent occurrence: there are two or three examples in the Spanish Gallery of the Louvre. There is another curious legend of St. Ildefonso which has furnished a subject for the Spanish artists. This was a vision of St. Leocadia, to whom he had vowed a particular

Sacred and
Legend. Art,
iL p. 301. worship, and who rose out of her sepulchre clad in a Spanish mantilla, in order to inform St. Ildefonso of the favour with which the Virgin regarded the treatise he had written in her praise; he had just time before she disappeared to cut off a corner of her mantilla, which was long preserved in her chapel at Toledo as a most precious relic. Mr. Ford mentions with admiration the bas-reliefs by Felise de Vigarny representing the principal events in the life of St. Ildefonso, which were executed in the reign of Charles V., about 1540.

ST. BAVON.

Flem. St. Bavo, or St. Baf.   *Ital.* San Bavone.   Patron saint of Ghent and
Haerlem.   Oct. 1, 657.

ST. BAVON is interesting, as we have a fine sketch of him in our National Gallery; and many pictures of him exist in the churches in Belgium.

He was a nobleman, some say a duke, of Brabant, and was born about the year 589: after living for nearly fifty years a very worldly and dissipated life, and being left a widower, he was moved to compunction by the preaching of St. Amand, the apostle of Belgium and first bishop of Maestricht. Withdrawing himself from his former associates, Bavon bestowed all his goods in charity, and then repaired to St. Amand, who received him as a penitent, and placed him in a monastery at Ghent. But this state of penance and seclusion did not suffice to St. Bavon: he took up his abode in a hollow tree in the forest of Malmedun near Ghent, and there he lived as a hermit; his only food being the wild herbs, and 'his drink the crystal well.' He is said to have died in his hermitage, somewhere about the year 657.

In the old Flemish prints and pictures he is represented either as a hermit, seated and praying in a hollow tree; or as a prince, in armour, and with a falcon on his hand. Among the penances he imposed on himself, was that of carrying a huge stone, emblematical of the burden of his sins, which is sometimes introduced as an attribute. The chapel erected in his honour is now the cathedral of Ghent, for which Rubens painted the great altar-piece. It represents the saint in his secular costume of a knight and a noble, presenting himself before Amand, bishop of Maestricht; he is ascending the steps of a church; Amand stands above, under a portico, and lower down are seen the poor to whom St. Bavon has distributed all his worldly goods. The original sketch for this composition London Nat. Gal. is the more valuable because of the horrible ill-treatment which the large picture has received from the hands of a succession of restorers. I find also the following representations of this saint:—

1. St. Bavon in his ducal robes, with a falcon on his hand; G. Huge, Sculp. statue over the door of the cathedral at Ghent.

2. St. Bavon in armour, with the falcon on his hand. Eng. J. Matham.

3. The slave of a nobleman, being possessed or mad, is Jordaens. Eng. restored by St. Bavon. The nobleman, in a balcony behind, looks down on the scene.

There is a story of St. Bavon which I do not remember to have seen represented, and which would be a beautiful subject for a picture. It is related that St. Bavon, one day after his Guizot, Hist. de la Civ. Fr. conversion, beheld coming towards him a man who had formerly been his slave, and whom he had, for some remissness in his service, beaten rigorously and sold to another master. And at the sight of him who had been his bondman, the Man of God was seized with an agony of grief and remorse, and fell down at his feet and said, 'Behold, I am he who sold thee, bound in leathern thongs to a new master; but, O my brother! I beseech thee remember not my sin against thee, and grant me this prayer! Bind me now hand and foot; beat me with stripes; shave my head, and cast me into prison: make me suffer all I inflicted on thee, and then perchance the Lord will have mercy and forget my great sin that I have committed against Him and against thee!' And the bondman, hearing these words, was astonished, and he refused to lay hands on the Man of God, his former master; but St. Bavon insisted the more, and at last, after much entreaty and many arguments, he yielded; and he took the Man of God and bound him, and shaved his head, and cast him into the public prison, where he remained for a certain time, deploring day and night the crime he had committed against his human and Christian brother.

In this legend, as M. Guizot well observes, the exaggeration of the details is of no importance; even the truth of the recital as a mere matter of fact is of little consequence. The importance of the moral lies in this: that the story was penned in the seventh century; that it was related to the men of the seventh century, to those who had incessantly before their eyes the evils, the iniquities, the sufferings of slavery; it was a protest in the name of the religion of Christ against such a state of things, and probably assisted in the great work of the abolition of slavery, begun by Pope Gregory the Great, in 604.

St. Giles.

Lat. Sanctus Ægidius.   *Ital.* Sant Egidio.   *Fr.* Saint Gilles.   *Sp.* San Gil.
Patron saint of the woodland.   Patron saint of Edinburgh ; of Juliers in
Flanders.   Sept. 1, 725.   ATTRIBUTE ;—a wounded hind.

'Ane Hynde set up beside Sanct Geill.'
SIR DAVID LINDSAY.

THIS renowned saint is one of those whose celebrity bears no proportion whatever to their real importance. I shall give his legend in a few words. He was an Athenian of royal blood, and appears to have been a saint by nature; for one day on going into the church, he found a poor sick man extended upon the pavement; St. Giles thereupon took off his mantle and spread it over him, when the man was immediately healed. This and other miracles having attracted the veneration of the people, St. Giles fled from his country and turned hermit; he wandered from one solitude to another until he came to a retired wilderness, near the mouth of the Rhone, about twelve miles to the south of Nismes. Here he dwelt in a cave, by the side of a clear spring, living upon the herbs and fruits of the forest, and upon the milk of a hind, which had taken up its abode with him. Now it came to pass that the king of France was hunting in the neighbourhood, and the hind, pursued by the dogs, fled to the cavern of the saint, and took refuge in his arms. The hunters let fly an arrow, and, following on the track, were surprised to find a venerable old man, seated there with the hind in his arms, which the arrow had pierced through his hand. Thereupon the king and his followers, perceiving that it was a holy man, prostrated themselves before him, and entreated forgiveness. (or, according to another legend, Wamba, king of the Goths.)

The saint, resisting all the attempts of the king to withdraw him from his solitude, died in his cave. But the place becoming sanctified by the extreme veneration which the people bore to his memory, there arose on the spot a magnificent monastery, and around it a populous city bearing his name and giving the same title to the counts of Lower Languedoc, who were styled comtes de Saint-Gilles.

The abbey of St. Giles was one of the greatest of the Benedictine communities, and the abbots were powerful temporal as well as spiritual lords. Of the two splendid churches which existed here, one has been utterly destroyed, the other remains one of the most remarkable monuments of the middle ages now existing in France. It was built in the eleventh century; the portico is considered as the most perfect type of the Byzantine style on this side of the Alps, and the whole of the exterior of the church is described as one mass of bas-reliefs. In the interior, among other curiosities of antique art, must be mentioned an extraordinary winding staircase of stone, the construction of which is considered a miracle of skill.[1]

St. Giles has been especially venerated in England and Scotland. In 1117, Matilda, wife of Henry I., founded an hospital for lepers outside the city of London, which she dedicated to St. Giles, and which has since given its name to an extensive parish. The parish church of Edinburgh existed under the invocation of St. Giles as early as 1359. And still, in spite of the Reformation, this popular saint is retained in our calendar.

---

[1] This staircase, called in the country 'La vis de Saint Gilles,' was formerly 'la but des pélerinages de tous les compagnons tailleurs de pierre.'— *Voyages au Midi de la France.*

4   St. Giles the Hermit.

He is represented as an aged man with a long white beard, and a hind pierced by an arrow is either in his arms or at his feet.   Sometimes the arrow is in his own bosom, and the hind is fawning on him.   In pictures his habit is usually white, because such pictures date subsequently to the period when the abbey of St. Giles became the property of the Reformed Benedictines, who had adopted the white habit.

Representations of St. Giles are seldom met with in Italy, but very frequently in early French and German art.[1]

[1] 'St. Giles standing in a transport of religious ecstasy before Pope Gregory IX.,' painted by Murillo for the Franciscan convent at Seville, is cited by Mr Stirling (*Artists of Spain*, p. 836) as 'St. Giles, the patron of the Greenwood,' but it represents a very different person; a St. Giles, more properly *il Beato Egidio*, who was one of the early followers of St. Francis of Assisi, and consequently wears the habit and cord of St. Francis.   The picture is now in England.

A very influential character of his time was St. Benedict of Anian, better known by his French name, Saint Benoît d'Aniane.

He was a Goth by race, a native of Maguelonne in Languedoc; and his name, before he assumed that of Benedict, is not known. His father sent him in his childhood to the court of king Pepin-le-Bref, where he was first page and then cupbearer, and distinguished himself as a military commander under Charlemagne. In the year 774 we find him a monk in the abbey of St. Seine, having been converted to a religious life by a narrow escape from drowning. Having vainly endeavoured to reform the monks of his monastery, we next find him a solitary hermit on the banks of the Anian, which flowed through the district in which he was born. A number of companions congregated around him, and he was enabled to construct an extensive monastery, into which he introduced the Benedictine Rule in all its pristine severity.

From Languedoc he was called by Louis-le-Débonnaire to Aix-la-Chapelle, where he assisted in the foundation of a large monastery near that city, the capital of Charlemagne and his successors; and we find him afterwards presiding in a council held especially for the reform of the monastic orders. At this time was promulgated a commentary upon the original Rule, which M. Guizot characterises as substituting narrow and servile forms for the large and enlightened spirit of the first founder.

Hist. de la Civilisation on France.

As this Saint Benoît d'Aniane had a great reputation for sanctity, effigies of him probably existed, and, if not destroyed, may still exist, in the churches of Languedoc. I have met with but one Italian picture in which he is represented. It commemorates the great incident of his life—the conversion of St. William of Aquitaine. This William was duke of Aquitaine in the time of Charlemagne, and a famous warrior and statesman of that day. Among other exploits, he obtained a signal victory over the Saracens, who about that period were ravaging the south of France. Converted by the preaching and admonition of St. Benedict d'Aniane, he withdrew from the world, and became a professed monk in a monastery which he had himself erected : he received the habit from the hands of St. Benoît, and died a few years afterwards in the odour of sanctity.

St. William of Aquitaine receiving the monastic habit from St. Benedict, is the subject of a picture by Guercino, now in the Academy at Bologna. The abbot is seated on a throne, and St. William, who kneels before him, is in the act of laying aside his helmet and cuirass.

Separate pictures of this St. William of Aquitaine, whose conversion is regarded as a great honour to the Benedictines, are often found in the edifices of the order. In general he is represented in armour, or in a monk's habit, with his armour and ducal crown lying beside him. There is a fine half-length of St. William, attributed to Giorgione, at Hampton Court.

A curious old print in the British Museum represents St. William kneeling, wearing a magnificent helmet ; his breviary on the ground, while his clasped hands embrace a standard : behind him is a shield, on which are three fleurs-de-lys and three crescents ; the latter, I suppose, in allusion to his victories over the Saracens.

There is a print after Lanfranco, representing the death of St. William : the blessed Virgin herself brings the holy water, a female saint dips her fingers into it, and an angel sustains him ; in the background the demons flee in consternation. He died in 812 or 813 ; and St. Benedict d'Aniane in 821.

St. Nilus, of Grotta Ferrata.

Ital. San Nilo. *Fr.* Saint Nil le jeune. Sept. 26, 1002.

THE name of this obscure Greek monk is connected in a very interesting manner with the history of art, and his story is mixed up with some of the most striking episodes in the history of mediæval Rome; but among the thousands of travellers, artists, students, and critics who have thronged his beautiful chapel at Grotta Ferrata during the last two hundred years, how few have connected its pictured glories there with the deep human interests of which they are the record and the monument !

St. Nilus was a Greek of Calabria, born near Tarentum. He was a man of a gentle and melancholy temperament, who, after many years of an active existence, and the loss of a wife whom he had tenderly loved, embraced in his old age a religious life : he became a monk of the Greek order of St. Basil, and, through his virtues and his intellectual superiority, in a few years he was placed at the head of his community. An invasion of the Saracens drove him from the east to the west of Italy. He fled to Capua, and there took refuge in the Benedictine convent of Monte Cassino, where he was received with all reverence and honour. There he composed Greek hymns in honour of St. Benedict, and the abbot assigned to him and his fugitive brotherhood a small convent dependent on Monte Cassino.

Pandolfo, prince of Capua, left a widow, Aloare, who at this time governed in right of her two sons. She had instigated these youths to murder their cousin, a powerful and virtuous noble ; and now, tortured by remorse, and fearful for the consequences to them, she sent for St. Nilus, confessed her crime, and entreated absolution ; he refused to give it, but upon condition that she should yield up one of her sons to the family of the murdered man, to be dealt with as they should think fit, as the only real expiation she could make. The guilty mother wept, and could not resolve on the sacrifice. Nilus then, with all the severity and dignity of a prophet, denounced her sin as unforgiven, and told her that the expiation she had refused of her own free will would ere long be exacted from her. The princess, terrified, entreated him to intercede for her, and endeavoured to force upon him a sum of money. Nilus flung the gold upon the earth, and turning from her, shut himself up in his cell. Shortly afterwards, the younger of the two princes assassinated his brother in a church, and for this sacrilegious fratricide he was himself put to death by order of Hugh Capet, king of France.

Nilus then quitted the territory of Capua, and took up his A.D. 990. residence at Rome, in the convent of St. Alexis on the Aventine, whither those who were diseased in body and mind repaired to the good saint for help and solace ; and many were the miracles

F

and cures wrought by his intercession : among others the cure
of a poor epileptic boy.

Rome was at this time distracted by factions : the authority
of the emperors of the East had been long set aside; that of the
emperors of the West was not yet established. The famous
Crescentius had been declared consul, and for a time, under his
wise and firm administration, liberty, order, and peace reigned
in the city. John XVI., a Greek by birth and an intimate
friend of St. Nilus, was then pope. On a sudden, the young
emperor, Otho III., appeared in Italy at the head of his barbarous legions; declared a relation of his own pope, under the
name of Gregory V.; put out the eyes of the anti-pope John,
and besieged Crescentius in the castle of St. Angelo. After a
short resistance Crescentius yielded on honourable terms; but
had no sooner given up the fortress, than the faithless emperor
ordered him to be seized, flung headlong from the walls, and
his wife Stephanie was abandoned to the outrages of the soldiers.

In the midst of these horrors, Otho and the new pope endeavoured to conciliate Nilus, whose virtues and whose reputation for sanctity had given him great power over the people: but
the old man rebuked them both as enemies of God. He wrote
to the emperor a letter of reproach, concluding with these words:
' Because ye have broken faith, and because ye have had no
mercy for the vanquished, nor compassion for those who had no
longer the power to injure or resist, know that God will avenge
the cause of the oppressed, and ye shall both seek mercy and
shall not find it.' Having despatched this letter, he shook the
dust from his feet, and departed the same night from Rome. He
took refuge first in a cell near Gaeta, and afterwards in a solitary
cavern near Frascati, called the *Crypta*, or Grotta, Ferrata.

Within two years Pope Gregory died in some miserable
manner, and Otho, terrified by remorse and the denunciations of
St. Nilus, undertook a pilgrimage to Monte Galgano. On his
return he paid a visit to Nilus in his hermitage at Frascati, and,
falling on his knees, besought the prayers and intercession of
the saint. He offered to erect, instead of his poor oratory, a
magnificent convent with an endowment of lands. Nilus refused
his gifts. The emperor, rising from his knees, entreated the

holy man to ask some boon before they parted, promising that, whatever it might be, he would grant it. Nilus, stretching forth his hand, laid it on the jewelled cuirass of the emperor, and said, with deep solemnity, ' I ask of thee but this, that thou wouldst make reparation for thy crimes before God, and save thine own soul ! ' Otho returned to Rome, where, within a few weeks afterwards, the people rose against him, obliged him to fly ignominiously, and he died, at the early age of twenty-six, poisoned by the widow of Crescentius.   In the same year St. Nilus died, full of years and honours, after having required Jan. 1002 of the brotherhood that they would bury him immediately, and keep the place of his interment secret from the people. This he did in the fear that undue honours would be paid to his remains, the passion for sanctified relics being then at its height.

The gifts which St. Nilus had refused were accepted by his friend and disciple Bartolomeo ; and over the cavern near Frascati arose the magnificent castellated convent and church of San Basilio of Grotta Ferrata.   In memory of St. Nilus, who is considered as their founder, the Rule followed by the monks is that of St. Basil, and mass is even now celebrated every day in the Greek language ; but they consider their convent as a dependency of Monte Cassino, and wear the Benedictine habit.

This community was long celebrated for the learning of the monks, and for the possession of the finest Greek library in all Italy ; now, I believe, incorporated with that of the Vatican. The Cardinal-Abbot Giuliano da Rovere, afterwards the warlike Julius IL, the patron of Michael Angelo, converted the convent into a fortress ; and in one of the rooms died Cardinal Consalvi.

But we must leave the historical associations connected with this fine monastery, for our business is with those of art.

About the year 1610, when Cardinal Odoardo Farnese was abbot of Grotta Ferrata, he undertook to rebuild a defaced and ruined chapel, which had in very ancient times been dedicated to those interesting Greek saints St. Adrian and his wife St. Natalia, whose story has been already narrated.   The chapel Legend. Art, was accordingly restored with great magnificence, re-dedicated il. 426. to St. Nilus and his companion St. Bartolomeo, who are regarded as the two first abbots; and Domenichino, then in his twenty-eighth year, was employed to represent on the wall some of the most striking incidents connected with the foundation of the monastery.

The walls, in accordance with the architecture, are divided into compartments varying in form and size.

In the first large compartment, he has represented the visit of Otho III. to St. Nilus; a most dramatic composition, consisting of a vast number of figures. The emperor has just alighted from his charger, and advances in a humble attitude to crave the benediction of the saint. The accessories in this grand picture are wonderful for splendour and variety, and painted with consummate skill. The whole strikes us like a well got up scene. The action of a spirited horse, and the two trumpeters behind, are among the most admired parts of the picture. It has always been asserted that these two trumpeters express, in the muscles of the face and throat, the quality of the sounds they give forth. This, when I read the description, appeared to me a piece of fanciful exaggeration; but it is literally true. If painting cannot imitate the power of sound, it has here suggested both its power and kind, so that we *seem* to hear. Among the figures is that of a young page, who holds the emperor's horse, and wears over his light flowing hair a blue cap with a plume of white feathers: according to the tradition, this is the portrait of a beautiful girl, with whom Domenichino fell violently in love, while he was employed on the frescoes. Bellori tells us that not only was the young painter rejected by the parents of the damsel, but that when the picture was uncovered and exhibited, and the face recognised as that of the young girl he had loved, he was obliged to fly from the vengeance of her relatives.

Bellori,
p. 180.

The great composition on the opposite wall represents the building of the monastery after the death of St. Nilus by his disciple and coadjutor St. Bartolomeo. The master builder, or architect, presents the plan, which St. Bartolomeo examines through his spectacles. A number of masons and workmen are busied in various operations, and an antique sarcophagus, which was discovered in digging the foundation, and is now built into

the wall of the church, is seen in one corner; in the background
is represented one of the legends of the locality. It is related
that when the masons were raising a column, the ropes gave
way, and the column would have fallen on the heads of the
assistants, had not one of the monks, full of faith, sustained
the column with his single strength.

One of the lesser compartments represents another legend.
The Madonna appears in a glorious vision to St. Nilus and St.
Bartolomeo in this very Grotta Ferrata, and presents to them
a golden apple, in testimony to her desire that a chapel should
rise on this spot. The golden apple was reverently buried in
the foundation of the belfry, as we now bury coins and medals,
when laying the foundation of a public edifice.

Opposite is the fresco, which ranks as one of the finest and
most expressive of all Domenichino's compositions. A poor
epileptic boy is brought to St. Nilus to be healed; the saint,
after beseeching the divine favour, dips his finger into the oil of

5   St. Nilus heals the Epileptic Boy. (From the fresco at Grotta Ferrata.)

a lamp burning before the altar, and with it anoints the mouth of the boy, who is instantly relieved from his malady. The incident is simply and admirably told, and the action of the boy, so painfully true, yet without distortion or exaggeration, has been, and I think with reason, preferred to the epileptic boy in Raphael's Transfiguration.

In a high narrow compartment Domenichino has represented St. Nilus before a crucifix: the figure of our Saviour extends the arm in benediction over the kneeling saint, who seems to feel, rather than perceive, the miracle. This also is beautiful.

St. Nilus having been a Greek monk, and the convent connected with the Greek order, we have the Greek fathers in their proper habits,—venerable figures portrayed in niches round the cornice. The Greek saints, St. Adrian and St. Natalia; and the Roman saints, St. Agnes, St. Cecilia, and St. Francesca, are painted in medallions.

A glance back at the history of St. Nilus and the origin of the chapel will show how significant, how appropriate, and how harmonious is this scheme of decoration in all its parts. I know not if the credit of the selection belongs to Domenichino; but, in point of vivacity of conception and brilliant execution, he never exceeded these frescoes in any of his subsequent works, and every visitor to Rome makes this famous chapel a part of his pilgrimage. For this reason I have ventured to enlarge on the details of an obscure story, which the beauty of these productions has rendered important and interesting.

Angel. (From the Chapel at Grotta Ferrata.)

The Benedictines in England, and in Germany.

THE introduction of the Order of St. Benedict into England, which took place about fifty years after the death of the founder, was an important era in our history—of far more importance than the advent of a king or the change of a dynasty. Many of the English Benedictines were, as individual characters, so interesting and remarkable, that I wish heartily they had remained to our time conspicuous as subjects of art. We should have found them so, had not the rapacity of Henry VIII. and his minions, followed afterwards by the blind fanaticism of the Puritans, swept from the face of our land almost every memorial, every effigy of these old ecclesiastical worthies, which was either convertible into money or within reach of the sacrilegious hand. Of Henry and his motives we think only with disgust and horror. The Puritans were at least religiously in earnest; and if we cannot sympathise with them, we can understand their stern hatred of a faith, or rather a form of faith, which had filled the world with the scandal of its pernicious abuses, while the knowledge or the comprehension of all the benefits it had bestowed on our ancestors lay beyond the mental vision of any Praise-God-Barebones, or any heavenly-minded tinker or stern covenanter of Cromwell's army. When I recall the history of the ecclesiastical potentates of Italy in the 16th century, I could almost turn Puritan myself: but when I think of all the wondrous and beautiful productions of human skill, all the memorials of the great and gifted men of old, the humanisers and civilisers of our country, which once existed, and of which our great cathedrals—noble and glorious as they are even now —are but the remains, it is with a very cordial hatred of the profane savage ignorance which destroyed and desecrated them.

Now if I dwell for a while on the legends of our old ecclesiastical worthies, and give a few pictures, rapidly sketched in words, of scenes and personages sanctified by our national traditions, it is not so much to show how they have been illustrated, but rather with a hope of conveying some idea as to the spirit and form in which they may be or ought to be, artistically treated.

In a cycle of our early English saints, wherever they are to be found,—whether in our old illuminated missals or in such decorations of our old churches as may survive in sculpture or be released from whitewash and plaster,—we should expect to meet with ST. HELENA, the mother of Constantine, and ST. ALBAN, our first martyr, taking precedence of the rest.

St. Helen,
A.D. 328,
Aug. 18.

Of St. Helen I will not say much here, for her legendary history belongs to another place. The early ecclesiastical writers fondly claim her as one of our native saints : all the best authorities are agreed that she was born in England; according to Gibbon at York; according to other authorities at Colchester; and the last-mentioned town bears as arms a cross with four crowns, in allusion to its claim, Helena being inseparably connected with the discovery, or the 'invention,' as it is not improperly termed, of the Holy Cross at Jerusalem. Some say she was the daughter of a mighty British prince, King Coilus or Coel (I suppose the 'Old King Cole' of our ballads), and that in marrying Constantius Chlorus she brought him a kingdom for her dowry. Others—but they are denounced as Jews and pagans—aver that she was the daughter of an innkeeper, and thence called Stabularia, literally *Ostler-wench;* while her Christian panegyrists insist that she obtained the name of Stabularia because she erected a church over the stable in which our Saviour was born. But I shall not enter further into the dispute concerning the birthplace and lineage of Helena. From remote antiquity the English have claimed her as their own, and held her in especial honour: witness the number of our old churches dedicated to her, and the popularity of her classical Greek name in all its various forms. In her old age she became

a Christian; and her enthusiastic zeal for her new religion, and the influence she exercised over the mind of her son, no doubt contributed to the extension of Christianity throughout the empire. For this she should be held in honour; and cannot, certainly, be reproached or contemned because of all the extravagant, yet often beautiful and significant, fictions and allegories with which she has been connected, and which served to lend her a popularity she might not otherwise have possessed. None of the old legends have been more universally diffused than the 'History of the True Cross;' and I believe that, till a darkness came over the minds of the people, it was, formerly, as well understood in its allegorical sense as the 'Pilgrim's Progress' is now. But this will be related in proper time and place. St. Helena as an English saint should stand in her imperial robes wearing the earthly crown and the celestial glory round her head, and holding the large cross, generally much taller than herself; sometimes she embraces the cross with both arms, and sometimes she is seen in companionship with her son Constantine, and they sustain the cross between them.

St. Helena is particularly connected with the Benedictines, for it was believed that her remains had been carried off from Rome about the year 863, and were deposited in the Benedic-

G

8   St. Helena and St. Constantine.   (Palma Vecchio.)

tine abbey of Hautvilliers in Champagne.   The disputes concerning the authenticity of these relics fill many pages of the
'Annales' of Mabillon.   Every one who has been at Rome
will recollect the superb sarcophagus of red porphyry in
which she once reposed, and which is now empty, as well as
her chapel in that lonely and beautiful church the 'Santa
Croce di Gerusalemme.'   But of these I will say no more at
present.

St. Alban.   ST. ALBAN, the famous English proto-martyr, was not a
A.D. 303,   monk, but, as the shrine dedicated to him became subsequently
June 22.   one of the greatest of our Benedictine institutions, I place
him here.

There is something particularly touching in the circumstances of his death, as related by Bede. He lived in the third century, in the reign of the Emperor Aurelian. In his youth he had travelled to Rome, conducted thither by his love of learning; and, being returned home, he dwelt for some time in great honour in his native city of Verulam. Though still in the darkness of the old idolatry, he was distinguished by the practice of every virtue, and particularly those of hospitality and charity. When the persecution under Diocletian was extended to the shores of Britain, a Christian priest pursued by the people took refuge in his house. Alban concealed him there, and, struck by the example of his resignation, and enlightened by his teaching, he became a Christian and received baptism. A few days afterwards he had the opportunity of proving the sincerity of his conversion. The stranger being pursued, Alban provided for his safety; then putting on the long raiment of the priest, he surrendered himself to the soldiers; and refusing equally to betray his guest or worship idols, he was condemned to death. He was first cruelly tortured, and then led forth to be beheaded. An exceeding great multitude, mostly Christians, followed him to the place of execution near the city. To reach it they were obliged to pass the river Coln; but so great was the multitude that it was impossible for them to go over the narrow bridge: the saint stood for a moment on the bank, and, putting up a short prayer, the waters miraculously divided, and the whole multitude passed dry-shod, to the number of a thousand persons. On reaching the summit of the hill, a most pleasant spot covered with bushes and flowers, St. Alban, falling on his knees, prayed that God would give him water, and immediately a living spring broke out before his feet, in which he quenched his thirst; and then bending his neck to the executioner, the head of this most courageous martyr was struck off, and he received the crown of life which God has promised to all who suffer for His sake.

Bede adds, that in his time there existed on the spot a church of wonderful workmanship; but in the subsequent wars and ravages of pagan nations the memory of the martyr had almost perished, and the place of his burial was forgotten;

until it happened, in the year 793, that the same was made
known by a great miracle.

For when Offa, king of the Mercians, was taking his rest on
his royal couch, he was admonished by an angel from Heaven,
that the remains of the blessed martyr should be disinterred,
and restored to the veneration of the people.   So King Offa
came to Verulam, and there they found St. Alban lying in a
wooden coffin; and there and then the pious king founded
a church, and in its vicinity arose the great Benedictine
monastery and the town of St. Alban's in Hertfordshire.

St. Alban being the first saint and martyr in England, the
abbot of St. Alban's had precedence over all others.

In some old effigies which remain of St. Alban he is represented like St. Denis, carrying his head in his hand.   His
proper attribute as martyr would be the sword and a fountain
springing at his feet; not *three* fountains, as in the effigies of
St. Paul.

We have all learned in our childhood the famous legend
which makes Gregory the Great the father of Christianity in
England, which tells how he became interested for the poor
benighted islanders, our fair-haired ancestors, (*non Angli sed
angeli!*) and represents St. Augustine of Canterbury as the first
Christian missionary in this nation.   But it appears to me that
our modern artists, and particularly the decorators of our
national edifices, are under a mistake in assuming this view to
be consonant with the truth of history.   St. Augustine preached
in England that form of Christianity which had been promulgated by the Hierarchs of the West.   He was the instrument
by which the whole island was brought under the papal power.
But Christianity and a knowledge of the Scriptures had shone
upon Britain three centuries at least before the time of Augustine.

The old traditions relating to the first introduction of Christianity into this land, are in the highest degree picturesque and
poetical.   As to their truth, I am rather inclined to sympathise

with the early belief in those ancient stories, which, if they
cannot be proved to be true, neither can they be proved to be
false. Now, everything that is possible *may* be true, and
everything that is improbable is not therefore false; which
being granted, it is a great comfort to be emancipated from the
severe limits prescribed by critical incredulity, and allowed
for a while to revel in the wider bounds allowed to a more
poetical and not wholly irreligious faith.

' Some,' says Dugdale, ' hold that, when Philip, one of the
twelve apostles, came to France, he sent Joseph of Arimathea
with Joseph, his son, and eleven more of his disciples hither,
who, with great zeal and undaunted courage, preached the
true and lively faith of Christ; and when King Arviragus
considered the difficulties that attended their long and
dangerous journey from the Holy Land, beheld their civil and
innocent lives, and observed their sanctity and the severities
of their religion, he gave them a certain island in the west
part of his dominions for their habitation, called Avalon,
containing twelve hides of land, where they built a church of
wreathen wands, and set a place apart for the burial of their
servants. These holy men were devoted to a religious solitude,
confined themselves to the number of twelve, lived there
after the manner of Christ and the apostles, and, by their
preaching, converted a great number of the Britons, who
became Christians.'

' Upon this ground,' says another writer, ' the ambassadors
of the kings of England claimed precedency of the ambassadors
of the kings of France, Spain, and Scotland in several councils
held in Europe; one at Pisa, A.D. 1409; another at Constance, v. Usher. De
Primo. Eccl.
A.D. 1414; another at Siena, A.D. 1424; and especially at Britt. p. 22.
Basle, A.D. 1434, where the point of precedency was strongly
debated : the ambassadors from France, insisting much upon
the dignity and magnitude of that kingdom, said, " 'Twas not
reasonable that England should enjoy equal privileges with
France;" but the ambassadors of England, insisting on the
honour of the Church, declared that the Christian faith was
first received in England, Joseph of Arimathea having come
hither with others, in the fifteenth year after the assumption of

the Virgin Mary, and converted a great part of the people
to the faith of Christ: but France received not the

Sacred and
Legend. Art,
ii. 341.

Christian religion till the time of Dionisius (St. Denis), by
whose ministry it was converted: and by reason hereof the
kings of this land ought to have the right of precedency,
for that they did far transcend all other kings in worth and
honour, so much as Christians were more excellent than
Pagans.'

Such is the legend of Glastonbury, that famous old abbey,
whose origin is wrapt in a wondrous antiquity; where bloomed
and still blooms the 'mystic thorn,' ever on the feast of the
Nativity, when, amid the snows of winter, every other branch
is bare of leaf and blossom; where sleeps King Arthur 'till
he comes again;' where Alfred found refuge when hunted by
his Danish foes, and matured his plans for the deliverance of
his country. And not at Glastonbury only, but at Bangor
and many other famous places, there were, before the coming
of St. Augustine, communities of religious men and women,
who lived according to the Eastern rule, as the Essenes of
Palestine and the Cenobites in Egypt, of whom I have spoken
in the lives of St. Paul and St. Anthony.

But Augustine the monk, whom the English call St. Austin,
was undoubtedly the first who introduced the Order of St.

Sacred and
Legend. Art,
i. 303.

Benedict into England. The Benedictines number St. Gregory
as one of their Order: it is not certain that he took the habit,
but he placed the convent which he had founded at Rome on
the Celian Hill under the rule of St. Benedict; and out of this
convent came the monk St. Augustine, and his companions,
whom Gregory selected as his missionaries to England. In
those days the coasts of England were, to the soft Italians, a
kind of Siberia for distance and desolation; and on their journey
these chosen missionaries were seized, we are told, 'with a
sudden fear, and began to think of returning home rather than
proceed to a barbarous, fierce, unbelieving nation, to whose
very language they were strangers;' and they sent Augustine
to entreat of their holy father, the Pope, that they might be
excused from this dangerous journey. We are not informed
how St. Gregory received Augustine: we only know that he

speedily sent him back with a brief but peremptory letter, beginning with these words, ' *Gregory, the servant of the servants of God, to the servants of our Lord.* Forasmuch as it had been better not to begin a good work than to think of desisting from that which is begun, it behoves you, my beloved sons, to fulfil the good work which, by the help of our Lord, you have undertaken.' So, Augustine being constituted chief and bishop over the future converts, they continued their journey, and landed in the Isle of Thanet, in Kent.

Now, the men of Kent had been, even from the earliest times, the most stiff-necked against the Christian faith, so that it was an old saying to express the non-existence of a thing, that it was not to be found ' *either in Christendom or in Kent.*' Notwithstanding, the Saxon King Ethelbert received St. Augustine and his companions very graciously, persuaded thereto by his wife Bertha, who was a Christian; and they entered by his permission the city of Canterbury, carrying on high the holy cross and the image of our blessed Saviour, and singing Hallelujahs.

Then they preached the Gospel, and King Ethelbert and his subjects were baptized and became Christians. It is recorded that the first Kentish converts received the rites of baptism and confirmation in a chapel near Canterbury, which the French princess Bertha had dedicated to her native saint, Martin of Tours.

But Augustine was not satisfied with converting the Saxons: he endeavoured to bring the ancient British Church to acknowledge the pope of Rome as its spiritual head, and himself as his delegated representative. The Britons were at first strongly opposed to what appeared to them a strange usurpation of authority; and their bishops pleaded that they could not lay aside their ancient customs and adopt the ceremonies and institutions of the Roman Church without the consent and free leave of the whole nation. (For before the time of Augustine the British Church acknowledged no obedience to Rome, but looked to its own metropolitan, the bishop of Caerleon-on-Uske, and derived Glaston-their customs, rites, and ordinances from the Eastern Churches.) bury. ' Therefore they desired that another synod might be called, because their number was small. This being agreed to, seven bishops and many learned men repaired thither; and on their way they consulted a certain holy and wise man who lived as an anchorite, and who advised them, saying, " If Augustine shall rise up when ye come near him, then he is a servant of God, and ye shall listen to his words; but if he sit still and show no respect, then he is proud and cometh not from God, and is not to be regarded." And when they appeared before Augustine, and saw that he sat still in his chair without showing any courtesy or respect to them, they were very angry, and, discoursing among themselves, said, " If he will not rise up now unto us, how much more will he condemn us when we are subject to him? " Then Augustine exhorted them to receive the rites and usages of the Church of Rome; but they excused themselves, saying that they owed no more to the bishop of Rome than the love and brotherly assistance which was due to all who held with them the faith of Christ; but to their own bishop they owed obedience, and without his leave they could not alter the ordinances of their Church. Then Augustine desired their conformity in three things only. 1. In the observation of Easter. 2. In the administration of baptism. 3. In their assistance by preaching among the English Saxons. And neither in these things could he obtain their compliance, for they persisted in denying him all power over them.' (I cannot but think that this conference between St. Augustine and the ancient British clergy would be a capital scene for a picture, and much better than the trite subjects usually chosen from this part of our history. To understand fully the conduct held by Augustine on this occasion, we should remember that it was then a question which divided the whole Christian world, whether the eastern or western patriarch should be acknowledged as the head of the universal Church ; and whether the Greek or the Roman ceremonial was to prevail. If it had not been for the obstinacy of St. Augustine, we might all have been now Greeks or Russians—dreadful possibility! But to continue the story.) ' Notwithstanding the opposition of the Britons, and contrary to the directions of his great and wise master St. Gregory, Augustine carried things with a high hand, and deprived the British bishops of their sees, which they had possessed for nearly 400 years, and this of his own will and power, and without any crime or sentence of a council. Further, he is accused of having incited the Saxons to rise up against the British Christians, and to have been the cause that Ethelfred, king of Northumberland, went up against the people of Chester, and slew the monks of Bangor, 1200 in number, and utterly destroyed that glorious monastery, in which were deposited many and precious records and monuments of British history.'

(The massacre at Bangor, which is described with picturesque circumstances by Bede, took place in 607, or later; and Augustine, who had received the pallium as first Primate of England in 601, died in 604.)

'This Augustine,' saith Capgrave, 'was very tall by stature; of a dark complexion; his face beautiful, but withal majestical. He always walked on foot, and commonly visited his provinces barefooted, and the skin on his knees had grown hard, through perpetual kneeling at his devotions; and further, it is said of him, that he was a most learned and pious man, an imitator of primitive holiness, frequent in watchings, fastings, prayers, and alms, zealous in propagating the church of his age, earnest in rooting out paganism, diligent in repairing and building churches, extraordinarily famous for the working of miracles and cures among the people. Hence his mind may have been puffed up with human vanity, which caused St. Gregory to admonish him.'

To this description I will add, that he ought to be represented wearing the black Benedictine habit, and carrying the pastoral staff and the Gospel in his hand, as abbot and as missionary. After the year 601, he may be represented with the cope, pallium, and mitre, as primate and bishop of Canterbury. The title of Archbishop was not in use, I believe, before the ninth century.

The proper companion to St. Augustine, where he figures St. Paulinus of York. as chief saint and apostle of England, would be St. Paulinus; who, in 601, was sent from Rome to assist him in his mission.

H

Paulinus preached through all the district north of the Humber,
and became the first Primate of York, where he founded the
cathedral, and afterwards died very old at Rochester, in 644.
His friends and converts, King Edwin and Queen Ethelburga,
may be grouped with him.

> But to remote Northumbria's royal hall,
> Where thoughtful Edwin, tutor'd in the school
> Of sorrow, still maintains a heathen rule,
> Who comes with functions apostolical?
> Mark him, *of shoulders curv'd, and stature tall,*
> *Black hair, and vivid eye, and meagre cheek,*
> *His prominent feature like an eagle's beak:—*
> A man whose aspect doth at once appal
> And strike with reverence.   *Wordsworth.*

This portrait of Paulinus, from a description left us by an
eye-witness, may be useful to artists: the epithet, '*thoughtful
Edwin,*' as well describes the king.

The conversion of Coifi, the Druid and high-priest of Thor,
is the most striking and picturesque incident in the life of St.
Paulinus of York. 'King Edwin gave his license to Paulinus
to preach the Gospel, and renouncing idolatry, declared that he
received the faith of Christ; and when he inquired of the
high-priest who should first profane the altars and temples
of the idols, he answered, "I!—for who can more properly
than myself destroy those things which I worshipped through
ignorance?" Then immediately, in contempt of his former
superstitions, he desired the king to furnish him with arms
and a horse, and mounting the same, he set forth to destroy
the idols (for it was not lawful before for the high-priest to
carry arms or ride on any but a mare). Having, therefore,
girt a sword about him, with a spear in his hand, he mounted
the king's charger, and proceeded to the idols. The multitude beholding it, concluded that he was distracted; but he,
when he drew near the temple, cast his spear into it, and
rejoicing in the knowledge of the true God, commanded
his companions to destroy the idols with fire.'[1] Here would

---

[1] The scene took place at Godmundham, in Yorkshire. Stukely says, in his
Itinerary, 'The apostle Paulinus built the parish church of Godmundham, where
is the font in which he baptized the heathen priest Coifi.'

have been a fine subject for Rubens! I recommend it to our artists; only they must be careful to preserve (which Rubens never did) the religious spirit; and in seeking the grand and dramatic, to avoid (as Rubens always did) the exaggerated and theatrical.

From the time of St. Augustine, all the monasteries already in existence accepted the rule of St. Benedict, and those grand ecclesiastical edifices which rose in England during the next 600 years were chiefly founded by or for the members of this magnificent order. They devoted their skill in art, their labour, their learning, and their wealth to admirable purposes; and as in these present more civilised times, we find companies of speculators constructing railways, partly for profit and expediency, and partly, as they say, to give employment to the poor, so in those early times, when we were only just emerging from barbarism, we find these munificent and energetic communities draining the marshes of Lincolnshire and Somersetshire, clearing the midland and northern forests, planting, building, and transcribing Bibles for the honour of God and the good of the poor; and though their cultivated fields and gardens, and their cloisters, churches, libraries, and schools, were laid waste, burned, and pillaged by the devastations of the Danes, yet the spirit in which they had worked survived, and their institutions were afterwards restored with more extensive means, and all the advantages afforded by improved skill in mechanical and agricultural science. I feel disappointment and regret while writing this, to be obliged to confine myself to the artistic representations of the early English Benedictines; yet, even within these narrow limits, I find a few who must be briefly commemorated; and I begin with one who is connected in an interesting manner with the history of Art in our country.

In the year 677, BENEDICT, or BENNET BISCOP, of a noble family in Northumberland, founded the two Benedictine monasteries of St. Peter's at Wearmouth, and St. Paul's at Jarrow, which became in process of time two of the most flourishing schools in England. *St. Bennet of Wearmouth.*

St. Bennet seems to have been a man, not only learned and accomplished as an ecclesiastic, but endowed with a sense of the beautiful, rare in those days, at least among our Saxon ancestors. Before his time there were scarcely any churches or chapels built of stone to be found in England. Glass in the windows was unknown; there were very few books, and fewer pictures. Bennet made no less than five journeys to France and Italy, and brought back with him cunning architects and carvers in stone, and workers in metal, whom he settled near his monastery: he brought glaziers from France, for the art of making glass was then unknown in England. Moreover, he brought with him a great quantity of costly books and copies of the Scriptures, and also many pictures representing the actions of our Saviour, in order, as it is expressly said, 'that the ignorant might learn from them as others did from books.' And further it is related that he placed in his monastery at Wearmouth 'pictures of the Blessed Virgin, of the twelve apostles, the history of the Gospel, and the visions of St. John. His church of St. Paul at Jarrow he adorned with many other pictures, disposed in such a manner as to represent the harmony between the Old and the New Testament, and the conformity of the figures of the one with the reality of the other. Thus, Isaac carrying the wood which was to make the sacrifice of himself, was explained by Christ carrying the cross on which he was to finish his sacrifice; and the brazen serpent was illustrated by our Saviour's crucifixion.' (From this we may gather how ancient, even in this country, was the system of type and antitype in Christian art, of which Sir Charles Eastlake has given a most interesting account in the notes to Kugler's Handbook, p. 216.) And further, St. Bennet brought from Rome in his last journey, a certain John, Abbot of San Martino, precentor (or teacher of music) in the Pope's chapel, whom he placed at Wearmouth to instruct his monks in the chanting the divine services according to the Gregorian manner, which appears to be the first introduction of music into our cathedrals. He also composed many books for the instruction of his monks and of those who frequented the schools of his monastery. Among the pupils of

Beda.

i.e. the Apocalypse.

St. Bennet was the Venerable Bede, who studied in his convent A.D. 735. during seven years.

After a long life of piety, charity, and munificence, embellished by elegant pursuits, this remarkable man died about the year 703.

St. Bennet Bi-oop.

He is represented as bishop, wearing the mitre and planeta, and bearing the pastoral staff; in the background, the two monasteries are seen, and the river Tyne flowing between them; —as in a little print by Hollar.

In association with this enlightened bishop, we ought to find St. Cuthbert of Durham; a saint in that age, of far greater celebrity and more extended influence, living and dead; yet looking back from the point where we now stand, we feel inclined to adjust the claims to renown more equitably. Perhaps we might say that St. Cuthbert represented the spirituality, and St. Benedict of Wearmouth the intellect, of their time and country.

St. Cuth-
bert.

Cuthbert began life as a shepherd, in the valley of the Tweed, not far from Melrose, where a religious house had recently sprung up under the auspices of St. Aidan. One of the legends of his childhood seems to have been invented as an instructive apologue for the edification of schoolboys. As St. Cuthbert was one day playing at ball with his companions, there stood among them a fair young child, the fairest creature ever eye beheld; and he said to St. Cuthbert, 'Good brother, leave these vain plays; set not thy heart upon them; mind thy book; has not God chosen thee out to be great in His Church?' but Cuthbert heeded him not; and the fair child wrung his hands, and wept, and threw himself down on the ground in great heaviness; and when Cuthbert ran to comfort him, he said, 'Nay, my brother, it is for thee I weep, that preferrest thy vain sports to the teaching of the servants of God;' and then he vanished suddenly, and Cuthbert knew that it was an angel that had spoken to him; and from that time forth, his piety and love of learning recommended him to the notice of the good Prior of Melrose, who instructed him carefully in the holy Scriptures. And it is related, that on a certain night, as Cuthbert watched his flocks by the river-side, and was looking up to the stars, suddenly there shone a dazzling light above his head, and he beheld a glorious vision of angels, who were bearing the soul of his preceptor St. Aidan into heavenly bliss; whereupon he forsook his shepherd's life, and entering the monastery of Melrose, he became, after a few years, a great and eloquent preacher, converting the people around, both those who were Pagans, and those who, professing themselves Christians, lived a life unworthy the name, and he brought back many who had gone astray ; for when he exhorted them, such a brightness appeared in his angelic face, that no man could conceal from him the most hidden secrets of the heart, but all openly confessed their faults and promised amendment. He was wont to preach in such villages as, being far up in the wild and desolate mountains, were considered almost inaccessible ; and among these poor and half-barbarous people, he would sometimes remain for weeks together, instructing and humanising them. Afterwards removing from Melrose to Landisfarne, he dwelt for some years as an anchorite in a solitary islet, on the shore of Northumberland, then barren, and infested by evil spirits, but afterwards called Holy Island, from the veneration inspired by his sanctity. Here he dug a well, and sowed barley, and supported himself by the labour of his hands ; and here, according to the significant and figurative legend, the angels visited him, and left on his table bread prepared in Paradise. After some years, Cuthbert was made bishop of Landisfarne, which was then the principal see of the Northumbrians (since removed to Durham), and in this office he was venerated and loved by all men, being an example of diligence and piety, 'modest in the virtue of patience, and affable to all who came to him for comfort;' and further, many wonderful things are recorded of him both while he lived and after his death, miraculous cures and mercies wrought through his intercession; and the shrine of St. Cuthbert became, in the North of England, a place of pilgrimage. It was often plundered, and on one occasion his relics were carried off by the Danes. Their final translation was to the Cathedral of Durham, where they now repose.

St. Cuthbert is represented as bishop, with an otter at his side, originally signifying his residence in the midst of waters. There is, however, an ancient legend, which relates that one night after doing penance on the shore in the damp and the cold, he swooned, and lay as one dead upon the earth ; but there came two otters out of the water, which licked him all over, till life and warmth were restored to his benumbed limbs. In this, as in so many other instances, the emblem has been translated into a fact, or rather into a miracle. The proper attribute of

St. Cuthbert is the crowned head of King Oswald in his arms; of whom, as associated with St. Cuthbert and often represented in early art, I will say a few words here.

ST OSWALD.   ST. OSWALD was the greatest of our kingly saints and martyrs of the Saxon line.   His whole story, as related by Bede, is exceedingly beautiful.   He had requested that a teacher might be sent to instruct him and his people in the Word of God; but the first who came to him was a man of a very severe disposition; who, meeting with no success in his mission, returned home.   Then Aidan, afterwards Prior of Melrose, rebuked this missionary, saying, he had been more severe to his unlearned hearers than he ought to have been; which good man, Aidan, being endued with singular discretion and all the gentler virtues, undertook to preach to the subjects of King Oswald, and succeeded wonderfully.

One of the most beautiful and picturesque incidents in the life of Oswald is thus related by Bede.

Having been dispossessed of his dominions by Cadwalla (or Cadwallader), king of the Britons, who, besides being a bloody and rapacious tyrant, was a heathen (this, at least, is the character given him by the Saxons), he lived for some time in exile and obscurity, but at length he raised an army and gave battle to his enemy.   And the two armies being in sight of each other, 'Oswald ordered a great cross of wood to be made in haste, and the hole being dug into which it was to be fixed, the king, full of faith, laid hold of it, and held it

Bede.   with both hands, till it was made fast by throwing in the earth.   Then raising his voice, he cried, "Let us all kneel down, and beseech the living God to defend us from the haughty and fierce enemy, for he knows that we have undertaken a just war, for the safety of our nation."   Then they went against the enemy and obtained a victory as their faith deserved.'

This King Oswald afterwards reigned over the whole country, from the Humber to the Frith of Forth, Britons, Picts, Scots, and English; but having received the Word of God, he was exceedingly humble, affable, and generous to the poor and strangers. It is related of him, that he was once sitting at dinner on Easter-day, and before him was a silver dish full of dainty meats; and they were just ready to bless the bread, when his almoner came in on a sudden, and told him there were some poor hungry people seated at his door, begging for food; and he immediately ordered the dish of meat to be carried out to them, and the dish itself to be cut in pieces and divided amongst them. And St. Aidan, who sat by him, took him by the right hand, and blessed him, saying, ' May this hand never perish!' which fell out according to his prayer. This most Christian king, after reigning justly and gloriously for nine years, was killed in battle, fighting against the pagan king of the Mercians. A great proof of the charity attributed to him, and a much greater proof than the sending a dish of meat from his table, was this—that he ended his life with a prayer, not for himself, but for others. For when he was beset with the weapons of his enemies, and perceived that he must die, he prayed for the souls of his companions; whence came an old English proverb, long in the mouths of the people, ' May God have mercy on their souls, as Oswald said when he fell.' His heathen enemy ordered his head and hands to be cut off, and set upon stakes, but afterwards, his head was carried to the church of Landisfarne, where it was laid as a precious relic in the tomb of St. Cuthbert, lying between his arms (hence in many pictures, St. Cuthbert holds the crowned head as his attribute); while his right hand was carried to his castle of Bamborough, and remained undecayed and uncorrupted for many years. 'And in the place where he was killed by the pagans, fighting for his country, infirm men and cattle are healed to this day.'—' Nor is it to be wondered at, that the sick should be healed in the place where he died, for whilst he lived, he never ceased to provide for the poor and infirm, and to bestow alms on them and assist them.' In the single figures he wears the kingly crown, and carries a large cross.

The whole story of St. Oswald is rich in picturesque subjects. The solemn translation of his remains, first to Bardney in Lincolnshire, by Osthrida, queen of the Mercians; and after-

I

wards to St. Oswald's, in Gloucestershire, by Elfleda, the
high-hearted daughter of Alfred, and her husband Ethelred,
should close the series.

In those devotional effigies which commemorate particularly
the Christianising of Northumbria by the early Benedictines,
we should find St. Benedict as patriarch, with St. Paulinus of
York, and St. Cuthbert of Durham. Or, if the monument
were to be purely Anglo-Saxon, we should have St. Oswald
between St. Cuthbert and St. Bennet of Wearmouth : where
female saints are grouped with these, we should find St.
Helena, St. Hilda of Whitby, and St. Ebba of Coldingham.

Dugdale.   ' In those early times,' says a quaint old author, ' there
were in England, and also in France, monasteries consisting
of men and women, who lived together like the religious
women who followed and accompanied the blessed apostles,
in one society, and travelled together for their advancement
and improvement in a holy life. From these women, these
monasteries were derived, and governed only by devout
women, so ordained by the founders in respect of the great
honour which they had for the Virgin Mary, whom Jesus on
the cross recommended to St. John the Evangelist. These
governesses had as well monks as nuns in their monasteries,
and jurisdiction over both men and women; and those men
who improved themselves in learning, and whom the abbess
thought qualified for orders, she recommended to the bishop,
who ordained them. Yet they remained still under her
government, and officiated as chaplains until she pleased to
send them forth upon the work of ministry. And among
these were Ebba, abbess of Coldingham; and St. Werburga,
abbess of Repandum in England; and St. Bridget of Kildare,
in Ireland, who had many monks under their charge.' ' And

St. Hilda.   more particularly HILDA, great-grandchild to King Edwin,
and abbess of Whitby, famous for her learning, piety, and
excellent government in the time of the Saxons, when, as Bede
relateth, she held her subjects so strictly to the reading of the
Scriptures and the performance of works of righteousness, that
many of them were fit to be churchmen and to serve at the

altar; so that afterwards, saith he, we saw five bishops who
came out of her monastery, and a sixth was elected, who
died before he was ordained. She was a professed enemy to
the extension of the papal jurisdiction in this country, and
opposed with all her might the tonsure of priests and the
celebration of Easter according to the Roman ritual. She
presided at a council held in her own monastery, and in
presence of King Oswy, when these questions were argued,
but being decided against her, she yielded.' 'She taught,'
says Bede, 'the strict observance of justice, piety, chastity,
and other virtues, and especially peace and charity, so that,
after the example of the primitive Christians, no person
was there rich, and none poor, all being in common to all,
and none having any property; and her prudence was so
great, that not only private individuals, but kings and princes,
asked and received her counsel in religious and worldly affairs.
The people adored her, and certain fossils which are found
there, having the form of snakes coiled up, are commonly
supposed to be venomous reptiles, thus changed by the
prayers of St. Hilda. And in the year of the incarnation
of our Lord 680, on the 17th of November, this most religious
servant of Christ, the Abbess Hilda, having suffered under an
infirmity for seven years, and performed many heavenly works
on earth, died, and was carried into Paradise by the angels,
as was beheld in a vision by one of her own nuns, then at
a distance, on the same night: the name of this nun was then
Bega; but she afterwards became famous under the name of
St. Bees.'

St Hilda should wear a rich robe over her Benedictine
habit, and hold in one hand her pastoral staff as abbess; in the
other hand, a book or books. St. Hilda and St. Benedict of
Wearmouth on each side of St. Cuthbert, might express the
sanctity, the learning, and, what modern authors would style,
the 'female element of civilisation,' proper to this early period.[1]

[1] In Hutchison's History of the Cathedral of Durham, there is a curious and
interesting catalogue of the subjects which filled the large stained glass windows,
before the wholesale destruction of those glorious memorials. Among them we find,
separately or in groups, and often repeated, St. Helena; St. Aidan (the instructor

ST. EBBA.

Of St. Ebba it is related, that when attacked in her monastery by a horde of Danish barbarians, she counselled her sisterhood to mutilate their faces, rather than fall a prey to the adversary; and they all consented. ' And when the Danes broke through the gates and rushed upon them, they lifted their veils, and showed their faces disfigured horribly, and covered with blood: then those merciless ravishers, starting back at such a spectacle, were about to flee; but their leaders, being filled with fury and disappointed of their prey, ordered the convent to be fired. So these most holy virgins, with St. Ebba at their head, obtained the glory of martyrdom.'

St. Ebba should bear the palm, and, being of royal lineage, she would have a double right to the crown as princess and as martyr.

CÆDMON.
A. D. 680.

v. Archæologia, vol. xxv.

Bede, b. iv. c. 24.

In the monastery of the Abbess Hilda, lived Cædmon the poet, whose paraphrase of Scripture history, in Anglo-Saxon verse, is preserved to this day. A copy exists in the Bodleian Library at Oxford, illuminated with antique drawings, most extraordinary and curious as examples of Saxon art.

The story of Cædmon, as related by Bede, appears to me very beautiful. ' He did not,' says Bede, ' learn the art of poetry from men, but from God; for he had lived in a secular habit till he was well advanced in years, being employed as one of the servants in the monastery.' And he knew nothing of literature, nor of verse, nor of song; so that when he was at table, and the harp came to him in his turn, he rose up, and left the guests, and went his way.

And it happened on a certain occasion, that he had done so, and had gone into the stable, where it was his business to care

---

of St. Cuthbert and St. Oswald), as bishop; St. Cuthbert, as patron saint and bishop, bearing the head of St. Oswald in his arms; St. Oswald himself, in princely attire, carrying a large cross,—and, again, St. Oswald ' blowing his horn;' and the Venerable Bede, who, at Durham, is *Saint Bede*, in a blue gown, and carrying his book. I have observed that, in the ancient stained glass, dark blue is often substituted for black in the dress of the monks; black, perhaps, being too opaque a colour. The figure of St. Bede still exists as a fragment.

for the horses; and he laid himself down to sleep. And in his sleep an angel appeared to him, and said, ' Cædmon, sing to me a song;' and he answered ' I cannot sing, and therefore I left the entertainment, and came hither because I could not sing.' And the other, answering him, said, ' You shall sing, notwithstanding.' He asked, ' What shall I sing?' And the angel replied, ' Sing the beginning of created beings.' Thereupon Cædmon presently began to sing verses in praise of God, the Father and Creator of all things. And awakening from his sleep, he remembered all he had sung in his dream, and added much more to the same effect in most melodious verse.

In the morning he was conducted before the Abbess Hilda, by whom he was ordered to tell his dream, and recite his verses; and she and the learned men who were with her, on hearing him, doubted not that heavenly grace had been conferred on him by our Lord: wherefore, the Abbess Hilda received him into her community, and commanded that he should be well instructed in the Holy Scriptures. As he read, Cædmon converted the same into harmonious verse. He sang the creation of the world, and the origin of man, and many other histories from Holy Writ; the terror of future judgment, the pains of hell, and the delights of heaven. And thus he passed his life happily, and as he had served God with a simple and pure mind, devoting his good gifts to his service, he died happily. That tongue which had composed so many holy words in praise of the Creator, uttered its last words while he was in the act of signing himself with the cross; and thus he fell into a slumber, to awaken in Paradise, and join the hymns of the holy angels, whom he had imitated in this world, both in his life and in his songs.[1]

St. Cuthbert and St. Hilda, with Cædmon the poet and Bede

---

[1] ' As Cædmon's paraphrase is a poetical variation mixed with many topics of invention and fancy, it has also as great a claim to be considered as a narrative poem as Milton's Paradise Lost has to be deemed an epic poem.' . . . ' In its first topic, the "fall of the angels," it exhibits much of a Miltonic spirit: and if it were clear that our illustrious bard had been familiar with Saxon, we should be induced to think that he owed something to the paraphrase of Cædmon.'—Turner's *History of the Anglo-Saxons*, vol. iii. p. 356.

the historian on either side, would form a very beautiful
and significant group. I do not know that it has ever been
painted; if *not*, I recommend it to the attention of artists—
particularly those who may be called upon to illustrate our
northern worthies.

Quitting the Northumbrians, we will take a view of the
Benedictine foundations in the midland districts among the
Mercians and East Anglians. Here we find a group of saints
not less eminent, and even more picturesque and poetical.

ST CHAD.
March 2, 669.
In those days lived four holy men, who were brothers, all
of whom had been educated in the monastery of St. Cuthbert.
Bede, b. iii.
c. 13; b. iv.
c. 3.
The eldest of these, whose name was Cedd, was desired by
Ethelbald, the son of King Oswald, to accept some land, on
which to build a monastery. Cedd, therefore, complying with
the king's request, chose for himself a place among craggy
and distant mountains, which looked more like lurking-places
of robbers, and retreats for wild beasts, than habitations for
men ;—' that the words of the prophet might be fulfilled, and
that where the dragons were wont to dwell, the grass and
corn should grow, and the fruits of good works should spring
up where beasts inhabited, or men who lived after the manner
of beasts.' There arose the Priory of Lastingham, in the
district of Cleveland, in Yorkshire.

A.D 669.
And, after many years, Cedd died of the plague, and his
younger brother Chad became abbot. And Chad was very
famous among the people for his holy and religious life; and
being of modest behaviour, and well read in the Holy Scriptures,
he was chosen to be bishop of the Mercians and Northumbrians:
Bede.
and he set himself to instruct the people—preaching the Gospel
in towns, in the open country, in cottages, in villages, and castles.
He had his episcopal see in the place called Lichfield—' the
field of the dead ; ' there he built a church, in which to preach
and baptize the people ; and, near to it, a habitation for himself,
where, in company with seven or eight brethren, he spent, in
reading and praying, any spare hours which remained to him

from the duties of his ministry. And after he had governed the Church there gloriously for two years and more, he had a vision, in which his brother Cedd, accompanied by the blessed angels, singing hymns and rejoicing, called him home to God; and the voices, after floating above the roof of the oratory, ascended to heaven with inexpressible sweetness. So St. Chad knew that he must depart; and having recommended his brethren to live in peace among themselves and towards all others, he died and was buried.

Such was the origin of the see and the cathedral of Lichfield, where, since the year 1148, the shrine of St. Chad was deposited, and held in great veneration by the people. Over the door of the present cathedral there is a figure of St. Chad throned as a bishop, restored from the old sculpture; but every other vestige of the saint perished at the time of the Reformation, or during the ravages of the civil wars. I do not know that St. Chad has any attribute proper to him in his individual character: as founder and first bishop of the see of Lichfield, he ought to wear the mitre and pastoral staff, and to hold the cathedral in his hand. A choir of angels singing, as they hover above his head, would be appropriate; or a storm and lightning in the background,— for it was his custom, when there was a tempest, to pray for mercy for himself and all mankind, considering the thunder, and the winds, and the darkness, as prefiguring the day of the Lord's judgment; 'wherefore,' said he, ' it behoves us to answer his heavenly admonition with due fear and love.'

ST. GUTHLAC would necessarily find a place in a series of the Mercian Saints. His story gave rise to the foundation of Croyland Abbey, one of the grandest of all the Benedictine communities, famous for its libraries and seminaries; and for the story of Turketel, so well and pleasantly told by Lord Campbell, that I only wish the pious old chancellor (I mean Turketel, of course) had been a saint, that I might have had the pleasure of inserting him here. Of St. Guthlac, who is not connected with any existing institutions or remains of art, there

ST. GUTH-
LAC.
A.D. 714.

is not much to say. The legend relates that 'at the time of his birth a hand of a ruddy splendour was seen extended from heaven to a cross which stood at his mother's door : ' and this vision prefigured his future sanctity. Nevertheless he grew up wild and lawless in wild and lawless times; and at the age of sixteen, gathering a band of military robbers, placed himself at their head: 'yet such was his innate goodness, that he always gave back a third part of the spoil to those whom he robbed.' After eight years thus spent, he began to see the evil of his ways : and the rest of his life was one long penance. He retired first to the monastery of Repton, rendered famous by St. Werburga; there he learned to read, and having studied the lives of the hermit fathers, he determined to imitate them. He retired to a vast marshy wilderness on the eastern shore, where was a sort of island, as much infested by demons as the deserts of Egypt. And they led St. Guthlac such a life, that the blessed St. Anthony himself had never been more tormented and scared by hideous shapes and foul temptations. Guthlac, trusting in his chosen protector, St. Bartholomew, defied the de-mons, and many times the blessed apostle visited him in person, and drove them into the sea. In the solitude where he dwelt, arose first an oratory; afterwards a most splendid church and monastery, built upon piles with wondrous art and wisdom, and dedicated to St. Bartholomew. The marshes were drained and cultivated, and good spirits (that is, health, peace, and industry) inhabited where foul spirits (disease, and famine, and savage ignorance) had dwelt before.

The ruins of Croyland Abbey cover twenty acres, and stand again in the midst of an unhealthy marsh. Remains of muti-lated but once beautiful sculpture adorn the eastern front. Among these is the figure of St. Guthlac, holding a whip, his proper

10 St. Guthlac. (Ancient English sculpture.)

attribute: this has been explained as alluding to his severe
penances; but among the relics left to the monastery by
St. Pega, the sister of St. Guthlac, is 'the whip of St.
Bartholomew,' with which I suppose he chastised and drove
away the demons which haunted the hermit saint: this is
the more probable interpretation of the attribute.   On the
antique bridge of Croyland is seen the throned figure of
Ethelbald, king or duke of Mercia, the first founder of this
great monastery.

The first Benedictine nunnery in England was that of
Barking, in Essex; and its first abbess St. Ethelberga, of whom
there is nothing related except that she led a most pious and
orderly life, governing her congregation with great wisdom,
studying the Scriptures, and healing the sick.   She is represented in the old missals with a pastoral staff and a book in her
hand.   As she was one of the few Saxon abbesses not of royal
birth, she should not wear the crown.

*St. Ethel-
berga.*

A still greater saint was Queen ETHELREDA, whom our
Anglo-Saxon ancestors regarded with peculiar veneration.   The
common people worshipped her under the name of St. Audrey,
and effigies of her formerly abounded in the old missals, in
stained glass, and in the decorative sculpture of the old ecclesiastical edifices in the eastern counties.   To her we owe the
foundation of the magnificent Cathedral of Ely; and the most
curious memorial which remains to us of her legendary life still
exists there.

*St. Ethel-
reda.*

*A.D. 679.
June 23.*

She was the daughter of Ina, king of the East Angles, and
Hereswida his wife; and was married at an early age to
Toubert, prince of the Gervii, receiving for her dowry the isle
of Ely.   Being left a widow at the end of three years, she was
married to Egfrid, king of Northumbria, with whom she lived,
say the historians, in a state of continency for twelve years.
She at length obtained his permission to withdraw entirely from
the world, and took the veil at Coldingham.   A year afterwards
she founded a monastery on her own lands at Ely, where she

K

lived for seven years in the practice of those religious austerities which were the admiration of the time, and gathered around her many virgins dedicated to God. Wonderful things are recorded of her by our early chronicles. When the beautiful lantern of Ely Cathedral was designed by Allan de Walsingham (sub-prior of Ely, and one of the most excellent architects of the time), the capitals of the great pillars which sustain it were carved with groups of figures representing the chief incidents in the life of Ethelreda, to whom the church, on its restoration by Bishop Ethelwold, had been originally dedicated.

A.D. 1342.

The subjects, taken in order, exhibit the chief incidents in her life :—

1. We have the marriage of Ethelreda to King Egfrid : her father, King Iua, gives her away.

2. She is represented making her religious profession : she has taken off her royal crown, and laid it on the altar; St. Wilfrid, bishop of York, pronounces the benediction; and Ebba, abbess of Coldingham, places the veil upon her head.

3. The third capital represents the miraculous preservation of the saint. It appears that King Egfrid repented of his concession, and threatened to drag her from her convent. She fled, attended by two companions, and took refuge on the summit of a rock, a promontory since called St. Ebb's Head. Egfrid pursued her to the foot of the rock, and would have accomplished his purpose, had not a sudden advance of the tide surrounded the rock so as to render it inaccessible; which was attributed to the prayers of the saint and her companions. King Egfrid retreated, and consoled himself by marrying another wife.

4. The fourth capital represents the miraculous dream of the saint. After her escape from Egfrid, she crossed the Humber, and sought repose in a solitary place, while her two virgins, whose names were Sewerra and Sewenna, watched beside her. In her sleep she had a vision, and dreamed that her staff, which she had stuck into the ground, had put forth leaf and branch, and had become a tall tree ; and, being much comforted, she continued her journey.

11   The Dream of St. Ethelreda.   (From the ancient sculpture in Ely Cathedral.)

5. The next pillar represents her receiving the pastoral staff, as abbess of Ely, from St. Wilfrid, archbishop of York; who, being cruelly persecuted by Ermenburga, Egfrid's second choice, had fled southwards, and taken refuge at Ely.

6. The sixth capital represents the sickness of St. Ethelreda, who is lying on her couch, with her pastoral staff in her hand, and her physician beside her. Another group in the same capital represents her interment.

7. The seventh capital commemorates a miracle of the saint, which is said to have occurred about 400 years after her death. There was a certain man whose name was Britstan, an usurer and a son of Belial. Being seized with a grievous sickness, he repented of his crimes, and resolved to dedicate himself to God in the monastery at Ely. But on his way thither he was over-taken by the officers of justice, and thrown into prison. He implored the protection of St. Ethelreda; and one night, in his

sleep, St. Benedict and St. Ethelreda appeared to him, and the former touching his fetters, they fell from his ankles, and he became free. In this group, an angel is in attendance on St. Ethelreda. The other figure represents St. Sexburga, her sister, who succeeded her as abbess.

8. The eighth and last capital exhibits two groups. In the first, St. Sexburga, St. Ermenhilda, and St. Werburga of Chester, are consulting together concerning the removal of the body of St. Ethelreda, which had rested in the common cemetery for sixteen years. In the second is seen the body of St. Ethelreda undecayed, with the royal crown on her head, while the attendants express their astonishment and admiration. On this her second burial, Ethelreda was laid in an antique marble sarcophagus most beautifully wrought, probably a relic of the Romans, but which the people supposed to have been constructed by angels expressly for the purpose.

The devotional figures of St. Ethelreda represent her richly dressed, as was usual with all the Saxon princess-saints of that time. St. Ethelwold of Winchester had a particular venera-
Coll. of the Duke of Devonshire. tion for her, and in his famous Benedictional she leads the choir of virgin saints, in a tunic of gold, with golden shoes, and a crown on her head. Her proper dress would be a rich mantle, clasped in front, worn over her black Benedictine habit; a crown, to denote her rank as princess; the white veil flowing underneath it; the pastoral staff in one hand, a book in the other. I do not know that she has any particular attribute to distinguish her from other royal abbesses; but the visionary tree which sprang from her staff might be introduced at her side.

p. 69 This very curious figure of St. Ethelreda, holding the Gospel in one hand, a lily (the emblem of her chastity) in the other, I give as a genuine specimen of Saxon art. It is taken from the Benedictional of Ethelwold, and was executed about the year 980.

St. Wer- bulga. St. Ethelreda had a niece, WERBURGA, daughter of Wulphere, king of the Mercians, to whom the Cathedral of Chester has been dedicated since the year 800; she being, with St. Oswald, still the tutelar saint of Chester. She was brought up

IMA CO
SĊE ÆÞEL
ÐR YÞE
ABB ACPE^R
PETYE VIRGIN

12   St. Ethelreda   (From an ancient Saxon miniature. A.D. 980.)

under her aunt, St. Ethelreda, at Ely, and altogether devoted
to good works, having founded many religious edifices, and
among others, the monasteries at Weedon, Trentham, Repton,
and Hanbury, over which she presided until her death, at
Trentham, about the year 708.

Her shrine at Chester was magnificent, and enriched with *v. King's Hist. of* many statues. 'A part of this shrine is now at the upper end *Chester.* of the choir, where it serves as a supporter to a fair pew erected
for the bishop of the diocese.'

I must mention here, Modwena, an Irish saint, of whom a *St. Mod-wena.* curious effigy existed at Stratford-on-Avon, and is engraved
in Fisher's Antiquities. King Egbert, says the legend, had an
epileptic son, whom none of the physicians of his court could
heal; and he was told that in Ireland, over the sea, there dwelt
a holy virgin who had power to cure such diseases; and thither

he sent his son with many presents, and the virgin healed the
boy.   But she refused the gifts of the king.   Then he invited
her into England; and, being surprised by her learning as well
as her sanctity, he built for her the monastery at Polesworth
in Warwickshire, and placed under her care and tuition his
daughter Edith, who became afterwards famous as St. Edith of
Polesworth.   St. Modwena, in this ancient picture above
referred to, wears the black habit of a Benedictine nun, and a
white veil; she holds a crosier in one hand, as first abbess of
Polesworth, and a book in the other.

In a group of the early Mercian saints, we ought to find St.
Chad as bishop, and St. Guthlac as hermit, St. Ethelreda and
St. Werburga as princesses and abbesses, conspicuous, and
admitting of a very beautiful variety in age, in dress, and in
character.

The period I have just reviewed, from about 650 to 750, was
remarkable for great mental activity and progressive civilisation, as well as for enthusiastic religious feeling.

In approaching the Danish invasions, which laid low our
ecclesiastical edifices, and replunged the whole island into a
state of temporary barbarism, we must pause for a while, and
take a view of those Anglo-Saxon Benedictines who became
Christian missionaries in foreign and (in those days) barbarous
lands.   The apostles of Friesland and Germany form a most
interesting group of saints in early German and Flemish art:
not less do they deserve to be commemorated among our own
national worthies.   At the head of these, we place

ST. BONIFACE, MARTYR.

Lat. and *Ger.* Sanctus Bonifacius. *Ital.* San Bonifaccio. Archbishop of
Mayence, and first primate and apostle of Germany. June 5, 755.

HABIT AND ATTRIBUTES.—He appears as bishop, wearing the episcopal
robes over the black Benedictine habit. In his hand is a book stained with
blood, or transfixed by a sword.

THE story of St. Boniface is one of the most beautiful and
authentic of the mediæval legends.   As one of the Saxon

worthies, educated in an English Benedictine convent and
connected with our own early history, he is especially interesting to us; his was a far different existence from that of
the good abbot of Wearmouth. His active eventful life, his ^{v. p. 51.}
sublime devotion, and his tragical death, afford admirable
subjects for Christian art and artists.

The sketch of the history and mission of St. Boniface, which
forms a striking passage in the 'Essays in Ecclesiastical Biography,' is so beautiful and comprehensive, that I venture to
insert it almost entire.

'In the Benedictine abbey of Nutsall, near Winchester, ^{or Nusoella}
poetry, history, rhetoric, and the Holy Scriptures were taught
in the beginning of the eighth century, by a monk, whom his
fellow-countrymen called Winfred, but whom the Church
honours under the name of Boniface. He was born at
Crediton, in Devonshire, of noble and wealthy parents, who
had reluctantly yielded to his wish to embrace the monastic
state. Hardly, however, had he reached middle life, when
his associates at Nutsall discovered that he was dissatisfied
with the pursuits by which their own thoughts were engrossed.
As, in his evening meditations, he paced the long conventual
avenue of lime-trees,—or as, in the night-watches, he knelt
before the crucifix suspended in his cell, he was still conscious
of a voice, audible though inarticulate, which repeated to him
the Divine injunction "to go and preach the Gospel to all
nations." Then, in mental vision, was seen stretching out
before him the land of his German ancestry; where, beneath
the veil of the customs described by Tacitus, was concealed
an idolatry of which the historian had neither depicted, nor
probably conjectured, the abominations. To encounter Satan
in this stronghold became successively the day-dream, the
passion, and the fixed resolve of Boniface; until, at length,
abandoning for this holy war the studious repose for which he
had already abandoned the world, he appeared, in his thirty-
sixth year, a solitary and unbefriended missionary, traversing
the marshy sands and the primæval forests of Friesland. But
Charles Martel was already there, the leader in a far different
contest. Nor, while the Christian mayor of the palace was

striking down the pagans with his battle-axe, could the
pathetic entreaties of the Benedictine monk induce them to
bow down to the banner of the Cross.   He therefore returned
to Nutsall, not with diminished zeal, but with increased knowledge.   He had now learned·that his success must depend on
the conduct of the secular and spiritual rulers of mankind,
and on his own connection with them.

  ' The chapter of his monastery chose him as their abbot, but
at his own request the Bishop of Winchester annulled the
election ; then, quitting for ever his native England, Boniface
pursued his way to Rome to solicit the aid of Pope Gregory II.
in his efforts for the conversion of the German people.'

  This was in the year 719 ; and it is said that on the occasion
of his visit to Rome he quitted his Anglo-Saxon name of Winfred, and assumed that of Boniface.   Having received his
mission from the Pope, he travelled into Thuringia and Bavaria :
he again visited Friesland, where Charles Martel now reigned
as undisputed master ; he penetrated into the wilds of Saxony,
everywhere converting and civilising the people, and founding monasteries, which, it should be remembered, was much
the same as founding colonies and cities.   In the year 732
Boniface was created Archbishop and Primate of all Germany ;
and soon afterwards King Pepin-le-Bref, whom he had crowned
and anointed, created him first Bishop of Mayence.   Into
the monasteries which he founded in Germany, he introduced
copies of the Holy Scriptures ; and in the midst of all his
labours and honours, he was accustomed to carry in his bosom
the Treatise of St. Ambrose, ' De Bono Mortis.'   In his
seventy-fourth year he abdicated his ecclesiastical honours,
and solemnly devoted the remainder of his life to the labours
of a missionary.

  ' Girding round him his black Benedictine habit, and deposit-
ing his Ambrose, "De Bono Mortis," in the folds of it, he once
more travelled into Friesland, and, pitching his tent on the
banks of a small rivulet, awaited there the arrival of a body of
neophytes, whom he had summoned to receive at his hands the
rite of confirmation.   Ere long a multitude appeared in the
distance advancing towards the tent ; not, however, with the

lowly demeanour of Christian converts drawing near their bishop, but carrying deadly weapons, and announcing by their cries and gestures, that they were pagans, sworn to avenge their injured deities against the arch-enemy of their worship. The servants of Boniface drew their swords in his defence; but, calmly and even cheerfully awaiting the approach of his enemies, and forbidding all resistance, he fell beneath their blows,—a martyr to the faith which he had so long lived and so bravely died to propagate. His copy of Ambrose, " De Bono Mortis," covered with his blood, was exhibited during many succeeding centuries at Fulda as a relic. It was contemplated there by many who regarded as superstitious and heretical some of the tenets of Boniface; but no Christian, whatever might be his own peculiar creed, ever looked upon that blood-stained memorial of him without the profoundest veneration. For, since the apostolic age, no greater benefactor of our race has arisen among men than the monk of Nutsall, unless it be that other monk of Wittemberg, who at the distance of seven centuries, appeared to reform and reconstruct the churches founded by the holy Benedictine.'[1]

Is not this a man whom we Anglo-Saxons might be proud to place in our ecclesiastical edifices?

In the single figures and devotional pictures St. Boniface is represented in the episcopal robes and mitre, the crosier in one hand, in the other a book transpierced with a sword. Or he is in the act of baptizing a convert, while he sets his foot on the prostrate oak, as a sign that he had overcome the Druid superstitions. Such figures are frequent in German art, and doubtless had once a distinguished place in the decorations of our own abbeys and cathedrals; but he is found there no longer.

He is seldom met with in Italian art. Bonifaccio, the Venetian, has represented the martyrdom of his patron saint; but I rather think that this is the Italian martyr Boniface, whose story has been related in the second volume of LEGEND-ARY ART.

Venice. S. Salvadore p. 256.

---

[1] Essays in Ecclesiastical Biography, i. 372.

L

The most splendid monument ever consecrated to St. Boniface is the Basilica which bears his name, and which was
founded by King Louis of Bavaria in 1835, in celebration of
the twenty-fifth anniversary of his marriage. The interior is
sustained by sixty-three pillars of white marble. The whole of
the choir and nave are covered with frescoes, executed by Professor Hess and his pupils; those in the choir represent our
Saviour, and on each side his mother Mary and St. John the
Evangelist; beneath, in a line, stand St. Benedict and the most
celebrated of those teachers of the Christian faith who preached
the Gospel in Bavaria,—St. Boniface, St. Willibald, St. Cor-
binian, St. Rupert, St. Emmeran, St. Cylien, and St. Magnus,
abbot of Füssen,[1] all of whom were Benedictines. Along the
upper walls, on each side of the central nave, runs a series of
compositions in thirty-six compartments, representing incidents in the lives of all those saints who preached the Gospel
throughout Germany, from the year 384 down to the baptism
of Wittikind in presence of Charlemagne in 785. Beneath
these thirty-six small compartments are twelve large compartments, containing on a larger scale scenes from the life of St.
Boniface, in each compartment two:—

1. The father of Winfred (afterwards Boniface), being healed
of a grievous malady by the prayers of his pious son, solemnly
devotes him to the priesthood. 2. Boniface receives the Benedictine habit. 3. He leaves the monastery at Nutsall, and
embarks at the port of Southampton for Rome. 4. He arrives
at Rome. 5. Pope Gregory II. consecrates him as missionary.
6. Boniface crosses the Alps into Germany. 7. He preaches
the Gospel in Friesland. 8. He receives the papal command
to repair to Rome. 9. Pope Gregory creates him bishop of the
new converts. 10. Returning to Germany he is miraculously
fed and refreshed in passing through a forest. 11. He hews
down the oak sacred to the German divinity Thor. 12. He

---

[1] In the Belle Arti at Venice, there is a charming picture by Cima da Conegliano of the incredulity of St. Thomas. On one side stands a bishop, called in
the catalogue St. Magnus; on what authority I do not know, nor why a
Bavarian bishop should be represented here, unless as the patron of the donor of
the picture.

founds the bishoprics of Eichstadt and Wurzbourg.   13. He
founds the great monastery of Fulda.   14. The solemn consecration of the monastery.   15. He receives into his monastery St. George of Utrecht as a child.   16. He crowns Pepin   March 1,752.
d'Heristal king of the Franks.   17. He is created first Archbishop of Mayence.   18. He resigns his archiepiscopal dignity, resumes the habit of a simple monk, and prepares to
depart on his second mission.   19. He suffers martyrdom at
the hands of the barbarians.   20. His remains are borne to
Mayence, and finally deposited in his monastery at Fulda.

I have given the list of subjects, because it will be found
useful and suggestive both to artists and travellers.   The
frescoes have been executed with great care in a large, chaste,
simple style.   I have etched the scene of the departure of St.
Boniface from Southampton.   The dress of the saint, the
short black sleeveless tunic over the white cassock, is the
travelling and working costume of the Benedictine monks.

In the time of St. Boniface, two Saxon brothers left   SS. EWALD.
England to preach the Gospel in Westphalia. These brothers,   A.D.695–7, or 700. Oct. 3
who were twins, were baptized by the same name, but, being
diverse in hair and complexion, were distinguished as ST.
EWALD THE BLACK and ST. EWALD THE FAIR. Having studied
for some time in Ireland, then famous for its seminaries of
learning, they embarked on their mission, encouraging each
other, and singing psalms and hymns by the way, and, passing through Friesland, reached in safety the frontiers of
Westphalia.   There they required to be conducted to the lord
of the country, that they might obtain his permission to
preach the Gospel among his people ; but the ignorant and
barbarous infidels of the neighbourhood fell upon them,
murdered them cruelly, and threw their bodies into the river.
A light was seen to hover above the spot, and search being
made, the bodies of the martyrs were found, and, by order of
Pepin d'Heristal, buried at Cologne, in the church of St.
Cunibert.   They are venerated as the patron saints of Westphalia.

There is a set of curious pictures illustrating the story of these brother martyrs, which appear to have been executed by Martin Hemskirk, for the church of St. Cunibert:—

1. The two brothers, distinguished as the Black and the Fair Ewald, stand together; the former carries a sword, the latter a club. 2. The brothers depart on their mission. 3. St. Ewald the Fair heals a possessed woman in presence of Radbrad, duke of Friesland. 4. The brothers defend their faith before the judge. 5. One of the brothers stands before a pagan emperor. 6. St. Ewald the Fair is beaten to death with clubs. 7. The Martyrdom of St. Ewald the Black. Two are engraved in the Boisserée Gallery.

I have etched the scene of the miracle. The attitude of St. Ewald is precisely that which I once saw assumed by a famous mesmerist, when throwing a patient into a mesmeric sleep.

Drayton, in his Polyolbion, celebrates a long list of the saints whom we sent from England to other countries, and among them he gives a conspicuous place to these brothers:

> So did the Ewaldi there most worthily attain
> Their martyr's glorious types, in Ireland first approv'd,
> But after, in their zeal, as need required removed,
> They to Westphalia went; and as they brothers were,
> So they, the Christian faith together preaching there,
> Th' old pagan Saxons slew, out of their hatred deep
> To the true faith, whose shrines brave Cullen still doth keep.

St. Swidbert, an English Benedictine monk, left his monastery in Northumberland to preach the Gospel to the heathen in Friesland and the duchy of Berg. He built a great monastery in Kaiserswerdt, on the Rhine, six miles below Dusseldorf. In a picture by B. de Bruyn he is represented as bishop, holding up a star in both hands, which may be a symbol of the rising light of the Gospel, which he preached in that district. He died in 713.

The companion picture, of the same size, represents St. Cunibert, who was Bishop of Cologne, and counsellor of King Dagobert and several of his successors, and he was also the intimate friend of Pepin d'Heristal. He governed the diocese of Cologne during thirty-seven years, and one of the most ancient churches of that ancient city bears his name. According to the legend, it was St. Cunibert who discovered the spot where St. Ursula and her companions lay buried, being directed thither by a dove. There is a curious picture of Munich Gal. this prelate painted by B. de Bruyn, one of the old Cologne school, probably for his church. He is represented as bishop, holding a church in his hand: his proper attribute is a dove.

I must mention one more of these old Benedictine mission- St. Lieven. aries, who has been illustrated in Flemish art. St. Lieven was born and educated in Ireland, then famous for its ecclesiastical schools. After being consecrated bishop in his native land, he was called on, or believed himself inspired, to preach the Gospel in the Low Countries, where so many martyrs had already preached, and he was destined to add to the number. While preaching and baptizing near Ghent, he was cruelly murdered, the infuriated pagans having first torn out his tongue, and then cut off his head. His hostess, a Christian Nov. 12, 654. lady, and her infant son (called St. Brictius, or St. Brice) were slain with him.

St. Lieven was a poet, and, among other productions, composed a hymn in honour of St. Bavon, within whose church, at Ghent, his remains are still preserved. He is sometimes represented as a bishop, holding his own tongue with a pair of tongs. Rubens painted the horrible Martyrdom of St. Lieven, Musée, Brussels. with most horrible skill, for the altar-piece of his chapel in the Jesuits' Church at Ghent.

Connected with St. Boniface and the early German martyrs and missionaries, in pictures, in architectural ornament, and in the stained glass of the German churches, we find two famous female saints, ST. WALBURGA and ST. OTTILIA.

The various names borne by the former saint, according to St. Wal-burga. the various localities in which she has been honoured, in Bavaria, Alsace, Poitou, Flanders, and England, testify to her popularity;—she is St. Walpurgis, Walbourg, Valpurge, Gualbourg, and Avangour. Her Anglo-Saxon name, Walburga, is the same as the Greek Eucharis, and signifies *gracious*. She was the niece of St. Boniface, and sister of St. Willibald. When her uncle and brother had decided on bringing over from England a company of religious women, to assist in their missions among the pagans, by teaching and by

A.D. 728.

example, Walburga, after passing twenty-seven years in the monastery of Winburn, in Dorsetshire, set forth with ten other nuns, and repaired to Mayence; thence her brother Willibald removed her to Eichstadt, and made her first abbess of the Benedictine nunnery at Heidenheim, about half way between Munich and Nuremburg. Walburga appears to have been a strong-minded and, for her time, a learned woman. She is the author of a Latin history of the life and mission of her brother Willibald; she governed her sisterhood with such a strong hand, and was so efficient in civilising the people around her, that, after the death of St. Willibald, she was called to Eichstadt, and for several years governed the two communities of monks and nuns. Her death took place about the year 778.

Like many of the religious women of that time, Walpurgis had studied medicine for the purpose of ministering to the poor. The cures she performed, either through faith or skill, were by the people attributed solely to her prayers. After her death she was laid in a hollow rock, near the monastery of Eichstadt, a spot where a kind of bituminous oil exuded from the stone. This oil was for a long time supposed to proceed from her remains, and, under the name of Walpurgis oil, was regarded by the people as a miraculous cure for all manner of diseases. The cave at Eichstadt became a place of pilgrimage. A beautiful church arose upon the spot; and other churches dedicated to St. Walburga are found, not only in Bavaria, but all over Flanders, and in Burgundy, Poitou, and Lorraine. There is a chapel dedicated to her honour in the Cathedral of Canterbury.

She died on the 25th of February; but, in the German and Belgic calendars, the 1st of May, the day on which she was enshrined as a saint, is recorded as her chief festival, and it was solemnised as such over all Germany. On this night, the famous *Walpurgis Nacht*, the witches held their orgies on the Blocksberg. For other wild and poetical superstitions connected with the name of Walpurgis, I must refer the reader to the notes of 'Faust,' and the writers on German ecclesiastical antiquities.

In German and Flemish art, St. Walburga is conspicuous.

She is represented, in the devotional figures, as wearing the habit of a Benedictine nun, with the crosier, as abbess of Heidenheim, and in her hand a vial or flask, which originally may have been intended to express, in a general way, her medical skill; but, latterly, the flask is always supposed to contain the miraculous oil which flowed under her shrine at Eichstadt.

Rubens painted for the church of St. Walburga at Antwerp, 1. The Voyage of the Saint and her companions from England to Mayence: they are in a small boat, tossed in a storm; 2. The Burial of St. Walburga.

The Voyage of St. Walburga is also among the frescoes painted by Hess, in the church of St Boniface, at Munich, and occupies the twenty-seventh compartment.

With St. Walburga should be represented her most famous St. Lioba. companion, St. Lioba, also singularly learned for the time, and a poetess. She was greatly loved and honoured by Charlemagne and his empress Hildegarde, who would willingly have kept her in their court as friend and counsellor, but she preferred the seclusion of her monastery. She died about the year 779, and was buried at Fulda by the side of St. Boniface.

It appears that some of the early Benedictine abbesses in England and Germany were 'ladies spiritual,' (as the bishops and abbots were 'lords spiritual,') and had large communities of monks, as well as nuns, under their rule and guidance. We are told that five of these 'ladies spiritual' signed the acts of the great council held at Beckenham. If it be easy to mock at all this, and to contemn a state of the Church in which women held a high, a venerable, and an influential position, let us first consider all that the women of these early times owed to the sanctity and teaching of such institutions, though even those sacred asylums could not always protect them from outrage and injustice. To this day, women must feel grateful

that thus was kept alive in the hearts and the consciences of
men that religious idea of the moral equality of women, that
reverence for womanhood, which the Divine Author of our faith
was the first to promulgate, which is enforced by his doctrine,
by his example, and by the most touching incidents of his
ministry on earth.

St. Ottilia.   St. Ottilia shares in the honours paid to St. Lucia as patron
saint against all diseases of the eyes.   She was the daughter of
Dec. 13, 720. Duke Adalrich of Alsace, and born blind; her father, who was
a heathen, then commanded that she should be carried out of
the house and exposed to perish, but her nurse fled with her to
a monastery.   Our Lord appeared to Erhard, a pious bishop in
the country of Bavaria, and said, ' Go to a certain monastery,
in which thou wilt find a little maiden of noble birth; baptize
her, and give her the name of Ottilia: and it shall be, that after
thou hast baptized her she shall recover her sight.'   Afterwards
her father repented, and dying, left to her all that he possessed.
She knowing that her father was tormented in Purgatory because of his cruelty, gave the first proof of her piety by delivering him from torment, by dint of prayers and tears; she built
a monastery at Hohenburg, in which she lived in great
austerity and devotion.   She
collected around her 130 nuns,
who walked with her in the
paths of Christian perfection;
and died abbess of Hohenburg
in 720.   She is the patron saint
of Alsace, and more particularly of the city of Strasbourg.

In consequence of her great
austerities and mortifications,
she has taken rank as martyr
in the Church, and is generally
represented as an abbess in the
black Benedictine habit; in
one hand a palm or a crosier,
in the other a book upon which

13   St. Ottilia.
(From an old German missal.)

St. Augine entering at Southampton.

venerable edifices of the most venerable city of Nuremberg.   He is
thus represented in the statue by
Peter Vischer; in a fine woodcut
by Albert Dürer, where he is standing under an arch adorned with
the armorial bearings of the city;
and in a most exquisite little print
by Hans Sebald Beham, where he
is seated under two trees, as
one reposing after a long journey,
yet still embracing his beloved
church.

The bas-reliefs on his shrine
exhibit four incidents of his life:
1. St. Sebald, accompanied by his
disciple, called by some Dionysius,
and   by   others   Deocari,   meets
Willibald   and   Winibald,   almost
dead   with   hunger   and   fatigue:
he transforms stones into bread,
and water into wine.   2. While
preaching to the people of Nuremberg, a wicked blasphemer mocks
at him and his doctrines; he prays

St. Sebald.
(From the statue by Peter Vischer.)

for a sign, and the earth opens to
swallow up his adversary; the man, half buried, calls aloud for
pardon and mercy, and the saint rescues him from perdition.
3. St. Sebald dwelt in a cell, whence he made almost daily
journeys to the city of Nuremberg to instruct the Christian
converts, and he was accustomed to rest in the hut of a poor
cartwright.   One day, in the depth of winter, he found his host
and all his family ready to perish with cold, for there was no
wood to make a fire.   The saint desired him to bring in the
icicles hanging from the roof of the house, and to use them for
fuel.   The grace and naïveté with which this quaint legend is
represented are particularly striking: the female figure, who,
on her knees, is feeding the fire with icicles; the attitude of

the saint, who is turning up the soles of his feet to the flame —are both admirable. 4. St. Sebald requiring fish, to keep a fast-day, desires the poor cartwright to go to the market and buy it. Now the lord of Nuremberg, being a tyrant and a pagan after the usual pattern, had prohibited his vassals from buying fish in the market till the inmates of the castle were supplied: the cartwright is seized, and his eyes are put out; but he is restored to sight by St. Sebald. This group is also beautifully managed, and the figure of the weeping wife is conceived and draped with truly Italian grace. The inscriptions on this wonderful shrine inform us that Peter Vischer began to cast it in 1508, and finished it with the assistance of his five sons, who, with their wives and children, dwelt under his roof, and shared his labours and his fame. The citizens of Nuremberg have been excellent Protestants for the last 300 years, and withstood most manfully the Catholic forces of the empire in 1632; but, happily, it never occurred to them to prove their sincerity or their piety by desecrating and destroying their monuments of art; and the shrine of St. Sebald— guarded by the twelve apostles, crowned with saintly teachers, while angels and seraphs, lovely Elysian forms, hover and cling like birds round its delicate tracery,—stands just where it did three centuries ago.

St. Benno, a German Benedictine, was Bishop of Meissen in Saxony, in the time of the Emperor Henry IV. After Henry was excommunicated in 1075, he attempted to make a forcible entry into the Cathedral of Meissen. Benno closed the doors against him, flung the key into the Elbe, and retired to Rome. On his return to his bishopric he recovered the key— miraculously, says the story; for he ordered a fisherman to cast his net in the river, and a fish being caught, the key was found within it. St. Benno is often represented in the old German prints with a fish in his hand; in the mouth of the fish, a key.

In the German Church at Rome (Sta. Maria dell' Anima) there is an altar-piece representing St. Benno and the miraculous recovery of the key. The painter, Carlo Saraceni, was one of the late Venetian School; and the picture, which is well coloured and animated, is, in arrangement and costume, an odd combination of the German and Venetian manner. St. Benno was canonised in the time of Luther, who made a most vigorous attack on the 'new idol set up at Meissen.' In the beautiful cathedral we may now look in vain for its intrepid bishop; we find, instead, the portraits of the intrepid reformer and his wife Catherine, by Lucas Cranach. Such are the changes on which pictures make us ponder—not idly nor irreverently.

We return to England.

One thing which particularly strikes us in the history of the early Benedictine communities, in England and elsewhere, is their perpetual feuds and tilts with the drinking, hunting, fighting barons around them; their quarrels, peaceful men though they were, with the seneschals and foresters who invaded their privileges and ignorantly opposed their plans of improvement.

Their fields, their gardens, and their mills had sprung up in heretofore uncultivated places, and were often grants of land reclaimed from some royal or baronial forest, in which the game, jealously preserved, trampled their fences, destroyed their corn, and worried their sheep. Our Norman kings—of one of whom it was said 'that he loved the tall stags as though they had been his children,' while of another it is related that he laid waste two hundred villages to make a hunting-ground—often interfered with the peaceful agricultural pursuits of the Church vassals. The Church, in her turn, had recourse to her spiritual weapons. Thus we find St. Hugh of Lincoln excommunicating the foresters of King John; and some of the earlier Church legends exhibit in a curious manner the feeling which existed between the two great powers in the state, the military and the ecclesiastical. But, as Mr. Turner observes, every battle which the churchmen fought against the king or the noble was, *then*, for the advantage of general freedom.

There is a most picturesque story of St. Anselm, archbishop of Canterbury, one of the most learned and distinguished of the

canouised churchmen of those times. The contemporary histories are full of his contests with that uncivilised and irreligious
barbarian, William Rufus. Anselm, as archbishop, presided in
the council wherein it was forbidden to sell the serfs with the
land as though they had been cattle, which was formerly the
custom in England. But the story I am now going to relate
exhibits him merely as opposed to the rude nobles of that age.
One day, as he was riding to his manor of Herse, a hare, pursued by the huntsmen and dogs, ran under the housings of his
mule, and cowered there for refuge : the hounds stood at bay ;
the foresters laughed; but St. Anselm wept, and said, 'This
poor hare reminds me of the soul of a sinner, beset by fiends
impatient to seize their prey.' And he forbade them to pursue
the creature, which limped away, while hounds and huntsmen
remained motionless as if bound by a spell.

The famous German legend of the hermit and the wild huntsman seems to have originated in a similar feeling.

I do not know that the pretty story of St. Anselm has ever
been represented in art; but the legend of Dale Abbey I found
illustrated in some old painted glass in Morley Church, in
Derbyshire. There are five small subjects. In the first, the
abbot, being aggrieved by the trespasses of the game which
had devoured his wheat in the green blade, is seen shooting
the deer with a crossbow. In the second, the king's foresters
complain of him, and the king has a label from his mouth on
which is written, ' Bring ye him before me.' In the third and
fourth he is in the presence of the king, who kneels at his feet,
and grants him as much land as between sun and sun he shall
encircle by a furrow drawn with his plough, to which he is to yoke
two stags caught wild from the forest : the inscriptions, ' *Go
take them and tame them;* ' ' *Go home and take ground with
the plough.*' In the fifth compartment he is ploughing with
the two stags; the inscription is, ' *Here St. Robert ploweth
with them.*'

There is a version of this legend in a collection of Ballads
by William and Mary Howitt; but the turn which they have
given to the story differs altogether from what I conceive to be
the real significance of the legend. The monks would hardly

have placed in their great window, over the altar, a series of
pictures commemorating their own trespasses: that they should
commemorate the wrongs done to them, the invasion of their
ancient charter, and the amends granted by the king, seems
perfectly intelligible.

These curious fragments of glass were brought from a window
of Dale Abbey, together with a part of the ruins, which have
evidently been used in building the north side of the little
church at Morley.

St. Edmund, King and Martyr.

A.D. 870.   Dec. 12.

THE history of Ragnar Lodbrog, and the first invasion of the
Danes, may be found in most of our chroniclers.   The ecclesiastical legend, as connected with St. Edmund the Martyr, is
exceedingly picturesque, and the real horrors are here softened
by a veil of religious poetry, and graceful and instructive
fiction.

Lodbrog, who was of the royal race of the Northmen, dwelt
on the coast of Denmark.   One day, taking his hawk on his
hand, he went out fowling in a small skiff.

A storm came on, and, after being tossed about for several
days, he was driven upon the English coast, at Redham in
Norfolk.   The people of the country carried him to Edmund
the king, who reigned over the East Angles.

Edmund was then in the bloom of youth, a gentle and
accomplished prince; and Lodbrog was struck with wonder at
the splendour of a court which so far exceeded in civilisation all
he had left in his own country.   Edmund, on his part, was
attracted by the immense strength of the Dane and his skill in
the chase.   But the king's huntsman envied his superiority;
and one day, when they were out hunting together, he trea-
cherously slew him, leaving his body in the wood.

Now Lodbrog had reared a greyhound in King Edmund's
court, which tarried by his master's body and watched it; but
after some days, being hungry, he returned to the king's house,

and, after being fed, again disappeared. When this had occurred several times, the servants, by the king's command, followed after the dog, and discovered the body of Lodbrog concealed in a thicket. The treacherous huntsman confessed his crime, and was sentenced by the king and his counsellors to be put alone into the boat which had brought Lodbrog to England, and set adrift on the sea; and the winds and the waves carried him to that part of the coast where dwelt Hinguar and Hubba, the sons of Lodbrog. They, seeing their father's boat, and concluding he had been murdered, burst into a most bitter weeping, and were about to put the huntsman to a cruel death; but he, doubly treacherous, saved himself by accusing King Edmund of the deed, whereupon they swore by all their gods that they would not leave unavenged the death of their father; and they collected a great fleet of ships, in which eight kings and twenty earls, with their followers, embarked and steered towards England. They landed in Northumbria, laid waste the whole country from the Tweed to the Humber, and then penetrated into East Anglia. They burned and destroyed everything before them, slew the monks of Croyland and Peterborough; ' and from this period,' says the historian of the Anglo-Saxons, ' language cannot describe their devastations: it can only repeat the words plunder, murder, famine, and distress; it can only enumerate towns and villages, churches and monasteries, harvests and libraries, burnt and demolished, and wounds inflicted on human happiness and human improvement which ages with difficulty healed.'

When they approached the dominions of Edmund, they sent him a haughty message, requiring of him that he would relinquish the half of his kingdom; whereupon Edmund called to him his counsellor Humbert, bishop of Helmham, and said to him, ' O Humbert! servant of the living God! and half of my life! the fierce barbarians are at hand, and oh! that I might fall, so that my people might thereby escape death; for I will not, through love of a temporal kingdom, subject myself to a heathen tyrant.' Then the bishop replied, ' Unless thou save thyself by flight, most beloved king, these fierce pirates will

presently destroy thee.' But the king absolutely refused to
fly; for, said he, ' I will not survive my faithful and beloved
friend; it is nobler to die for my country, than to forsake it.'
Then, calling in the messenger, he thus addressed him :—
' Stained as ye are with the blood of my people, ye deserve
the punishment of death; but, following the example of
Christ, I will not pollute my hands with your blood. Go
back to your master, and tell him, that though you may rob
me of the wealth and of the kingdom which Divine Providence bestowed on me, you shall not make me subject to an
infidel. After slaying the servants, slay also the king, whom
the King of kings will translate into heaven, there to reign
for ever.'

When the most blessed King Edmund had sent back the
messenger with these words, he advanced boldly against the
enemy with all the forces he could raise, and met the Danes
near the town of Thetford, and gave them battle; and after
great slaughter on both sides, King Edmund retreated, and was
afterwards surrounded by Hinguar and Hubba, who had united
their forces. He took refuge in the church with his friend
Humbert, whence he was dragged by the barbarians, bound to
a tree, and, after been scourged, shot with arrows, ' until,' as
the old legend expresses it, ' his body was stuck as full of darts
as is the hedgehog's skin with spines.' At length they cut off
his head; and with him suffered his friend and inseparable
companion, Bishop Humbert.

or Nov. 20.   This happened on the 12th day of December, in the year
870, in the twenty-ninth year of his age.

When the Christians came forth from their hiding-places,
they sought everywhere for the remains of the martyred king :
and then appeared a wonderful and unheard-of prodigy, for they
found a huge grey wolf of the wood watching over the severed
head. Then they, taking it up boldly and reverently, carried
it to the place of interment, followed by the wolf. And, after
many years, a great church and monastery was erected over
his remains; and around them rose a town, called, in memory
of him, Bury St. Edmunds, which name it retains to this day.

In the old effigies, St. Edmund bears an arrow in his hand,

1. S. Sebald.　　2. S. Emald.

which is his proper attribute, and is sometimes accompanied by the 'grey wolf' crouching at his side.

Contemporary with this martyred king, we find the preceptor *St. Neot.* and kinsman of the great Alfred, St. Neot. He was a monk of Glastonbury, and it is recorded of him that he visited Rome seven times, was very learned, mild, religious, fond of singing; 'humble to all, affable in conversation, wise in transacting business, venerable in aspect, severe in countenance, moderate even in his walk, sincere, upright, calm, temperate, and charitable.' This good man is said to have reproved Alfred for his faults, and consoled him in his misfortunes. He lived for a time in a wild solitude in Cornwall, and died in 878. Two towns in England bear his name.

He should be represented as an aged man with a venerable beard, wearing the black habit of his Order, and a pilgrim's staff and wallet, to signify his frequent journeyings.

St. Swithen shared with St. Neot the glory of educating *St. Swithen July 2, 862.* our Alfred. He was chancellor under Egbert and Ethelwolf, and 'to him,' says Lord Campbell, 'the nation was indebted for instilling the rudiments of science, heroism, and virtue into the mind of the most illustrious of our sovereigns.' He also accompanied Alfred on his pilgrimage to Rome. He was Bishop of Winchester; a learned, humble, and charitable man; a devout champion of the Church, and munificent in building, like most of the prelates of that time. It is related of him that while presiding over the erection of a bridge near his city of Winchester, a poor old woman complained to him that some insolent workman had broken all the eggs in her basket; whereupon the good bishop restored them all; or, according to the popular legend which converts this simple act of justice and charity into a miracle, he *restored* the broken eggs by making them whole. He had ordered that his body should be buried among the poor, outside the church, 'under the feet of the passengers, and exposed to the droppings of the eaves from

N

above.' When his clergy attempted to remove the body to a more honourable tomb inside the church, there came on such a storm of rain as effectually stopped the procession; and this continued for forty days without intermission, till the project was abandoned, and his remains were suffered to rest in the humble grave he had chosen for himself. St. Swithen figures in our Protestant calendar as the *Jupiter Pluvius* of our Saxon ancestors; and, in this character, perhaps a waterspout would be his most appropriate attribute: but he has some graver claims to reverence. He ought to be conspicuous in a series of our southern canonised worthies, bearing the cope, mitre, and pastoral staff as bishop, and the great seal as chancellor; and, thus distinguished, he should be placed in connection with the kingly Alfred, the wise St. Neot, St. Dunstan the skilful artificer, and St. Ethelwold the munificent scholar.

ST. DUNSTAN.

A.D. 988.   May 19.

In the history of our earlier English hierarchy, St. Dunstan stands out a conspicuous figure; but the colours in which he is portrayed are as contrasted as night and day. In the hands of some of our historians he appears a demon of ambition and cruelty. I recollect that my own early impressions of him, after reading sentimental versions of the story of Edwin and Elgiva, were revolting; I could think of him only as a bigoted and ferocious priest. The story of the Devil and the red-hot tongs, adding a touch of the grotesque, completed the repulsive picture. More extensive sources of information, and awakened reflection and comparison, have considerably modified these impressions. Dunstan was, in fact, one of the most striking and interesting characters of the times; and not merely as a subject of art, but as being himself an artist, he must be commemorated here.

He was born in the year 925, in the beginning of the reign of Athelstan, the grandson of Alfred. His early years were passed in the neighbourhood of Glastonbury, where he afterwards became a professed monk. He profited by all the means of instruction which that great seminary placed at his disposal. He became not only learned in books, but an accomplished scribe, and made himself master of those arts which, according to the rule of the Order, were carried on within the walls. He was a painter, a musician, and an excellent artificer in metal. He constructed an organ ' with brass pipes, filled with air from the bellows, and which uttered a grand and most sweet melody.' Bede. In those days, when a complete and well-written copy of the Scriptures was a most precious possession, such volumes were frequently enclosed in caskets of metal, adorned with figures of our Saviour, the Virgin, and the apostles; or guardian angels spread their wings over them, as over the ark of old. Some curious and elegant specimens of the piety and skill of the early monks are still preserved, and arts were thus kept alive which would else have perished. Dunstan, like St. Eloy, whose story Sacred and Legend. Art, has been already related, was a cunning artificer in metals. ii. 353. ' To have excelled his contemporaries in mental pursuits, in the fine arts, though then imperfectly practised, and in mechanical labours, is evidence of an activity of intellect, and an ardour for improvement, which proclaim him to have been a superior personage, whose talents might have blessed the world.' He Turner's Anglo- repaired at a very early age to court, where he was at first Saxons. much beloved by King Edmund, who took particular delight in his musical talent, which was then rare, and which, added to his skill in mathematics, his mechanical dexterity, and the power he obtained over the king, exposed him to the imputation of sorcery. His enemies persuaded the king that he was assisted by a demon; and Edmund reluctantly drove him from his presence. Some time afterwards, as the king was hunting, having outstripped his courtiers, it happened that the stag and the hounds in pursuit, coming suddenly to the edge of a precipice, fell over, and were dashed to pieces. The king, following at full speed, and seeing the precipice, endeavoured to rein in his horse. But unable to do so, and seeing his impending destruction, he recommended himself to God in prayer,—recalling, and at the same time repenting, his injustice to Dunstan. His horse, on reaching the edge of the precipice, instead of tumbling headlong, stood still, trembling and panting. The king was saved; he sent for Dunstan, who had retired meantime to his cell at Glastonbury, where he was occupied with his usual pursuits, and restored him to favour.

The famous story of the Devil seems to be referred to this period. One night, as Dunstan was working at his forge, the most terrible howls and cries were heard to proceed from his cell. The Devil, as he related, had visited him in the form of a beautiful woman, and endeavoured to tempt him from his holy work. He had seized the disguised demon by the nose with his red-hot tongs, which had caused him to roar with pain, and to flee discomfited.[1] A much more beautiful legend is that which relates that on a certain day, as Dunstan sat reading the Scriptures in his cell, his harp, which hung on a peg against the wall, sounded, untouched by human hands, for an angel played on it the hymn *Gaudete animi*, to the great delight and solace of the holy man. Dunstan was a poet and an artist; and later poets have heard in the chords of a harp, swept by the ' desultory breeze,' now the ' full celestial choir,' chanting ' the lofty anthem ; ' now the wailing of an imprisoned spirit; and anon the soft complainings of love. There needs no miracle here.

There was a certain royal lady at this time, whose name was Ethelfreda, who particularly admired the talents of Dunstan, and venerated his sanctity. For her he is said to have designed the pattern of a robe which she embroidered with her own hands. The probability is, that Dunstan drew the design for some vestment for the church service, or covering for an altar, such as it was then, and is even now, considered an act of religion to prepare and to decorate. Dunstan returned to court and became the minister and favourite of the king, who appointed him abbot of Glastonbury, and his treasurer. Edwin succeeded, and, from his accession, appears to have resisted the power of Dunstan. His character has of course suffered in the hands of

---

[1] One would have thought that fire being the natural element of the demon, he might have taken it more easily. The same story is told of St. Eloy. And the reader will probably recollect the incident, also related by himself, of Luther throwing his inkstand at the Devil. Such fancies may be interpreted without the imputation of deliberate falsehood calculated for a certain purpose.

the ecclesiastical historians, who represent him as abandoned to vice, and Elgiva not as his wife, but as his mistress. He drove Dunstan from his court. His subjects rebelled against him, and raised his brother Edgar to a share of the throne. Edwin died about the age of twenty, and Edgar became sole king. Dunstan was now at the height of power. He was made successively Bishop of Worcester, of London, and at length Archbishop of Canterbury. Mr. Turner represents Dunstan as having intro- *Hist. of the* duced the Benedictine Order into England; but there had existed *Anglo- Saxons.* no other Order in England from the time of St. Augustine of Canterbury. The fact is, that he introduced the reform of the Benedictine rule; restored its discipline; and used all the means which his energy, his talents, and his influence placed at his disposal, to extend and exalt his already powerful Order.

In the year 960 he made a journey to Rome, was received there with great honour by Pope John XII., from whose hands he received the pallium as Primate of the Anglo-Saxon nation. Returning to England, he set himself assiduously to found monasteries and schools, and to extend everywhere the taste for knowledge and the civilising arts. His miracles, his supernatural arts, and his visions, form a large part of the ecclesiastical history of his time. He relates himself a vision in which he beheld the espousals of his mother, for whom he entertained the profoundest love and veneration, with the Saviour of the world, accompanied with all the circumstances of heavenly pomp, amid a choir of angels. One of the angels asked Dunstan why he did not join in the song of rejoicing? when he excused himself on account of his ignorance. The angel then taught him the song. The next morning, St. Dunstan assembled his monks around him, and, relating his vision, taught them the very hymn which he had learned in his dream, and commanded them to sing it. Mr. Turner calls this an *impious* story, whereas it is merely one form of those old allegorical legends which are figurative of the mystic espousals of the soul, or the Church (as in the marriage of St. Catherine), and which appear to have been suggested by the language and imagery of the Canticles.

St. Dunstan died at Canterbury in 988.

The few representations which remain to us of St. Dunstan must be considered as devotional. I have not as yet met with any dramatic or historical pictures relating to his life, which, however, abounds in picturesque incidents. A drawing from his own hand has been most erroneously described as 'St. Dunstan on a throne, and a monk kissing his feet:' however outrageous the pride of Dunstan, he never would have dared such an exhibition of presumption. The drawing, of which I

15　St. Dunstan kneeling at the feet of Christ. (From a pen-drawing by himself, existing in the Bod. Lib., Oxford, and engraved in Hick's Thesaurus.)

give a faithful (reduced) transcript, represents our Saviour throned, holding a sceptre, and Dunstan himself prostrate before him.

A miniature, in which St. Dunstan is enthroned, and B. Museum MS. three ecclesiastics kneel at his feet, one wearing the *black*, the other the *white* Benedictine habit, and the third the dress of a priest or canon regular, is also very curious, and of a much B. Museum later period.

St. Dunstan seated, writing, is engraved in ' Strutt's Regal and Ecclesiastical Antiquities,' from an ancient MS.

In a series of pictures from the life of St. Dunstan, the scene with Edwin and Elgiva would of course find a place, and the sentiment would vary according to the view taken of his character. Either he would appear as the venerable ecclesiastic, as one clothed with Divine authority reproving a licentious boy unmindful of the decencies and duties of his high station ; or as a fierce and cruel priest, interfering to sever the most holy ties and to crush the most innocent affections. This last is the view taken by Mr Taylor in the drama of ' Edwin the Fair,' and by Wordsworth :—

> The enthusiast as a dupe
> Shall soar, and as a hypocrite can stoop,
> And turn the instruments of good to ill,
> Moulding a credulous people to his will—
> Such DUNSTAN.

In connection with St. Dunstan, we must not forget St. Edith of Wilton, one of the most interesting of the princess-nuns of the Anglo-Saxon race. She was the daughter of King Edgar by Wilfrida, a beautiful nun, whom he had carried off forcibly from her seclusion. For this sacrilege, Edgar was placed by St. Dunstan under an interdict for seven years. Wilfrida, as soon as she could escape from the power of the king, again took refuge in her convent, and there brought forth a daughter, Editha, whom she educated in all the learning of the times, and who was a marvel for her beauty as well as her sanctity and her learning. She refused to attend her father's court, but expended the rich dowry he gave her in founding the nunnery at Wilton, which, since the Reformation, has been the seat of the earls of Pembroke. This St. Edith should be grouped with St. Dunstan and St. Ethelwold and St. Denis of France. She should be young and beautiful, and richly dressed; for, even at the time when all the

sainted princesses wore costly garments, she was remarkable for
the splendour of her attire. On this account being rebuked
by St. Ethelwold, she replied that the judgment of God,
which penetrated through the outward appearance, was alone
true and infallible. 'For,' said she, 'pride may exist under
the garb of wretchedness; and a mind may be as pure under
these vestments as under your tattered furs.' And the holy
man, being so answered by this wise and royal lady, held his
peace.   St. Edith died soon after the consecration of the
church she had built in honour of St. Denis, being in her
twenty-third year.

St. Edward the Martyr.

A.D. 978.

As King Edward, the son of Edgar, was one day weary with
hunting and very thirsty, he left his attendants to follow the
dogs, and hearing that his stepmother Elfrida and his brother
Ethelred were living in a certain village named Corvesgate, he
rode thither, unattended, in quest of something to drink; in his
innocence suspecting no harm, and judging the hearts of others
by his own. His treacherous stepmother received him with
caresses, and, kissing him, offered him the cup; and as he
drank it off, one of her servants stabbed him in the back with a
dagger. Finding himself wounded, he set spurs to his horse,
and his attendants coming up, followed him by the track of his
blood, and found his body mangled and bleeding in the forest.
The wicked woman Elfrida, and her son Ethelred, ordered the
body of Edward to be ignominiously buried at Wareham, in the
midst of public rejoicing and festivity, as if they had buried his
memory and his body together; but Divine pity came to his aid,
and ennobled the innocent victim with the grace of miracles, for
a celestial light was shed on that place, and all who laboured
under any infirmity were there healed. And when multitudes
from all parts of the kingdom resorted to his tomb, his murderess
Elfrida, being severely reproved by Dunstan, and struck with
remorse, would also journey thither; but when she mounted her

v. Chronicle of William of Malmsbury.

Corfe-Castle.

horse, he, who before had outstripped the winds and was full of ardour to bear his royal mistress, now by the will of God stood immovable; neither whip nor spur could urge him forward; and Elfrida, seeing in this the hand of God, repented of her crime, and, alighting from her horse, walked humbly and barefooted to the tomb. His body was taken up, and he was buried with great honour in the nunnery which had been endowed by his ancestor, Alfred the Great, at Shaftesbury.

St. Edward is represented as a beautiful youth, with the diadem and flowing hair, holding in one hand a short sword or sceptre, and in the other the palm as martyr; further to distinguish him, the scene of his assassination is frequently represented in the background. This incident, from its tragical and picturesque circumstances, has always been a favourite subject with English artists. I am not sure that the title of martyr properly belongs to St. Edward, for his death was not voluntary, nor from any religious cause. The Anglo-Saxons regarded his memory with devout reverence, but as a patron-saint he was not so popular as his namesake, Edward the Confessor.

St. Edward, King and Confessor.

A.D. 1066. Jan. 5.

THE effigies of St. Edward were formerly common in our ecclesiastical edifices, and are still to be found. I shall give his legendary history here as it is represented in the singular bas-reliefs in his chapel in Westminster Abbey, of which there are accurate engravings in Carter's 'Specimens of Ancient Sculpture.'

1. King Ethelred had by his first wife Edmund Ironside; and by his second wife, Queen Emma, he had Alfred. The queen was near her second confinement, when Ethelred assembled his council to deliberate on the concerns of his kingdom, and whom he should appoint to succeed him; some inclined towards Edmund on account of his great bodily strength, others towards Alfred. St. Dunstan, who was present, prophesied the short life of both these princes, therefore the council decided in favour

Camden's Remains, ed. 1654, p. 484.

o

of the unborn child, afterwards Edward the Confessor; and
all the nobles then present took the oath of fealty to him,
dans le sein de sa mère.

In the bas-relief, Queen Emma, standing in the centre,
is surrounded by prelates and nobles, who seem to do her
homage.

This same Queen Emma afterwards married Canute, and,
during the reign of Edward, was accused of many crimes; she
was said to have hated her son, to have refused him aid from
her treasures, 'to have loved Canute more when living than
her first husband, and more commended him when dead'—
an unpardonable sin in the eyes of the Saxons, though
excusable, considering the contrasted characters of the cruel,
slothful Ethelred, and the warlike fiery-spirited Dane. She
cleared herself by walking blindfold and unhurt over eleven
red-hot ploughshares; ever since a favourite legend with the
English.

2. The second compartment represents the birth of King
Edward the Confessor, which took place at Islip in Oxfordshire.
Hist. of Oxfordshire. ' In the chapel, not many years since, there stood the very font
wherein that religious prince St. Edward the Confessor received
the sacrament of baptism, which font being rescued from
profane uses, to which it had been condemned during the
Commonwealth, was placed by Sir Henry Brown on a pedestal,
and adorned with a poem rather pious than learned.'

3. In the third compartment we have the coronation of the
saint, on Easter-day 1043.

4. A large sum of money having been collected for the tribute
called *Danegelt*, it was conveyed to the palace, and the king was
called to see it; at the sight thereof he started back, exclaim-
ing, that he beheld a demon dancing upon the money, and
rejoicing: thereupon he commanded that the gold should be
restored to its owners, and released his subjects from that
grievous tribute. In the bas-relief the money is represented
in casks, and upon these casks there seems to have been a
figure of a demon, which has been broken away.

5. Hugolin, the king's chamberlain, one day took some money
out of a coffer in the king's bedchamber, leaving it open, the,

king being then on his couch. A young man who waited on the king, believing him to be asleep, put his hand into the coffer, took out a handful of gold, went away and hid it; he then returned a second time, took another handful; and again a third time, on which the king cried out, 'Nay! thou art too covetous! take what thou hast, and be content; for, if Hugolin come, he will not leave thee one penny:' whereupon the young man ran out of the room and escaped. When Hugolin returned, he began to lament himself because of the robbery. 'Hold thy peace,' replied the king; 'perhaps he who hath taken it hath more need of it than we have: what is left is sufficient for us.'

6. King Edward partaking of the Eucharist before the altar at Westminster, attended by Leofric, earl of Chester (the husband of Godiva), had a vision of the Saviour standing in person on the altar.

7. The king of the Danes had assembled an army for the purpose of invading England, and, on going on board his fleet, fell over into the sea and was drowned; which circumstance was miraculously made known to King Edward in a vision. In the bas-relief the Danish king is floundering in the sea.

8. The king, the queen, and Earl Godwin, the queen's father, are seated at table; in front is the contest between Harold and Tosti, two boys, the sons of Godwin: the king, looking on, foretold the destruction of both, through their mutual enmity.

9. On Easter-day, as the king was seated at table, he was observed to smile, and then to look particularly grave. After dinner, being asked by Earl Harold and the Abbot of Westminster the reason of his smiling, he told them that at that moment he had had a vision of the Seven Sleepers of Ephesus, and that while he looked they turned from the right side, on which they had rested for two hundred years, and were to lie seventy-four on their left side, during which time the nation would be visited by many sorrows; which prophecy came to pass when the Normans invaded England. _{Sacred and Legend. Art, ii. 198.}

10 and 12 represent the legend of St. John the Evangelist, which has been already related. _{Sacred and Legend. Art, i. 141.}

11 represents the king's miraculous power of healing, a gift

which was popularly believed to have descended to all his anointed successors down to the time of Queen Anne.

13. The pilgrims deliver to the king the ring which they had received from St. John the Evangelist.

14 represents the dedication of the church of St. Peter at Westminster.

A short time afterwards, in the year 1066, on the eve of the Epiphany, St. Edward the Confessor died, 'and was buried in the said church, which he first, in England, had erected after that kind of style which, now, all attempt to rival at a great expense.'

In the reign of Henry III. the church was rebuilt, and a splendid chapel and shrine erected to the memory of the founder. The architect of the shrine is said to have been Pietro Cavalini, an Italian painter, some of whose works remain in the church of

16   Richard II. with his three protectors, St. John the Baptist, St Edmund, and St. Edward the Confessor. From an ancient diptych, now at Wilton. (Sketch from Hollar's print.)

Assisi; but of the paintings which he is supposed to have executed on the walls of this chapel, no trace remains.

The single devotional figures of St. Edward the Confessor represent him in the kingly robes, the crown on his head, in one hand the sceptre surmounted with a dove (as in the effigy on his seal), in the other the ring of St. John. He has a long beard, a fair complexion, and a mild serene countenance. The ring is his proper attribute: in the beautiful coronation of the Virgin Kensington in the collection of Prince Wallerstein, the figure of St. Edward Pal. the Confessor appears in the lower part of the picture holding the ring, and a letter which is supposed to contain the message of St. John: this is quite un-English in character and conception, and the introduction of our Saxon king into foreign devotional subjects very unusual.

St. Thomas of Canterbury.

St. Thomas à Becket. *Lat.* Sanctus Thomas Episc. Cantuariensis et Martyr. *Ital.* San Tomasso Cantuariense. *Fr.* Saint Thomas de Cantorbéri. Dec. 29, 1170.

THE story of Becket in connection with the annals of England is to be found in every English History: the manner in which it is related, the colour given to his actions and character, vary considerably in all; the view to be taken of both had become a question, not of justice and truth, but of religious party. Lord Campbell, in his recent and admirably written life of Becket, as chancellor and minister of Henry II., tells us that his vituperators are to be found among bigoted Protestants, and his unqualified eulogists among intolerant Catholics. After stating, with the perspicuity of a judge in equity, their respective arguments and opinions, he sums up in favour of the eulogists, and decides that, setting aside exaggeration, miracle, and religious prejudice, the most merciful view of the character of Becket is also the most just. And is it not pleasant, where the imagination has been so excited by the strange vicissitudes and picturesque scenes of his varied life, the judgment so dazzled by his brilliant and generous qualities, the sympathies so touched by the tragic circumstances of his death, to have our scruples set at rest, and to be allowed to admire and to venerate with a good conscience; and this too on the authority of one accustomed to balance evidence, and not swerved by any bias to extreme religious opinions? But it is not as statesman, chancellor, or prelate, that Becket takes his place in sacred Art. It is in his character of canonised saint and martyr that I have to speak of him here. He was murdered or martyred because he pertinaciously defended the spiritual against the royal authority; and we must remember that in the eleventh century, the cause of the Church was in fact the cause of the weak against the strong, the cause of civilisation and of the people against barbarism and tyranny; and that by his contemporaries he was regarded as the champion of the oppressed Saxon race against the Norman nobility.

I must not allow myself to dwell upon the scenes of his secular career. The whole of his varied life is rich in materials for the historical painter, offering all that could possibly be desired, in pomp, in circumstance, in scenery, in costume, and in character. What a series it would make of beautiful subjects, beginning with the legend of his mother, the daughter of the Emir of Palestine, who, when his father Gilbert à Becket was taken prisoner in the crusade, fell in love with him, delivered him from captivity, and afterwards followed him to England, knowing no words of any Western tongue except *Gilbert* and *London*, with the aid of which she found him in Cheapside; then her baptism, her marriage, the birth of the future saint; his introduction to the king; his mission to Rome; his splendid embassy to Paris; his single-handed combat with Engleran de Trie, the French knight; the king of England and the king of France at his bedside when he was sick at Rouen; his consecration as archbishop; his assumption of the Benedictine habit; his midnight penances, when he walked alone in the cloisters bewailing his past sins; his washing the feet of the pilgrims and beggars; his angry conference with the king; their reconciliation at Friatville; his progress through the city of London,

when the grateful and enthusiastic people flung themselves in
his path and kissed the hem of his garment; his interview with
the assassins; his murder on the steps of the altar; and, finally,
the proud king kneeling at midnight on the same spot, sub-
mitting to be scourged in penance for his crime:—I know
not that any one of these fine subjects has been adequately
treated.   There was, in a recent exhibition, a little picture
of the arrival of the Emir's daughter at her lover's door in
Cheapside, where the dark-eyed, dark-haired, cowering maiden   Armitage.
is surrounded by a crowd of wondering fair-haired Londoners,
which was excellently drawn and conceived, only a little too
pale in the colouring: and the murder has often been painted,
but never worthily.

The sole claim of Becket to a place in sacred Art lies in his
martyrdom, and the causes which immediately led to it; and to
these, therefore, I shall confine myself here.

Thomas à Becket, on being promoted to the see of Canterbury, resigned the chancellorship; and throwing aside the
gay and somewhat dissipated manners which had made him
a favourite with his sovereign, he became at once an altered
man.

'The universal expectation was, that Becket would now play   v. Lord
the part so successfully performed by Cardinal Wolsey in a   Campbell's
                                                               Lives of the
succeeding age; that, chancellor and archbishop, he would   Chancellors
continue the minister and personal friend of the king; that he
would study to support and extend all the prerogatives of the
crown, which he himself was to exercise; and that, in the palaces
of which he was now master, he would live with increased magnificence and luxury.   When we judge of his character, we must
ever bear in mind that all this was easily within his reach; and
that if he had been actuated by love of pleasure or mere vulgar
ambition, such would have been his career.'   But very different
was the path which he resolved to pursue.

From this time his history presents us with one long scene
of contention between a haughty, resolute, and accomplished
prince, and a churchman determined to maintain at once the
privileges of the Church, and his own rank of spiritual father to

the king and people of England.   It was a contest for power in which the intrepid archbishop was brought into collision, not merely with the king, but with many of the nobility, and some of the Norman prelates whom he had excommunicated for contumacy.   Henry, driven desperate at last by the indomitable zeal and courage of his adversary, was heard to exclaim, 'Of the cowards that eat my bread, is there none that will rid me of this upstart priest?'

The words, uttered in a moment of exasperation, had scarcely left his lips when they were acted on.   Four of his Norman attendants, Reginald Fitzurse, William Tracy, Hugh de Morville, and Richard Brito, bound themselves by oath to put the refractory priest to death.   They came over to Canterbury, and, though they at first entered the presence of Becket unarmed, he seems to have anticipated their fatal purpose.   'In vain,' said he, 'you menace me; if all the swords in England were brandished over my head, their terrors could not move me.   Foot to foot you would find me fighting the battle of the Lord!'   They rushed in a fury from his presence, and called their followers to arms.   The rest of the story I give in the words of Lord Campbell :—

'In this moment of suspense, the voices of the monks singing vespers in the adjoining choir were heard; and it being suggested that the church offered the best chance of safety, Becket agreed to join the worshippers there, thinking that at all events, if he was murdered before the altar, his death would be more glorious, and his memory would be held in greater veneration by after ages.   He then ordered the cross of Canterbury to be carried before him, and slowly followed his friends through the cloister. He entered the church by the north transept, and hearing the gates barred behind him, he ordered them to be reopened, saying, that the temple of God was not to be fortified like a castle.   He was ascending the steps of the choir, when the four knights, with twelve companions, all in complete armour, burst into the church, their leader calling out, "Hither to me, ye servants of the king!"   As it was now dusk, the archbishop might have retreated and concealed himself, for a time at least, among the crypts and secret passages of the building, with which he was well acquainted; but, undismayed, he turned to meet the assassins, followed by his cross-bearer, the only one of his attendants who had not fled. A voice was heard, "Where is the traitor?" Silence for a moment prevailed; but when Fitzurse demanded, "Where is the archbishop?" he replied, "Here I am; the archbishop, but no traitor! Reginald, I have granted thee many favours; what is thy object now? If you seek my life, let that suffice; and I command you, in the name of God, not to touch one of my people." Being again told that he must instantly absolve the prelates whom he had excommunicated, the Archbishop of York and the Bishop of Salisbury, he answered, "Till they make satisfaction I will not absolve them." "Then die," said Tracy. The blow aimed at his head only slightly wounded him, as it was warded off by the faithful cross-bearer, whose arm was broken by its force. The archbishop, feeling the blood trickle down his face, joined his hands and bowed his head, saying, "In the name of Christ, and for the defence of his Church, I am ready to die." To mitigate the sacrilege, they wished to remove him from the church before they despatched him; but he declared he should there meet his fate, and, retaining the same posture, desired them to execute their intentions or their orders, and, uttering his last words, he said, "I humbly commend my spirit to God, who gave it." He had hardly finished this prayer, when a second stroke quickly threw him on his knees, and a third laid him prostrate on the floor at the foot of the altar. There he received many blows from each of the conspirators, and his brains were strewed upon the pavement.

'Thus perished, in the fifty-third year of his age, the man who, of all the English chancellors since the foundation of the monarchy, was of the loftiest ambition, of the greatest firmness of purpose, and the most capable of making every sacrifice to a sense of duty, or for the acquisition of renown.' (I think, however, Lord Campbell should not have placed the two motives together thus, as though he had deemed them equal.) 'I cannot,' he adds, 'doubt Becket's sincerity, and almost all will agree that he believed himself to be sincere;' and I will add, in conclusion, that perishing as he did, voluntarily,

P

resolutely, and in support of what he considered as the right-
eous cause, it is not, perhaps, without reason that he has been
styled a *martyr*, even where he would not be allowed the
dignity of a saint.

His monks buried him in the crypt at Canterbury; and it
is related, that as they carried him to his resting-place, chanting with trembling and fear the Requiem for the dead, the
voices of the angels were heard singing a loud and harmonious
Lætabitur justus, the beginning of the Service of the Martyrs;
and the monks stopped in their mournful chant, being
amazed; then, as inspired, they took up the angelic strain,
and thus, the heavenly and the earthly voices mingling
together in the hymn of praise and triumph, they bore the
holy martyr to his tomb.

Considering the extraordinary veneration once paid to St.
Thomas à Becket throughout all Christendom, but more especially in England, it seems strange that we may now seek
through the length and breadth of our land, and find not a
single memorial left of him.

The Church which he had defended canonised him, and held
up his name to worship; within two years after his death, his
relics were laid in a rich shrine, the scene of his martyrdom
became a place of pilgrimage to all nations, and the marble
pavement of Canterbury Cathedral may be seen at this day worn
by the knees of his worshippers.[1] But the power which he
had defied, the kingly power, *uncanonised* him, desecrated his
shrine, burned his relics, and flung his ashes into the Thames.
By an act in council of Henry VIII., it was solemnly decreed
'that Thomas à Becket was no saint, but a rebel and a
traitor; that he should no longer be called or esteemed a saint;
that all images and pictures of him should be destroyed, all

---

[1] ' There, to whose sumptuous shrine the near succeeding ages
So mighty offerings sent, and made such pilgrimages;
Concerning whom, the world since then hath spent much breath,
And many questions made, both of his life and death:
If he were truly just, he hath his right—if no,
Those times were much to blame that have him reckoned so.'
DRAYTON'S *Polyolbion*. Song 24.

festivals held in his honour should be abolished, and his name and remembrance erased from all documents, under pain of royal indignation and imprisonment during his Grace's pleasure.' This decree was so effective in England, that the effigies of this once beloved and popular saint vanished at once from every house and oratory. I have never met, nor could ever hear of, any representation of St. Thomas à Becket remaining in our ecclesiastical edifices:[1] and I have seen missals and breviaries, in which his portrait had been more or less carefully smeared over and obliterated. But with regard to the representations of St. Thomas of Canterbury in Roman Catholic countries, where alone they are now to be found, there are some particulars to be noted which appear to me curious and interesting.

St. Thomas was martyred in 1170; and canonised by Pope Alexander III. in the year 1172. In that year William the Good, king of Sicily, began to build the magnificent church of Monreale, near Palermo, the interior of which is incrusted with rich mosaics; and among the figures of saints and worthies we find St. Thomas of Canterbury, standing colossal in his episcopal robes, with no attribute but his name inscribed. It is the work of Byzantine artists, and perhaps the earliest existing effigy of Thomas à Becket in his saintly character. In the year 1178, the great abbey of Aberbrothock was founded in his honour, by William the Lion, king of Scots. A few years later, about 1200, Innocent III., being pope, presented to the little church of Agnani, the place of his birth, a cope and mitre richly embroidered. On the cope we find, worked with most delicate skill, and evidently from excellent original drawings, thirty-six scenes from sacred story; and among these is the martyrdom of Becket: on the mitre he is again represented. I saw careful tracings of these subjects made upon the embroidered originals; the colours, I was told by the artist, being but little faded. This cope is not quite so ancient as the famous

---

[1] I am informed by an obliging correspondent, that in the very ancient church of the village of Horton, in Ribblesdale, there exists a head of St. Thomas à Becket, still to be seen in the east window over the altar.

dalmatica in the Vatican, but is almost as beautiful, and even more elaborate.

These examples show how early and how effectually the Church had exalted the saintly fame of Thomas à Becket. In the former instance, the appearance of our English saint in a Sicilian church, his figure designed and executed by Greek artists, seems incomprehensible till explained by the recollection that William the Good married the Princess Joanna of England, daughter of Henry II. She arrived in Sicily in the year 1177, and William probably thought to honour his bride, and certainly intended no dishonour to his father-in-law, by placing within the glorious temple he was then building the worshipped image of the man whom that father-in-law had assassinated. Altogether the circumstances seem to me curiously illustrative of the feelings and manners of that time.

In the devotional figures, St. Thomas is represented wearing the chasuble over the black Benedictine habit, and carrying the crosier and Gospels in his hand. When represented as martyr, he is without the mitre, and the blood trickles from a wound in his head, or he has a battle-axe or sword struck into his head. He is, in every instance I can remember, beardless. The observer must be careful to distinguish these martyr-effigies of St. Thomas Archbishop and Martyr, from those of St. Peter Martyr, the Dominican Friar.

Though I suppose no *authentic* effigy of him now exists, yet those which we possess seem to have been done from some original portrait existing in his time.

Brit. Mus. There is a beautiful and very rare little print by Vorstermann, executed in England, and, from the peculiar character, I suppose from some original document not named.

Verona. In his church at Verona, dedicated to him in 1316, is placed *Bologna.* the scene of his martyrdom. I found him standing by the *San Salvador.* throned Virgin in a picture by Girolamo da Treviso; and again *Venice.* in a picture by Girolamo da Santa Croce, where he is seated on *San Silvostro.* a throne, and surrounded by a company of saints: a most beautiful picture, and a capital work of the master. A small picture in distemper on panel, of the martyrdom of St. Thomas, used to

17   Thomas à Becket. (After a print by Vostermann.)

hang over the tomb of King Henry IV. at Canterbury, and is
engraved in Carter's 'Specimens.'

I remember to have seen a very old representation of the
murder of St. Thomas à Becket, in which the faithful cross-
bearer is standing by the altar, with outstretched arm, as if
defending his lord; and another in which King Henry, kneeling
before the tomb of Becket, and his shoulders bared, is scourged
by four Benedictine monks.

In a beautiful Psalter which belonged to Queen Mary, elaborately illuminated by French artists, there is a complete series
of groups from the life of Thomas à Becket, beginning with the
baptism of his Eastern mother, and ending with the penance of
King Henry.

In the ancient representations of his martyrdom, the assassins
are handed down to the execration of the pious, by having their
names written underneath, or they are distinguished by their
armorial bearings. Morville bears the *Fretty fleurs-de-lis;*
Tracy, *or, two bars* or *bandlets gules;* Brito, *three bears' heads*

Eng. in
Strutt's Re-
gal and Eccl.
Antiq.,Supp.

muzzled; Fitzurse, *three bears passant,* in allusion to his name. I have seen also a French print of the martyrdom of St. Thomas,

1 S   Penance of Henry II.   (From old stained glass.)

in which the fierce Norman assassins are habited in the full court costume of Louis XV.[1]

With St. Thomas à Becket I conclude this sketch of the most popular and distinguished of our Anglo-Saxon saints; those who,

[1] There is at Chatsworth a picture by Johan Van Eyck, styled the ' Consecration of Thomas à Becket as Archbishop of Canterbury,' an important and beautiful composition of seventeen figures.   I mention it here, but I am doubtful about the subject.   A very beautiful picture of the same school, now in the possession of Sir Charles Eastlake, which used to be styled ' The Burial of St. Thomas à Becket,' is, I am persuaded, the burial of St. Hubert.

as subjects of art, have represented, or might properly represent, in a characteristic manner, the early religious tendencies of our nation.   The Conquest introduced us to a new
celestial hierarchy.   First came St. Michael, the favourite
patron of William of Normandy, who landed at Hastings on
the day of the feast of the archangel.   Matilda of Scotland,
the wife of Henry I., popularised St. Giles.   The French
princes and nobles connected with our Norman kings brought
over their French patrons, St. Martin, St. Maur, St. Maurice,
St. Radegonde, and that 'Sainte Demoiselle Pécheresse,'
Mary Magdalene.   The Crusaders introduced a long array of
poetical Greek patrons,—St. George, St Catherine, St.
Nicholas, St. Barbara, &c.,—of whom I have already spoken
at length.   The French and the Eastern saints were the
patrons of the dominant race, and represented the religious
feelings of the aristocracy and the chivalry of the country.
Henry III., to conciliate the Saxons, gave to his eldest son a
name dear and venerable to his English subjects, and placed
him under the protection of St. Edward the Confessor.   When
Edward III. gave the password at the siege of Calais, it was
'Ha, St. Edward!   Ha, St. George!' and the Normans—
with more, perhaps, of policy than piety—associated with
their hereditary patrons the martyr saints of the Anglo-
Saxons; but this was seldom.   The English meanwhile clung
to their own native saints; among the people, the Edwards
and Edmunds and Oswalds, the Austins and Audrys and
Cuthberts, gave way very slowly to a companionship with the
outlandish worthies of a new dynasty: and it is amusing to
find that, in adopting these, the popular legends, in a truly
national spirit, claimed them as their own.   According to
the local traditions, St. George's father and mother lived in
Warwickshire, and St. Ursula assembled her virgins at
Coventry.

The religious Orders which sprang up after the eleventh
century brought over to us of course their own especial saints
and patriarchs.   I confess I find no proof that these ever became very popular in England, as subjects of religious Art:

or that their effigies, even before the Reformation, prevailed
in our ecclesiastical edifices to any great degree.   It does not
appear that St. Bernard, St. Francis, St. Dominick, ever
superseded St. Cuthbert, St. Dunstan, and St. Thomas à
Becket.

But it was the reverse abroad, and we turn once more to
the splendours of foreign Art.

10

20   St. Benedict.   St. Romualdo.
            (From a picture in the National Gallery.)

The Reformed Benedictines.

FOR about three centuries after the death of St. Benedict we
find his Order extending in every direction throughout Christendom ; so that when Charlemagne inquired whether any other
religious Order existed in his dominions, he was informed that
from east to west, and from north to south, only Benedictines
were to be found throughout the length and breadth of his
empire.   M. Guizot, in his view of the reign of Charlemagne,
gives us a 'tableau' of the celebrated men who were in his

Q

service as ministers, counsellors, secretaries: they were all
ecclesiastics of the Benedictine Order; and we have seen,
that in England almost all the leading men who figured as
statesmen, as scholars, and as legal functionaries, from the
seventh to the twelfth century, belonged to the same religious
community.

But it appears that, from the middle of the ninth to the
middle of the eleventh century, the intellectual superiority of
the Benedictines, and their moral influence over the people,
Dark Ages. declined. As far as I can judge, Mr. Maitland has triumphantly proved, that the common notion of the universal
ignorance, and laziness, and depravity of the monks, even
during this period, has been much exaggerated; still, the
complaints of the ecclesiastical writers of the time, writers of
their own Order,—there were no other,—prove that manifold
disorders had crept into the religious houses, and that the
primitive rule of the founder, particularly that chapter which
enjoined manual labour, was neglected or evaded by the monks.
If there appeared among them some men more conscientious
or more enlightened, who denounced, or endeavoured to reform
these abuses, they were in some instances imprisoned or even
murdered by their own companions; oftener they withdrew in
disgust, and hid themselves in deserts, to avoid what they
could neither heal nor prevent. The number of these solitaries
was so great, that every forest, every woodland glade, or
rocky glen, had its hermit cell, and in all the romances,
legends, and poems of the time, some holy hermit is sure to
figure as one of the chief actors.

The first successful attempt to restore the strict institutions
of St. Benedict was made in France, in the famous monastery
of Clugni, by the Abbot Odo, between 927 and 942: but as
these monks of Clugni, however important in the page of
history, are comparatively insignificant in Art, I pass them
over for the present. In Italy the reform began in the
following century under Romualdo and Gualberto, two very
remarkable characters, who occur very frequently in the early
Florentine works of art, but rarely in any other.

St. Romualdo, Founder of the Order of Camaldoli.

Feb. 7, 1027.

The habit entirely white—white hood and girdle.

Romualdo, descended from one of the noblest families of Ravenna, that of the Onesti, was born about the year 956; his father, Sergius, gave him the usual education of a young nobleman of that time. In his youth he was fond of hunting, but when he chased the boar through the pine forests of Ravenna, he would slacken his bridle, and become, almost unconsciously to himself, absorbed in contemplation of the beauty and quietude of the scene. Then he would sigh forth a prayer or two, and think of the happiness of those who dwell in peace far from the vain pleasures and deceits and turmoil of the world.

His father, Sergius, was a man of a far different spirit,—worldly, haughty, grasping, and violent. Believing himself aggrieved by a near relation, on the subject of a succession to a certain pasture, in the course of the dispute he challenged his adversary, and slew him on the spot. Romualdo, then a young man of twenty, was present on this occasion; and, struck with horror and compunction, he believed himself called upon to expiate the crime of his father by doing penance for it himself. He retired to the monastery of Sant Apollinare *in Classe*, about four miles from the city of Ravenna; and there, in a fit of disgust and despair, assumed the habit of the Order of St. Benedict. He passed seven years in the convent, but was scandalised by the irregularity of the monks, and the impunity with which the fundamental rules of a religious Order were daily and hourly transgressed. The idea of restoring to the monastical institutions that purity and that spiritual elevation of which he fondly believed them capable, took possession of his mind, and the rest of his long life was one of perpetual struggle in the cause. He was slandered and vilified by the corrupt monks, his life threatened, often in danger; but his enthusiastic faith and firmness overcame all. After a conflict of about thirty years, he found himself at the head of some hundreds of reformed monks, and had become celebrated throughout the whole of the north of Italy.

The parent monastery was founded by Romualdo, in a solitary glen among the Apennines, near Arezzo; called from the family name of its original owners, the *Campo Maldoli;* hence the appellation of the Order. It is one of the strictest of all the monastic institutions. The congregations of the Camaldolesi remind us in some respects of those of the ancient Egyptian hermits; they are devoved to the perpetual service of God, in silence, contemplation, and solitude; they neither converse nor eat together, but live in separate huts, each of which has its little garden, for that part of the institute of St. Benedict which enjoined manual labour is retained.

Romualdo died in 1027, according to his legend, at the great age of one hundred and twenty years; according to more probable accounts, at the age of seventy. Dante has placed him in his Paradiso 'among the spirits of men contemplative.'

c. 2.

Figures of St. Romualdo are met with only in pictures painted for the houses of his Order, and are easily recognised. He wears the white habit with loose wide sleeves, a long white beard descending to his girdle, and leans upon a crutch: we have such a picture in our National Gallery, painted by Taddeo Gaddi, either for the convent at Camaldoli, or, which is more probable, for that of the 'Angeli,' a foundation of the Camaldolesi at Florence, now suppressed. It is one of the two compartments entitled in the catalogue ' Saints;' the Virgin and Child having evidently formed the centre group. St. Romualdo sits on the right in front; his pendant in the opposite wing being St. Benedict with his rod. Thus we have the two patriarchs of the Order most conspicuously placed. With St. Benedict, beginning at the top, we have St. Ambrose with his music-book, St. Francis, St. Stephen, St. Paul, St. Catherine, as patroness of theologians and schoolmen, St. John the Baptist, St. Mark (holding his Gospel open at the text ch. xvi. v. 16); and in company with St. Romualdo we find St. Gregory, St. Philip,

v. p. 113.

St. Laurence, St. Dominick, St. John the Evangelist, St. Peter, and (I think) St. Bernard, the great scholar and polemic of his time, as pendant to St. Catherine.

'The Vision of St. Romualdo' is the only subject I have seen from his life. It is recorded in his legend, that, a short time before his death, he fell asleep beside a fountain near his cell; and he dreamed, and in his dream he saw a ladder like that which the patriarch Jacob beheld in his vision, resting on the earth, and the top of it reaching to heaven; and he saw the brethren of his Order ascending by twos and by threes all clothed in white. When Romualdo awoke from his dream, he changed the habit of his monks from black to white, which they have ever since worn in remembrance of this vision. *Perhaps the same which Dante alludes to, Purg. c. v.*

The earliest example is a small picture by Simone Avanzi, which I saw in the Bologna Gallery. The latest, and a justly celebrated picture, is the large altar-piece by Andrea Sacchi, painted for the church of the Camaldolesi at Rome; the saint, seated under a tree, leaning on his staff, and surrounded by five of his monks, is pointing to the vision represented in the background. It has been a question whether Andrea has not committed an error in representing St. Romualdo and his companions already in white, supposing the alteration to have been made in consequence of the vision. But the picture ought perhaps to be understood in a devotional and ideal sense, as Romualdo pointing out to his recluses the path to heaven. *Rome. Vatican. Engr Musée Napoléou.*

Although the Camaldolesi have not been remarkable as patrons of art, their order produced a painter of great importance in his time—Lorenzo, called from his profession Don Lorenzo *Monaco;* and another painter named Giovanni, who belonged to the same convent, 'Degli Angeli,' already mentioned. Several pictures from this suppressed convent are in the Florence Academy, and one in which Don Giovanni Monaco assisted Frate Angelico. In the Gallery of the Uffizi is a beautiful Adoration of the Magi by Don Lorenzo. *Sacred and Legend.Art. i. 86.* *Fl. Acad. No. 15.*

St. John Gualberto, Founder of the Order of Vallombrosa.

Ital. San Giovanni Gualberto.   *Fr.* S. Jean Gualbert, or Calbert.
July 12, 1073.

The proper habit is a pale ash colour or light grey ; the monks now wear a black cloak, and, when abroad, a large hat.

SAINT JOHN GUALBERTO appears only in the Florentine pictures, and I have never seen his beautiful legend represented in a manner worthy of its picturesque and poetical associations and grave moral significance.

Giovanni Gualberto was born at Florence of rich and noble lineage. His father, who was of high military rank, gave him a good education according to the ideas of the time ; he excelled in all manly exercises, and entered on the active and brilliant career of a young Florentine noble, in the days when his native city was rising into power and opulence as a sovereign state.

When he was still a young man, his only brother, Hugo, whom he loved exceedingly, was murdered by a gentleman with whom he had a quarrel. Gualberto, whose grief and fury were stimulated by the rage of his father and the tears of his mother, set forth in pursuit of the assassin, vowing a prompt and a terrible vengeance.

It happened, that when returning from Florence to the country house of his father on the evening of Good Friday, he took his way over the steep, narrow, winding road which leads from the city gate to the Church of San Miniato-del-Monte. About half way up the hill, where the road turns to the right, he suddenly came upon his enemy, alone and unarmed. At the sight of the assassin of his brother, thus as it were, given into his hand, Gualberto drew his sword. The miserable wretch, seeing no means of escape, fell upon his knees and entreated mercy : extending his arms in the form of a cross, he adjured him by the remembrance of Christ, who had suffered on that

day, to spare his life.   Gualberto, struck with a sudden
compunction, remembering that Christ when on the cross
had prayed for his murderers, stayed his uplifted sword,
trembling from head to foot; and after a moment of terrible
conflict with his own heart, and a prayer for Divine support,
he held out his hand, raised the suppliant from the ground,
and embraced him in token of forgiveness.   Thus they parted;
and Gualberto, proceeding on his way in a sad and sorrowful
mood, every pulse throbbing with the sudden revulsion of feeling, and thinking on the crime he had been on the point of
committing, arrived at the church of San Miniato, and, entering, knelt down before the crucifix over the altar.   His rage
had given way to tears, his heart melted within him; and as
he wept before the image of the Saviour, and supplicated
mercy because he had shown mercy, he fancied, that, in gracious reply to his prayer, the figure bowed its head.[1]   This
miracle, for such he deemed it, completed the revolution
which had taken place in his whole character and state of
being.   From that moment the world and all its vanities became
hateful to him; he felt like one who had been saved upon the
edge of a precipice: he entered the Benedictine Order, and
took up his residence in the monastery of San Miniato.   Here
he dwelt for some time an humble penitent; all earthly ambition
quenched at once with the spirit of revenge.   On the death
of the Abbot of San Miniato, he was elected to succeed him,
but no persuasions could induce him to accept of the office.
He left the convent, and retired to a solitude amid the
Apennines about twenty miles from Florence, the Vallombrosa, renowned for its poetical as well as its religious
associations.

Here he took up his abode, and built himself a little hut
in company with two other hermits.   But others, attracted
by his sanctity, collected around him; the number increased
daily, all regarding him as their head, and he found it necessary to introduce some order into his community.   He therefore gave to his disciples the rule of St. Benedict, renewing

[1] This crucifix is preserved in the church of the Trinità at Florence, which
belongs to the Vallombrosan Order.

those strict observances which for three centuries had been
almost laid aside; adding also some new obligations—for
example, that of silence. The rule, however, was considerably
less severe than that of the Camaldolesi.

This new institution received the confirmation of the Pope,
and the founder lived to see twelve
houses of his Order spring up
around him. One of the most celebrated of these, next to the parent
institution at Vallombrosa, was the
monastery of the Salvi, about two
miles from Florence: it is now
ruined and deserted, but the vast
space it covers shows its former
magnificence. In the refectory still
exists Andrea del Sarto's Last
Supper, to which many a pilgrimage is still made. The church of
the Trinità at Florence, so familiar
to those who have dwelt there, also
belongs to the monks of Vallombrosa.

St. John Gualberto died in 1073.
The devotional figures of this saint,
which are to be found only in the
pictures painted for the convents
of his Order, exhibit him in the
light-grey habit, and in general
holding a cross in his hand, sometimes also a crutch. He is generally beardless.

21 St. John Gualberto. (F. Angelico.)

With regard to the subjects from his life, some of them are
of extreme interest in the history of Florentine Art. I have
always regretted that the most beautiful and most affecting
incident in his story, the meeting with the murderer on the
road to San Miniato, has never been worthily treated. The
spot where the meeting took place has been consecrated to

memory by a small tabernacle surmounted by a cross, within
which the scene is represented; and I remember, in the
churches at Florence and in the convents of the Order of Vallombrosa, several miserably bad pictures of this incident,
where Gualberto is generally an armed cavalier on horseback, ^{Fl. Santa Trinità.}
and the murderer kneels at his stirrup entreating mercy.
There may possibly exist better examples, but I have not met
with them.   As the Order increased in importance and in
riches, the subjects selected by the monks were those relating
to the religious life of their founder, and to the legends connected with it.   The following are the most important:—

1. John Gualberto, among his other virtues, was remarkable
for his simplicity and his humility.   On a certain occasion,
visiting one of his dependent monasteries, that of Moscetta, ^{or Moscera.}
over which he had placed, as superior, one of his disciples,
named Rudolfo, he found that this man had expended in the
embellishment of his convent a large portion of the sums en- ^{v. Southey's Poems. Ballad of S. Gualberto}
trusted to him, having enriched it with marbles, columns,
and other decorations.   Gualberto sternly reproved this vainglory, and prophesied the impending destruction of the convent, which soon after took place from a sudden inundation
of the mountain torrents, which carried away great part of the
newly-constructed edifice.

2. Gualberto had distinguished himself by his constant
enmity to the practice of simony then common in the Church.
Pietro di Pavia, a man of infamous character, having purchased
by gold the archbishopric of Florence, Gualberto denounced
him for this and other malpractices.   Pietro sent a body of
soldiers, who burnt and pillaged the monastery of San Salvi,
and murdered several of the monks.   Gualberto persisted in
his accusation; but such was the power of this wicked and
violent prelate, that he would probably have prevailed, if one
of the monks of Vallombrosa had not demanded the ordeal
of fire, at that time in legal use.   He passed between the
flames triumphantly, and the archbishop was deposed.   This
monk, afterwards known as Peter Igneus, is commemorated
among the worthies of the Order.   I have seen this incident
represented in pictures; he is seen passing in his white habit

Fl. Acad. between two fires in the midst of a crowd of spectators, St. John Gualberto standing by :—as in a small picture by Andrea del Sarto.

3. It is related of Gualberto, as of other saints, that when his monks were driven to extremity by want, he multiplied the viands upon the table.

4. One of his monks being grievously tormented by the demon when on his sick-bed, Gualberto came to his assistance, and, holding up the cross which he usually carried in his hand, he exorcised the tormentor.

Fl. Acad. When the figure of a cardinal is introduced into pictures painted for this Order, as in the magnificent Assumption by Perugino, it represents St. Bernard degli Uberti, a celebrated Fl. Acad. abbot of Vallombrosa. The same cardinal is introduced into a group of saints, ' St. Michael, St. John the Baptist, St. John Gualberto, and the Cardinal St. Bernard;'—one of the grandest pictures ever painted by Andrea del Sarto.

A.D. 1514. The most beautiful monument relating to the history of Gualberto is the series of bas-reliefs by Rovezzano, now in the Florence Gallery. At the time when the remains of the saint were about to be translated from the convent of Passignano to that of the Salvi, Rovezzano was employed to build a chapel and a shrine to receive them. Of the shrine, which was of exquisite beauty, but little remains except this series of five compositions :—1. Gualberto exorcises the demon from the couch of the monk Fiorenzo. 2. The monks, while performing service in the choir, are attacked by the soldiers of the archbishop and his partisans. 3. Peter Igneus, having received the blessing of his superior, passes uuhurt through the fire. 4. The death of the saint surrounded by his weeping monks. 5. The translation of the relics of St. John Gualberto. The blind, the lame, and other afflicted persons throw themselves in the way of the procession.

These charming works, among the most finished remains of Italian sculpture in its best time, were injured by the brutal and ignorant German soldiery, during the invasion of Italy in 1530. Yet, mutilated as they are, they remain, for grace, expression, and delicacy of finish, worthy of being reckoned among the miracles of Art. They are now to be seen on the walls of a little corridor on the north side of Fl. Gal. the sculpture gallery at Florence.

It is interesting to find these Vallombrosan hermits not only in possession of one of the finest libraries in all Italy, until despoiled by the French of its rarest books and manuscripts; but, from a very early period, among the most munificent patrons of Art.[1]

The pictures painted for them have been abstracted from their shrines, and are now only found on the walls of galleries and academies; but surely it is a species of injustice to look upon them without reference to their original destination. For the Vallombrosans, Cimabue painted his Madonna, famous in Fl. Acad the history of the revival of Art, and for a long time preserved in the Trinità at Florence; for them, Signorelli painted the chapel of San Miniato; for them, Perugino painted the Assumption in the Academy,—once over the high altar in the church at Vallombrosa; for them, Andrea del Sarto painted his Cenacolo B. Salvi. and the 'Quattro Santi.' In the groups of saints painted for Fl. Acad this Order, we shall generally find St. Benedict as patriarch; St. John Gualberto as founder; St. Michael the archangel the celestial patron and protector of the community; and San Bernardo *Cardinale*, already mentioned. I have seen strange mistakes made with regard to these pictures; such mistakes as diminish greatly their interest and significance. Thus, San

---

[1] Raphael, on his journey over the mountains from Urbino to Florence, in 1508, spent some days at Vallombrosa, and painted the portraits of Don Biagio, the General of the Order, and Don Baldassare, the Abbot of the Monastery. (*Passavant*, i. 115.) These two heads, after being preserved for three hundred years among the treasures of the convent, were removed, in 1813, to the Academy, and, when I was there, they hung in the little side-room, beneath the beautiful groups of angels by Granacci. In the catalogue they are attributed to Perugino, but are, without doubt, by Raphael. I hardly know in what words to express my feeling of their wonderful beauty. They are nearly life-size, yet finished like exquisite miniatures, and, with the intense expression and colour of Titian, have an elevation of sentiment, a delicacy and precision in the drawing, to which Titian never attained. Not long ago, I heard a distinguished writer of the present day—an artist, too— express his opinion, that 'Raphael had been overrated.' One might as well say that Shakespeare had been overrated. I would be content to rest the question of his supereminence as a painter on these two heads alone.

Bernardo Cardinale is confounded with St. Bernard of Clairvaux
when he wears the mitre as abbot; or with St. Jerome when he
wears the cardinal's hat. The same figure in Botticelli's Coronation of the Virgin is called, in the catalogue, *St. Dominick.*
So in a beautiful Nativity painted for the Camaldolesi, St.
Romualdo, in his monk's habit, and leaning on his crutch, is
styled St. Joseph.

There were formerly Vallombrosan nuns, and I believe they
still exist. The foundress was Rosana, the wife of Ugolotto
Caccianemici of Faenza, afterwards beatified as *Sant' Umiltà*
(Saint Humility). There is a curious effigy of her, with incidents
from her life, by Bufalmacco. In one of these she is preaching
continence to her husband, reminding us of St. Cecilia and St.
Valerian; in another she has persuaded her husband to assume
the monastic habit. These quaint little pictures are of great
value as memorials; genuine works of Bufalmacco—the friend
and butt of Giotto and Boccaccio—being extremely rare.

Guido Aretino, the greatest musician of his time, and the
inventor of the modern system of notation in music, was originally a monk of Vallombrosa.

A.D. 1310.

Fl. Acad.

v. Rio, Poésie
Chrétienne.
Lord Lind-
say, ii. p. 86.
Sacred and
Legend. Art,
ii. 202.

THE CARTHUSIANS.

THE Carthusian Order was founded in 1084, by Bruno, a monk
of Cologne. The first seat of the Order was the famous monastery at Chartreux, near Grenoble (afterwards known as *la grande
Chartreuse*, and which gave its name to the Order, and all the
affiliated foundations). Another contemporary monastery rose
at La Torre, in Calabria. Both were reared by Bruno himself
in his lifetime.

Of all the reformed Benedictine congregations, the Order of
the Carthusians is the most austere, but it is also the most
interesting. As a community, the Carthusians have never
exhibited the ambitious self-seeking of the Franciscans and the
Dominicans. They have been less in alliance with the Church

as a power; more in alliance with religion as an influence. In
their traditional origin, and the early legends connected with
their founder Bruno, there is something wildly poetical: in
the appearance of the monks themselves, in their ample white
robes and hoods, their sandalled feet and shaven heads, (for
the tonsure is not with them partial, as with other monks,)
there is something strangely picturesque. Their spare diet,
their rigorous seclusion, and their habits of labour, give them
an emaciated look, a pale quietude, in which, however, there
is no feebleness, no appearance of ill-health or squalor: I never
saw a Carthusian monk who did not look like a gentleman.
The sumptuous churches and edifices of this self-denying
Order date from the 16th century; about that period we find
the first application of their increasing funds to purposes of
architecture and artistic decoration. They had previously
been remarkable for their fine libraries and their skill in
gardening. They were the first and the greatest horticulturists
in Europe: of the Carthusians it may emphatically be said,
that wherever they settled, 'they made the desert blossom as
the rose.' When they built their first nest amid the barren
heights of Chartreux, they converted the stony waste into a
garden. When they were set down amid the marshes at
Pavia, they drained, they tilled, they planted, till the unhealthy
swamp was clothed, for miles around, with beauty and fertility:
it is now fast sinking back to its pristine state, but that is not
the fault of the few poor monks, who, after years of exile,
have lately been restored to their cells, and wander up and
down the precincts of that wondrous palace-like church, and
once smiling garden, like pale phantoms come back to haunt
their earthly homes.

It is remarkable that, with all their sumptuous patronage of
art, and all their love of the beautiful in nature, these religious
recluses have never been accused of deviating personally from
the rigid rule of their Order, which has been but slightly modified since the days of Peter of Clugni, who, writing of them
about fifty years after the death of their founder Bruno, has
left us such a striking, and almost fearful, description of their
austerities. The rule was the severest ever yet prescribed. To

the ordinances of St. Benedict, which commanded poverty,
chastity, obedience, and daily labour, was added almost
perpetual silence; only once a week they were allowed to
walk and discourse together. They fasted rigorously eight
months out of the twelve; flesh was absolutely forbidden
at all times, even to the sick; of the pulse, bread, and water
to which they were confined, they made but one meal a day,
and that was eaten separately, and in silence, except on
certain festivals, when they were allowed to eat together.
They were enjoined to study, and to labour with their hands;
their labour consisted in cultivating their fields and gardens,
and in transcribing books, by which, in the commencement
of the institution, they supported and enriched their community. Mr Ford speaks of the Carthusian monks at Paular,
as paper-makers and breeders of sheep on a large scale. The
libraries in the Carthusian convents have always been well
filled with books, even from the first institution of the Order.
St. Bruno, who had been an eminent scholar and teacher, was
careful to provide good books at a great expense, and these
were transcribed and multiplied by the monks with most
praiseworthy industry. When the Count de Nevers, who had
been much edified by their sanctity, sent them a rich present
of plate for their church, they sent it back as useless to them.
He then sent them a quantity of parchment and leather for
their books, which they accepted with gratitude.[1]

Handbook of Spain.

---

[1] The several parts of which the Bible consists, were in the Middle Ages considered more in the light of separate and independent books than they are now,
when the Bible is accepted as one book, and it is even difficult to procure the Old
Testament and the New Testament bound separately. We find MS. copies of the
Pentateuch, the Book of Job, the Prophecies, the Four Gospels, the Revelation,
the Canonical Epistles, all in separate volumes. The copying of the whole Bible
was a very long and laborious undertaking; and many apologues and legends were
invented to encourage and extol the merits of so vast a performance. I give one
quoted in Mr Maitland's work :—

'A monk, who was a scribe, wrote out the whole volume of the divine law;
but he was a great transgressor, and after his death there was a sharp contention
for his soul : the evil spirits brought forward his innumerable sins; the angels
counted up the letters in the volume he had written as a set-off against the same
number of sins. At length the letters were found in a majority of one, by virtue of which the monk was spared for a while for reformation in this life.'—*Dark
Ages,* p. 268.

Peter of Clugni, writing to Pope Eugenius, to complain of some contention relative to the election of a Superior of the Carthusians, thus expresses his admiration of the Order generally :—

' I thought, and I do not believe I was wrong, that theirs was the best of all the Latin systems, and that they were not of those who strain at a gnat and swallow a camel : that is, who make void the commandment of God for the traditions of men ; and, tithing mint, and anise, and cummin, and (according to one Evangelist) every herb, neglecting the weightier matters of the law, judgment, mercy, and faith. For they do not consider the kingdom of God as consisting principally in meats and drinks, in garments, in labours and the like, though these, wisely managed, may do that kingdom of God good service ; but in that godliness of which the Apostle says, "Bodily exercise is profitable to little, but godliness is profitable to all things, having promise of the life that now is, and of that which is to come." These holy men feast at the table of wisdom ; they are entertained at the banquet of the true Solomon, not in superstitions, not in hypocrisy, not in the leaven of malice and wickedness, but in the unleavened bread of sincerity and truth.'

I have said enough of the Carthusians to show what interest attaches to their connection with Art ; but, at first sight, it appears unaccountable, that while the institution of the Order dates from the year 1084, we do not find that the Carthusians or 1086. figure in very early Art. This is explained by the circumstance that their founder and patriarch, Bruno, was not canonised for more than 500 years after his death. The Order had increased in numbers, in possessions, and in influence, but the monks remained secluded, laborious, and unambitious. At length Bruno was declared a *Beato* by Leo X.—the most humble and self-denying of ascetics was beatified by the most luxurious A.D. 1514 and profligate of churchmen !—and he was finally canonised by Gregory XV. in 1623.

Of course, all the single devotional figures of Bruno, as saint and patriarch, date subsequently to this period ; he wears the peculiar habit of his Order, the white scapular, which, hanging down before and behind, is joined at the side by a band of the same colour, about six inches wide. The hands are usually crossed on the bosom, the head declined, and the whole attitude expresses contemplation and humility.

Manuel
Pereyra,
1647.

Stirling's Sp.
Art, p. 578.

There was a fine statue of St. Bruno over the porch of the hospital of the Carthusians, in the Alcalá at Madrid. This effigy was so much admired by Philip IV., that the coachman who drove him about Madrid had general orders to slacken his pace when-
ever the royal carriage passed it, in
order that the king might have leisure
to dwell upon it for a few moments.
This statue I have not seen, but it
could hardly surpass the fine characteristic figure by Houdon, in the Certosa at Rome. This, for simplicity and
contemplative repose, far exceeds another figure of the same saint,—the

A.D. 1746. colossal statue by Sloedtz, in St.
Peter's, erected soon after the
canonisation of the saint.

Instead of relating in detail the life
of St. Bruno, I will give it here as
represented by Le Sueur in the series
of pictures painted for the cloisters
of the Chartreuse at Paris, in 1649;
purchased from the monks, and trans-

22

St. Bruno reading the Pope's letter.
(Le Sueur.)

ferred to Versailles, in 1776; and now in the Louvre, where the twenty-two pictures fill one room :—

1. Raymond, a learned doctor of Paris, and canon of Notre Dame, teaching theology to his pupils.

Bruno, born at Cologne, was the son of rich and noble parents, who, proud of his early distinction in letters, sent him to finish his studies in the theological school at Paris, under a celebrated teacher and preacher, whose name was Raymond. In this picture Raymond is instructing his auditors from the pulpit, and Bruno, under the lineaments of a beautiful youth, is seated in front,—a book under his arm, and listening with deep attention.

2. The death of Raymond.

This learned doctor, venerated by the people for his apparent piety and austere virtue, lies extended on his deathbed. A priest, attended by two young students, one of whom is Bruno, presents the crucifix. A demon at the pillow appears ready to catch the fleeting soul. This may have suggested to Reynolds the imp upon the pillow of Cardinal Beaufort; but in

23   St. Bruno.   (Statue by Houdon, in the Certosa at Rome.)

both instances it is a fault of taste which we expect to meet with and excuse
in the early ages of Art, but which is inexcusable in painters of the seventeenth and eighteenth centuries.

3. The fearful resurrection of Raymond.

'Now Raymond, being greatly venerated for his apparent sanctity, was
carried to the grave attended by a great concourse of the people ; and as
they were chanting the service for the dead, just as they came to the words
"Responde mihi quantas habes iniquitates," the dead man half raised himself
from his bier, and cried, with a lamentable voice, " *By the justice of God I
am accused !* " thereupon the priests laid down the bier, and put off the interment till the following day.   Next day they again formed in procession,
and as they chanted the same words, "*responde mihi*," the dead man again
rose up and cried out with a more dreadful voice, " *By the justice of God I
am judged !* " and then sank down on his bier as before.   Great was the
consternation of the people, and they put off the conclusion of the obsequies

S

till the third day, when, just as they had begun to chant the same verse, trembling for the result, the dead man again rose up, crying with a terrible voice and look, "*By the justice of God I am condemned!*" Upon this, priests and attendants, half dead with fear and horror, flung the body out into a field, as unworthy of Christian burial.' In the picture the ghastly terror of the incident is given with the highest dramatic power without the slightest exaggeration; and the effect of the awful incident on Bruno, who stands behind the officiating priest, prepares us for the next scene.

4. St. Bruno kneeling before a crucifix in an attitude of profound meditation; in the background they throw the body of the canon into an unhallowed grave.

5. St. Bruno teaches theology in the school at Rheims.

6. St. Bruno, after long meditation on the dangers of the world, engages six of his friends to follow him into a life of penance and seclusion.

7. St. Bruno and his companions prepare to set off for Grenoble, but first they distribute all their worldly possessions in alms to the poor.

8. Hugo, bishop of Grenoble, had a dream, in which he beheld seven stars move before him, and remain stationary above a certain spot in his diocese. When Bruno and his six companions appeared in his presence and made their request for a spot of ground on which to found a retreat from the world, he saw the interpretation of his vision, and bestowed on them a rocky and barren hollow near the summit of a mountain, about six leagues from Grenoble.

9. Bruno and his companions, preceded by St. Hugo on his mule, journey to the village of Chartreux.

A.D. 1084.   10. St. Bruno founds the monastery afterwards celebrated under the name of 'La Grande Chartreuse.' In the picture he is examining the plan presented by an architect, while masons and other artificers are seen at work in the background.

11. St Hugo, bishop of Grenoble, invests St. Bruno with the habit of his Order.

12. The rule which Bruno drew up for his brotherhood is confirmed by Pope Victor III. Though in this picture, and others of the same subject, St. Bruno is represented as giving a written rule to his monks, it is certain that his ordinances were not reduced to writing till after his death.

13. St. Bruno, wearing the chasuble as abbot, receives several young men into his Order. Among those who are present is the father of one of the novices, who seems to lament the loss of his son.

14. Urban II., raised to the pontificate in 1088, had been one of the disciples of St. Bruno when he taught in the university of Rheims. On his accession to the supreme spiritual power, he sent for St. Bruno to aid him in the administration of his affairs. The picture represents St. Bruno reading the letter, while the monks around him exhibit disquiet and consternation. Several of these refused to be separated from him, and followed him to Rome.

15. St. Bruno is received by Pope Urban II.

16. The Pope desired to make St. Bruno archbishop of Reggio ; but he absolutely declined the honour. In the picture, St. Bruno in his coarse white habit kneels before the Pope : prelates and cardinals in rich dresses are standing round.

17. St. Bruno, unable to endure the cares and turmoils of the court, retired to a desert in Calabria. He is seen lying on the ground, and looking up at a glory of cherubim in the skies.

18. He obtained leave from Urban to found a convent for his Order in Calabria. In the picture he is seen praying in his cell, while several of his monks are employed in clearing and cultivating the ground.

19. Roger (or Ruggiero), Count of Sicily and Calabria, being out on a hunting expedition, lost himself in the wilderness, and discovered the hermitage of St. Bruno. In the picture he finds the holy man praying in his rocky cell, and, kneeling before the entrance, entreats his blessing.

20. Shortly afterwards, this same Count Roger of Sicily besieged Capua, and while asleep in his tent he beheld in a vision St. Bruno, who warned him that one of his officers had conspired with the enemy to betray his army. The Count, awaking, is enabled to guard against the meditated treachery.

21. The death of St. Bruno, who expires on his lowly pallet, surrounded by his monks. His death took place in 1100. This is one of the most striking pictures of the whole series.

22. The last picture represents the apotheosis of the saint. He is carried up by angels, his white habit fluttering against the blue sky. Not a pleasant picture, nor gracefully arranged.

I have described these subjects as painted by Le Sueur ; but the same incidents have been often repeated and varied by other painters, employed to decorate the edifices of the Carthusian Order. Whatever might have been the austerities of the monks, their churches and monasteries were in later times sumptuous. Zurbaran was employed in the Chartreuse of Santa Maria de las Cuevas, near Seville, already 'rich in architecture, in tombs, plate, jewels, carvings, books, and pictures, and celebrated for its groves of orange and lemon trees, on the banks of the Guadalquiver,' and represented the life of the founder and the fortunes of the Order in twenty-eight pictures.

No one ever painted the Carthusians like Zurbaran, who studied them for months together while working in their cloisters. 'Every head looks like a portrait; their white draperies chill the eye, as their cold hopeless faces chill the heart ;' but the faces are not always cold and hopeless. The

Stirling's Sp. Painters.

Ford's Handbook of Spain.

Stirling.

24   St. Bruno praying in the desert.   (Andrea Sacchi.)

fine head in the Munich Gallery, styled 'St. Bruno with a
skull,' is probably a study of a Carthusian monk, after nature,
and nothing can exceed the intense devotional aspiration of
the upward look and parted lips.

The series of the life of St. Bruno, painted for the Chartreuse
of Paular by Vincenzio Carducho, consists of fifty-four large
pictures.   Twenty-six represent scenes from the life of St.
Bruno, and twenty-six are consecrated to the exultation of the
Order.   Both the series of Zurbaran, and that of Carducho,
comprise the subjects from the story of the Carthusian martyrs
—a dark page in our English history.

The Charter-House was suppressed by Henry VIII., after
existing from 1372: it was founded by Sir Walter Manny, of
chivalrous memory; and the history of the dissolution of the

monastery, and the fate of the last unhappy monks, is feelingly related in Knight's 'London.' The prior Haughton and eleven Carthusian monks were hanged, drawn, and quartered; one of the quarters of Haughton's body being set over the gate of his own monastery. 'Ten others were thrown into prison, a prey to the most horrible tyranny, neglect, filth, and despair, till they all, but one, died under the treatment,' and *he* was afterwards executed. 'Whatever we may think of their opinions, these men were truly martyrs; deliberately dying, because they would not accept of mercy offered on condition of violating their vows and belying their conscience.' In the series by Carducho, two pictures represent the monks in their white robes, dead or dying, and chained to the pillars of their dungeon; and open doors give a view of Catholic martyrs in the hands of grim Protestant tormentors. In the third, three Carthusians are hurried off to execution on a hurdle drawn by horses, which are urged to their full speed by their rider, in the dress of a Spanish muleteer.

This whole series has been removed from Paular to the Museum at Madrid, where it is placed in the first hall as we enter. Mr. Stirling's observations on the present locality of these pictures are in such good taste, and so often applicable to other changes of the kind, that I give the passage entire:—

'Like many other trophies of Spanish Art, these fine works of Carducho have lost much of their significance by removal from the spot for which they were painted. Hung on the crowded walls of an ill-ordered museum, his Carthusian histories can never again speak to the heart and the fancy as they once spoke in the lonely cloister of Paular, where the silence was broken only by the breeze as it moaned through the overhanging pine-forest, by the tinkling bell or the choral chant of the chapel, or by the stealing tread of some mute white-stoled monk, the brother and the heir of the holy men of old, whose good deeds and sufferings and triumphs were there commemorated on canvas. There, to many generations of recluses, vowed to perpetual silence and solitude, these pictures had been companions; to them the painted saints and martyrs had become friends; and the benign Virgins were the sole objects within these melancholy walls to remind them of the existence of woman.

'In the Chartreuse, therefore, absurdities were veiled, or criticism awed, by the venerable genius of the place; while in the Museum, the monstrous legend and extravagant picture, stripped of every illusion, are coolly judged of on their own merits as works of skill and imagination. Still, notwith-standing their present disadvantages of position, these pictures vindicate the high fame of Carducho, and will bear comparison with the best history ever painted of the Carthusian Order.'

St. Hugh of
Grenoble.
April 1, 1132.

But neither Carducho nor Le Sueur have equalled Zurbaran in characteristic expression. I recollect a picture by him in the Aguado Gallery, which represents a curious legend of St. Hugo. Hugo, it will be remembered, was Bishop of Grenoble when Bruno founded the first Chartreuse. He frequently left his bishopric, and resided among the Carthusians as a humble brother of the Order, devoting himself for months to a life of austerity and seclusion. On one occasion, when he appeared in the refectory, he found the monks seated motionless, for although it was a festival, they were not permitted to eat any flesh whatever, and, no other food being obtainable, fowls had been served up before them. In this picture seven Carthusians, looking very grave, and some with their white cowls drawn over their heads, as if resigned to fasting and despair, are seated at table; the aged bishop, in purple vestments, attended by a page, stands in the foreground, and by the sign of the cross converts the fowls into tortoises.[1] Of Hugo of Grenoble it is related, that for forty years he was troubled and haunted by Satan after a very singular fashion. The demon was conti-nually whispering to his mind intrusive questionings of the providence of God in permitting evil in this world. Hugo firmly believed that such thoughts could only come by dia-bolical suggestion. He endeavoured to repel them by fast-ing, prayer, and penance, and he complained bitterly to his spiritual father, the Pope, that he should be, in despite of his will thus grievously tormented. The pope, Gregory VII.,

[1] Not into *turtle*. The small land-tortoise was considered as fish. There is a similar picture in the Museum at Madrid, mentioned by Mr. Stirling (Artists of Spain, 771).

A legend similar to this of St. Hugo is related of St. Ulrich, first bishop and patron saint of Augsburg. On a fast-day he converted flesh into fish; and in German prints and pictures he is represented with a fish in his hand, as in the fine woodcut of Albert Dürer, in which he stands with St. Erasmus and St. Nicholas (*Sacred and Legend. Art*, ii. 290, 327, 334). Where there is a key with the fish, it is St. Bruno.

(the great and sagacious Hildebrand,) possibly smiled to himself at the simplicity of the good bishop, and assured him it was only a trial of his virtue. Nevertheless, in spite of Pope and penance, these perplexing doubts pursued him to the grave, without, however, obtaining any dominion over his mind or disturbing his faith.

St. Hugo of Grenoble died in 1132.

It is necessary to distinguish between this St. Hugh of Grenoble, and another St. Hugh, also a Carthusian, and connected in an interesting manner with our own ecclesiastical history. He was sent here in 1126, by Pope Urban III., and consecrated Bishop of Lincoln. To him we owe the rebuilding of the cathedral, which had been destroyed by an earthquake; the greater part remains as this good bishop left it,—one of the most splendid and perfect monuments of the best period of Gothic architecture. The shrine of the founder, rich in gold and gems, and yet more precious for its exquisite workmanship, stood behind the choir. It was confiscated and melted down at the Reformation. Such memorials of St. Hugh as offered no temptation to Henry VIII., were destroyed by those modern Vandals, the Cromwellian soldiery, who stabled their horses in the nave of the cathedral, and the sole memorial of this excellent and munificent priest, within the glorious precincts raised by his piety, is the stained glass in the rose window of the south transept. This contains several scenes from his life, confused and dazzling, from the rude outlines and vivid colouring, so that the only one I could make out distinctly was the translation of his remains, when the two kings of England and Scotland bore him on their shoulders to the porch of the cathedral.

His name is retained in our calendar, November 17th.

Devotional pictures of St. Hugo are rare. Here is one; it p. 198 represents him in the Carthusian habit, over it the episcopal robes, the mitre on his head and the pastoral staff in his hand.

By his side a swan, his proper attribute, which is here the emblem of solitude, in which he delighted. He has sometimes three flowers in his hand, or an angel who defends him against

25

St. Hugh presenting a votary.
(From a picture in the Boisserée Gallery.)

the lightning, emblems mentioned in the German authorities, but not explained.

ST. HUGH MARTYR.

There was a third St. Hugh, a *little* St. Hugh of Lincoln, who was not indeed a monk, but his story is one of the late monkish legends. The popular hatred of the Jews, in the eleventh and twelfth centuries, is set forth, and not exaggerated, in the tale of Ivanhoe. It should seem that our ancestors

regarded the whole Jewish nation as if they had been the iden-
tical Jews who crucified our Saviour; as if every individual
Jew represented, to their imaginations, the traitor Judas. To
this fanatic hatred was added, on the part of the people, envy
of their riches; on that of the ecclesiastics, jealousy and fear
of the superior intelligence and medical and astrological skill
of some distinguished individuals of that detested race. I will
not dwell upon the fearful excesses of cruelty and injustice
towards this oppressed people, in our own and other countries;
though I must touch upon the horrible reprisals imputed to
them, and which served as excuses for further persecutions.
There are a number of stories related of their stealing little
children, and crucifying them on their Easter feast, in ridicule
of the God and Saviour of the Christians. Of these real or
imaginery victims, we have four who were canonised as saints : A.D. 1137.
St. William of Norwich, St. Hugh of Lincoln, St. Richard of A.D. 1255.
A.D. 1182.
Pontoise, and St. Simon of Trent. A.D. 1472.

Chaucer has given the story of one of these little Christian
martyrs in the Prioress's Tale; he places the scene in Asia,
but concludes with a reference to 'young Hugh of Lincoln, in
like sort laid low.' The tale, as modernised by Wordsworth,
is in everybody's hands.

St. Hugh of Lincoln is represented as a child about three
years old, nailed upon a cross; or as standing with a palm in
one hand, and a cross in the other. There is a picture attri- Engraved
buted to Agostino Caracci, representing St. Simon of Trent,
as a beautiful boy, holding a palm in one hand, and in the
other the long bodkin with which those wicked Jews pierced
his side.

The effigies of these little martyrs, which used to occur frequently in the churches, kept alive that horror of the Jews
which is so energetically expressed in the Prioress's Tale. Such
atrocious memorials of religious hatred are now everywhere
banished, or exist only in relics of the old stained glass.

26   St. Bernard of Clairvaux.   (Angelico da Fiesole.)

THE CISTERCIANS.

ANOTHER and a far more important reform in the Order of St.
Benedict took place in 1098, when Robert de Molesme founded
at Cisteaux (or Citeaux), about twelve leagues to the north of
Chalon-sur-Saone, the first abbey of the Cistercians, in a
desert spot, described as 'overgrown with woods and brambles,
wholly unfrequented by men, and the habitation of wild
beasts.

Of all the branches of the Benedictine Order, this was the
most popular.   It extended, in a short time, over France,
England, and Germany; produced innumerable learned men,
popes, cardinals, and prelates; and numbered, within a century
A.D. 1128.   after its foundation, 3000 affiliated monasteries.   In England
their first seat was Waverley, in Surrey; and Furness and
Fountains, Kirkstall, Bolton, Tintern, and many other abbeys,

magnificent even in ruin, belonged to this famous Order. In Spain, the noble military Orders of Calatrava and Alcantara were subject to it. In France, the most celebrated of the numerous dependent monasteries was that of Clairvaux in A.D. 1115. Champagne.

The habit adopted by the Cistercians, at the time they placed their Order under the especial protection of the Virgin Mary, was white, the colour consecrated to her purity; and, according to a legend of the Order, assumed by her express command, intimated in a vision to ST. BERNARD,—the great saint of the Cistercians, the man who mainly contributed to render the Order illustrious throughout Christendom, and the only member of it who is conspicuous as a subject of Art.

ST. BERNARD OF CLAIRVAUX.

Lat. Sanctus Bernardus Doctor mellifluus. *Ital.* San Bernardo di Chiara-
valle, Abbate. *Ger.* Der Heilige Bernhard. *Fr.* Saint Bernard.
Aug. 20, 1153.

The habit white, a long loose robe with very wide sleeves, and a hood or cowl : he has sometimes the mitre and crosier as abbot. The attributes are—a book, or a roll of papers, always in his hand ; often a pen or ink-horn ; sometimes a demon fettered at his feet, or chained to a rock behind him.

IF I were called upon to enter on the life and character of St. Bernard in relation to the history of his time ; to consider him as the religious enthusiast and the political agitator; as mixed up with the philosophy, the theology, the wars, the schisms, the institutions, of an age which he seemed to have informed with his own spirit, while in fact he was only the incarnation, if I may so express myself, of its prejudices and its tendencies —then I might fairly throw down the pen, and confess myself unequal to the task; but, luckily for me, the importance of St. Bernard as a subject of Art bears no proportion to his import-ance as a subject of history. It is not as the leading ecclesiastic and politician of his age,—it is not as the counsellor of popes and kings,—it is not as the subtle theological disputant, —it is not as the adversary of Abelard and Arnold de Brescia, that he appears in painting and sculpture. It is as the head of a dominant Order, and yet more as the teacher and preacher, that we see him figure in works of art; and then only occasionally; for he is far less popular than many saints who never exercised a tithe of his influence,—whose very existence is comparatively a fiction.

A.D. 1090. Bernard was born at the little village of Fontaine, near Dijon. His father was noble, a lord of the soil. His mother, Alice, was an admirable woman; all the biographies of Bernard unite in giving her the credit of his early education. He was one of a large family of children, all of whom were fed from the bosom of their mother; for she entertained the idea that the infant, with the milk it drew from a stranger's bosom, imbibed also some portion of the quality and temperament of the nurse: therefore, while her children were young, they had no attendant but herself. They all became remarkable men and women; but the fame of the rest is merged in that of Bernard, who appears, indeed, to have moulded them all to his own bent.

After pursuing his studies at the university of Paris, Bernard entered the reformed Benedictine monastery of Citeaux. He was then not more than twenty, remarkable for his personal beauty and the delicacy of his health; but he had already, from the age of fifteen, practised the most rigorous self-denial: he had been subject to many temptations, but surmounted them all. It is related that, on one occasion, he recollected himself at the moment when his eyes had rested with a feeling of pleasure on the face of a beautiful woman, and, shocked at his own weakness, he rushed into a pool of water more than half frozen, and stood there till feeling and life had nearly departed together.

He was about twenty-five, when the abbey of Citeaux became so overcrowded by inmates, that his abbot sent him on a mission to found another monastery. The manner of going forth on these occasions was strikingly characteristic of the age;—the abbot chose twelve monks, representing the twelve apostles, and placed at their head a leader, representing Jesus Christ, who, with a cross in his hand, went before them. The gates of the convent opened,—then closed behind them,—and they wandered into the wide world, trusting in God to show them their destined abode.

Bernard led his followers to a wilderness called the *Valley of* A.D. 1114. *Wormwood,* and there, at his bidding, arose the since renowned abbey of Clairvaux. They felled the trees, built themselves huts, tilled and sowed the ground, and changed the whole face of the country round: till that which had been a dismal solitude, the resort of wolves and robbers, became a land of vines and corn, rich, populous, and prosperous.

In a few years the name of Bernard of Clairvaux had become famous throughout the Christian world. His monastery could no longer contain those who came to place themselves under his guidance. On every side the feudal lords appealed to him to decide differences and to reconcile enemies; the ecclesiastics, to resolve questions of theology. He was the great authority on all points of religious dicipline; he drew up the statutes of the Templars; Louis VI. appointed him arbiter between the rival popes, Anacletus and Innocent II., and Bernard deciding in favour of the latter, the whole Church received the fiat with perfect submission. He was then in his thirty-ninth year. He was afterwards sent to reconcile the disputes between the clergy of Milan and those of Rome, and succeeded. He was commissioned by Eugenius III. to preach a second crusade. He succeeded here also, unhappily; for his eloquent adjurations so inflamed the people, that those who refused to take up the cross were held in scorn, and had a distaff put into their hands, in mockery of their effeminate cowardice. Bernard was invited to assume the command of the multitude he had excited to take up arms; but he had the wisdom to decline. He remained at home studying theology in his cell; and of those whom his fiery exhortations had impelled to the wars of Palestine, few, very few returned.

The people raged against Bernard for a false prophet; but their rage was transient as violent. He defended himself boldly and eloquently, affirming that the armies of the crusaders were composed of such a vile, insubordinate, irreligious crew, that they did not deserve to be protected by Heaven. If they had been betrayed, defeated, destroyed; if the flood, the plague, the sword, had each had a part in them, it was in just punishment of the vices and the crimes of the age. He bade them go home and repent:—and they did so.

Worn out by fatigues, missions, and anxieties, by long and frequent journeys, by the most rigorous fasts and penances, the health of this accomplished and zealous monk gave way prematurely; and, retiring to his cell, he languished for a few years, and then died, in the sixty-third year of his age. Twenty years after his death he was canonised by Alexander III.

The virtues and the talents of Bernard lent a dreadful power to his misguided zeal, and a terrible vitality to his errors. But no one has ever reproached him with insincerity. In no respect did he step beyond his age; but he was, as I have already said, the impersonation of the intellect of that age; and, in a period of barbarism and ignorance, he attracts us, and stands out in the blood-soiled page of history like a luminous spot surrounded with shadow. Of his controversy with Abelard it is not necessary to speak. Had the life of Abelard been as pure from moral stain as that of Bernard, he might possibly have had a better chance against his great adversary.

The writings of St. Bernard are of such authority that he ranks as one of the fathers of the Catholic Church. It was said of him (and believed) that when he was writing his famous homilies on 'The Song of Songs, which is Solomon's,' the holy Virgin herself condescended to appear to him, and moistened his lips with the milk from her bosom; so that ever afterwards his eloquence, whether in speaking or in writing, was persuasive, irresistible, supernatural.

In devotional pictures a monk in the white habit of the Cistercian Order, with a shaven crown, little or no beard, carrying a large book under his arm, or with writing implements before him, or presenting books to the Madonna, may be generally

27   St. Bernard writing the praises of the Virgin.

assumed to represent St. Bernard. His peculiar attributes however, are—1. The demon fettered behind him; the demon, having the Satanic, and not the dragon form, is interpreted to signify heresy. 2. Occasionally three mitres on his book or at his feet, as in a picture by Garofalo, signify the three bishoprics he refused,—those of Milan, Chartres, and Spires. 3. He has *Dresden Gal.* also the bee-hive as symbol of eloquence, in common with Chrysostom and Augustine; but here it alludes also to his title of *Doctor mellifluus*. 4. The mitre and crosier, as abbot of Clairvaux, are also given to him,—but rarely.

In old German art he may be found
occasionally with the black mantle over
the white tunic, as in this figure.

He is often grouped with other Benedictine saints,—St. Benedict or St. Romualdo,—or he is embracing the instruments of the Passion, a subject frequently
met with in the old French prints.

The subject called 'the Vision of St.
Bernard' must be considered as mystical
and devotional, not historical.   St. Bernard, as we have seen, was remarkable
for his devotion to the Blessed Virgin:
one of his most celebrated works, the
Missus est, was composed in her honour
as Mother of the Redeemer; and in eighty
sermons on texts from the Song of Solomon, he set forth her divine perfection as
the Selected and Espoused, the type of
the Church on earth.   Accordingly, the
Blessed Virgin regarded her votary with
peculiar favour.   His health was extremely feeble; and once, when he was
employed in writing his homilies, and
was so ill that he could scarcely hold the

23   St. Bernard.

pen, she graciously appeared to him, and comforted and restored him by her divine presence.   Of this graceful subject.
there are some charming examples :—

Giottino.
Fl. Acad.

1. He is kneeling before a desk, the pen in his hand; the
Virgin above, a graceful veiled figure, comes floating in, sustained by two angels; as in a picture by Giottino.   The little
etching I have appended will give an idea of the composition.

Fl. Chiesa
de la Badia.

2. St. Bernard is writing in a rocky desert, seated at a rude
desk formed of the stump of a tree.   The Virgin stands before
him, attended by angels, one of whom holds up her robe.   On
the rock behind him is inscribed his famous motto, *Sustine et
abstine* (Bear and forbear).   I give an etching of this group

from the large picture by Filippino Lippi. In the original composition the demon is seen chained to the rock behind St. Bernard, and there are monks in the background; these I have omitted for want of space. The figure of the Virgin is singularly noble and graceful; the angels, as is usual with Filippino, are merely handsome boys.

3. He is seated writing, and looking round to the Virgin, who enters on the opposite side attended by two angels. Behind St. Bernard stand St. Philip and St. Bartholomew. A beautiful version of the subject. *Munich Gal. Perugino.*

4. He is sustained amid clouds, the pen in his hand, looking up at the Madonna and infant Saviour, who are surrounded by a choir of red seraphim: Mary Magdalen stands near. This visionary representation is extremely characteristic of the painter,—original, fantastic, but also elegant. *Louvre. Cosimo Roselli.*

I have seen several other instances, by Fra Bartolomeo; by Murillo; and one by Benozzo Gozzole in the collection of M. Joly de Bamville, in which the figures are half-length. The leading idea is in all the same, and easily recognised.

5. The Virgin nourishes St. Bernard with milk from her bosom. This subject occurs only in the later schools of art, and must be taken in a mystical and religious sense. It is a literal and disagreeable version of a figure of speech too palpable for representation. Yet genius has overcome these objections, and Murillo's great picture is cited as a remarkable example of his skill in treating with dignity and propriety a subject which, in many hands, might have suggested opposite ideas. 'The great abbot of Clairvaux, seated amongst his books, and with jars of lilies on the table, as an emblem of his devotion to Our Lady, is surprised by a visit from that celestial personage. As the white-robed saint kneels before her in profound adoration, she bares her beautiful bosom, and causes a stream of milk to fall from thence upon the lips of her votary, which were from that time forth endowed with a sweet persuasive eloquence that no rival could gainsay, no audience resist. Above and around the heavenly stranger cherubs disport themselves in a flood of glory; and on the ground lie the abbot's *The finest example by Murillo. Stirling's Sp Painters, p. 914*

U

crosier and some folios bound in pliant parchment, like
those which once filled the conventual libraries of Spain, and
which Murillo has often introduced into his pictures. The
chaste and majestic beauty of the Virgin almost redeems the
subject.' The etching will give an idea of the arrangement of
the picture, but, of course, not of the wonderful expression and
colouring.

· I believe it is well known that the fine stained glass in the
choir of Lichfield Cathedral was brought from a Cistercian
nunnery near Liege (the abbey of Herekenrode, ruined and
desecrated in the French revolutionary wars). On one of these
windows, the third on the north side of the choir, we find this
mystical legend very beautifully expressed. St. Bernard kneels
at the feet of the Virgin, looking up with passionate devotion ;
she prepares to bare her bosom. Behind him stands his sister,
the Abbess St. Humbeline. The workmanship dates between
1530 and 1540, when the nuns rebuilt their convent, and employed the best artists of the Low Countries to decorate it. The
designs for these windows I should refer to Lambert Lombard,
the first, and by far the best, of the Italianised Flemish school
of the sixteenth century.

The historical subjects from the life of St. Bernard are very
few.

Bartsch,
xlii. 11.
He was in the habit of lecturing his monks every morning
from some passage in Scripture. This scene is represented in a
rare old engraving by Benedetto Montagna.

Masaccio.
At Berlin there are two little pictures from the early life of
St. Bernard. 1. As a child, his mother consecrates him to the
service of the Church ; 2. His habit having fallen into the fire,
he takes it uninjured from the flames. And in the same gallery
is a curious picture representing St. Bernard holding his crosier
and book ; and around this central figure six small subjects from
his life.

Some other incidents in the life of St. Bernard would be admirable for art. As, for instance, the building of his monastery,
where he and his white monks, scattered in the wilderness, are

felling the trees, while others are praying for divine strength and aid; or the preaching of the Crusade in various countries and among various conditions of men; but I have not met with either of these subjects.

It is related that, when he was abbot of Clairvaux, his sister Humbeline, who had married a nobleman, came to pay him a visit borne in a litter, and attended by a numerous retinue of servants: he, scandalised by so much pride and pomp, refused to see her. She then desired to see another brother, who was also in the convent, who in like manner rejected her. She burst into tears, and entreating on her knees that her saintly brother would instruct her what she ought to do, he condescended to appear at the gate, desired her to go home, and imitate her mother. Humbeline afterwards became a model of humility and piety, and ended her life in seclusion. This conference between the brother and the sister would be a fine subject for a painter.

In the Boisserée Collection there is a very curious picture entitled ' St. Bernard in the Cathedral of Spires,' (Der Heilige Bernhard im Dom zu Speir,) which for a long time embarrassed me exceedingly, as I dare say it has others. At length I found the legend. It is related, that when St. Bernard was preaching the Crusade in Germany, he entered the Cathedral of Spires, accompanied by the Emperor Conrad, and a splendid retinue of prelates and nobles. There, in presence of all, he knelt down three times as he approached the altar, reciting the famous hymn to the Virgin. The first time, he exclaimed, ' O Clemens!' the second, ' O Pia!' the third time, ' O dulcis Virgo Maria!' In memory of the saint and of this incident these words were inscribed on the pavement where he had knelt, and the Salve Regina was sung every day in the choir. These memorials were preserved, and this custom retained, till the magnificent Cathedral of Spires, almost equal to that of Strasbourg, was desecrated and turned into a military station in the beginning of the French Revolution. The picture I have alluded to, represents, in the centre, St. Bernard kneeling in the black habit, which is very unusual; and rather fat and clumsy, which is not characteristic, for he was of a fair complexion, and spare and delicate temperament. The three inscriptions are visible on the pavement. The Emperor Conrad stands on the right, with his courtiers and warriors ; on the left, a bishop and an abbot with attendants. The picture is gorgeous in colour, and very curious as an historical memento.

Dante, whose great poem is a reflection of the religious feelings prevalent in his time, has given St. Bernard a most distinguished place in the ' Paradiso ' (c. xxxi.) The poet, looking round, finds that Beatrice has left his side, and that her place is filled by that ' teacher revered,' St. Bernard, upon whom, with great propriety, devolves the task of presenting him to the Virgin, who, in turn, is to present him to her divine Son. St. Bernard then breaks forth into that sublime address to the Virgin-mother, which Petrarch has imitated, and Chaucer has translated. This leading idea, this *rapport* between the Virgin and St. Bernard, must be borne in mind, for it is constantly reproduced in the pictures painted for the Cistercian Order ; and I shall have much to say on this subject in the ' Legends of the Madonna.'

In pictures executed for the French, Flemish, and German churches, St. Bernard is often found in companionship with his friend and contemporary St. Norbert, bishop of Magdeburg, founder of the Premonstratensians ; for whom the reader will turn to the Augustins, further on.

THE CONGREGATION OF MONTE OLIVETO.

WE must bear in mind that there are *three* St. Bernards repre-sented in art ;—the great abbot of Clairvaux, whose history has just been given ; St. Bernard degli Uberti, abbot of Vallombrosa, and cardinal, already mentioned ; and a third St. Bernard, distinguished as San Bernardo dei Tolomei, who is more properly the *Beato Bernardo*, for I do not find that he has been regularly canonised ; he was born in 1272, of an illustrious family of Siena, and for some years was distinguished as a learned professor of law in his native city; but the dominant passion of the age reached him, and he was still in the prime of life when, seized with religious compunction, he withdrew from the world to a mountain, about ten miles from Siena, called the Monte Uliveto, or Mount of Olives. Others joined him; they erected cells and an oratory in the usual manner; and thus was founded the 'Olivetani,' or 'Congregation of the Blessed Virgin of Monte Oliveto.' Bernardo placed his new Order under the Rule of St. Benedict, and gave them the white habit. The Order was confirmed by Pope John XXII. in 1319. The principal saints represented in the churches and monasteries of the Olivetani are St. Benedict, as patriarch, and St. Bernard of Clairvaux, the patron saint of their founder. Only in late pictures do we find the founder himself, generally in the white Benedictine habit, with a branch of olive in his hand, in allusion to the name of his Order. In a picture by Salviati he kneels before the Madonna, and at his feet is a small model of a hill, with an olive tree, and a cell at the summit. In a picture by Pamfilo he receives from the Blessed Virgin branches of olive.

Monaci Bianchi di Monte Uliveto.

Bologna S. Cristina.

Cremona Church of S. Lorenzo.

The saint who figures in the Olivetan foundations as the boast of their Order, is St. Francesca Romana, as her name implies, a Roman saint. Effigies of her abound in Rome; we even meet with them on the outer walls of the houses. Her convent, in the Torre de' Spechi is (or was) the best seminary in Rome for young women of the higher classes. Many who have visited Rome of late years will remember the splendour and interest of her festival, when the doors of this school are thrown open to all visitors.

March 9, 1440.

She was born in 1384; the daughter of Paolo di Bassi and his wife Jacobella. She was baptized in the church of Sant' Agnese, in the Piazza Navona, and, from her childhood, displayed the most pious dispositions. Her parents married her, against her inclination, to Lorenzo Ponziano, who was rich and noble; but she carried into her married life the same spiritual virtues which had distinguished her in early youth. Every day she recited the Office of the Virgin from beginning to end. She was particularly remarkable for her charity and humility.

Instead of entering into the pleasures to which her birth and
riches entitled her, she every day went, disguised in a coarse
woollen garment, to her vineyard, outside the gate of San Paolo,
and collected faggots, which she brought into the city on her
head, and distributed to the poor.   If the weight exceeded her
womanly strength, she loaded therewith an ass, following after
on foot in great humility.

In the lifetime of her husband, with whom she lived in the
most blessed union, she had already collected a congregation of
pious women, whom she placed under the Rule of St. Benedict;
but they pronounced no irrevocable vows, and were merely
dedicated to works of charity, and the education of the young.
A.D. 1425. After her husband's death she joined these sisters, and became
their Superior.   In recompense of her piety, she was favoured
with ecstatic visions, and performed surprising miracles.   It is
related, that on a certain day the provision of bread was found
to be reduced to a few small pieces, hardly enough for two
persons (the number to be fed was fifteen); this being told
to the saint, she merely replied, 'The Lord will provide for
us.'   Then, calling for the bread, she laid it on the table, and,
having blessed it, there was found to be abundance for all.
On another occasion, as she was reciting the Office of the
Virgin in her vineyard, there came on a storm of rain,
by which the sisters were wet to the skin, while she remained
perfectly dry.   Further, it is related that, like St. Cecilia,
she was everywhere attended by an angel visible to herself
alone.

After many years passed in a life of sanctity, regarded with
enthusiastic reverence and affection, not only by the Romans,
but in all the neighbouring states, she died in the house of her
son Baptista Ponzani, who lived at that time near the church of
St. Cecilia in Trastevere.   She had gone to comfort him with
maternal solicitude in some visitation of sorrow or sickness, but
was seized with fever, and expired in the arms of her sisterhood,
who had assembled round her bed, while the bereaved poor
prayed and wept at her door.

She was canonised by Paul V. in 1608.   All pictures of her
date of course after that time; and as the Caracci were then at

the height of their celebrity, the best pictures of her are from
their school.

The church now dedicated to St. Francesca Romana was
formerly that of St. Maria Nuova, rendered celebrated as the
scene of her prayers, vigils, and ecstatic trances.   It is situated
in a locality of majestic interest, near the extremity of the
Forum, between the grand remains of the Basilica of Constantine
and the ruins of the temple of Venus and Rome (on part of the
site of which it stands), and close to the arch of Titus.   She is
represented in the dress of a Benedictine nun, a black robe and
a white hood or veil; and her proper attribute is an angel, who
holds in his hand the book of the Office of the Virgin, open at
the words, ' *Tenuisti manum dexteram meam, et in voluntate*   Psal. lxxiii.
tua deduxisti me, et cum gloria suscepisti me ;' which attribute is   23. 24.
derived from an incident thus related in the acts of her canonisation.   Though unwearied in her devotions, yet if, during her

20   St. Francesca Romana.   Domenichino (from the fresco at Grotta Ferrata).

prayers, she was called away by her husband or any domestic
duty, she would close her book, saying that ' a wife and a
mother, when called upon, must quit her God at the altar, and
find Him in her household affairs.'   Now it happened once,
that, in reciting the Office of Our Lady, she was called away
four times just as she was beginning the same verse, and,
returning the fifth time, she found that verse written upon the

page in letters of golden light by the hand of her guardian angel. This charming and edifying legend is introduced in most of the pictures of St. Francesca; occasionally, however, she is kneeling before a pix, while, from the consecrated wafer within it, rays proceed and fall upon her breast, in allusion to the name of her Order, the ' Oblate.'

Turin Gal. There is a fine picture by Guercino, of St. Francesca Romana seated, holding the book of the Office of the Virgin, a basket of bread beside her, while a young angel, clothed in the albe worn by boys who serve at the altar, his hands crossed on his bosom, stands reverentially before her. This picture was painted for Emanuel II. of Savoy, about 1656.

'The Vision of St. Francesca,' painted by Nicolò Poussin, represents her kneeling in supplication. The Virgin appears to her from above, holding in her extended hands a number of broken or blunted arrows; figures of the dead and dying lie on the ground. This alludes to the supposed cessation of an epidemic disease in Rome through the prayers of the saint.

Bologna.
Malvasia,
ii. 132. ' St. Francesca restores a dead child, and gives him back to his mother,' is the subject of a picture by Tiarini, remarkable for true and dramatic expression.

The marble bas-relief by Bernini in the crypt of her church at Rome, in which she is seated with her book and her angel, is, for him, unusually grand and simple.

Pictures of St. Francesca are to be found in the convents of the Congregation of Monte Oliveto.

St. Carlo Borromeo is represented sometimes in companionship with St. Francesca; they stand as *pendants* to each other, or kneel together before the same altar. Where they are thus placed in connection, it is because the one founded the sisterhood of the *Oblate* at Rome, the other introduced the brotherhood of the *Oblati* into Milan, and became the Superior of the institution, for which reason I place him here.

and his uncle Pope Pius IV. created him cardinal and archbishop of Milan at the age of twenty-three.[1]   He lived in the
Court of Rome as his uncle's chief counsellor and favourite,
not only without reproach, but an object of reverential wonder
for the singular combination of youthful modesty and candour
with the wisdom and the self-government of maturer years.
He was a good deal under the dominion of the Jesuits at
this time, who seemed to have inspired him with prudence,
without either corrupting his native sincerity or weakening
his fervid charity.   On the death of his elder brother, Count
Frederigo, he succeeded to the hereditary honours of his
family, and left Rome to take possession at once of his
heritage and his diocese; he was then in his twenty-sixth
year.   His fame had gone before him, and the people of
Milan received him as a second St. Ambrose.   Not so the
ecclesiastics; they dreaded the arrival of a young apostle
whose whole life was in singular contrast with their own;
who came among them armed with bulls and edicts for the
reformation of abuses and the restoration of the Church
revenues to their proper channels—the maintenance of an
active and efficient clergy and the relief of the poor.   Having
assembled a convocation for these purposes, and distributed
in charity the immense personal property he had inherited,
he was suddenly called back to Rome, to attend his uncle on
his death-bed; in this sacred duty he was assisted by St.
Philip Neri.   His subsequent influence in the conclave procured the election of Pius V., who endeavoured to detain the
young archbishop at Rome; but in vain.   St. Charles felt
that his duty called him to the government of his diocese; and,
from this time, his life presents a picture of active charity, of
self-denying humility, only to be equalled by the accounts we
have of the primitive apostles and teachers of Christianity.   All
his own private revenues, as well as those of his diocese, were
expended in public uses: he kept nothing for himself, but what
sufficed to purchase bread and water for his diet, and straw

A.D. 1565.

A.D. 1566.

---

[1] He was cardinal by the title of *Santa Prassede* (see Sacred and Legendary
Art, ii. 243).   I was much astonished to find in the Duomo at Milan an altar
dedicated to this peculiarly Roman saint, till I remembered that San Carlo was
titular *Cardinal di Santa Prassede.*

The Vision of St Bernard.
after Murillo.

St. Charles, who believed himself mortally wounded, made them a sign to kneel down again, and, without stirring from the spot, or a change in his countenance, finished his prayer. It was found that the ball had bruised him, and several small shot had penetrated his clothes, but he was otherwise unhurt. The people, in their enthusiastic veneration, attributed his safety to the direct interposition of Heaven, to a miracle operated in his favour. He, meanwhile, shut himself up for a few days, and solemnly re-dedicated to God the life which had been spared to him.

The other memorable incident of his life was the plague at Milan in 1575. It had been preceded by a scarcity, in which St. Charles ministered to his people like a beneficent angel. He sold his principality of Oria, and gave the produce, forty thousand crowns, for their relief. When the pestilence broke out, he was at Lodi : while all the higher clergy and the nobles were flying from Milan in different directions, St. Charles calmly took his way thither, and entered the city in spite of the remonstrances of his vicars, replying only, that it was the duty of the shepherd to die for his flock. During the continuance of the plague, which carried off some thousands of the people, he preached every day, distributed medicine and relief to the sick and poor, administered the last sacraments to the dying, and assisted in burying the dead. Three several times he walked barefoot through the city, wearing his purple robes as cardinal, and with a halter round his neck ; then, kneeling before the crucifix in the cathedral, he solemnly offered himself as a sacrifice for the people. Twenty-eight priests voluntarily joined him in his ministry, and it is recorded that neither himself nor any of these caught the infection.

In considering the life and character of St. Charles Borromeo, we cannot but feel that in earnestness and goodness lies a power beyond all other power which God has given to man. It is clear that he was not a man of large intellect. The admirable good sense he exhibited on several occasions, was at other times clouded by the most puerile superstition. He was not *wiser* than the men of his creed and time, except in so far as he was *better:* he was better, because he lived up to the creed he professed. If he was a rigid disciplinarian in external forms, he was most rigid to himself. He took no interest whatever in politics, and, after he had possession of his diocese, not much in science, in art, or in literature, though he extended education on every side and to all classes. Neither did he owe his boundless influence over the people to any external advantages. He had a sallow meagre visage, a very aquiline nose, a dark complexion, a high but narrow forehead; his features, altogether, presenting almost a caricature of the Italian physiognomy. He was tall and thin, and stooped in his gait from bodily weakness; he had a bad voice, and stammered, yet he was one of the most forcible and eloquent of preachers. He died on the 4th of November 1584, and, true to his spiritual vocation to the very last, he was heard to breathe out, with a sort of dying rapture, the words ' *Ecce, venio!* ' and so expired, having lived on this earth forty-six years.

He was canonised by Pope Paul V. in 1610, and his remains were afterwards consigned to the rich shrine in which, guarded merely by the reverential piety of all denominations of Christians, they now repose; for, amid the changes and revolutions of Italy, as yet no one has dared to violate the sanctity of his chapel, or take away a jewel from among the offerings of his votaries. What the good saint himself would have thought of the gold, silver, gems, and crystal lavished upon him, we can all imagine and believe. This thought has always intruded with a disagreeable and discordant feeling in the visits I have paid to his chapel, panelled with silver, and glittering with heaped-up treasures; the dead form arrayed in splendid pontificals, the black skeleton head crowned with the jewelled mitre, shocked me. ' Upon the sarcophagus, and all around, we find repeated ^{v. Murray's Handbook, Milan.} the motto of San Carlo, *Humilitas*, reading its lesson, and almost reproaching the sumptuous decorations of the house of death.'

In crossing the Simplon into Italy, the colossal statue of San Carlo, standing on an eminence near the shore of his native lake, the Lago Maggiore, and visible for many miles around, is one of the first objects which strike the traveller. It was erected in 1696, and is nearly seventy feet high; the attitude

is majestic; the proportions agreeable to the eye, when viewed
from a distance, though lost when near; and the hand is
extended in benediction over the district which still reveres
him as ' *Il buon Santo.*'

The Company of Goldsmiths at Milan raised to him a statue
of pure silver, as large as life, which stands in the sacristy of
the cathedral.

The best devotional figures represent St. Charles in his
cardinal's robes, barefoot, carrying the crosier as archbishop;
a rope round his neck, one hand raised in benediction. In
all the Italian pictures he is distinguished by the peculiar
physiognomy which has been preserved in authentic portraits:
the thin beardless face, mild dark eyes, rather large mouth,
and immense aquiline nose.

Of the many pictures which exist of him, I shall notice only
the most remarkable, all of which belong to a late period of art.

His portrait by Guido is in his fine church in the Corso at
Rome; another, by Philippe de Champagne, is at Brussels.

Muséo R. Berlin. We have ' San Carlo kneeling, with angels around him,' by L.
Milan, Brera. Caracci, and the same subject by Annibal. He stands beside
the figure of the dead Christ, to whom an angel points, by C.
Procaccino: the same subject by L. Caracci. San Carlo pre-
sented by the Virgin to our Saviour,—one of the best pictures
of Carlo Marratti,—is over the high altar of San Carlo-in-
Rome. Corso. In the late Milanese pictures he is often represented
with St. Catherine and St. Ambrose; also with St. Francesca
Romana, for the reason given in her life; and with St. Philip
Neri, his friend and contemporary.

When the citizens of Bologna added him, about the year
1615, to the list of their patron saints, he became a favourite
subject in the then flourishing Bologna school. All the three
Caracci, Guido, Guercino, Lanfranco, Garbieri, and Brizio,
have left pictures of him. In Guido's magnificent Pietà, his
masterpiece, St. Charles stands below with the other protectors
of Bologna, St. Petronius, St. Dominick, St. Francis, St. Pro-
culus, St. Florian. The head of San Carlo is on the right,—
beautiful for devout feeling, besides being a characteristic
portrait.

Among the incidents of his life, the two principal are, the plague at Milan, and the attempt to assassinate him. In the subjects taken from his conduct during the pestilence, he is sometimes represented standing amid the dead and dying, and administering the sacrament—a subject frequently painted;— or, prostrate before the altar, he offers himself a sacrifice for his afflicted people. Of this last incident, the finest example I know is the picture by Le Brun: yet the sentiment, as it seems to me, is weakened, not enhanced, by the introduction of the attendant behind, who, lifting up the rich robe, shows to his companion the feet of the saint streaming with blood (he had walked barefoot through the streets of Milan). But Le Brun has always a touch of the theatrical—always painted in a wig. I give a sketch from this picture, taken from the celebrated engraving by Edelinck.

90   St. Charles Borromeo.

The procession through the streets of Milan during the pestilence, by Pietro da Cortona, is over the high altar of *San Carlo-ai-Catinari* at Rome, where no less than three churches are dedicated to him.

Before I close this brief account of San Carlo, it seems worth recording that his name is associated with music, as well as painting and sculpture. In the middle of the sixteenth century the style of music performed in the churches had become so secular and depraved in taste and style, that the Council of Trent took the matter in hand as a scandal to religion; and Pius IV. ' nominated a commission to advise upon the question, whether music was to be permitted in the churches or not.' The decision was long doubtful. ' The Church required that the words should be distinctly articulated, and the musical expression adapted to them. The musicians affirmed that this was not to be attained according to the laws of their art.' Carlo Borromeo was at the head of this commission, and the very strict opinions of this ' great ecclesiastic ' on all matters of Church discipline rendered it most probable that judgment would be given against that heaven-descended art which had been so profanely abused. ' But,' adds the historian, ' happily the right man appeared at the critical moment.' That man was PALESTRINA. When his great Mass, since known and celebrated as the ' *Mass of Pope Marcellus*,' was performed before Pius IV., St. Charles, and the other members of the commission, they were unable to resist its majestic solemnity, its expressive pathos; and ' by this one great example the question was for ever set at rest.'

Ranke Hist. of the Popes. i. 50s.

From a fresco by Matteo di Gualdo at Assisi.

32   St. Philip Neri : an angel holds the Gospel from which he preaches.

In connection with St. Charles Borromeo, we find his contemporary and intimate friend ST. PHILIP NERI.

Effigies of this saint, who was canonised in 1622, belong, San Filippo
of course, to the later schools of art, and none are very good. 26, 1595.
He is, himself, extremely interesting as founder of one of the
most useful, practical, and disinterested of all the religious
communities, that of the Oratorians.[1]

1 When I visited the elegant little church of the Oratorians, recently erected
near Alton Towers, I found portrayed on the window over the high altar the following saints. In the centre, as patron of the church, St. Wilfred of York ; on
his right, St. Benedict (I presume St. Bennet of Wearmouth), and St. Ethelburga ;
on his left, St. Chad of Lichfield, and St. Hilda of Whitby. From this selection
I presume that the Oratorians consider themselves as derived from the Benedictine
Order.

Y

He was born in 1515, the son of a Florentine lawyer, and descended from one of the oldest Tuscan families. In 1533 he repaired to Rome in search of employment, and became a tutor in the family of a nobleman. He was already distinguished as a profound and elegant scholar and conscientious teacher, and yet more for his active charity. His superior intellect, his persuasive eloquence, his spotless life, rendered him a very influential personage in the religious movement of the sixteenth century. As the adviser and almoner of St. Charles Borromeo, he had great power to do good, and he used it for noble and practical purposes.

Ranke gives us a striking picture of Filippo Neri in few words. ' He was good-humoured, witty, strict in essentials, indulgent in trifles. He never commanded; he advised, or perhaps requested: he did not discourse, he conversed: and he possessed, in a remarkable degree, the acuteness necessary to distinguish the peculiar merit of every character.'

He associated with himself, in works of charity, several young ecclesiastics, members of the nobility, and students in the learned professions at Rome, who, under his direction, were formed into a community, and devoted themselves to the task of reading the Scriptures, praying with the poor, founding and visiting hospitals for the sick, &c. They were bound by no vows; there was no forced seclusion from the ordinary duties of life. They took the name of Oratorians, from the little chapel or oratory in which they used to assemble round Filippo to receive his instructions.

Cardinal de Berulle introduced the *Pères de l'Oratoire* into France in 1631, and they have lately been established in England. After a long, useful, and religious life, Filippo Neri died in 1595, at the age of eighty-two.

Gregory XIII., in confirming the congregation of the Oratory in 1575, bestowed on Filippo Neri and his companions the church of S. Maria della Vallicella. After the death of the saint it was entirely rebuilt, not, certainly, in very good taste, yet it is one of the most superb churches in Rome. It still belongs to the Oratorians. Here, after his canonisation in 1622, a chapel was dedicated to San Filippo by his Florentine kinsman Nero de' Neri, and in it is placed the mosaic copy after the fine picture by Guido which represents the saint in an ecstasy of devotion. In the oratory is preserved the books, the crucifix, the bed, and some other relics of this benevolent saint. I do not know that he is distinguished by any particular attribute. The sketch is from v. p. 16L his statue in St. Peter's, executed by Algardi.

St. Philip Neri was the spiritual director of the Massimi family; it is in his honour that the Palazzo Massimi is dressed up in festal guise every 16th of March, as those who have been at Rome at that period will well remember. The annals of the family relate, that the son and heir of Prince Fabrizio Massimi died of a fever at the age of fourteen, and that St. Philip, coming into the room amid the lamentations of the father, mother, and sisters, laid his hand upon the brow of the youth, and called him by his name, on which he revived, opened his eyes, and sat up. 'Art thou unwilling to die?' asked the saint. 'No,' sighed the youth. 'Art thou re- Litta, 'Memorie,' &c. signed to yield thy soul to God?' 'I am.' 'Then go,' said Philip. ' *Va, che sii benedetto, e prega Dio per noi!* ' The boy sank back on his pillow with a heavenly smile on his face, and expired.

This incident, so touching as a well-authenticated fact, so needlessly exalted into a miracle, is the subject of a very beautiful picture by Pomerancia, painted by order of Prince Fabrizio, and placed in the church of Vallicella. The family portraits in this picture are from life; the head of the saint bending over Paolo; the beautiful expression in the face of the dying youth; the surprise of the father; the devout thankfulness of the pious mother; the two sisters, who kneel with clasped hands and parted lips, watching the scene—are rendered with much dramatic power.

When I was at Rome in 1846, Pius IX. performed a service in the family chapel of the Massimi in memory of this incident. The prince received all visitors in state, and the halls and corridors of this once magnificent but now dilapidated palace were thronged with people of all classes: some who came there in honour of the saint; others, as a mark of respect to the family; others, like myself, merely as spectators of a strange and animated scene—a sort of religious ' at home.'

It is worth remarking and considering, that at the very time when St. Charles Borromeo, San Filippo, and their companions and disciples, were setting an example of Christian charity at Rome, the massacre of St. Bartholomew was enacted in France by those who professed the same faith; and the same Pope who encouraged St. Charles in his spiritual reforms, and assisted St. Philip Neri in his works of charity, and in his efforts for the moral regeneration of Italy, struck the medal *in honour* of the massacre of the Huguenots! Such are the moral and religious inconsistencies which make the devils sneer, and the angels weep.

I must not conclude these notices of the Reformed Benedictines in their connection with Art, without a few words on the Port-Royalists and the Trappistes. The renowned convent of Port-Royal-des-Champs was a foundation of the Cistercians in the sixteenth century. The account of the fortunes of this community, and of the noble conduct of La Mère Angélique and her nuns, which forms no unimportant page of French history, has been recently given to us by Sir James Stephen; and his brief, but earnest and eloquent, summary of their wrongs, and feminine and Christian heroism, must lend a new interest to every memorial connected with them. They were persecuted to the grave because they refused to certify, by their signatures, that they knew what they did *not* know, and believed what they did *not* believe. If they were not saints and martyrs of the Church, yet saints they were in the true and original sense of the word; for they lived holily, worked faithfully, suffered patiently, resisted humbly, and died at last, as their historian expresses it, ' martyrs of sincerity, strong in the faith that a lie must ever be hateful in the sight of God, though infallible popes should exact it, or an infallible church, as represented by cardinals and confessors, should persuade it.'

Nor can I refrain from numbering among these martyr-nuns the noble Jacqueline Pascal (the sister of the great Pascal), with her large poet mind, and woman's softest gifts, who died broken-hearted because she had in evil hour signed that formal lie. She had previously written to La Mère Angélique,—'Je sais bien qu'on dit que ce n'est pas à des filles à défendre la vérité, mais si ce n'est pas à nous à défendre la vérité, c'est à nous à mourir pour la vérité.' Yet for the sake of peace she was induced to sign, and died of that malady for which earth has no cure—a wounded conscience ; a martyr to truth, which she could not violate and live.[1]

The eldest daughter of the painter Philippe de Champagne had become a nun in the convent of Port-Royal, about the year 1650. Champagne was a religious man, but he was also a rich and prosperous man, holding an office at court ; and having lost two children by death, he was unwilling to resign to a nunnery the only one left : she persisted, however, and he consented perforce. She took the vows under the abbess Angélique, second of that name, a woman of genius, virtue, and learning. Of this excellent abbess there remains a portrait by Champagne : where it is now, I do not know ; but the portraits of her father and her mother, Arnauld-D'Andilly and his wife, Madlle. Le Febre, are in the Louvre. The first is one of the finest portraits ever produced by the French school : the second is rather hard in the execution ; but it is a face of such peculiar character,—

Nos. 389, 1824.

---

[1] When the commissioner of the Archbishop of Paris was sent to examine into the condition and confession of faith of the nuns of Port-Royal, Sœur Jacqueline was one of those interrogated. After a searching examination on grace, election, and so forth, which she met unflinchingly, the commissioner concluded with a home question : 'N'avez-vous point de plaintes à faire ?' R. 'Non, monsieur ; par la grâce de Dieu je suis parfaitement contente.' D. 'Mais cela est étrange ! Quand je vais quelquefois voir des Religieuses, elles me tiennent des deux heures de suite à me faire des plaintes, et je ne trouve point cela ici !' R. 'Il est vrai, monsieur, que par la grâce de Dieu nous vivons dans une très-grande paix et une grande union. *Je crois que cela vient de ce que chacune fait son devoir sans se mêler des autres.*'—*Vie de Jacqueline de Pascal*, par Victor Cousin.

so spiritualised, so refined from all earthly alloy, with such a
tinge of pale, religious contemplation, such a look of transparent
purity, without any of the charms of youth,—that, once seen,
it leaves an indelible impression upon the mind. This portrait
hangs nearly opposite that of her husband ; they ought to hang
side by side.   In the same gallery we find Philippe de Champagne's most celebrated picture, known as ' *Les Religieuses.*'
I give a sketch from it here.   It represents the daughter of

33   Two Nuns of Port-Royal. (Philippe de Champagne.)

Champagne who had been ill of a fever, and given over by her
physician, restored by the prayers of one of the sisterhood,
Catherine Agnes by name.   This picture, remarkable for the
simplicity, and purity, and religious repose of the treatment,
seems to have been painted with earnest feeling and good-will,
to please his daughter, and as an offering of paternal gratitude.
The nuns wear the white habit and black hoods proper to their
Order ; and are distinguished by a red cross on the breast, the
badge of the Port-Royalists.

The Trappistes, another late community of reformed Cister-

cians, is the most austere of all; and remarkable as having A.D. 1644.
originated in an age of general luxury, profligacy, and ir-
religion.

The romantic story of the conversion of the Abbé de
Rancé, who, on hastening to an assignation with his mistress,
the beautiful Duchess de Montbazon, found her dead in the
short interval of his absence, and laid out in her coffin under
circumstances of peculiar horror, is well known, and would
afford many picturesque subjects; but as they would hardly
belong to *religious* art, properly so called, I pass them over.
De Rancé, on founding his famous institution of La Trappe,
seems to have taken as his *device* the text, ' In the midst of
life we are in death;' and imposed as conditions, perpetual
silence, perpetual labour, perpetual contemplation of our
mortality. Not only all art and all ornament, but all literature, was banished. That in the mind of De Rancé there
was, after the shock he had received, a touch of the morbid
or the mad,—that even in his gloomy retreat he was haunted
by that ' enervating thirst for human sympathy which had
distinguished him in the world,'—seems clear and intelligible; yet the numbers of those who resorted to him, who
lived and died under his terrible ordinations—lived happily
and died calmly—shows us that there are forms of moral
suffering, and mental disease, for which we might provide
more appropriate asylums than either the hospital or the
madhouse.

Early Royal Saints.

I HAVE given a sketch of the most eminent of our Anglo-Saxon princes, who were canonised through the influence of the Benedictine Order in England; confining myself to those who have either figured, or ought, as I presume, to figure, in the illustration of our early ecclesiastical history. I shall now, in order to keep this department of my subject quite distinct, place together those Royal Saints who flourished throughout Christendom in early times; who either preceded the institute of St. Benedict, or whom we find in connection with that illustrious Order in religious Art or through historical associations.

I know not how it may be with others, but to me the effigies of the Royal Saints are not satisfactory. They are all, of course, historical personages, but they do not figure as such in sacred Art; and whatever space they may fill in the page of history—though it be that of a whole era, like Charlemagne —however distinguished as actors in the world's drama, however reverenced for virtues which the world seldom sees in high places—still, in their saintly character, they are not, with one or two exceptions, eminent or interesting. As connected with Art they are comparatively unimportant, both in regard to what they represent and what they suggest. For, be it remembered, they do not represent history; neither do they personify an attribute of Divine power, nor embody a truth, nor set forth an example; which is the reason, I suppose, that for one real St. Charlemagne or St. Clotilda, we have ten thousand St. Christophers and St. Catherines. In considering these royal Saints we must in the first place, and in all cases, set the saint above the sovereign, and put history out of our minds, and its stern facts and judgments out of our memories. Now this is not easy: in some cases it is not possible; hence the legendary fictions connected with many of these stately and glorified personages disturb rather than excite the fancy, for here the real and ideal do not blend well together. When Constantine, with the celestial nimbus round his head, figures as the hero of a religious legend, he becomes as mere a fiction as Charlemagne starting amid his magicians and paladins at the sound of Orlando's horn. Unluckily for these pictured or poetical creations, we can hardly in either case set aside the image in our minds of the *real* Constantine, the *real* Charlemagne: and the reality is more perplexing, more painful, when it disturbs our religious, than when it interferes with our poetical, associations. The Charlemagne of Ariosto is delightful; the *Saint* Constantine of Church history is to me disgusting. There should not intrude repugnance and offence and the risk of a divided feeling, where the idea conveyed ought to be either abstract, or at least gracious and harmonious, and the feeling completely reverential. Now in the case of historical or political personages, whose effigies are placed before us in the character of superior beings, they are involuntarily subjected to a judgment such as crowned kings must be prepared to endure, but which in regard to crowned saints is in some sort profane;—' For the glory of the celestial is one, and the glory of the terrestrial is another.' Therefore, I repeat, the effigies of sainted potentates and princes are unsatisfactory. As it is out of the question to deal with them otherwise than in the religious and artistic point of view, they may be passed over briefly.

We should, in the first place, distinguish between those who were canonised for services and submission to the Church or for the interest of churchmen, and those who were canonised —so to speak—in the hearts of the people, long before an ecclesiastical decree had confirmed their exaltation, for virtues difficult and rare on a throne—beneficence, clemency, self-denial, humility, active sympathy with the cause of humanity and the general good, as far as they understood it. To the former class belong St. Constantine, St. Henry, St. Ferdinand, and a crowd of others; to the latter class belong St. Charle-

magne, St. Elizabeth, and perhaps a few more. In giving a
reason for the canonisation of the Empress Cunegunda, the
writer of her life remarks, that those who are placed in high
stations must necessarily be to very many the occasion of
eternal salvation or of eternal perdition : that, as far as the
wide circle of their influence and example extends, they cannot rise without raising the standard of virtue around them ;
they cannot fall without dragging down others into the abyss
of sin. 'Therefore,' he argues, 'a greater degree of glory or
of punishment than would be the lot of common men is the
just and everlasting portion of the rulers of men.'

I shall now take them in order.

At their head stand Constantine and Charlemagne, often
together, as patrons respectively of the Greek and the Latin
Churches. St. Constantine rarely stands alone in Western
Art. Notwithstanding his famous donation of the central
territory of Italy to the popes of Rome (which Ariosto has so
irreverently placed in the moon with Orlando's lost wits), I
have seldom seen him figure in any situation where his Christian merits took precedence of his imperial greatness,—not
even in the 'Hall of Constantine' in the Vatican, where
Raphael has done his best to glorify him. It is still the
emperor, and not the saint; and when Sylvester receives the
act of donation, *he* is throned, and the imperial Constantine
humbly presents it on his knees. The 'Legend of St. Constantine and St. Sylvester' I have already given at length ;
the emperor plays, throughout, the secondary personage in
that curious fiction. In an assemblage of the Blessed in a
Last Judgment, a Paradiso, a Coronation of the Virgin, and
such subjects, it is usual to find Constantine and Charlemagne
standing together: the former bearing the long sceptre, or
the standard with the cross (the Labarum), and, in Italian
Art, always in the classical costume; the latter in a suit of
armour, a long mantle often trimmed with ermine; a sword,
or a globe surmounted by a small cross, in one hand; and in
the other a book—either as the great legislator of his time,

St. Con-
stantine,
May 21.

Sacred and
Legend. Art,
ii. 313.

or because he ordered the translation of the Scriptures to be carefully corrected and widely promulgated.

The most ancient representation of Charlemagne in his saintly character I have yet met with is a fragment of Mural painting preserved in the Christian Museum in the Vatican; the head only, wearing the kingly crown surmounted by the aureole; he has a short, square yellowish beard, and a refined and rather melancholy face: I describe from memory, but it impressed me as having a portrait-like air, as a head I would have given to Alfred.

St. Charle-
Magne,
Jan. 28.

The copies of the Gospels which Charlemagne ordered to be transcribed and distributed to various religious institutions were sometimes illuminated by Greek artists, whom he had invited from Constantinople. Two of these MSS. are in the National Library at Paris. The drawing of the figures is as rude as that of St. Dunstan; the colours vivid, the ornaments fanciful. An *Evangelistarium*, copied and illuminated for the use of Charlemagne and his empress Hildegarde, was presented to Napoleon on the birth of his son, and was in the ex-king's private library in the Tuilleries: I know not if it still exists there. Napoleon liked to be considered as a second Charlemagne; and Charlemagne assumed the name and attributes of King David.[1] He occurs perpetually in the French missals: in Angelico's exquisite coronation of the Virgin, he kneels at the foot of the Divine throne, on the left of the picture; and has three crowns embroidered on his robe, representing his dominion over France, Germany, and Italy. In order to represent the embodied religious and intellectual spirit of those times, the imperial saint should stand between his secretary and chronicler Eginhardt, and the wise Saxon monk Alcwin, 'le confident, le conseiller, le docteur, et, pour ainsi dire, le premier ministre intellectuel de Charlemagne:' and thus accompanied, I should not object to see him with a halo round his head.

p. 94.

Guizot.

---

[1] So Alcwin occasionally addresses him in his letters,—'Très-excellent et digne de tout honneur, Seigneur Roi David!' Alcwin had been educated in the Benedictine Monastery of York under St. Wilfred.—*Guizot: Cours d'Histoire Moderne*, Leçon 22.

In France, Germany, and Italy, Charlemagne stands at the head of the Royal Saints; but in a chronological series, St. Clotilda and St. Sigismond should precede him.

A.D. 584.
Jan. 3. CLOTILDA, the Christian wife of the fierce and warlike Clovis, was a princess of Burgundy. She is said to have christianised France, and occurs frequently in French pictures and illuminated missals and breviaries. She is usually represented in the royal robes, with a long white veil and a jewelled crown : she is either bestowing alms on the poor, or kneeling in prayers; or attended by an angel holding a shield, on which are the three *Fleurs-de-lys*. By her prayers and alms she hoped to obtain the conversion of her husband, who, for a long time, resisted her and the holy men whom she had called to her aid. At length, as the historians tell us, Clovis having led his army against the Huns, and being in imminent danger of a shameful defeat, recommended himself to the God of his Clotilda : the tide of battle turned; he obtained a complete victory, and was baptized by St. Remi, to the infinite joy of Clotilda. On this occasion, says the legend, not only was the cruse of holy oil miraculously brought by a dove (figuring the Holy Ghost), but, owing to a vision of St. Clotilda, the lilies were substituted in the arms of France for the three frogs or toads Collection of
Sir J. Tobin. (*crapauds*) which Clovis had formerly borne on his shield. In the famous Bedford missal, presented to Henry VI. when he was crowned King of France, this legend, with appropriate and significant flattery, is introduced in a beautiful miniature : an angel receives in heaven the celestial lilies, descends to earth, and presents them to St. Remi, who receives them reverently in a napkin, and delivers them to Clotilda; lower down in the picture, she bestows the emblazoned shield on her husband. Such is the famous legend of the *Fleurs-de-lys*, the antique emblems of purity and regeneration, how often since trailed through blood and mire ! St. Clotilda displayed some qualities not quite in harmony with her saintly character. When, in her old age, her two younger sons had seized the children of their eldest brother Chlodomir, and demanded of her whether she would prefer death or the tonsure for her grandsons, she

exclaimed passionately, ' Better they were dead, than shaven monks!' They took her at her word, two of the princes were immediately stabbed. The third escaped, fled to a monastery, assumed the cowl, and became famous as SAINT CLOUD; who or Clodoaldus, A.D. 560. should be represented as a Benedictine monk, with the kingly crown at his feet.

ST. SIGISMOND of Burgundy was the cousin of Clotilda. At A.D. 525, May 1. this time, Gaul was divided between the Arians and the Catholics; the Catholics triumphed, and those who perished on their side became consequently canonised martyrs. Sigismond was one of these: his father Gondubald, an Arian, had murdered the parents of Clotilda. When Sigismond succeeded to the throne of Burgundy, he became a Catholic, and was distinguished by his piety: he, however, like the pious Constantine, put his eldest son to death, on the false accusation of a cruel stepmother; and while repenting his crime in sackcloth and ashes, he prayed that the punishment due to him might fall upon him in this world, rather than the next. His prayers were heard; the sons of Clotilda invaded his kingdom, took him prisoner, and avenged the crimes of his father Gondubald, by putting him to death. The body of Sigismond was flung into a well; and thence, some years afterwards, removed to the convent of St. Maurice. It is his connection (as a saint Sacred and only) with St. Maurice and Legend. Art, ii. 411.

34   St. Sigismond.

the Theban Legion which has popularised St. Sigismond in
Italy. He is one of the patrons of Cremona. In a chapel dedicated to him there, Francesco Sforza celebrated his marriage
with Bianca Visconti, the heiress of Milan. As a monument at
once of his love, his gratitude, and his piety, he converted the
little church into a most magnificent temple, glorious with
marbles and pictures, and shrines of wondrous beauty. The
painters of the Cremona school, rarely met with out of Italy,
cannot be better studied than in the church of St. Sigismond.
I made a pilgrimage thither one hot dusty day (it is two miles
from the city gate), and I remember well the feeling with which
I put aside the great floating draperies which hung before the
portal, and stepped out of the glaring sunshine into the perfumed
air and subdued light, and trod the marble pavement, so cool
and lustrous, and leaned, unblamed, against the altar-steps, to
rest me. I was quite alone; and, for many reasons, that church
of San Gismondo dwells in my remembrance. Yet the pictures,
though interesting as examples of a particular school of art,
were not to me attractive, either in style or subject, excepting
always the grand altarpiece of Giulio Campi. It represents
the Madonna and Child enthroned; and Francesco Sforza and
Bianca Maria Visconti, as duke and duchess of Milan, presented
by St. Chrysanthus and St. Daria, with St. Sigismond and St.
Jeromo standing on each side. The choice of the attendant
saints appears unintelligible, till we remember that the nuptials
which gave Sforza the sovereignty of Milan and Cremona were
celebrated on the feast of SS. Chrysanthus and Daria; that the
church was dedicated to St. Sigismond, and the monastery to
St. Jerome. The picture is splendid,—like Titian; and the
dress of St. Sigismond in particular, with its deep crimson and
violet tints, quite Venetian in the intense glow of the colouring.
The describer of this picture in Murray's Handbook mentions
'the shrinking timidity in the figure of Bianca.' There is no
such thing: on the contrary, she looks like a gorgeous bride who
had brought two duchies to her husband. But this is a digression;—I must turn back to the old royalties of Germany and
Gaul. How is it there were no Royal Saints among the powers
and principalities of Italy? I find none: not even the 'great

v. Sacred and
Legend. Art.

Oct. 25, 1441.

Countess Matilda,' whose munificent piety almost doubled the possessions of the Church of Rome.

Next after Charlemagne we find St. Wenceslaus and St. Ludmilla, familiar to all who have visited Prague.

A school of art, distinct from German Art, and of which we know little or nothing in England, flourished in Bohemia about the middle of the fourteenth century. Charles IV., king of Bohemia and emperor, who held his court at Prague, decorated his churches and palaces with altarpieces and frescoes ; not only employing native artists, but inviting to his capital others from foreign countries; among them an Italian, one of the school of the Giotteschi, called from his birthplace Tomaso di Mutina (*i.e.*, Thomas of Modena). By this painter, by Theodoric or Dietrich of Prague, and by Carl Skreta Ritter Ssotnowsky von Zaworzic—('Phœbus ! what a name !' after the musical nomenclature of Italian Art !)—I saw, when I was in Bohemia and Austria, various pictures, and am only sorry I did not then pay more attention to the peculiar and national subjects represented,—the legendary worthies and patron saints of Bohemia.

The earliest apostles of the Sclavonic tribes, the Moravians, Bohemians, Hungarians, and Bulgarians, were two Greek monks of the Order of St. Basil, known as St. Cyril and St. Methodius, and connected in a very interesting manner with the history of religious Art. Cyril was learned and eloquent, a philosopher and a poet; Methodius was considered an excellent painter of that time, when his country produced the only painters known. These two monks departed together, by order of the patriarch of Constantinople, to preach to the savage nations along the shores of the Danube. Bogaris, the king or chief of Bulgaria, having heard of the art of Methodius, required of him that he should paint a picture in the hall of his palace, and that it should be ' something terrible,' to impress his subjects and vassals with awe. Methodius accordingly

painted the Day of Judgment, representing at the summit our
Lord seated in glory, and surrounded with angels; on his
right, the resurrection of the blessed, and on his left, the doom
of sinners, swallowed up in flames, and tormented by the most
hideous demons.   When the king desired to have the interpretation of this 'terrible' picture, Cyril, who was as eloquent
in words as Methodius was in colours and forms, preached to
the barbarian monarch and his attendants such a sermon as
converted them all on the spot.   Their mission was extended
successfully through the surrounding nations.   While Methodius *painted* the doctrines of the Christian faith, Cyril explained
them in the language of the people, invented for them a
written alphabet, translated portions of the Gospel, and obtained from Pope Nicholas the privilege of celebrating the
divine service in the Sclavonic tongues.   These two saints are
generally represented together, as St. Methodius the painter,
and St. Cyril the philosopher.   The former holds in his hand
a tablet, on which is a picture of the Day of Judgment; the
latter holds a large book.   Thus they stand in a fine marble
group in the cathedral at Prague.

Another missionary who carried the light of the Gospel into
or Albert. Bohemia was St. Adelbert, an Anglo-Saxon Benedictine from
the kingdom of Northumbria.   He converted Ludmilla, the
grandmother of Wenceslaus, venerated through northern
Germany and Denmark as St. Wenzel.   Ludmilla carefully
educated the young prince in her own faith.   Meantime, his
brother Boleslaus had been brought up by his heathen mother
Drahomira in all the dark errors of paganism.   The characters
of the two princes corresponded with the tenets they respectively embraced.   Wenceslaus was as mild, merciful, and just,
as Boleslaus was fierce, cruel, perfidious.   Bohemia was divided
by the two parties, the Christian and the heathen; and at
length Boleslaus and his wicked mother conspired to assas-
St. Lud-
milla,
A.D. 927.
Sept. 16. sinate Ludmilla, as being the great protectress of the Christians, and the enemy of their native gods.   The hired murderers
found her praying at the foot of the cross in her private oratory,
and strangled her with her own veil.   Thus she became the
first martyr-saint of Bohemia.

33   St. Ludmilla. (E. Max.)

The turn of Wenceslaus came next; he had valiantly met his enemies in the field, though not even the atrocities of Drahomira could induce him to forget his duty to her as a son. According to the legend, two angels from heaven visibly protected Wenceslaus in battle; but they forsook him, apparently, when, by the arts of his mother, he was entrapped to pay her a visit, and slain by the hand of his brother at the foot of the altar and in the act of prayer. *A.D. 938, Sept. 28.*

Wenceslaus lived at the time when the passion for relics had spread over all Christendom. On a visit which he paid to his friend Otho I., that warlike emperor bestowed on him certain relics of St. Vitus and St. Sigismond. Thus in the Bohemian pictures we have St. Wenceslaus and St. Sigismond, all glorious in their princely robes, their crowns and palms, and shining armour; St. Ludmilla, with her palm and her veil; St. Vitus, as a beautiful boy with a cock on his book; St. George; and St. Procopius, a holy Bohemian prince who turned hermit in the eleventh century, and is represented with a doe at his side and a crown at his feet. *Sacred and Legend. Art, 2nd edit.*

St. Wenceslaus is represented robed and armed as Duke of Bohemia, carrying the shield and standard with the black

A A

90   St. Procopius.

Imperial eagle (a privilege granted to him by Otho I.), and
his palm as martyr.

In the Imperial Gallery at Vienna is a very curious altarpiece, with the Virgin and Child enthroned in the central
compartment: on one side St. Wenceslaus; on the other St.
Palmatius, inscribed

'Quis opus hoc finxit? Thomas de Mutina pinxit.'

Augiolo Ca-   Another picture in which St. Wenceslaus, a colossal figure, is
roselli, 1653.   standing with the same attributes, while an angel brings him
the crown of martyrdom. In the background is a pedestal,
on which is depicted a bas-relief, exhibiting the murder of
the saint by his wicked brother. The painter, Angiolo Caro-

selli, was one of the numerous artists in the employment of Rudolph II.

In the gallery of the Academy there is (or was) a series of pictures representing the life and martyrdom of Wenceslaus, by Carl Skreta, who, notwithstanding his terrible name, was a very good painter, particularly of portraits.

The martyrdom of St. Ludmilla I found represented in a curious old fragment of a bas-relief, standing in the Church of St. Laurence at Nuremberg. A fine marble statue by a native Bohemian sculptor, Emanuel Max, has recently been set up in the Church of St. Vitus at Prague, from which I give a sketch.

ST. HENRY of Bavaria was one of those princes who earned their canonisation by boundless submission to the Church. He was born in the year 972, was elected emperor in 1002, and died at Rome in 1024. He founded and endowed, in conjunction with his wife Cunegunda, the magnificent cathedral and monastery of Bamberg in Franconia, and many other convents and religious edifices in Germany and Italy. His brother the Duke of Bavaria, and other princes of the empire, reproached him for expending not only his patrimony but the public treasures in these foundations; they even made this an excuse for their rebellion against him. But Henry showed himself not less valiant than he was devout. He defeated his adversaries in the field, and then earned his title of saint by pardoning them all freely, and restoring to them their possessions. He undertook an expedition against the idolatrous nations of Poland and Sclavonia, partly for their conversion, and partly for their subjection. On going forth to this war he solemnly placed his army under the protection of the three holy martyrs St. Laurence, St. George, and St. Adrian, and, as already related, girded on the sword of the last-named warlike saint, which had been long preserved as a precious relic in the church of Walbeck. The legend goes on to assure us that his saintly protectors were seen visibly fighting on his side, and that through their divine aid he defeated the infidels,

St. Henry, Emperor. A.D. 1024, July 14.

Sacred and Legend. Art, ii. 429.

and obliged them to receive baptism.   As a memorial of his
victory arose the beautiful church of Merseberg.   He also led
an army to the very extremity of Italy, and drove the Saracens
from their conquests in Apulia.   These were services rendered
not only to the Church, but to Christendom ; and it seems
clear that though the piety of Henry was deeply tinctured by
the fanaticism and superstition of the times in which he lived,
he possessed some great and some good qualities.   He professed a particular veneration for the Virgin, and it was his
custom in his warlike expeditions, whenever he entered a city
for the first time, to repair immediately to a church dedicated
to the Mother of the Saviour, and there to pay his devotions.
On one occasion when visiting the abbey of Verdun, he was
seized with such a weariness of soul, such a disgust for the
pomps and cares of his position, that he was about to renounce the world, and take the habit of a monk.   The prior,
Richard of Verdun, told him that the first vow required of
him would be *obedience*.   The emperor expressed his readiness
to obey; thereupon the prior enjoined him to retain his kingly
office and discharge his duties.   ' The emperor,' said he,
' came hither to learn obedience, and he practises this lesson
by ruling wisely.'

St. Cune-
gunda.
March 3,
1040.
Henry, on assuming the imperial dignity, married the
beautiful and pious princess Cunegunda, daughter of Sieg-
fried, Count of Luxembourg, who shares her husband's celestial,
as she shared his earthly crown.   She is *Saint* Cunegunda,
adored by her people while living, and the subject of innumerable legends and ballads since her death.   After a union
of several years, during which they lived together in love and
harmony, but by mutual consent in the strictest continence,
the holy Empress was suspected of infidelity to her husband;
and Henry, though perfectly convinced of his wife's immaculate purity, was somewhat affected by the malicious reports
concerning her.   Cunegunda herself would willingly have submitted to these accusations as a trial sent from Heaven to test
her patience and humility ; but considering that Providence
had placed her in a position of life wherein an evil example
would cause much mischief and scandal, she appealed to the

St. Cunegunda walking over the red-hot ploughshares.

trial by ordeal, and, having walked unhurt over the burning ploughshares, she was acquitted. This story of the Empress Cunegunda is as popular in German Poetry and German Art, as the story of our Queen Emma, the mother of the Confessor, was formerly in England. Henry endeavoured to make his wife amends for the indignities to which she had been exposed, by treating her with more respect and tenderness than ever, but she obtained his permission to retire from the world, and withdrew to the cloister. Henry died in 1024, and was interred in his cathedral of Bamberg. Cunegunda, on his death, assumed the Benedictine habit, and not only set an example of piety and charity, but of industry, working continually with her hands when not engaged in prayer; for this most holy Empress had often on her lips the words of St. Paul, that 2 Thess. iii. 8. those who did not work had no right to eat.   She died in 1040, and was buried at Bamberg, by the side of her husband. The influence of the monks of Bamberg, which became one of the greatest of the Benedictine communities, procured the canonisation of their founder, Henry, by Eugenius III., in 1152, and that of Cunegunda by Innocent III. in 1200.

The single devotional figures of St. Henry exhibit him in complete armour, wearing the imperial crown ; in one hand, his sword, or the orb of sovereignty; in the other he usually holds the Cathedral of Bamberg.

The effigies of Cunegunda represent her as Empress, wearing a long veil under her diadem; and in her hand she also bears the Cathedral of Bamberg as joint founder,—or it may be the Church of St. Stephen at Bamberg, of which she was sole founder.   In a print by Hans Burgmair, she is stepping over the red-hot ploughshares, and holds a ploughshare in her hand.

Henry, having been a great protector of religion in Italy as well as in Germany, is sometimes found in Italian pictures, particularly at Florence, where

38   St. Henry.   (I. v. Melom.)

he built and endowed the Church of San Miniato, so famous in Florentine story.   The legend of 'St. Laurence and the Emperor Henry' occurs frequently in old Florentine Art.   I found in the Pitti Palace a picture representing St. Henry and

St. Cunegunda standing with a lily between them,—emblem of their chastity.

The most beautiful monument to the sanctity and glory of this imperial pair is their sepulchre or shrine in the Cathedral of Bamberg. They lie together, under a rich Gothic canopy, arrayed in their imperial robes; the heads and hands are admirably sculptured; but finer still are the bas-reliefs which decorate the pedestal or sarcophagus on which they recline. There are four subjects:—1. Cunegunda undergoes the fiery ordeal, a beautiful composition of eight figures. 2. Cunegunda pays, out of her dower, the architects and masons who are building the Church of St. Stephen at Bamberg. 3. Henry, in his last illness, takes leave of his wife. 4. Henry receives the last offices from the Bishop of Bamberg. 5. The legend of St. Laurence, which I have already related at length. These sculptures, contemporary with the bronzes of Peter Vischer at Nuremberg, were executed, under the auspices of a bishop of Bamberg, by Hans Thielmaun of Wurzburg. In delicacy of workmanship and dramatic feeling, they equal some of the finest contemporary works of Italy. *Sacred and Legend. Art. ii. 161.* *between 1499 and 1513.*

In the courtyard of the castle at Nuremberg, there stood, and I hope still *stands*, a lime-tree, said to have been planted by Cunegunda, and, for her sake, religiously guarded by the people. It was, when I saw it, almost in the last stage of decay, though still preserving its vitality. This memorial, though it concerns *Nature*, not *Art*, deserves to be mentioned.

Of St. Stephen, king at Hungary, there is not much to be said with reference to Art. He was the first *Christian* king of that country, and succeeded his father Duke Geysa, about the year 998. Geysa and his wife received baptism late in life from the hand of St. Adelbert, the Northumbrian missionary; and, as a sign of their new faith, gave the name of the Christian proto-martyr to their eldest son. Stephen found his country barbarous and heathen; and he left it comparatively civilised and Christianised. Having subdued the pagan nations around, and incorporated them with his own people, he sent ambassa- *St. Stephen A.D. 1038, Sept. 2.*

dors to Rome with rich offerings to request the papal benediction and the title of king. The Pope, Sylvester II., sent him in return a royal diadem, and a cross to be borne before his army. This crown was preserved at Presburg, and is the same which was placed on the fair head of Maria Theresa on the memorable day of her coronation. What may have become of it since 1848 I do not know.

St. Stephen married Gisela, the sister of St. Henry, a princess 'full of most blessed conditions.' Unhappily, all their children died before their parents. The eldest son, a youth of singular beauty of person and great promise, is styled St. Emeric by the Hungarians, and associated with his father as an object of reverential worship.

St. Stephen is considered as the apostle and legislator of Hungary. In common with those saints who have triumphed over paganism, he bears the standard with the cross; and is usually represented with this attribute, dressed in complete armour, wearing the kingly crown, and holding the sacred sword, which was also preserved among the regalia of Hungary. He is introduced into groups of the Blessed where the object has been to compliment those sovereigns of Spain or Austria who were connected with Hungary, but I do not recollect ever meeting with him in Italian Art.

A picture in the Vienna Gallery, and which appears to have been painted for Maria Theresa, represents St. Stephen receiving the crown sent to him by Pope Sylvester in 1003.

St. Leopold.
A.D. 1136,
Nov. 15.

ST. LEOPOLD, Margrave of Austria, was born in 1080. In 1106 he married Agnes, the beautiful and youthful widow of Frederic, Duke of Suabia; by her he was the father of eighteen children, eleven of whom survived him; and, after a long and most prosperous reign, he died in 1136.

The virtues of this prince were certainly conspicuous in the age in which he lived. The history of his life and actions shows that he had a deep religious feeling of his responsibility

as a governor of men, a just mind, a merciful and kindly disposition; but these virtues, and many more, would not, in all probability, have procured him the honours of a saint, had he not
founded during his lifetime the magnificent monastery of
Kloster-Neuburg, on the banks of the Danube. It is related
that, on a certain day soon after their marriage, Leopold and
Agnes stood in the balcony of their palace on the Leopoldsberg
(a site well known to those who have resided in Vienna), and
they looked round them over the valley of the Danube, from the
borders of Bohemia on one side, to the confines of Hungary on
the other, with the city of Vienna lying close at their feet.
And, as they stood there, hand in hand, they vowed to commemorate their love, and their gratitude to Heaven who had
given them to each other, by building and endowing an edifice
for the service of God. Just then the breeze caught and lifted
the bridal veil of Agnes, and it went floating away upon the
air till lost to view. About eight years afterwards, as Leopold
was hunting in the neighbouring forest, he saw at a distance
a white and glittering object suspended from a tree; and on
spurring his horse towards it, he recognised the veil of Agnes,
and recollected their joint vow. He immediately ordered the
wilderness to be cleared, and on that spot arose the Kloster-
Neuburg; around it, a once flourishing town, and some of the
richest and most productive vineyards in Austria. This convent,
when I visited it some years ago, was a seminary; the old
Gothic church and cloisters had been partly rebuilt in the worst
ages of Art, in the worst possible taste; but the library was
still fine and extensive, and the veil of Agnes and the shrine
of St. Leopold were *then* preserved among the treasures of the
place.

It was at the request of the monks of Kloster-Neuburg that
Leopold was canonised by Pope Innocent VIII., in 1485.
He has since been revereuced as one of the patron saints of
Austria, and it is in this character that he is represented in
German Art; I have never met with him in an Italian pic-
ture. His canonisation was celebrated with great pomp, and
he became popular as a saint all over Germany just before the
Reformation, and at the time when Mabuse, Lucas Cranach,

Albert Durer, L. van Leyden, and other early German artists,
flourished.   In the Vienna Gallery are two devotional figures
of St. Leopold.   One of these, *attributed* to Holbein, represents
him standing, as prince and saint, in complete armour, with
a glory round his head, and a coral rosary in his hand.   The
other, by Lucas Cranach, also represents him in complete
armour, with spear and shield, and in companionship with
St. Jerome, who in the old pictures is often the representative of a life of religious seclusion—of ' the cloister ' in its
general sense.   They are placed together as the patrons
of the Kloster-Neuburg, whence, I presume, this picture
originally came.

There is a fine woodcut by Albert Durer, executed in
compliment to his patron the Emperor Maximilian, and representing the eight guardian saints of Austria.   Among them
stands St. Leopold, wearing his ducal crown (with which
crown, brought from Kloster-Neuburg for the purpose, I saw
the ex-emperor Ferdinand crowned Archduke of Austria in
1835).   The others are—St. Quirinus, as bishop; St. Maximilian, as bishop and martyr; St. Florian the martyr, in
complete armour; St. Severinus, an obscure saint considered
as the first apostle of Austria (whose relics are honoured
at San Severino in Naples), in the Benedictine habit; St.
Coloman, as pilgrim (one of the earliest missionaries), St.
Poppo, as abbot of Stavelo (of whom it is recorded that he
persuaded the Emperor St. Henry to abolish the barbarous
combats between men and beasts); and St. Otho, as bishop
of Bamberg.

Another rare and curious woodcut by Albert Durer represents the Emperor Maximilian on his knees before the
First Person of the Trinity, who stands on a raised throne,
arrayed as a high priest, and holding the orb of sovereignty.
Beside Maximilian stands the Virgin with the infant Christ;
she is saying ' *Lord, save the king, and hear us when we call
upon thee!* '   St. Andrew, kneeling on his jewelled cross,
St. Barbara, St. George, St. Leopold, St. Sebastian, and St
Maximilian, appear to be assisting the emperor in his
devotions.

Sacred and
Legend. Art.
II. 428.

A.D. 492.

A.D. 1048.

A.D. 1139.

89   St. Ferdinand. (From a picture by Murillo.)

ST. FERDINAND OF CASTILE was the son of Alphonso, king
of Leon, and Berengaria of Castile.   After a union of several
years, and the birth of four children, Alphonso and Berengaria
were separated by a decree of the Pope, because, being within
the prohibited degrees of consanguinity, they had married
without a dispensation. Their children were, however, declared
legitimate.   Berengaria returned to her father, the king of
Castile, and lived retired in his court; but she exercised during
her whole life an extraordinary influence over the mind of her
eldest son, Ferdinand, and his obedience to her even to the
hour of his death was that of a docile child. When Berengaria
succeeded to the throne of Castile, she gave up her rights to her

El Santo
Rey.
Don Fer-
nando II.
A.D. 1152.
May 30.

son, and shortly afterwards on the death or his father he succeeded to the throne of Leon, thus uniting for ever the two kingdoms; and from this time it may be said that Berengaria and her son reigned together, such complete union existed between them. He married Joan, Countess of Ponthieu; and she vied with her husband in duty and love to the queen-mother. In reading the chronicles of the royal houses of Spain, the murders, treasons, tragedies which meet us in every page, it is refreshing to come upon this record of domestic confidence, fidelity, and affection, lasting through a long series of years: we feel there must have been admirable qualities, shall I say *saintly* qualities, on which this peace, and trust, and tenderness were founded. But history does not dwell upon them: and St. Ferdinand owed his canonisation less to his virtues than to his implacable enmity against the Moors. Mr. Ford, who is not given to praising saints, styles him, ' the best of kings and bravest of warriors.' His piety, if tinctured with the ferocious fanaticism of the times, was conscientious, and the *nature* of Ferdinand was neither ambitious nor cruel. He had made a solemn vow never to draw his sword in Christian conflict, and in his wars against the infidels he was constantly victorious. Moreover, it is related in the Spanish chronicles, that, at the great battle of Xeres, Santiago himself appeared visibly at the head of his troops, combating for him, and, while thousands of the Moors were left dead on the field, on the side of the Christians there fell but one knight, who had refused before the battle to pardon an injury.

Handbook of Spain.

But neither his victories, nor his magnificent religious foundations, leave so pleasing an impression of the character of Ferdinand as one speech recorded of him. When he was urged to replenish his exhausted coffers, and recruit his army by laying a new tax on his people, he rejected the counsel with indignation: ' God,' said he, ' in whose cause I fight, will supply my need. I fear more the curse of one poor old woman than a whole army of Moors ! '

After driving the infidels from Toledo, Cordova, and Seville, he was meditating an expedition into Africa, when he was seized with sickness, and died as a Christian penitent, a cord round his neck and the crucifix in his hand. He was buried in the Cathedral of Seville, and was succeeded by his son, Alphonso the Wise, in 1152. His only daughter, Eleonora of Castile, who inherited the piety and courage of her sainted father, married our Edward I. She it was who sucked the poison from her husband's wound.

It was not till 1668 that Ferdinand was canonised by Clement IX., at the request of Philip IV., and 'the greatest religious festival ever held at Seville' took place in 1671, on the arrival of the Pope's bull. Of course the pictures of him as *saint* are confined to Spain, or at least to Spanish Art, and can date only from this late period. But the Spanish School of Seville was then in all its glory, and as Philip IV. was a munificent patron of Art, the painters hastened to gratify him by multiplying effigies of his sainted ancestor.

St. Ferdinand, as Mr. Stirling tells us in his beautiful book, 'Annals of the Artists of Spain.' founded the Cathedral of Burgos, 'which points to heaven with spires more rich and delicate than any that crown the cities of the imperial Rhine. He also began to rebuild the Cathedral of Toledo, where during four hundred years artists swarmed and laboured like bees; and splendid prelates lavished their princely revenues to make fair and glorious the temple of God entrusted to their care.' There is preserved in the convent of San Clemente at Seville a portrait of St. Ferdinand, 'a work of venerable aspect, of a dark dingy colour, and ornamented with gilding;' reckoned authentic and contemporary. When Ferdinand VII., in 1823, wished to borrow this portrait for the purpose of having it copied, the nuns of San Clemente would not allow it to leave their custody.

Devotional pictures of San Fernando represent him in complete armour, over which is thrown a regal mantle; he wears the kingly crown, surmounted by the celestial glory. He has sometimes a drawn sword in his hand, sometimes it is the orb of sovereignty. In the arms of the city of Seville he is throned as patron saint, with the two famous bishops St. Isidore and St. Lauriano on either side.

There are five pictures of San Fernando by Murillo; one of Eng. by

Arteaga in
the *Fiestas
de Sevilla.* them, a fine head, is supposed to be a copy of the portrait in
San Clemente. The sketch given above is from the small full-
length in the Madrid Gallery.

In the Spanish Gallery of the Louvre are two figures of St.
Ferdinand, attributed to Zurbaran, but probably by some later
painter. I recollect a fine San Fernando among the Spanish pictures in the possession of Lord Clarendon. Another picture in
my list I must mention, from its characteristic Spanish feeling ;
' St. Ferdinand bringing a faggot to burn a heretic,' by Valdès.

St. Casimir.
1448,
March 4. Of St. Casimir of Poland there is nothing to be remarked
except his enthusiastic piety and his early death. He was the
third son of Casimir IV. of Poland and Elizabeth of Austria ;
and, from his childhood, a gentle-spirited and studious boy,
whom no influence or teaching or example could rouse to
active pursuits, or waken to ambition, or excite to pleasures :
and thus he grew up in his father's half-barbarous court, and
among his warlike brothers, a being quite of a different order ;
a poet, too, in his way, composing himself the hymns he sung
or recited in honour of the Virgin and the saints. After refusing the crown of Hungary, he became more and more
retired and austere in his habits. At length he fell into a decline
and died in 1483. He was canonised by Leo X. at the request
of his brother Sigismond the Great ; and became patron saint
Fl. Pisa Pal. of Poland. He is represented as a youth in regal attire ; a
lily in his hand, a crown and sceptre at his feet. Or, he holds
in his hands his hymn to the Virgin beginning,

'Omni Die
Dic Mariæ
Mea laudes anima ! '

while the lily and the crown lie on a table beside him ; as in
an elegant little picture by Carlo Dolce. When Casimir V.
abdicated the crown of Poland, and became abbot of the Benedictine convent of St. Germain-des-Près at Paris, he introduced
the worship of his patron saint, and the young St. Casimir is
often found in French prints.

Other royal saints who are particularly connected with the
Mendicant Orders will be found in their proper place.

The Augustines.

THE Augustine Order has been so widely scattered, its origin
is so uncertain, it has been broken up into so many denominations, and the primitive rule so variously modified, that it is
difficult to consider the whole community as one body of men,
animated by one spirit, and impressed with a certain definite
character, as is the case with the Benedictines and Franciscans
and the Dominicans.

There is no occasion to enter into the much disputed question
of the origin of this famous Order.   In tracing its history in
connection with Art, it is sufficient to keep in mind the only two
facts which, on looking over the best ecclesiastical authorities,
stand out clear and intelligible before us.

I. The Augustines claim as their founder and patriarch the
great Doctor and Father of the Church, St. Augustine; and in
every language they bear his name: in Italian, *Agostini*, *Padri
Agostiniani;* in German, *Augustiner.*

It is related in his Life, that he assembled together a number
of persons religiously and charitably disposed, who solemnly
renounced the cares and vanities of this world, threw their
possessions into a common stock, and dedicated themselves to
the service of God and the ministry of the poor.   Similar communities of women were likewise formed under his auspices ;
and such, they aver, was the origin of the ' Rule of St. Augustine.'

II. At the same time, it is not clear that this great Father
and Teacher of the Church contemplated the institution of a
religious Order such as was founded by St. Basil in the East
and afterwards by St. Benedict in the West; or that any such

Order existed until the middle of the ninth century. About that period, all the various denominations of the Christian clergy who had not entered the ranks of monachism—priests, canons, clerks, &c.—were incorporated, by the decrees of Pope Leo III. and the Emperor Lothaire, into one great community, and received as their rule of discipline that which was promulgated by St. Augustine. Thenceforward, we have the regular and secular canons (*Canonici regolari e secolari*) of Augustine, and all those personages who had been dedicated to a holy life, or to the duties of the priesthood, in the first centuries after the apostolic ages, were retrospectively included in the Augustine community.

In the time of Innocent IV., all the hermits, solitaries, and small separate confraternities, who lived under no recognised discipline, were registered and incorporated by a decree of the Church, and reduced under one rule, called the rule of St. Augustine, with some more strict clauses introduced, fitting the new ideas of a conventual life. There was some difficulty in compelling these outlying brethren to accept a uniform rule and habit, and bind themselves by monastic vows. Innocent IV. died before he had completed his reform, but Alexander IV. carried out his purpose; not, however, without calling a miracle to his assistance, for just at the critical moment, St. Augustine himself deigned to appear : he was dressed in a long black gown, tattered and torn, in sign of poverty and humility; round his waist he wore a leathern strap and buckle, and carried in his hand a scourge; and he gave the Pope to understand that the contumacious hermits were to take forthwith the Augustine habit, and submit themselves to the monastic rule, under pain of the scourge, freely and not *metaphorically* applied. At length these scattered members were brought into submission, and the whole united into one great religious body, under the name of *Eremiti* or *Eremitani Agostini*, hermits or friars of St. Augustine; in English, Austin-Friars. This was about forty years after the introduction' of the Franciscans and Dominicans.

A.D. 1254.

The Augustines, as I have observed, branch out into a great variety of denominations; and the rule is considered as the parent rule of all the monastic orders and religious congregations not included in the Benedictine institution, and to number among its members all the distinguished characters and recluses who lived from the fourth to the sixth century.

The first great saint of the Order who figures as a subject of Art is of course St. Augustine himself, whose effigy is generally conspicuous in the houses and conventual churches bearing his name : not chiefly as one of the four Latin fathers (in this character he is to be found in most religious edifices), but more especially as patriarch and founder of the Augustine Order; not always in the rich episcopal cope and mitre, but with the black frock, leathern girdle, and shaven crown of an Augustine friar : not seated with the other great Fathers in colloquy sublime on the mysteries and doctrines of the Church, but dispensing alms, or washing the feet of our Saviour under the guise of a pilgrim ; or giving the written rule to the friars of his Order; or to the various religious communities who, as Lanzi expresses it, ' fight under his banner,—*militano sotto la sua bandiera.*' All these subjects I have already discussed at length, with reference to the life and character of St. Augustine as a Father of the Church ; and, therefore, I shall say no more of them here. *St. Augustine.* *Sacred and Legend. Art, i. 296.*

St. Monica, the mother of St. Augustine, is also a favourite subject in the pictures painted for this Order. She is usually considered as the first Augustine nun. In the Santo-Spirito at Florence, which belongs to the *Eremiti*-Agostiniani, we find St. Monica seated on a throne, surrounded by twelve women of the Capponi family, and in another chapel of the same church she and her son stand together. *St. Monica.*

St. Antony and St. Paul, the primitive hermits, with all the curious legends relating to them, are generally to be found in the edifices of the Augustine friars, either as examples of hermit life, or as belonging to the community. Of these ancient worthies I have already spoken at length in a former volume. *Sacred and Legend. Art, ii. 368.*

The Augustine writers also number among the early saints

c c

of their Order St. Patrick and St. Bridget of Ireland.   It is true
that nearly every vestige of these two memorable personages
has been destroyed or mutilated; but not the less do they live
in the hearts of the people, familiar names in their household
talk, mixed up with many wild, strange, incongruous legends,
but still representing to them the traditions of their ancient
civilisation; the memories of better times, before their religion
was proscribed and their country confiscated.

St. Patrick.
A.D. 464.
March 17.

St. Patrick, who styles himself 'a Briton and a Roman,'
was carried away captive into Ireland when a youth of sixteen,
and was set to tend the herds of his master.   Being born of
Christian parents, he turned his misfortune to good account,
making his captivity a school of patience and humility.   The
benighted condition of the people among whom he dwelt filled
him with compassion; and when afterwards he made his escape
and was restored to his parents and his home, he was haunted
by visions, in which he beheld the yet unborn children of these
Irish pagans stretching forth their little hands and crying to
him for salvation.   So he returned to Ireland, having first
received his mission from Pope Celestine, and preached the
word of God; suffering with patience all indignities, affronting
all dangers and fatigues with invincible courage, converting
everywhere thousands by his preaching and example, and
gaining over many disciples who assisted him most zealously
in the task of instructing and converting these barbarians.   He
himself preached the kingdom of Christ before the assembled
kings and chiefs at Tara; and though Niell, the chief monarch,
refused to listen to him, he soon afterwards baptized the kings
of Dublin and Munster; and the seven sons of the king of
Connaught.   After forty years of unremitting labour in teaching
and preaching, he left Ireland not only Christianised, but full
of religious schools and foundations, which became famous in
Western Europe and sent forth crowds of learned men and
missionaries; and having thus founded the Church of Ireland,
and placed its chief seat at Armagh, he died and was buried
at Down, in the province of Ulster.

The story of St. Patrick exorcising the venomous reptiles

from his adopted country has the same origin as the dragon
legends of the East, and the same signification. It is merely
one form of the familiar allegory figuring the conquest of
good over evil, or the triumph of Christianity over Paganism.

It is related that St. Patrick consecrated many women to
the service of God, finding them everywhere even more ready
to receive the truth than the men ; and among these, was St.
Bridget or Brigida. The mother of this famous saint was a
beautiful captive, whom her father, a powerful chieftain, had
taken in war. The legitimate wife of the chief became jealous
of her slave, and cast her out of the house like another Hagar.
So she brought forth her child in sorrow and shame ; but two
holy men, disciples of St. Patrick, took pity on her, baptized
her and her daughter,—and Bridget grew up in wisdom and
beauty, and became so famous in the land, that her father
took her home, and wished to have married her to a neighbouring chief, but Bridget would not hear of marriage. She
devoted herself to the service of God, the ministry of the poor,
and the instruction of the people, particularly those of her
own sex ; and retired to a solitary place, where was a grove
of oaks, which had once been dedicated to the false gods.
There she taught and preached, healing the sick, and restoring sight to the blind ; and such was the fame of her sanctity
and her miraculous power, that vast crowds congregated to
that place, and built themselves huts and cells that they
might dwell in her vicinity ; and, particularly, many women
joined themselves to her, partaking of her labours, and imi-
tating her example : and this was the first community of
religious women in Ireland. Kildare, ' the cell or place of
the oak,' became afterwards one of the most celebrated convents
and most flourishing cities in Ireland. Here was preserved,
unextinguished, for many centuries, the sacred lamp which
burned before her shrine.

The Church of St. Patrick and St. Bridget, at Down, was
destroyed by Sir Leonard Grey in the reign of Henry VIII.
Other memorials of these patrons perished in the desolating
wars of Elizabeth ; and whatever religious relics, dear and
venerable to the hearts of the Irish, may have survived the

St. Bridget,
or St. Bride.
A.D. 500.
Feb. 1.

first period of the Reformation were utterly swept away by the savage Puritans under Cromwell. In London the name of St. Bridget survives in the beautiful Church of St Bride in Fleet Street, and the Palace (now the Prison) of Bridewell.

In any pictured memorial of the former civilisation and spiritual glories of Ireland, if such should ever be called for, St. Patrick and St. Bridget ought to find a place; for they represent not merely the Church of the Roman Catholics, but the first planting of the Church of Christ in a land till then filled with the darkest idolatry; and the two should always stand together.

St. Patrick may be represented in two ways; either as missionary and apostle, or as the first bishop and primate of the Church of Ireland.

As the apostle of Ireland he ought to wear a gown with a hood, and a leathern girdle; in one hand a staff and wallet, in the other the gospel of Christ; he should not be represented old, because, though dates are very uncertain, it is most probable that he was still a young man when he first came to Ireland. At his feet or under his feet should be a serpent. The standard with the cross, the proper attribute of the missionary saints who overcome idolatry, would also belong to him.

As bishop he should wear the usual episcopal insignia, the mitre, the cope, the crosier; the gospel in his hand, and at his side a neophyte looking up to him with reverence.

St. Bridget may also be represented in two different characters. She may wear the ample robe and long white veil always given to the female Christian converts; in one hand the cross, in the other the lamp,—typical at once of heavenly light or wisdom (as in the hand of St. Lucia), and also her proper attribute as representing

> 'The bright lamp that shone in Kildare's holy fane,
> And burn'd through long ages of darkness and storm,'—

and which her female disciples watched with as much devotion us the Vestal Virgins of old the sacred fire. An oak-tree or a grove of oaks should be placed in the background.

She may also be represented as first abbess of Kildare; and as this abbey became afterwards a famous Franciscan community, St. Bridget might with propriety be represented as the Irish St. Clara, in the long grey habit and black hood, bearing the pastoral staff. This would be much less appropriate as well as less picturesque than the former representation, but I believe the old effigies would thus exhibit her.

Next to the patriarch St. Augustine, the great saint of the Order is ST. NICHOLAS OF TOLENTINO.

He was born about the year 1239, in the little town of St. Angelo, near Fermo. His parents having obtained a son through the intercession of St. Nicholas, bestowed on him the name of the beneficent bishop, and dedicated him to the service of God. He assumed the habit of an Augustine friar in very early youth; and was distinguished by his fervent devotion and extraordinary austerities, so that it was said of him that 'he did not *live*, but languished through life.' He was also an eloquent preacher, and unwearied in his ministry. As for his miracles, his visions, and his revelations, they are not to be enumerated. He died in 1309, and was canonised by Pope Eugenius IV. in 1446. St. Nicholas A.D. 1309, Sept. 10.

According to the legend, the future eminence and sanctity of this saint were foretold by a star of wonderful splendour, which shot through the heavens from Sant' Angelo, where he was born, and stood over the city of Tolentino, where he afterwards fixed his residence. For this reason the devotional effigies of St. Nicholas of Tolentino represent him in the black habit of his Order, with a star on his breast; and sometimes he carries the Gospel as preacher of the Word, and a crucifix wreathed with a lily,—the type of his penances and his purity of life. a version of the ' Star in the East.' Nat. Gal.

He is generally young, of a dark complexion, and an ardent meagre physiognomy.

Fl. Santo-Spirito. There is a fine statue of this saint by Sansovino.

'St. Nicholas of Tolentino crowned by the Virgin and St. Augustine,' is a picture attributed to Raphael.

Nat. Gal. A charming little picture by Mazzolino da Ferrara, exhibiting all his characteristics, represents St. Nicholas of Tolentino kneeling before the Virgin and Child. The head of the saint is a master-piece of finish and expression, but has not the wasted nor the youthful features generally given to him.

40   St. Nicholas of Tolentino.

It is related of this St. Nicholas that he never tasted animal food. In his last illness, when weak and wasted from inanition, his brethren brought him a dish of doves to restore his strength. The saint reproved them, and, painfully raising himself on his couch, stretched his hand over the doves, *Leuchtenberg Gal.* whereupon they rose from the dish and flew away. This legend is the subject of a small but very pretty picture by Garofalo.

Another picture by the same painter represents St. Nicholas restoring to life a child laid at his feet by its disconsolate mother.

'In the year 1602, the city of Cordova was visited by the

plague; and the governor, Dion Diego de Vargas, caused the image of St. Nicholas of Tolentino (it was the day of his festival), to be carried through the streets in solemn procession to the Lazaretto. Father G. de Uavas met the procession, bearing a large crucifix; thereupon the saint stretched forth his arms, and the figure of Christ stooping from the cross embraced St. Nicholas; and from that hour the pestilence was stayed.' This miraculous incident is the subject of a picture by Castiglione, from which there is a print in the British Museum.

A much more interesting saint is the good Archbishop of Valencia, ST. THOMAS DE VILLANUEVA, called the ALMONER, glorious in the pictures of Murillo and Ribalta; but he lived in the decline of Italian art, and I do not know one *good* Italian picture of him.

St. Thomas A.D. 1555. Sept 17.

Thomas of Villanueva, the son of Alphonso Garcia and Lucia Martinez of Villanueva, was born in the year 1488. The family was one of the most ancient in Valencia, but his parents, who were of moderate fortune, were remarkable only for their exceeding charity, and for lending money without interest, or furnishing seed for their fields, to the poor people around them. Their son inherited their virtues. When he was a child only seven years old, he used to give away his food to the poor children, and take off his clothes in the street, to throw them over those who were in rags. The vocation for the ecclesiastical life was too strongly exhibited to be gainsayed by his parents. After studying for fourteen years at Alcala and at Salamanca, he entered the Augustine Order at the age of thirty: and I find it remarked in his Life, that the day and hour on which he pronounced his vows as an Augustine friar were the same on which Luther publicly recanted and renounced the habit of the Order.

After two years' preparation, by retirement from the world, penance and prayer, Thomas de Villanueva became a distinguished preacher, and soon afterwards prior of the Augustines

at Salamanca. He was regarded with especial veneration by
the Emperor Charles V., who frequently consulted him on the
ecclesiastical affairs of his empire. It is recorded, that when
Charles had refused to pardon certain state criminals, though
requested to do so by some of his chief counsellors, the Grand
Constable, the Archbishop of Toledo, and even his son Don
Philip, he yielded at once to the prayer of St. Thomas, declar-
ing that he looked upon his request in the light of a Divine
command.

In the year 1544, Charles showed his respect for him by
nominating him Archbishop of Valencia. He accepted the
dignity with the greatest reluctance: he arrived in Valencia
in an old black cassock, and a hat which he had worn for
twenty-six years; and as he had never in his life kept anything
for himself beyond what was necessary for his daily wants, he
was so poor, that the canons of his cathedral thought proper
to present him with four thousand crowns for his outfit: he
thanked them gratefully, and immediately ordered the sum to
be carried to the hospital for the sick and poor, and from this
time forth we find his life one series of beneficent actions. He
began by devoting two-thirds of the revenues of his diocese to
purposes of charity. He divided those who had a claim on
him into six classes:—first, the bashful poor, who had seen
better days, and who were ashamed to beg; secondly, the poor
girls whose indigence and misery exposed them to danger and
temptation; in the third class were the poor debtors; in the
fourth, the poor orphans and foundlings; in the fifth, the
sick, the lame, and the infirm; lastly, for the poor strangers
and travellers who arrived in the city, or passed through it,
without knowing where to lay their heads, he had a great
kitchen open at all hours of the day and night, where every
one who came was supplied with food, a night's rest, and a
small gratuity to assist him on his journey.

In the midst of these charities he did not forget the spiritual
wants of his people; and, to crown his deservings, he was a
munificent patron of art.

Artists of
Spain, p. 353.
' Valencia,' says Mr. Stirling, 'was equally prolific of saints,
artists, and men of letters. Its fine school of painting first

grew into notice under the enlightened care of the good archbishop. He encouraged art, not to swell his archiepiscopal
state, but to embellish his cathedral, and to instruct and im-
prove his flock.' Among the painters who flourished under
his auspices, was Vicente de Juanes, the head and founder of
the Valencian School;—'His style, like his character, was grave
and austere: if Raphael was his model, it was the Raphael of
Perugia; and whilst his contemporaries El Mudo and El
Greco were imbuing Castilian Art with the rich and volup-
tuous manner of the Venetian School, he affected the antique
severity of the early Florentine or German masters.' He was
particularly remarkable for the combination of majesty with
ineffable mildness and beneficence which he threw into the
heads of our Saviour. We can easily imagine that such a
painter, both in his personal character and his genius, was
fitted to please the good Archbishop of Valencia; and not the
least precious of the works which Juanes left behind him is
the portrait, from life, of St. Thomas of Villanueva, which
now hangs in the sacristy of the cathedral. He appears robed
and mitred, 'with that angelic mildness of expression, that
pale and noble countenance, which accorded with the gentleness of his nature.' This picture was painted when Juanes
was in the prime of his life and powers, and his excellent
patron declining in years.

Thomas de Villanueva died in 1555. To the astonishment
of the people, he left no debts, in spite of the enormous sums
he had spent and given; and thenceforth it was commonly said
and believed that his funds, when exhausted, had been re-
plenished by the angels of God. On his death-bed he ordered
all the ready money in his house to be distributed to the
parish poor; and sent all his furniture and goods to the
college he had founded in Valencia. There remained nothing
but the pallet on which he lay; and that he bequeathed to the
jailer of the prison, who, as it appears, had become one of the
instruments of his charity. He was followed to the grave by
thousands of the poor, who bewailed the loss of their benefactor; and, already canonised in the hearts of his people, he
was declared a *Beato* in the year 1618, by Paul V. At the

*or Juan de
Juanes.
Stirling.*

Stirling.

D D

same time it was ordained that in his effigies an open purse should be placed in his hands instead of the crosier; with the poor and infirm kneeling around him; and thus we find him represented, though the crosier is not always omitted. Most of the pictures of St. Thomas de Villanueva which are now commonly to be met with in the churches of the Augustines, both in Italy and in Spain, have been painted since 1688, the year in which the bull of his canonisation was published by Alexander VII. It can easily be imagined that he was most popular in his own country. 'There were few churches or convents on the sunny side of the Sierra Morena without some memorial-picture of this holy man,' but the finest beyond all comparison are those of Murillo.

Lord Ashburton's picture, perhaps the most beautiful Murillo in England next to that of Mr Tomline, represents the saint as a boy about six or seven years old dividing his clothes among four ragged urchins. The figures are life-size. This picture was formerly in the collection of Godoy, by him presented to Marshal Sebastiani, from whom it was purchased by the late Lord Ashburton in 1815. The small original sketch of the composition is in the same collection.

The picture called the 'Charity of San Tomas de Villa Nueva,' which Murillo preferred to all his other works, and used to call 'his own picture,' was one of the series painted for the Capuchins at Seville. 'Robed in black (the habit of his Order), and wearing a white mitre, St. Thomas *the Almoner* stands at the door of his cathedral, relieving the wants of a lame half-naked beggar who kneels at his feet. His pale venerable countenance, expressive of severities inflicted on himself, and of habitual kindness and good-will towards all mankind, is not inferior in intellectual dignity and beauty to that of St. Leander.'

Sacred and
Legend. Art,
h. 300.

There is a fine picture of the same subject, but differently treated, in the Louvre; and another, brought from Seville about 1805, was purchased by Mr Wells of Redleaf, and recently sold.

F. ed.
Ribalta.

In the college of Valencia, which he founded, is a grand picture of St. Thomas 'surrounded by scholars,' (?) parts of

which, says Mr. Ford, ' are as fine as Velasquez.' This must
have been painted, however, long after the death of the saint.

ST. JOHN NEPOMUCK.

Ital. San Giovanni Nepomuceno. *Ger.* S. Johannes von Nepomuk. Canon
Regular of St Augustine. Patron Saint of Silence and against Slander.
Protector of the Order of the Jesuits. In Bohemia and Austria, the
patron saint of bridges and running water.

CHARLES IV., Emperor of Germany, of whom I have already ^{p. 175.}
spoken, died in the year 1378, after having procured, by lavish
bribery to the electors, the succession of the empire for his
son Wenceslaus IV. In his early childhood his father had
invited Petrarch to superintend his education : the wise poet
declined the task, and it may be doubted if even *he* could
have made anything of such untoward material. The history
of the long and disgraceful reign of this prince does not, fortunately, belong to our subject : it is sufficient to observe that
he obtained from his people the surnames of the *Slothful* and
the *Drunkard;* and from historians, that of the Modern
Sardanapalus. He married the Princess Joan of Bavaria, a
beautiful and virtuous princess : she was condemned to endure
alternately his fits of drunkenness, of ferocity, and fondness,
and her life was embittered and prematurely brought to a close
by his cruelty and his excesses.

She had for her confessor and almoner a certain excellent
priest, called, from the place of his birth, John of Nepomuck.
This good man pitied the unfortunate Empress, and, knowing
that for misery such as hers there was no earthly remedy, he
endeavoured by his religious instructions to strengthen her to
endure her fate with patience and submission.

Wenceslaus, in one of his fits of mad jealousy, sent for John,
and commanded him to reveal the confession of the Empress.
The priest remonstrated, and represented that such a violation
of his spiritual duties was not only treachery, but sacrilege.
The Emperor threatened, entreated, bribed, in vain. The

confessor was thrown into a dungeon, where he was kept for a few days in darkness and without food. He was again brought before the Emperor, and again repelled his offers with mild but most resolute firmness. Wenceslaus ordered him to be put to the torture. The unhappy Empress threw herself at her husband's feet, and at length by her prayers and tears obtained the release of the saint. She ordered his wounds to be dressed, she ministered to him with her own hands ; and as soon as he was recovered he reappeared in the court, teaching and preaching as usual. But, aware of his dangerous position, he chose for the text of his first sermon the words of our Saviour, *Yet a little while and ye shall not see me,* and sought to prepare himself and his hearers for the fate he anticipated.

A few days afterwards, as he was returning home from some charitable mission, the Emperor, preceiving him from the window of his palace, was seized with one of those insane fits of fury to which he was subject ; he ordered his guards to drag him to his presence, and again repeated his demand. The holy man, who read his fate in the eyes of the tyrant, held his peace, not even deigning a reply. At a sign from their master the guards seized him, bound him hand and foot, and threw him over the parapet of the bridge into the waters of the Moldau.

A.D. 1383,
May 16.

He sank ; but, says the legend, a supernatural light (five stars in the form of a crown) was seen hovering over the spot where his body had been thrown, which when the Emperor beheld from his palace, he fled like one distracted, and hid himself for a time in the fortress of Carlstein.

Meantime the Empress wept for the fate of her friend, and the people took up the body and carried it in procession to the Church of the Holy Cross.

From this time St. John of Nepomuck was honoured in his own country as a martyr, and became the patron saint of bridges throughout Bohemia. In the year 1620, when Prague was besieged by the Imperialists, during the Thirty Years' war, it was commonly believed that St. John of Nepomuck fought on their side ; and on the capitulation of Prague, and subsequent conquest of Bohemia, the Emperor Ferdinand and the

Jesuits solicited his canonisation, but the papal decree was not published till the year 1729.

The rest of the history of Wenceslaus would here be out of place, but it may be interesting to add that the unhappy Empress died shortly after her director; that Wenceslaus was deprived of the empire, and reduced to his hereditary kingdom of Bohemia, which, during the last few years of his life, was distracted and laid waste by the wars of the Hussites.

On the bridge at Prague, and on the very spot whence he was thrown into the river, stands the statue of St. John of Nepomuck. He wears the dress of a canon of St. Augustine; in one hand the cross, the other is extended in the act of benediction; five stars of gilt bronze are above his head. This is the usual manner of representing him; but I have seen other devotional effigies of him, standing with his finger on his lip to express his discretion; and in some of the old German prints he has a padlock on his mouth, or holds one in his hand. He is of course rare in Italian Art, and only to be found in pictures painted since his canonisation. There is one by Giuseppe Crespi, in which he is pressing the crucifix to his heart, painted about 1730; and another by the same painter in which he is confessing the Empress. She is kneeling by the confessional, and he has the attribute of the five stars above his head. Neither of these pictures is good.

San Giovanni Nepomuceno che affettuosamente stringe al petto il crocifisso. Turin Gal.

St. John of Nepomuck, or, as he is called there, San Juan Nepomuceno, became popular in Spain, but at so late a period that the pictures which represent him in the Jesuit churches and colleges there are probably worthless. I have before me a Spanish heroic poem in his praise, entitled *La Eloquencia del Silencio, Poema Heroico, Vida y Martyrio del gran Protomartyr del Sacramental Sigillo, Fidelissimo Custodio de la Fama y Protector de la Sagrada Compañia de Jesus;* dedicated significantly to the Jesuit confessor of Philip V., William Clarke by name. In the opening stanza St. John is compared to Harpocrates, and in the frontispiece he is seen attended by an angel with his finger on his lip; underneath is the bridge and the river Moldau, on which is the body of St. John Nepo-

muck with five stars over it. I lived for some weeks under the
protection of this good saint and ' Protomartyr of the Seal of
Silence,' at the little village of Traunkirchen (by the Gmun-
den-See in the Tyrol), where his effigy stood in my garden,
the hand extended in benediction over the waters of that
beautiful lake. In great storms I have seen the lightning play
round his head till the metal stars became a real fiery nimbus
—beautiful to behold !

ST. LORENZO GIUSTINIANI, of Venice, was born in 1380, of
one of the oldest and noblest of the Italian families.   His
mother, Quirina, the young and beautiful widow of Bernardo
Giustiniani, remained unmarried for his sake, and educated
him with the utmost care and tenderness.   He appears to
have been a religious enthusiast even in his boyhood, and
believed himself called to the service of God by a miraculous
vision at the age of nineteen.   As he was the eldest son, his
family was anxious that he should marry; but he fled from
his home to the cloister, and took refuge with the Augustine
hermits at San-Giorgio-in-Alga.   The next time he appeared
at the door of his mother's palace, it was in the garb of
a poor mendicant friar, who humbly begged an alms, *per i
poveri di Dio*.   His mother filled his wallet in silence, and
then retired to her chamber to pray, perhaps to weep—whether
tears of gratitude or grief, who can tell ?

He became distinguished in his retirement for his indefatigable care of the poor, his penances, and his mortifications
(which were, however, private), and was held in such general
esteem and veneration that he was created Bishop of Castello
by Pope Eugenius IV.   And a few years afterwards, on the
death of the Patriarch of Grado, the patriarchate was transferred to Venice, and Lorenzo was the first who bore that title.

The whole of his long life was spent in the quiet performance of his duties, and the most tender and anxious care for
the people committed to his charge.   He wore habitually his
coarse black gown, slept on straw, and devoted the revenues of
his diocese to charitable and religious purposes.   He died, amid

the prayers and tears of the whole city, in 1455. The people believed that the republic had been saved from plague, war, and famine, by his prayers and intercession, and did not wait for a papal decree to exalt him to the glories of a saint. They built a church in his honour, and placed his effigies on their altars, two hundred years before his canonisation, which took place in 1690 by a decree of Alexander VIII., who was a Venetian.

The portrait of San Lorenzo was painted during his life by Vittore Carpaccio, and is engraved in the great work of Litta. There is a fine half-length figure in marble over his tomb in San Petro di Castello. Both these represent him with the spare yet benign lineaments we should have given to him in fancy, and in the simple dress of a priest or canon. I do not know that he has any particular attribute. This characteristic sketch is from a contemporary picture by Gentil Bellini; and is singular, because he has the nimbus, and is attended (in the original) by angels bearing the crosier and mitre, although not canonised.

'Memorie delle Famiglio Italiane,' &c.

Venice. S. Maria dell' Orta.

41   St. Lorenzo Giustiniani.

Pictures of this amiable prelate abound in the churches of Venice and Palermo. The best I have seen was painted about the time that Clement VII. had declared him a Beato, and represents him standing in a niche on an elevated step; three canons of his order are looking up to him; St. John the Baptist, St. Augustine, and St. Francis, stand in front.

Pordenone, Venice Acad.

There is also a fine picture by Il Prete Genovese, in which San Lorenzo, during a famine, is distributing in charity the precious effects, plate, and vestments belonging to his church.

Venice. al Tolentini.

A.D. 1160,
Sept. 4.
St. Rosalia of Palermo, of whose festival we have such a
gorgeous description in Brydone's ' Sicily,' would be claimed
by the Augustines as belonging to their order of hermits ; for
which reason I place her here.

She was a Sicilian virgin, of noble birth, who, in her sixteenth year, rejected all offers of marriage, and withdrew
secretly to a cavern near the summit of Monte Pellegrino—
that rocky picturesque mountain which closes in the Bay of
Palermo on the west; and there she devoted herself to a
life of solitary sanctity, and there she died unknown to all.
But, when she had ascended into bliss, she became an intercessor before the eternal Throne for her beautiful native city,
which she twice saved from the ravages of the plague. Happily,
after a long interval, her sacred remains were discovered
lying in a grotto, uncorrupted—such virtue was in her
unsullied maiden purity !—and on her head a wreath of roses
from Paradise, placed there by the angels who had sung her
to rest.   Her name, inscribed by herself, was found on the
rock above.   She was thenceforth solemnly inaugurated as
the patroness of Palermo ; and in the year 1626, through the
credit of the Sicilian Jesuits, she was canonised by Pope
Urban VIII.

On the summit of Monte Pellegrino stands the colossal
statue of the virgin saint, looking to the east over the blue
Mediterranean, and seen from afar by the Sicilian mariner—
at once his auspicious beacon, and his celestial protectress.

Her grotto has become a church, and a place of pilgrimage,
and statues and pictures of her abound through the locality.
She is not usually represented in the religious habit, but in a
brown tunic, sometimes ragged ; her hair loose.   She is generally recumbent in her cavern, irradiated by a celestial light,
and pressing a crucifix to her bosom, while angels crown her
with roses.   Such a picture, by a late Sicilian painter,
Tyrone
House.
probably Novelli, I saw in Dublin, in the possession of Mr.
Alex. Macdonnell.   Sometimes she is standing, and in the
act of inscribing her name on the rocky wall of her cavern.

As a subject of painting, St. Rosalia is chiefly interesting
for the series of pictures painted by Vandyck, soon after her

canonisation, for the Jesuits' Church at Antwerp. One of these is now at Palermo: two are at Munich;—the Vision of St. Rosalia; and the saint ascending into heaven with a company of angels, one of whom crowns her with roses; a fourth, very grand and beautiful, represents St. Rosalia glorified and crowned with roses by the infant Saviour. We must be careful not to confound St. Rosalia with the Magdalen, or with St. Cecilia, or with St. Dorothea.

Spedale de' Sacerdotl. Eng. by Vorstermann. Vienna.

Eng. by P. Pontius.

Another Augustine saint whom we find occasionally in pictures is Clara di Monte-Falco, styled in her own country *Saint* Clara; but, as she was never regularly canonised, her proper title is the ' Beata Clara della Cruce di Monte-Falco.' This beautiful little city crowns the summit of a lofty hill, seen on the right as we travel through the Umbrian valleys from Foligno to Spoleto. Here she was born about the year 1268, and here she dwelt in seclusion, and shed over the whole district the perfume of her sanctity and the fame of her miracles and visions. She is represented in the dress of her Order, the black tunic fastened by a leathern girdle, black veil, and white wimple, which distinguishes her from her great namesake, the Abbess St. Clara of Assisi. This Beata Clara is met with in the Augustine churches. There is a picture of her in the Santo Spirito at Florence.

Of the various communities which emanated directly from the Augustine Order, properly so called, the earliest which has any interest in connection with art is one with a very long name—the PREMONSTRATENSIANS.

St. Norbert, Founder.

Ital. San Norberto, Fondatore de' Premostratesi. *Ger.* Stifter der Prä-
monstratenser-Orden. May 6, 1134.

St. Norbert, whose effigy occurs frequently in French and
Flemish Art, was a celebrated preacher and religious reformer
in the eleventh century. He was born at Cologne; he was a
kinsman of the Emperor Henry IV.; and though early intended for the ecclesiastical profession, in which the highest
dignities awaited his acceptance, he for several years led a
dissolute life in the Imperial court.

One day, as he was riding in pursuit of his pleasures, he was
overtaken by a sudden and furious tempest; and as he looked
about for shelter, there fell from heaven a ball of fire, which
exploded at his horse's feet, burned up the grass, and sank deep
in the earth. On recovering his senses, he was struck with
dismay when he reflected what might have been his fate in the
other world had he perished in his wickedness. He forsook his
evil ways, and began to prepare himself seriously for the life of a
priest and a missionary. He sold all his possessions, bestowed
the money on the poor, reserving to himself only ten marks of
silver, and a mule to carry the sacred vestments and utensils for
the altar; and then, clothed in a lambskin, with a hempen cord
round his loins, he set out to preach repentance and a new life.

After preaching for several years through the northern provinces of France, Hainault, Brabant, and Liège, he assembled
around him those whose hearts had been touched by his eloquence, and who were resolved to adopt his austere discipline.
Seeing the salvation of so many committed to his care, he
humbly prayed for the Divine direction; and thereupon the
blessed Virgin appeared to him in a vision, and pointed out to
him a barren and lonesome spot in the valley of Coucy, thence
called *Pré-montré*. Hence the name adopted by his community, ' the Premonstratensians.' The Virgin likewise dictated the fashion and colour of the habit they were to adopt;
it was a coarse black tunic, and over it a white woollen cloak,
in imitation of the angels of heaven, 'who are clothed in white

*Pratum
Mon-
stratum.*

The Charity of St. Thomas de Villanova.

are thoroughly German, and I suppose it was painted before
Bernard v. Orlay had studied in the school of Raphael.

'St. Norbert in a vision receiving the habit of his Order from
the hand of the Virgin,' was painted by Niccolo Poussin.

Two pictures from his life are in the Brussels Gallery. 1.
He consecrates two deacons. 2. He dies, surrounded by his
brotherhood, in the act of benediction. The pictures are not
very good.

I know but one other saint of this Order, who has found a
place in the history of Art, and his legend is very graceful.

A.D. 1236,
April 7. St. Herman was the son of very poor parents, dwelling in
the city of Cologne. His mother brought him up piously,
giving him the best instructions she could afford. Every day,
as he repaired to school, he went into the Church of St. Mary,
and, kneeling before the image of Our Lady, said his simple
prayer with a right lowly and loving and trusting heart. One
day he had an apple in his hand, which was all he had for his
dinner, and, after he had finished his prayer, he humbly offered
his apple in childish love and faith to the holy image, 'which
thing,' says the legend, 'pleased our Blessed Lady, and she
stretched forth her hand and took the apple and gave it to our
Lord Jesus, who sat upon her knee; and both smiled upon
Herman.' The young enthusiast took the habit of the Premonstratensians, and edified his monastery by his piety, his
austerities, and his wonderful visions. He had an ecstatic
dream, in which the Virgin descended from heaven, and
putting a ring upon his finger, declared him her espoused.
Hence he received from the brotherhood the name of Joseph.
He died in 1236.

Vienna Gal. The vision of St. Herman-Joseph has been represented by
Vandyck. He kneels, wearing the white cloak over the black
tunic, and is presented by an angel to the Virgin, who touches
his hand. The pretty legend of the child offering the apple I
do not remember to have seen.

THE SERVI, OR SERVITI.

EVERY one who has been at Florence must remember the Church of the ' Annunziata ; ' every one who remembers that glorious church, who has lingered in the cloisters and the *Cortile*, where Andrea del Sarto put forth all his power— where the *Madonna del Sacco* and the *Birth of the Virgin* attest what he could *do* and *be* as a painter,—will feel interested in the Order of the SERVI. Among the extraordinary outbreaks of religious enthusiasm in the thirteenth century, this was in its origin one of the most singular.

Seven Florentines, rich, noble, and in the prime of life, whom a similarity of taste and feeling had drawn together, used to meet every day in a chapel dedicated to the Annunciation of the Blessed Virgin (*then* outside the walls of Florence), there to sing the *Ave* or evening service in honour of the Madonna, for whom they had an especial love and veneration. They became known and remarked in their neighbourhood for these acts of piety, so that the women and children used to point at them as they passed through the streets and exclaim, ' *Guardate i Servi di Maria!* ' (Behold the *servants* of the Virgin!) Hence the title afterwards assumed by the Order.

The passionate devotion of these seven enthusiasts was increased by their mutal sympathy and emulation, till at length they resolved to forsake the world altogether, and distributing their money to the poor, after selling their possessions, they retired to Monte Senario, a solitary mountain about six miles from Florence. Here they built for themselves little huts, of stones and boughs, and devoted themselves to the perpetual service of the Virgin. At first they wore a plain white tunic, in honour of the immaculate purity of their protectress; it was then the favourite religious garb; but one of the brotherhood was honoured with a vision, in which the holy Virgin herself commanded them to change their white tunic for a black one, ' in memory of her maternal sorrow and the death of her Divine Son : ' the habit was thenceforward black.

These seven *Santi Fondatori dei Servi* were Buonfiglioli ᴬ·ᴰ· 1239.

Monaldi, Giovanni Manetti, Benedetto Antellesi, Gherardo
Sostegni, Amadio, Ricovero Lippi, and Alessio Falconieri.
They were all allied to the noblest families of Florence, and,
as their Order grew in fame and sanctity, their native city be-
came proud of them. I remember in the private chapel of the
Casa Buonarotti (still the residence of the representative of
Michael Angelo) a series of lunettes, in which all the renowned
Florentine saints are seen as walking in procession, led by
John the Baptist and Santa Reparata, the patron saints of the
city. The *Padri Serviti*, in their black habits, form part of
this religious company. At their head walks St. PHILIP BEN-
OZZI, the chief saint of the Order, who has been called the
founder, but it existed fifteen years before he joined it in 1247.

San Filippo
Beniti, or
Benizzi.
August 23,
1285.

Filippo Benozzi began life as a physician. In general, I
think, the study of medicine and surgery does not prepare the
mind for intense devotional aspirations; yet I have heard of
young men studying for the medical profession, who, after
going through a probation in the hospitals, unable to bear the
perpetual sight of bodily suffering, and yet subdued at once
and elevated by such spectacles, have turned to the Church,
and become 'healers of the sick' in another sense.

Such a one was Filippo Benozzi. After studying at Paris
and at Padua, then, and down to recent times, the best schools
of medicine in Europe, he returned to Florence, with the title
of Doctor, and prepared to practise his art. He had a tender and a thoughtful character; the sight of physical evil
oppressed him,—he became dissatisfied with himself and the
world. One day, as he attended mass in the Chapel of the

Acts viii. 29.

Annunziata, he was startled by the words in the epistle of the
day, ' Draw near and join thyself to the chariot.' And going
home full of meditation, he threw himself on his bed. In his
dreams he beheld the Virgin seated in a chariot; she called
to him to draw near, and to join her *servants*. He obeyed
the vision, and retired to Monte Senario, where such was his
modesty and humility, that the brethren did not for a long
time discover his talents; and great was their astonishment
when they found they had among them a wise and learned
Doctor of the University of Padua! He soon became dis-

tinguished as a preacher, and yet more as a reconciller of differences, having set himself to allay the deadly hereditary factions which, at that time, distracted all the cities of Tuscany. He prevailed on the Pope, Alexander IV., to confirm the rule of the Order, preached through the chief provinces of Italy, and at Avignon, Toulouse, Lyons, Paris, gaining everywhere converts to his peculiar adoration for the Virgin, and at length died General of his Order in 1285.

His memory has from that time been held in great veneration by his own community; but it was not till 1516 that Leo X. (himself a Florentine) allowed his festival to be celebrated as a *Beato*. This was a great privilege, which the Serviti had long been desirous to obtain, and it led to the formal canonisation of their saint in 1671. It was on the occasion of his Beatification under Leo X., or soon after, that Andrea del Sarto was called to decorate the cloisters of the Annunziata. Florence. Vasari gives a most amusing account of the contrivances of the sacristan of the convent (a certain Fra Mariano) to get the work done as well and as cheaply as possible. He stimulated the vanity of rival artists; he pointed out the advantage of having their works exhibited in a locality to which such numbers of the devout daily resorted; he would not hold out the hope of large pay, but he promised abundance of prayers; and he dwelt on the favour which their performances would, no doubt, obtain from the Blessed Virgin herself, to whose especial honour, and that of her newly exalted votary, they were to be consecrated. He obtained not *all*, but in great part what he desired. Andrea painted on one side of the Cortile two scenes from the life of the Madonna,—the birth of the Virgin, and the adoration of the Magi; and on the other side the life of San Filippo Benozzi. Of the first I will not say anything at present; every figure in those sublime groups is familiar to the student and the lover of Art. Baldovinetti painted on the same side the birth of our Saviour; and Franciabigio his chef-d'œuvre, the Marriage of the Virgin. Of the six frescoes from the life of San Filippo, Cosimo Roselli painted the first, where he takes the habit of the Serviti. The five others are by Andrea. 2. S. Filippo, on his way to the court of the Pope at Viterbo, gives his only shirt to a poor leper. 3. Some gamblers and profligate young men mocked at the devotion of the saint, and pursued him with gibes and insults as he ascended, with three of his brotherhood, the Monte Senario. A storm came on: the brethren drew their cowls over their heads, and quietly pursued their way; the scoffers ran for shelter to a tree, and were killed by the lightning. This is one of the best of the series, admirable for the fine landscape and dramatic felicity with which the story is told. 4. San Filippo heals a possessed woman. 5. The death of the saint, also very beautiful. 6. Miracles performed by his relics after his death: his habit is placed on the head of a sick child, who is immediately healed. The fine figure of the old man in red drapery, leaning on his stick, is the portrait of Andrea della Robbia, one of the family of famous sculptors.

In the cloisters, over the door which leads into the church, Andrea del Sarto painted the *Riposo*, so celebrated as the 'Madonna del Sacco.' And, on the walls, Bernardino Pocetti, Mascagni, and Salimbeni, clever mannerists of the sixteenth century, painted a series of subjects from the lives of the original founders of the Order, of which the best (by Pocetti) represents the recovery of a child drowned in the Arno, by the prayers of Amadio. This fresco is celebrated under the name of the *Anegato*, or *Affogato*, 'The Drowned Boy.' On the whole, the black robes of the personages give to these frescoes a spotty and disagreeable effect, and they are not in any respect first rate: yet they are interesting when considered in reference to their locality and the history of the origin of the Order. Out of Florence, St. Philip Benozzi and his companions are not conspicuous as subjects of Art, though the Order became popular and widely extended. In 1484 the Serviti were added to the Mendicant Orders, and from that time are styled *Frati*. Father Paul Sarpi, the Venetian, so famous in the political and literary history of Italy, was of this Order, and would be properly styled *Fra Paolo*.

THE TRINITARIANS.

The Order of the Most Holy Trinity, for the Redemption of Captives.

OF the many communities, male and female, which emanated from the Augustine Rule, the most interesting are those which were founded for purposes of mercy and charity, rather than for self-sanctification through penance and seclusion. These have, however, afforded comparatively but few subjects, either in painting or sculpture.

Among the suffering classes of our Christendom, from the tenth to the fifteenth century, none were more pitiable than the slaves and prisoners. The wars of that period had a peculiar character of ferocity, enhanced by the spirit of religious hatred: prisoners on both sides were most inhumanly treated. The nobles and leaders were usually ransomed, often at the price of all their worldly goods; the poorer classes, and frequently women and children, carried off from the maritime cities and villages, languished and toiled in a hopeless slavery, 'captives in the land of their enemies.'

ST. JOHN DE MATHA was born at Faucon in Provence, in 1154, of noble parents. As usual, we find that his mother, whose name was Martha, had educated him in habits of piety, and consecrated him early to the service of God. St. John de Matha, Feb. 8, 1213.

He, being a student in the University of Paris, became famous there for his learning and holiness of life;—and, being ordained priest, at his first celebration of divine service he beheld a vision of an angel clothed in white, having a cross of red and blue on his breast, and his hands, crossed over each other, rested on the heads of two slaves, who knelt on each side of him. And believing that in this vision of the mind God spoke to him, and called him to the deliverance of prisoners and captives, he immediately sold all his goods, and forsook the world, to prepare himself for his mission. 'He retired to a desert place, where, at the foot of a little hill, was a fair, clear, and cold fountain, to which a white hart did daily resort for refreshment, whence it was called in Latin *Cervus frigidus*, and in French *Cerfroy*; and here, with another holy and benevolent man, named Felix de Valois, the two together arranged the institution of a new Order for the Redemption of Slaves, and travelled to Rome to obtain the approbation of the Pope.'

When they came to Rome they were courteously received by Pope Innocent III., who having been favoured with the like vision of an angel clothed in white with two captives chained (and on this occasion one captive was a Christian, and the other a Moor, showing that in this charitable foundation there was to be no distinction of colour or religion), 'his Holiness did forthwith ratify the Order, and, by his command, they assumed the white habit, having on the breast a Greek cross of red and blue; the three colours signifying the Three Persons of the Most Holy Trinity: the white, the Father Eternal: the blue, which was the traverse of the cross, the Son as Redeemer; and the red, the charity of the Holy Spirit: and he appointed that the Brotherhood should be called The Order of the Holy Trinity, for the Redemption of Captives.'

This being settled, John de Matha and Felix de Valois—the Clarkson and Wilberforce of their time—returned to France, and they preached the redemption of captives through the whole country, collecting a number of followers who devoted themselves to the same cause. They were then called *Mathurins*, and the name survives in a street of Paris, near which was one of their first establishments, but the parent monastery was that of Cefroy. The Pope also gave them, at Rome, the church and convent since called S. Maria della Navicella, on the Monte Celio, well known to those who have been at Rome, for its solitary and beautiful situation, and for the antique bark which stands in front of it, and from which it derives its name.

Having collected a large sum from the charitable, John sent two of his brotherhood to the coast of Africa, to negotiate for an exchange of prisoners, and for the redemption of slaves. They returned with 186 redeemed Christians. The next year John went himself to Spain, preaching everywhere the cause of captives and slaves; then passing over to Tunis, he returned with 110 redeemed captives. On a third voyage, in which he had ransomed 120 slaves, the infidels, furious at seeing him depart, cut up the sails of the ship into fragments, and broke away the rudder. The mariners were in despair at being thus abandoned to the winds and waves. But John, trusting in his good cause, replaced the torn sails with his mantle and those of his brotherhood; and, throwing himself on his knees, prayed that God himself would be their pilot. And behold it was so; for gentle winds wafted them into the port of Ostia. But the health of John de Matha was so completely broken, that he found himself unable to proceed to France, and the last two years of his life were spent at Rome, where, in the intervals of a lingering malady, he passed his time in visiting the prisons and preaching to the poor. And thus he died in the exercise of those charities to which, from early youth, he had devoted himself.

St. John de Matha is represented in a white habit, with a blue and red cross upon his breast, fetters in his hand or at his feet, and, in general, the vision of the angel with the two captives is placed in the background. The peculiar cross and white habit distinguish him from St. Leonard, whose beautiful legend has been already related. *Sacred and Legend. Art, ii. 396.*

Mr. Stirling mentions a picture representing the Virgin giving San Juan de Mata a purse of money for the redemption of captives, painted by a certain Fray Bartolomé, who belonged to the Order; and his effigy is common in the old French prints. *Artists of Spain, p. 1224.*

His companion, St. Felix de Valois, wears the habit of an Augustine hermit, and is represented sitting in a contemplative attitude by the side of a fountain, at which a stag or hind is drinking. There is a series of ten pictures, by Gomez, representing the lives of these two companion saints ; but the subjects are not mentioned.

I remember a singular mosaic of a circular form, executed by Giovanni Cosmata about 1300, and certainly for this Order. It represents Christ enthroned, and loosing the fetters of two slaves who kneel on each side. One of these slaves is white, and the other is a negro. I have lost my note of the church in which this mosaic exists, but it is probably to be found in S. Maria della Navicella. *Rome.*

St. Rade-
gunda
August 13,
587.

A.D. 564.

The first founders of the Trinitarians placed themselves especially under the protection of St. Radegunda, whose effigy is often to be found in the houses of the Order, and in connection with the legend of Juan de Matha. The story relates that Radegunda was the daughter of Berthaire, king of Thuringia, and that in her childhood she was carried away into captivity with all her family by Clothaire V., king of France, who afterwards married her. 'And this queen was a virtuous lady, much devoted to prayer and alms-deeds, often fasting, and chastening herself with hair-cloth, which she wore under her royal apparel. And one day, as she walked alone in the gardens of her palace, she heard the voices of prisoners on the other side of the wall, weeping in their fetters, and imploring pity; and remembering her early sorrows, she also wept. And, not knowing how to aid them otherwise, she betook herself to prayer, whereupon their fetters burst asunder, and they were loosed from captivity. And this Queen Radegunda afterwards took the religious habit at the hands of St. Médard, bishop of Noyon, founded a monastery for nuns at Poitiers, and lived in great sanctity, ministering to the poor.' She is represented with the royal crown, under which flows a long veil; she has a captive kneeling at her feet, and holding his broken fetters in his hand.

Dugdale.

When the Order of the Trinitarians was introduced into England by Sir William Lucy of Charlecote, on his return from the Crusade, he built and endowed for them Thellesford Priory in Warwickshire, 'and dedicated it to the honour of God, St. John the Baptist, and St. Radegunda.'

THE ORDER OF OUR LADY OF MERCY.

St. Peter
Nolasco.
Jan. 13, 1258.

AMONG the converts of St. John Matha, when he preached the deliverance of captives in Languedoc, was the son of a nobleman of that country, whose name was Peter Nolasque, or Nolasco. In his youth he had served in the Crusade against the Albi-

genses, and afterwards became the tutor or governor of the
young king, James of Aragon.   Struck with the miseries of Don Jayme, el Conquistador.
war, which he had witnessed at an early age, and by the fate
of the Christians who were kept in captivity by the Moors, he
founded, in imitation of San Juan Mata, a
community for the redemption of slaves
and captives, and prisoners for debt, to
which he gave the name of 'The Order of
Our Lady of Mercy.'   This foundation was
at first military and chivalrous, and consisted of knights and gentlemen, with
only a few religious to serve in the choir.
The king, Jayme el Conquistador, not only
placed himself at their head, but gave them

42 Badge of the Order
of Mercy.

as a perpetual badge his own arms.   From Barcelona the
Order extended far and wide, and Peter Nolasco was the first
General or Superior.   From this time his long life was spent
in expeditions to the various provinces of Spain, then under
the dominion of the Moors ; to Majorca, and to the coast of
Barbary, whence he returned with many hundreds of redeemed
slaves.   He died in 1258.

The Fathers of the Order of Mercy, which had lost its military character, and become strictly religious, obtained the
canonisation of their founder in 1628.   The Spanish painters
thereupon set themselves to glorify their new saint ; and the
convents of the Order of Mercy, particularly *La Merced* at
Seville, were filled with pictures in his honour.

St. Peter Nolasco is represented as an aged man wearing
the white habit, and on his breast the shield or arms of King
James, the badge of the Order : this distinguishes him from
all monks wearing the white habit.   Zurbaran painted a great
number of pictures from his life.   Two of the best of these are
in the Museum at Madrid :—1. St. Peter Nolasco beholds in a
vision his patron, St. Peter the Apostle, who appears to him
on a cross with his head downwards.   2. An angel shows him
in a vision the city of Jerusalem : the angel is vulgar, the
kneeling saint very fine.   Several other pictures belonging to
the same series, and obtained apparently from the same con-

vent (La Merced at Seville), were in the Soult Gallery, and others were among the Spanish pictures collected by King Louis Philippe, and formerly in the Louvre.

Connected with this Order, and often associated with St. Peter Nolasco, is another Saint, Raymond Nonnatus, called by the Spaniards San Ramon, who died in 1240, just after being created a cardinal by Gregory IX. In consequence of the peculiar circumstances attending his birth, he obtained the surname of *Nonnatus*, and is in Spain the patron saint of midwives and women in travail. Mr. Stirling mentions a picture of San Ramon, in which he is represented as having his lips bored through with a red-hot iron, and a padlock placed on his mouth; according to the legend, this was the barbarous punishment inflicted on him while, in his vocation as a Friar of Mercy, he was redeeming Christian captives among the Moors. Several interesting pictures in the Soult Gallery relate to this saint, and not to St. Raymond de Peña-forte, who was quite a different person, and belonged to the Dominican Order.[1] One of these pictures (in the Soult Catalogue, No. 22) represents a chapter of the Order of Mercy held at Barcelona, in which St. Raymond Nonnatus, habited as Cardinal, presides, and St. Peter Nolasco is seated among the brethren. Another (No. 24 in the same Catalogue) represents the funeral obsequies of St. Raymond: he is extended on a bier, wearing the mitre as general and grand vicar of the Order, with the cardinal's hat lying at his feet. The Pope and the King who assist at the ceremony are Gregory IX. and St. James of Aragon. Both these pictures formed part of the series painted by Zurbaran for the *Merced* at Seville. Another, which was in the Spanish Gallery of the Louvre, represents St. Raymond wearing the white habit and badge of the Order, and the mitre as grand-vicar. In the Catalogue it is called, by some extraordinary mistake, *San Carmelo*.

In the legend of St. Peter Nolasco it is related, that when he was old and infirm, two angels bore him in their arms to the foot of the altar in order to receive the sacrament, and then carried him back to his cell. This is one of the com-

---

[1] The history of St. Raymond de Peñaforte is given further on.

43   St. Peter Nolasco. (Claude de Mellan.)

monest subjects from the life of St. Peter Nolasco, and it
admits of great beauty in the treatment. There were two or
three specimens in the Standish Gallery in the Louvre.[1]   This
sketch is from the masterpiece of Claude Mellan, a famous
French engraver. The print was published in 1628, in the
year in which St. Peter was canonised.

San Pedro Nolasco finding the choir of his convent occupied   Cathedral
by the Virgin and a company of angels (in a fine picture by   Granada.

---

[1] Since the year 1848, the pictures composing the Standish Gallery and the
Spanish Gallery of the Louvre, all the private property of King Louis Philippe,
have been packed up, and their present destination is unknown to me. The Soult
Gallery was sold and dispersed on the 19th May 1852.

Boccanegra), and San Pedro Nolasco correcting the novices of his Order (by Salcedo), are mentioned by Mr. Stirling.[1]

A favourite subject in these convents is Our Lady of Mercy, *Nuestra Senora de la Merced.* She is represented standing, crowned with stars, and wearing on her breast the badge of the Order, which she likewise holds in her hand. The attendant angels bear the olive, the palm, and broken fetters, in sign of peace, victory, and deliverance.

THE BRIGITTINES.

or Birgitta.

Wulpho
Fulco. or
Foulques.

Oct. 8.

THE last of these branches of the Augustine Order which it is necessary to mention in connection with Art is that of the Brigittines, founded by St. Bridget of Sweden, whom we must be careful not to confound with St. Bridget the primitive saint of Ireland. This St. Bridget was of the royal blood of Sweden; at the age of sixteen she married Ulpho, Prince of Norica in Sweden, and was the mother of eight children. She was singularly devout, and inspired her husband and children with the same sentiments. After the death of her husband she retired from the world; and she built and endowed, at a great expense, the monastery of Wastein, in which she placed sixty nuns and twenty-four brothers, figuring the twelve apostles and seventy-two disciples of Christ. She prescribed to them the Rule of St. Augustine, with certain particular constitutions which are said to have been dictated to her by our Saviour in a vision. The Order was approved in 1363 by Urban V., under the title of the Rule of the Order of our Saviour. But the nuns always bore the name of the Brigittines. She was said to have been favoured by many revelations, which were afterwards published. She died in the odour of sanctity in 1373, was canonised by Boniface IX. in 1391, and has since been regarded as one of the patron saints of Sweden.

[1] The first of these pictures must represent, I think, St. Felix de Valois, of whom, and not of St. Peter Nolasco, the vision is recorded.

She is represented of mature age in the dress of a nun, wearing the black tunic, white wimple, and white veil, which has a red band from the back to the front, and across the forehead; this distinguishes the habit from that of the Benedictines. She has the crosier, as first abbess of the Order, and sometimes the pilgrim's staff and wallet, to express her various pilgrimages to Compostella and to Rome. The earliest representation I have seen of this saint is a curious old woodcut in possession of Lord Spencer, of which there is an imitation in Otley's History of Engraving. It represents her writing her revelations. As her disciples considered her inspired, the holy Dove is generally introduced into the devotional representations of this saint. In the Church of the Hospital of St. John at Florence, there is a fine picture of ' Santa Brigitta giving the Rule to her nuns,' by Fra Bartolomeo. In the Berlin Gallery are two curious pictures representing this saint at a writing-table, and one of her visions;—called there by mistake St. Catherine of Siena.

No. 1105.
Lorenzo di
Pieto.

One of the daughters of St. Bridget distinguished for her extreme piety, became Superior of the community after the death of her mother, and was canonised under the name of St. Catherine of Sweden.

The Order of the Brigittines was introduced into England by Henry V., and had a glorious nunnery, Sion House, near Brentford, which, at the Reformation, was bestowed on the Duke of Northumberland, and still continues in possession of his descendants. The nuns, driven from their sacred precincts, fled to Lisbon, where they found protection and relief; and their Order still exists there, but in great poverty. Some of the beautiful relics and vestments which they had carried away from Sion, and religiously preserved in all their wanderings, are now in the possession of the Earl of Shrewsbury.[1]

In the Madrid Gallery there is a most beautiful picture by Giorgione, representing a lovely female saint offering a basket of roses to the Madonna, and behind her a warrior saint with

---

[1] Among these, a cope of wonderful beauty, embroidered all over with scriptural subjects worked in silk and gold, was in the collection of ' Works of Mediæval Art,' exhibited in the Adelphi (April 1850).

his standard. This is called in the Madrid catalogue, by some strange mistake, *St. Bridget and her husband Fulco.* There can be no doubt that it represents two saints very popular at Venice, and often occurring together in the Venetian pictures of that time, St. Dorothea and St. George, with their usual attributes.

To the Augustines belong the two great Military Orders, the Knights Templars (1118) and the Knights of St. John of Jerusalem, afterwards styled of Malta (1092). The first wear the red cross on the white mantle ; the second, the white cross on the black mantle. They may thus be recognised in portraits; but in connection with sacred Art I have nothing to record of them here.

The Mendicant Orders.

THE FRANCISCANS. THE DOMINICANS. THE CARMELITES.

THE three great Mendicant Orders arose almost simultaneously in the beginning of the thirteenth century.

The Carmelites, as we shall see, claim for themselves a very high antiquity : and for their founder, no other than the prophet Elijah himself. These claims the Roman Church has not allowed; neither do we find the Carmelites, at any time, an influential Order; nor are they conspicuous in early Art; and in modern Art they are interesting for one saint only, the Spanish St. Theresa. On the other hand, the Franciscans and Dominicans are so important and so interesting in every respect, so intimately connected with the revival of the Fine Arts and their subsequent progress, and so generally associated and contrasted in the imagination, that I shall give them the precedence here ; and I shall say a few words of them in their relation to each other before I consider them separately.

In the Introduction, and in the preceding chapters, I have touched upon that wonderful religious movement which, in the thirteenth century, threw men's minds into a state of fusion. I have described some of its results. Without doubt, the most important, the most memorable of all, was the portentous twin-birth of the two great mendicant communities of St. Francis and St. Dominick. Their founders were two men of different nations—differing yet more in nature, in temperament and character,—who, without any previous mutual understanding, had each conceived the idea of uniting men under a new religious discipline, and for purposes yet unthought of.

In the year 1216, Dominick the Spaniard, and Francis of Assisi, met at Rome. They met and embraced,—each re-

cognising in the other the companion predestined to aid the
Church in her conflict with the awakening mental energies, so
long repressed; and in her attempt to guide or crush the
aspiring, inquiring, ardent, fevered spirits of the time.   Some
attempts were made to induce them to unite into one great
body their separate institutions.   Dominick would have com-
plied : it may be that he thought to find in Francis an instrument as well as an ally.   Francis, perhaps from an intuitive
perception of the unyielding, dogmatic character of his friend,
stood aloft.   They received from Innocent III. the confirmation
of their respective communities, ' and parted,' as it has been
well expressed, ' to divide the world between them.'   For,
before the end of the century,—nay, in the time of one generation,—their followers had spread themselves in thousands,
and tens of thousands, over the whole of Christian Europe,
and sent forth their missionaries through every region of the
then known world.

Both had adopted, as their fundamental rule, that of St
Augustine ; and hence it is that we meet with pictures of the
Franciscans and Dominicans in the churches of the Augustines :
whereas I do not remember meeting with pictures of the Mendicant Orders in any of the Benedictine houses and churches ;
such must, therefore, be rare, if they occur at all.

In fact, from the beginning, the monks had been opposed
to the friars, as, in earlier times, the secular clergy had been
opposed to the monks.

The monastic discipline had hitherto been considered as
exacting, in the first place, seclusion from the world; and
secondly, as excluding all sympathy with worldly affairs.   This,
at least, though often departed from in individual cases, was
the fundamental rule of all the *stricter* Benedictine communities, who, as it seems to me, wherever their influence had
worked for good, had achieved that good by gathering the
people to them,—not by lowering themselves to the people.
They were aristocratic, rather than popular communities.

The Franciscans and Dominicans were to have a different
destination.   They were the spiritual democrats ; they were to
mingle *with* the people, yet without being *of* the people : they

were to take cognisance of all private and public affairs; of all those domestic concerns and affections, cares and pleasures, from which their vows personally cut them off.   They were to possess *nothing* they could call their own, either as a body or individually; they were to beg from their fellow-Christians food and raiment:—such, at least, was the original rule, though this article was speedily modified.   Their vocation was to look after the stray sheep of the fold of Christ; to pray with those who prayed; to weep with those who wept; to preach, to exhort, to rebuke, to advise, to comfort, without distinction of place or person.   The privilege of ministering in the offices of religion was not theirs at first, but was afterwards conceded. They were not to be called *Padri*, fathers, but *Frati, Suori,* brothers and sisters of all men : and as the Dominicans had taken the title of *Frati Predicatori,* preaching brothers; so Francis, in his humility, had styled his community *Frati Minori, Frères Mineurs,* Minorites, or lesser brothers.   In England, from the colour of their habits, they were distinguished as the *Black-Friars* and the *Grey-Friars,* names which they have bequeathed to certain districts in London, and which are familiar to us at this day: but it does not appear that the Mendicant Orders ever possessed, in England, the wealth, the power, or the popularity of the Benedictines.

One important innovation on the rules and customs of all existing religious communities was common to the Franciscans and Dominicans; and while it extended their influence, and consolidated their power, it was of incalculable service to the progress of civilisation and morals,—consequently to the cause of Christianity.   This was the admission into both communities of a third class of members (besides the professed friars and nuns), called the Tertiary Order, or Third Order of Penitence. It included both sexes, and all ranks of life; the members were not bound by vows, nor were they required to quit their secular occupations and domestic duties, though they entered into an obligation to renounce secular pleasures and vanities, to make restitution where they had done wrong, to be true and just in all their dealings, to be charitable to the extent of their

means, and never to take up weapon except against the enemies
of Christ. Could such a brotherhood have been rendered
universal, and could Christians have agreed on the question,
' whom, among men, Christ himself would have considered as
his enemies ? ' we should have had a heaven upon earth, or at
least the Apostolic institutions restored to us ; but, with every
drawback caused by superstition and ignorance, by fierce, cruel
and warlike habits, this institution, diffused as it was through
every nation of Europe, did more to elevate the moral standard
among the laity, more to Christianise the people, than any
other that existed before the invention of printing. It is
necessary to keep this ' Third Order ' in mind, to enable us to
understand some of the stories and pictures which will be
noticed hereafter ; those, for instance, which relate to St. Ives
and St. Catherine of Siena.

The distinction between the Franciscans and Dominicans
lay not in essentials, but merely in points of discipline, and
difference of dress.

In pictures the obvious, and, at first sight, the only apparent
distinction between the two Orders is the habit ; we should
therefore be able, at a glance, to tell a Franciscan from a
Dominican by its form and colour. This is so essential a
preliminary that I shall here describe the proper costume of
each, that the contrast may be impressed on the memory.

The habit of the Franciscans was originally grey, and it is
grey in all the ancient pictures. After the first two centuries
the colour was changed to a dark brown. It consists of a
plain tunic with long loose sleeves,—less ample, however, than
those of the Benedictines. The tunic is fastened round the
waist with a knotted cord. This cord represents symbolically
the halter or bridle of a subdued beast, for such it pleased
Francis to consider the body in its subjection to the spirit.
A cape, rather scanty in form, hangs over the shoulders, and
to the back of the cape is affixed a hood, drawn over the head
in cold or inclement weather.

The Franciscan nuns wear the same dress, only instead of a
hood they have a black veil.

The habit of the Dominicans is a white woollen gown, fastened round the waist with a white girdle: over this a white scapular (a piece of cloth hanging down from the neck to the feet, like a long apron before and behind): over these a black cloak with a hood. The lay brothers wear a black scapular.

The Dominican nuns have the same dress, with a white veil.

The members of the Third Order of St. Francis are distinguished by the cord worn as a girdle. Those of the Third Order of St. Dominick have the black mantle or the black scapular over a white gown; the women, a black cloak and a white veil.

The Dominicans are always shod. The Franciscans are generally barefoot, or wear a sort of wooden sandal, called in Italy a *zoccolo;* hence the name of *Zoccolanti,* sometimes given in Italy to the Franciscan friars.

The dress, therefore, forms the obvious and external distinction between the two Orders. But, in considering them in their connection with Art, it will be interesting to trace another and a far deeper source of contrast. As the two communities have preserved, through their whole existence of six hundred years and more, something of that character originally impressed by their founders, so in pictures, and in all the forms of Art, we feel this distinctive character as sensibly as we should the countenance and bearing of two individuals. I mean, of course, in genuine Art, not in factitious Art—Art as the interpreter, not the imitator.

Two celebrated passages in Dante give us the key to this distinct character, rendered by the great painters as truly as by the great poet. Paradiso, c. xi.

Dominick was a man of letters; a schoolman, completely armed with all the weapons of theology; eloquent by nature; sincere, as we cannot doubt; in earnest in all his convictions; but, as Dante portrays him, *Benigno ai suoi ed ai nemici crudo:* c. xii.

> The holy wrestler, gentle to his own,
> And to his enemies terrible.

In other words, unscrupulous, inaccessible to pity, and 'wise as the serpent,' in carrying out his religious views and purposes.

Francis, on the contrary, was a wild and yet gentle enthusiast, who fled from the world to espouse the 'Lady Poverty;' a man ignorant and unlettered, but of a poetical nature, passionate in all its sympathies;—in Dante's words, *Tutto serafico in ardore.* ' The one like the cherub in wisdom, the other like the seraph in fervour.' The first would accept nothing from the Church but permission to combat her enemies; the latter, nothing but the privilege of suffering in her cause. And the character of the combatant and penitent, of the *active* and the *contemplative* religious life, remained generally and externally impressed on the two communities, even when both had fallen away from their primitive austerity of discipline.

The Dominicans, as a body, were the most learned and the most energetic. We find them constantly arrayed on the side of power. They remained more compact, and never broke up into separate reformed communities, as was the case afterwards with the Franciscans. Their greatest canonised saints were men who had raised themselves to eminence by learning, by eloquence, by vigorous intellect or resolute action.

The Franciscans aspired to a greater degree of sanctity and humility, and a more absolute self-abnegation. They were most loved by the people. They were among the Catholics of the thirteenth century what the Methodists of the last century were with us. Their most famous saints were such as had descended from worldly power and worldly eminence, to take refuge in their profession of lowly poverty and their abject self-immolation, rendered attractive to the high-born and high-bred by the very force of contrast. The Franciscans boast of several princely saints; which is not, I believe, the case with the Dominicans. The latter have, however, one canonised martyr in their ranks—their famous St. Peter—more glorious in their own estimation than all the Franciscan royalties together; but on this point, as we shall see, opinions differ. He was certainly the incarnate spirit of the Order.

I have taken here the picturesque and poetical aspect of the
two Orders, which, of course, is that which we are to seek for
in sacred Art, where a fat jovial Franciscan would be a
solecism: a gross, arrogant, self-seeking Dominican, not less
so. As the painters employed by each generally took their
models from the convents in which, and for which, they worked,
we may read no unmeaning commentary on the progressive
history of the two communities in the pale, spiritual, thoughtful, heavenward look of the friars in the early pictures; and
the commonplace and often basely vulgar heads which are so
hatefully characteristic of the degenerate friarhood in some of
the later pictures, and more particularly in the second-rate
Spanish and Bolognese schools.

Very interesting and very significant to the thoughtful
observer are those pictures which represent in companionship
the chief saints of the two Orders: as where St. Francis and

44   St. Dominick and St. Francis.
          (From a picture formerly in the Spanish Gallery of the Louvre.)
                              H H

St. Dominick are embracing each other; or stand on each side
of the throne of the Virgin; or are jointly trampling on the
world and sustaining the Church and the cross between them,
as in this little sketch from a Spanish picture.

And we can sometimes tell at a glance for which of the two
Orders the picture was painted, by observing the degree of
relative importance and dignity given to the figures. As, for
instance, in a picture where St. Dominick stands pointing to
the Virgin, while St. Francis and St. Clara are kneeling;
painted, of course, for the Dominicans. Or where St. Francis
receives his awful seraphic vision, while St. Dominick is
standing by; painted, of course, for the Franciscans. And
when the Mendicant Orders had attained the height of their
power and popularity, we find the Augustines exceedingly
anxious to assert their own superiority as the primitive Order,
and to represent St. Augustine as giving the rule to St. Francis
and St. Dominick. Andrea del Sarto painted a picture, by
command of the Augustine Hermits, in which St. Augustine
stands in an attitude of great dignity, expounding the doctrine
of the Trinity; St. Francis stands meditating, and St. Peter
the Dominican consults an open volume; St. Lawrence, St.
Sebastian, and St. Mary Magdalene are listening around.
The introduction of the last three personages expresses the
right assumed by the Augustines of including in their Order
all those sacred worthies who lived between the first and the
sixth centuries. The picture is one of wonderful beauty, and,
with this interpretation of its significance and its intention,
may be read like a page out of a book.

Florence.
Pitti Pal.

Of the munificent patronage extended by the Franciscans
and Dominicans to every branch of Art,—of the great artists
they produced from their ranks,—I have given a general
sketch in the Introduction. In looking at the pictures produced by them or for them, it will be well and wise and just
to recollect, not merely their connection with the progress of
Art, but with the progress of human culture and social
amelioration. Equally beautiful and candid is the testimony

borne to their deserts by Sir James Stephen, in his 'Ecclesiastical Sketches.'

'So reiterated,' he says, 'and so just have been the assaults on the Mendicant Friars, that we usually forget that, till the days of Martin Luther, the Church had never seen so great and effectual a reform as theirs. . . . Nothing in the histories of Wesley or of Whitfield can be compared with the enthusiasm which everywhere welcomed them, or with the immediate and visible result of their labours. In an age of oligarchal tyranny, they were the protectors of the weak; in an age of ignorance, the instructors of mankind; and in an age of profligacy, the stern vindicators of the holiness of the sacerdotal character and the virtues of domestic life.'

If an earnest English Protestant could thus write of them in the nineteenth century, we may be permitted to look with some sympathy and respect on the effigies which commemorated what they were—what they acted and suffered, during the thirteenth and fourteenth; and this in spite of their dingy draperies, and what Southey pleasantly calls their 'bread and water' expression.

45 A Franciscan. (Zurbaran.)

THE FRANCISCANS.

In pictures painted for the Franciscans, we expect of course to find, conspicuous in their grey or brown habits, and girded with the knotted cord, the worthies of their own Order. And in entering a church or convent belonging to any of the Franciscan communities, whether under the name of Minorites, Capuchins, Minims, Observants, Recollects, the first glance round the walls and altars will probably exhibit to us, singly or grouped, or attending on the Madonna, their eight principal saints, called in Italian *I Cardini dell' Ordine Serafico;*—'The Chiefs of the Seraphic Order.'

In the first and highest place St. Francis, as the *Padre Serafico*, patriarch and founder.

St. Clara, as the *Madre Serafica*, first Franciscan nun and foundress of the *Povere Donne* (Poor Clares).

St. Bonaventura, *il Dottore Serafico*, the great prelate of the Order, sometimes as a simple Franciscan friar, sometimes as cardinal; often grouped with St. Clara, and with St. Louis.

St. Antony of Padua. He generally figures as the *pendant* to St. Francis, being the second great luminary and miracle-worker of the Order; he is very conspicuous in Spanish Art.

St. Bernardino of Siena, the great preacher and reformer of the Order.

Then the three princely saints: St. Louis, king of France; St. Louis, bishop of Toulouse; and the charming St. Elizabeth of Hungary, with her crown on her head, and her lap full of roses, conspicuous in German Art.

Following after these, and of less universal popularity, we find—

St. Margaret of Cortona, in Italian pictures only.
St. Ives of Bretagne.
St. Eleazar of Sabran.
St. Rosa di Viterbo.
(These four belonged to the Third Order of Penitence.)
St. John Capistrano.
St. Peter Regalato.
And chiefly in Spanish pictures—
St. Juan de Dios.
St. Felix de Cantalicio.
St. Peter of Alcantara.
St. Diego of Alcalá.

Any works of Art in which we find one or more of these personages conspicuous, we may safely conclude to have been originally executed for a community of Franciscans, or for the purpose of being placed in one of their churches.

A single instance of a picture dedicated to the honour of the Franciscan saints is to be found in a grand altarpiece in the Church of San Bernardino at Verona, of which it is written in Murray's Handbook,—'No lover of Art should pass through Verona without seeing this picture:' and I venture to add my

testimony to its exceeding beauty.   The Virgin and Child are
seated in glory; and on each side are St. Francis and St.
Antony of Padua, nearly on an equality with the celestial
personages.   Around these, and mingled with the choir of
angels, are seven beautiful seraphic or allegorical figures,
bearing the attributes of the Seven Cardinal Virtues.   Below
on the earth stand six Franciscan saints; on the right of the
Virgin, St. Elizabeth of Hungary, St. Bonaventura, and St.
Louis, king; on the left, St. Eleazar of Sabran, St. Louis of
Toulouse, and St. Ives; below these in the centre is seen the
half-length of the votary who dedicated this fine picture, a
certain Madonna Caterina de' Sacchi, who appears veiled and
orCavazzola. holding a rosary.   The lower group, painted by Paolo
Morando, is much superior to the upper part of the picture.
A.D. 1522. Morando died young while he was at work upon it, and it was
finished by Francesco Morone.

Some of these saints are personally so interesting, their lives
and actions so full of matter and so significant, that it is with
difficulty I refrain from following out the track of thought suggested to my own mind: and though, as Wordsworth writes—

> ' Nuns fret not at their convent's narrow room,
> And hermits are contented with their cell,'

I *could* sometimes feel inclined to fret at the narrow limits of
artistic illustration within which I am bound.   But, without
further pause, I must now endeavour to show through what
real or imaginary merits each has earned his or her meed of
glorification, and by what characteristic attributes they are to
be recognised and distinguished from each other.

ST. FRANCIS OF ASSISI.

Lat. Sanctus Franciscus, Pater Seraphicus.   *Ital.* San Francesco di Assisi.
Fr. Saint François d'Assise.   Oct. 4, 1226.

Habit, grey or dark brown, girded with a hempen cord.   Attributes: 1.
The stigmata; 2. The skull; 3. The crucifix; 4. The lily; 5. The lamb.

THE father of this famous saint, Pietro Bernardone of Assisi,
was a rich merchant, who traded in silk and wool.   His

mother's name was Pica. He was christened Giovanni; but his father, who carried on large dealings with France, had intended his eldest son to be his chief agent and successor, and had him taught early to speak the French language : this was, for the time and locality, a rare accomplishment, and his companions called him *Francesco—the Frenchman.* The name superseded his own, and remained to him through life ; by that name he became celebrated, venerated, canonised ; and it has since been adopted as a common baptismal name through Western Christendom.

Francis, in his boyish years, was remarkable only for his vanity, prodigality, and love of pleasure. He delighted especially in gay and sumptuous apparel; but he was also compassionate, as ready to give as to spend, and beloved by his companions and fellow citizens. Thus passed the first fifteen or sixteen years of his life. In a quarrel between the inhabitants of Assisi and those of Perugia, they had recourse to arms. Francis was taken prisoner, and remained for a year in the fortress of Perugia ; on this occasion he showed both patience and courage. On his return home, he was seized with a grievous fever, and languished for weeks and months on a sick bed. During this time, his thoughts were often turned towards God ; a consciousness of his sins, a feeling of contempt for the world and its vanities, sank deep into his mind. He had been brought in his young years so near to death, that life itself took a shade from the contemplation.

Soon after his recovery he went forth, richly dressed as usual, and met a poor man in filthy ragged garments, who begged an alms for the love of God. Francis, looking on him, recognised one who had formerly been ranked with the richest and noblest of the city, and had held a command in the expedition against Perugia. Melted with compassion, he took off his rich dress, gave it to the mendicant, and, taking the other's tattered cloak, threw it round his own shoulders. That same night, being asleep, he had a vision, in which he fancied himself in a magnificent chamber, and all around were piled up riches and jewels innumerable, and arms of all kinds marked with the sign of the cross; and in the midst stood the figure of Christ, who said to him, 'These are the riches reserved for my servants, and the weapons wherewith I arm those who fight in my cause.' And when Francis awoke, he thought that Providence had intended him for a great captain, for he knew not yet his true vocation. Soon afterwards he went into the Church of San Damiano to pray. Now this church, which stands not far from the eastern gate of Assisi, was then, as it is now, falling into ruin; ard as he knelt before a crucifix, he heard in his soul a voice which said to him, 'Francis, repair my Church, which falleth to ruin!' He, not understanding the sense of these words, believed that the church wherein he knelt was signified; therefore he hastened home, and, taking some pieces of cloth and other merchandise, sold them, and carried the money to the priests of San Damiano for the reparation of the church. Whereat his father, being in great wrath, pursued him to bring him back; but Francis fled, and hid himself for many days in a cave, being in fear of his father. At length, taking heart, he came out, and returned to the city; but changed, pallid, worn with hunger, his looks distracted, his garments soiled and torn, so that no one knew him, and the very children in the streets pursued him as a madman. These and all other humiliations Francis now regarded as the trials to which he was called, and which were to usher him on his path to regeneration. His father, believing him frantic, shut him up, and bound him in his chamber; but his mother, having pity on her own son, went and delivered him, and spoke to him words of comfort, entreating him to have patience, and to be obedient to his parents, and not to shame them and all their kindred by his wild unseemly deportment. As he persisted, his father took him before the bishop, a mild and holy man; and when Francis beheld the bishop, he flung himself at his feet, and abjuring at once parents, home, heritage, he tore off his garments, and flung them to his father, saying, 'Henceforth I recognise no father but him who is in heaven!' Then the bishop wept with admiration and tenderness, and ordered his attendants to give Francis a cloak to cover him; it was of the coarsest stuff, being taken from a beggar who stood by; but Francis received it joyfully and thankfully as the first fruits of that poverty to which he had dedicated himself.

He was then in his twenty-fifth year, and from that time forth he lived as one who had cast away life.

His first care was to go to an hospital of lepers, to whom he devoted himself with tender and unwearied charity. This was in him the more meritorious, because previous to his conversion he could not look upon a leper without a feeling of repugnance, which made him sick even to faintness.

Then he went wandering over those beautiful Umbrian mountains from Assisi to Gubbio, singing with a loud voice hymns (*alla Francese,* as the old legend expresses it, whatever that may mean), and praising God for all things;—for the sun which shone above; for the day and for the night; for his *mother* the earth, and for his *sister* the moon; for the winds which blew in his face; for the pure precious water, 'Acqua ca-tu e and for the jocund fire; for the flowers under his feet, and for pretiosa.' the stars above his head;—saluting and blessing all creatures, cundo.' whether animate or inanimate, as his brethren and sisters in the Lord.

Thus in prayer, in penance, in charity, passed some years of his life. He existed only on alms, begged from door to door, and all but what sufficed to stay the pangs of hunger was devoted to the reparation of the Church of San Damiano and other churches and chapels in that neighbourhood. Among these was a little chapel dedicated to the 'Queen of Angels,' S. Maria- in the valley at the foot of the hill on which Assisi stands. gel. Here he inhabited a narrow cell, and the fame of his piety and humility attracted to him several disciples. One day, being at mass, he heard the text from St. Luke, 'Take nothing for your journey, neither staves, nor scrip, nor bread, nor money, nor two coats:' and regarding this as an immediate ordinance, he adopted it as the rule of his life. He was already barefoot, poorly clad, a mendicant for the food which sustained him. There was but one superfluity he possessed; it was his leathern girdle. He threw it from him, and took one of hempen cord,

I I

which being afterwards adopted by his followers, they have been thence styled by the people *Cordeliers.*

Having thus prepared himself for his mission in the manner commanded in the Gospel, he set forth to preach repentance, charity, humility, abnegation of the world,—a new life, in short; and everywhere he preached without study, trusting that God would put into his mind what he ought to utter for the edification of others.

It was, as I have said, a time of great and general suffering —of sorrow, and of change—of mental and moral ferment. Men's minds were predisposed to be excited by the marvellous, and melted by the pathetic, in religion; and the words of Francis fell upon them like sparks of fire upon the dry summer grass. Many, excited to enthusiasm by his preaching, joined themselves to him; and among these his earliest disciples, four are especially mentioned and commemorated,—Silvestro, Bernardo, Leo, and Giles (or Egidio). His first female disciple was a maiden of noble family, Clara d'Assisi, whose story I shall have to relate hereafter.

It being necessary to bind his followers together, and to him, by a rule of life which should be literally that of the apostles, he made the first condition absolute poverty; his followers were to possess *nothing* — hence the picturesque allegory of his espousals with The Lady Poverty, to which I shall have to return. Meantime, to pursue the course of his life, he repaired to Rome to obtain the sanction of the Pope for his new institution. Innocent III. was too cautious to lend himself at first to what appeared the extravagance of a fanatic enthusiast. Francis, being repulsed, retired to the Hospital of St. Antony; but that night, as is related by St. Bonaventura, the Pope was admonished by a dream, in which he beheld the walls of the Lateran tottering and about to fall, while the poor enthusiast whom he had rejected in the morning sustained the weight upon his shoulders. The Pope, on awaking, sent for him, confirmed the rule of his Order, and gave him a full dispensation to preach. St. Francis then returned to his humble cell in the Porzioncula,[1] and built

---

[1] The term *Porzioncula*, which occurs so perpetually in reference to the pictures

other cells around for his disciples.   He gave to his followers
the name of '*Frati Minori*,' to signify the humility and the
submission enjoined them, and that they should strive everywhere, not for the first and highest place, but for the last and
lowest.   They were not to possess property of any kind, nor
would he allow any temporal goods to be vested in his Order:
nor would he suffer during his life any building or convent in
it, that he might say with perfect truth he possessed nothing.
The spirit of Holy Poverty was to be the spirit of his Order.
He prescribed that the churches built for them should be low
and small, and all their buildings of wood; but, some representing to him that wood is in many places dearer than stone,
he struck out this last condition.   To extreme austerity he
joined profound humility of heart; he was in his own eyes the
basest and most despicable of men, and desired to be so reputed
by all.   If others commended him, he replied humbly, 'What
every one is in the eyes of God, that I am and no more.'   He
was endowed with what his biographer calls an extraordinary
'gift of tears;' he wept continually his own sins and those of
others; and, not satisfied with praying for the conversion of

---

of St. Francis, is, I believe, sometimes misunderstood. It means, literally, 'a
small portion, share, or allotment.' The name was given to a slip of land, of a
few acres in extent, at the foot of the hill of Assisi, and on which stood a little
chapel; both belonged to a community of Benedictines, who afterwards bestowed
the land and the chapel on the brotherhood of St. Francis. This chapel was then
familiarly known as the 'Capella della Porzioncula.' Whether the title by which
it has since become famous as the S. Maria-degli-Angeli ('Our Lady-of-Angels'),
belonged to it originally, or because the angels were heard singing around and
above it at the time of the birth of St. Francis, does not seem clear: at all events,
this chapel became early sanctified as the scene of the ecstacies and visions of the
saint: here, also, St. Clara made her profession: particular indulgences were
granted to those who visited it for confession and repentance on the 5th of August,
and it became a celebrated place of pilgrimage in the fourteenth century. Mr.
Ford tells us that in Spain the term *Porzioncula* is applied generally to distinguish
the chapel or sanctuary dedicated to St. Francis within the Franciscan churches.
The *original* chapel of the Porzioncula now stands in the centre of the magnificent
church which has been erected over it. The church and chapel were both much
injured by an earthquake in 1832, but the chapel was restored from the old
materials, and the exterior is adorned with frescoes by Overbeck. It is a small
building—might contain, perhaps, thirty persons; but I did not take the measure-
ment: it looks small under the lofty dome of the edifice which now encloses it,
and also the 'narrow cell' near it, called the '*Stanza di S. Francesco*.'

the heathen, he resolved to go and preach to the Mahometans in Syria, and to obtain the crown of martyrdom: but he was driven back by a storm. Afterwards, in 1214, he set forth to preach the gospel in Morocco. But in travelling through Spain he was stopped by sickness and other obstacles, so that he did not on this occasion proceed to Africa; but, after performing many miracles in Spain, and founding many convents, he returned to Italy.

Ten years after the first institution of his Order, St. Francis held the first General Chapter in the plain at the foot of the hill of Assisi. Five thousand of his friars assembled on this occasion. This famous Chapter is called, in the history of his Order, the 'Chapter of Mats,' because they had erected booths covered with mats to shelter them. They gave themselves no care what they should eat or what they should drink, for the inhabitants of Assisi, Spoleto, Perugia, and Foligno supplied them with all they needed; and such was the general en- *afterwards* thusiasm, that the Cardinal Protector Ugolini, and Francis *Gregory IX.* himself, were obliged to moderate the austerities and mortifi- cations to which the friars voluntarily subjected themselves. On this occasion he sent missionaries into various countries, reserving to himself Syria and Egypt, where he hoped to crown his labours by a glorious martyrdom for the cause of Christ. But it was not so ordered.

He arrived at Damietta, he penetrated to the camp of the infidels, and was carried before the Sultan. The Sultan asked him what brought him there? to which he replied, that he had come there to teach him and his people the way of eternal salvation. In order to prove the truth of his mission, he desired that a fire should be kindled, and offered to pass through it if the Sultan would command one of his Imauns to pass with him. As the Sultan refused this, Francis offered next to throw himself into the fire, provided the Sultan and all his people would embrace Christianity. The Sultan declined this likewise; but looking on Francis with the Oriental feeling of respect and compassion, as one idiotic or insane, he sent him back guarded to Damietta, whence he returned to Italy without having the satisfaction of either gaining a soul to Christ or shedding his blood for his sake. As some amends for this disappointment, he had the joy of hearing that five of his missionaries, whom he had sent to Morocco, had there suffered a cruel martyrdom.

Four years after his return, he obtained the confirmation of his Order from Pope Honorius; resigned his office of Superior, and retired to a solitary cave on Monte Alverna. There he *or Lavorna.* was visited by ecstatic trances, by visions of the Virgin and our Saviour, and it is said that he was sometimes raised from the ground in a rapture of devotion. It was on this occasion that he was favoured with an extraordinary vision, which I cannot venture to give otherwise than in the words of his biographer. 'After having fasted for forty days in his solitary cell on Mount Alverna, and passed the time in all the fervour of prayer and ecstatic contemplation, transported almost to heaven by the ardour of his desires,—then he beheld, as it were, a seraph with six shining wings, bearing down upon him from above, and between his wings was the form of a man crucified. By this he understood to be figured a heavenly and immortal intelligence, subject to death and humiliation. And it was manifested to him that he was to be transformed into a resemblance to Christ, not by the martyrdom of the flesh, but by the might and fire of Divine love. When the vision had disappeared, and he had recovered a little from its effect, it was seen that in his hands, his feet, and side, he carried the wounds of our Saviour.

Notwithstanding the interpretation which might easily be given to this extraordinary vision, it has remained an article of belief, on the testimony of St. Bonaventura, that these wounds were not only *real,* but impressed by supernatural power. The title of the SERAPHIC has since been given to St. Francis and to his Order. He wished to have concealed the favour which had been vouchsafed to him; but notwithstanding his precautions, the last two years of his life became, in various ways, a period of perpetual manifestation. He suffered meantime much from sickness, pain, weakness, and blindness caused by continual tears. He hailed the approach of death with rapture: and desired, as a last proof of his humility, that his body should be carried to the common place of execution, a rock outside the walls of Assisi, then called the *Colle d'Inferno*, and buried with the bodies of the malefactors. He dictated a last testament to his friars, in which he added to the rule already given, that they should work with their hands, not out of a desire of gain, but for the sake of good example, and to avoid idleness. He commanded that those who did not know how to work should learn some trade. But Pope Nicholas III. afterwards abrogated this last precept.

When he felt the approach of death, he ordered himself to be laid upon the bare earth, and endeavoured with a trembling voice to recite the 141st Psalm: he had reached the last verse, *Bring my soul out of prison*, when he ceased to breathe. His body was carried to the city of Assisi, and those who bore it paused on their way before the Church of San Damiano, where Clara and her nuns saluted it, and weeping, kissed his hands and his garments. It was then carried to the spot which he had himself chosen, and which became from that time consecrated ground.

A.D. 1226.

Two years after his death, in the year 1228, he was canonised by Gregory IX., and in the same year was laid the foundation of that magnificent church which now covers his remains. To all those who contributed, either by the work of their hands or by their wealth, indulgences were granted. Almost all the princes of Christendom sent their offerings; and the Germans were particularly distinguished by their liberality. The city of Assisi granted the quarries of marble: the inhabitants of all the neighbouring towns sent their artists to decorate the temple within and without. The body of St. Francis was transported thither in the month of May 1230; and, contrary to the usual custom with regard to the remains of the Roman Catholic saints, it has ever since reposed there entire and undisturbed.

Were all other evidence wanting, we might form some idea of the passionate enthusiasm inspired by the character of St.

Francis, and the popularity and influence of his Order, from the incalculable number of the effigies which exist of him. They are to be found of every kind, from the grandest creations of human genius, down to a halfpenny print, and are only rivalled in profusion and variety by those of the Madonna herself. In this case, as in some others, I have found it necessary to class the subjects, noticing only the leading points in the artistic treatment, and the most remarkable examples under each head, so as to assist the reader to discriminate the merit, as well as to comprehend the significance, of the representation.

But even a classification is here difficult. I shall begin with those subjects which must be considered as strictly devotional. They are of two kinds :—

46 St. Francis. (Giunta Pisano.)

I. The figures which represent St. Francis standing either alone or in a *Sacra Conversazione;* or enthroned, as the *Padre Serafico,* the patron saint and founder of his Seraphic Order.

II. Those which represent him in prayer or meditation as the devout solitary, the pattern of ascetics and penitents.

The earliest known representation of St. Francis has almost the value and authenticity of a portrait. It was painted by Giunta Pisano a few years after the death of the saint, and under the directions of those who had known him during his life: it is a small full-length, in the sacristy of his church at Assisi; which when I was there, hung high over a door with a curtain drawn before it, rather, as it seemed, to preserve

than to conceal it. He is standing—a long meagre figure—
long out of all proportion,—wearing the grey habit and the
cord; holding a cross in his right hand, and in the left
the Gospel: the face is small; the forehead broad; the features delicate and regular; the beard black, thin, and short;
the expression mild and melancholy. Another very ancient
figure, with the hood drawn over the head, and in the hand
a scroll, on which is written *Pax huic*, exists at Subiaco, and
is supposed to have existed there since the time of Gregory
IX. (the same Cardinal Ugolini who was the friend of St.
Francis, and 'Protector' of the Order). A third, by Mar-
garitone di Arezzo, also with the hood drawn over the head,
the Gospel in one hand, the other raised in benediction, is
still preserved in the Church of Sargiano near Arezzo. The
character of head in these effigies is nearly the same, and
is, or ought to be, the authority for succeeding painters; and
the best have not widely departed from this peculiar type
—no doubt the true one. But it has either been set aside

altogether or most grossly
caricatured by later painters,
and more particularly by the
German and Spanish schools.
I have seen heads of St.
Francis, mere coarse versions
of the burly sensual friars we
meet begging in the streets
of Italy or Spain; and reminding us rather of Friar
Tuck in Ivanhoe, or the disguised bandit in Gil Blas,
than of the fervent ascetic
—the tender-hearted and
poetical enthusiast.

But even where the true
character of head is neglected
or degraded, we distinguish
St. Francis from all other
saints wearing the same habit,

47   S . FRANCIS.   (Simon Memmi.)

by the stigmata (or wounds of Christ) in his hands and feet; and he is often in the act of opening his tunic and displaying the wound in his side: these are proper to him, and, together with the crucifix and the skull, common to other saints, are the almost unfailing attributes in the countless effigies which exist of him. The lamb and the lily, as symbols of meekness and purity, are also given to him.

When St. Francis is grouped with other saints, or stands near the throne of the Madonna or at the foot of the cross, he has generally a crucifix in his hand, more seldom the lily, and in the early pictures he is often distinguished only by the habit and physiognomy. When St. Francis and St. Dominick stand together, the crucifix is given to the former, the lily to the latter.

I have seen some devotional figures of St. Francis which deviate from the usual version; and shall mention one or two, which, though expressive, are exceptional:—

1. In a picture by Sassetta, he is standing within a glory of seraphim, his hands extended in the form of a cross: over his head are three angels, with the symbols of poverty, chastity, and obedience: under his feet the worldly vices, as pride, gluttony, heresy, the latter being distinguished by the printing press,—a curious and, for the time, significant attribute. (48) *[Eng. in Rossini's 'Storia della Pittura,' pl. 60.]*

2. He stands holding a flaming seraph in his hand, to denote his title of the *Seraphic*, as in a picture by Sano di Pietro of Siena. I observe there is often something fanciful and peculiar in the attributes chosen by the Siena school. *[Acad. Siena.]*

3. He stands on a throne, delivering the Franciscan cords to Religion, who distributes them to various persons, popes, princes, &c. This picture was painted for the Franciscans of Bologna. *[Agostino Caracci. Bologna Gal.]*

4. He stands between St. Clara and St. Elizabeth, who here represent piety and charity, as in a small Spanish picture. *[Louvre. Sp. Gal.]*

Very different are those pictures which represent St. Francis as the devout penitent; the example at once, and the consoler, of the broken and contrite spirit. He is usually kneel-

K K

48   St. Francis in a glory of Seraphim.   (Sassetta, 1444.)

ing in a gloomy solitude, or in his cell, barefoot, his grey or
brown tunic ragged or patched; and either with hands
clasped, and head bowed down over a crucifix, the symbol of
redemption; or over a skull, the emblem of mortality; or with
arms outspread, and eyes raised to heaven, where there is

40   St. Francis. (Cigoli.)

usually a vision of angels, or the Virgin, or the Trinity.
Some of these ascetic or ecstatic figures are wonderful for
expression ; and none have excelled Cigoli in Italy, and Zurbaran in Spain, in the representation of the hollow-eyed, wan,
meagre, yet ardent and fervent recluse.

I cannot remember any of these penitential figures by the
very ancient painters; but in the late Bologna and Florentine
schools, and more especially in Spanish Art, they abound.

A second class of subjects, which are not strictly devotional,
nor yet historical, I will call *mystical.* They represent some
vision or incident of his life, not as a fact, but as conveying a
significance more than meets the eye, and proper for religious
edification.

1. 'St. Francis receiving the Stigmata,' is the most im-

OVERBECK

GIGOLI

SPADA

GIOTTO

BADALOCCHI.

LAURI

DOMENICHINO

with his appearance, desired him to come into his study and
wait while he sketched him: but before the sketch was completed the poor wretch swooned from exhaustion: Cigoli seized
the moment, and transferred to his canvass the wasted features
almost fixed in the languor of death. I am not sure that the
result is quite satisfactory; for the swoon is too painfully
natural: it ought to be a trance rather than a swoon.

2. A much more agreeable subject is that styled 'The
Vision of St. Francis.' The Virgin mother, descending in a
glory of light and attended by angels, places in his arms her
Divine Son. This is not an early subject, but, once introduced,
it soon became a favourite one both with the painters and the
people. The contrast afforded was precisely of that kind which
the later artists delighted in; equally violent in the forms and
the sentiment. On one side kneels the visionary, with features
wan and worn, and fatigued with emotion, with tattered
raiment, and all the outward signs of sordid misery: on the
other we behold the Virgin, loveliest and most benign of female
forms, bending from her heavenly throne; and the infant
Saviour smiling as if fresh from Paradise. The subject admits
of great variety, without departing from the leading idea, for
sometimes St. Francis holds the divine Child in his arms with
an air of reverential tenderness, while the Virgin looks down
upon both with maternal benignity; and sometimes the
Child, seated in her lap, extends his hand to the prostrate
saint, who, with half-closed eyes, as if fainting with excess of
bliss, just touches that hand with reverential lips. A choir of
angels generally completes the mystic group; and the locality
varies with the taste of the painter, being sometimes a
landscape, sometimes the interior of the Porzioncula, where,
according to the legend, the vision occurred, and in memory of
which almost every Franciscan church in Spain has its Porzioncula, or chapel dedicated to the Vision of St. Francis. In this
subject it is necessary to distinguish St. Francis from other
saints who were favoured with a similar vision; and more
especially from St. Antony of Padua, who wears the same
habit. In general, St. Francis may be recognised by the

stigmata; he is rather aged, with more or less beard; while St.
Antony is, or *ought* to be, young, beardless, of a beautiful
countenance, with a lily beside him.   Where the infant Christ
stands beside the saint or on his book, it is probably St. Antony.
Where the saint is prostrate, and almost in a trance before the
Virgin and Child, it is probably St. Francis.

It is a mistake, and a gross departure from the proper religious feeling, to represent St. Francis caressing the infant
Saviour as a father would caress his child; yet this is what we
find in many of the later pictures, in which, but for the habit,
he might be mistaken for St. Joseph.

There is a very daring and original version of this vision of
St. Francis in a picture by Murillo.   Here it is no longer the
blessed Infant leaning from his mother's bosom, but the crucified Saviour who bends from his cross of agony; and while St.
Francis, with outstretched arms, and trampling a globe under
his feet, symbol of the world and its vanities, looks up with the
most passionate expression of adoration and gratitude, the
benign Vision gently inclines towards him, and lays one hand
on his shoulder, while the other remains attached to the cross:
two choral angels hover above.   This may possibly be intended
to represent the vision in San Damiano.

Museum,
Seville.

3. 'St. Francis shivering in his cell in the depth of winter,
a demon whispers to him suggestions of ease and luxury; he
repels the temptation by going out and rolling himself in the
snow on a heap of thorns; from the thorns sprinkled with his
blood spring roses of Paradise, which he offers up to Christ
and the Madonna.'   This altogether poetical and mystical
subject refers to the famous vision in the Porzioncula.   There
is an example in the Louvre, wherein St. Joseph and St.
Dominick stand by as spectators.   There is another by
Murillo, in which a flight of cherubim shower the roses on the
saint.

No. 582,
New Cata-
logue.

Madrid Gal.

4. 'St. Francis, languishing in sickness, an angel descends
from heaven to solace him with music:' styled also 'The
Ecstasy of St. Francis.'   This is a beautiful subject often

gracefully treated, but never, at least as far as I know, in a
truly poetical and religious spirit. In general, St. Francis is
in his cavern, leaning back with eyes half closed, or sustained
by an angel, while another angel sounds the viol above. Or it
is a choir of angels, singing in a glory; but this is a less
orthodox conception. A singular version of this subject represents St. Francis almost fainting with ecstasy; the angelic
visitant, hovering above, touches his viol and 'makes celestial
music:' meanwhile St. Bernard, seated near with his ample
white robes and his book, seems to have paused in his studies
to listen.

Louvre,
No. 1042

5. 'St. Francis espouses Poverty, Chastity, and Obedience.'
Giotto was the first who treated this subject; whether he
derived the original idea from a celebrated passage in Dante's
Paradiso, or Dante from him, has been disputed: both the poet
and the painter allegorised the old Franciscan legend as given
by St. Bonaventura long before their time; and the inventor
of the apologue was certainly Francis himself. 'Journeying to
Siena, in the broad plain between Campiglia and San Quirico,
St. Francis was encountered by three maidens, in poor raiment,
and exactly resembling each other in age and appearance, who
saluted him with the words, "Welcome, Lady Poverty," and
suddenly disappeared. The brethren not irrationally concluded that this apparition imported some mystery pertaining
to St. Francis, and that by the three poor maidens were
signified Chastity, Obedience, and Poverty, the beauty and
sum of evangelical perfection: all of which shone with equal
and consummate lustre in the man of God, though he made
his chief glory the privilege of poverty.'

This legend is very literally rendered in a small picture in
the possession of Count Demidoff, from which I give a sketch.
Below, St. Francis meets the three virgins in the plain; and
above, they are seen floating away, distinguished by their
attributes.

The treatment of this subject in the lower church of Assisi
is altogether different. The whole allegory is elaborately
worked out, and it has been supposed with reason that Giotto

50   St. Francis encounters Poverty, Chastity, and Obedience.   (School of Giotto.)

was indebted to his friend Dante for many particulars in the
conception.   The vault of the choir is divided into four com-

partments. In the first we have the allegory of 'The Fortress of Chastity,' to which St. Francis appears ascending; while through a window appears Chastity herself, as a young maiden, praying; two angels floating in the air present to her the palm and the volume of the Holy Scriptures.

The second compartment represents Obedience, who is figured as an angel, robed in black, placing the finger of the left hand on·his mouth, while with the right he passes the yoke over the head of a Franciscan friar kneeling at his feet. On one hand is Prudence, on the left Humility. Above this group, and attended by kneeling angels, stands St. Francis in his habit: two hands appear as coming out of heaven, holding apparently the knotted cord of the Franciscans.

The third compartment, 'The Espousals of St. Francis with the Lady Poverty,' was certainly suggested by a passage in Dante's Paradiso, or suggested that passage. The scene is a rocky wilderness: Poverty,—

> The Dame to whom none openeth pleasure's gate
> More than to death,—

stands in the midst, emaciated, barefoot, in a tattered robe, her feet among thorns, which a youth is thrusting against her with a staff, and a dog barks at her; she is attended by Hope and Charity as bridesmaids, herself being thus substituted for Faith. St. Francis places the ring upon her finger, while our Saviour, standing between them, at once gives away the bride and bestows the nuptial benediction. For the corresponding passage in Dante I may refer to the Divina Commedia. Kugler says, 'A tradition ascribes these paintings collectively to Dante, who was an intimate friend of the artist, and even recalls him from the other world to reveal them in a dream to the painter.' But as Dante was apparently alive, and in communication with Giotto, at the time these frescoes were painted, he needed not to come 'from the other world' to reveal his suggestions. *Paradiso, c. xi.*

The fourth compartment of the vault remains to be described. It exhibits the glorification or apotheosis of the saint. He is seated on a throne, wearing the rich embroidered robe of a

deacon (from his great humility he had refused any higher
ecclesiastical honour): he holds in one hand the cross, in the
other the written rule of his Order. On each side are choirs of
angels, who hymn his praise; others in front, bearing lilies in
their hands, have a truly angelic and ethereal grace.

I shall now proceed to the historical representations taken
from the life and miracles of St. Francis.

The history of this saint, in a series of subjects, may be
found very commonly in the churches and convents belonging
to his Order.[1]

About 1308.   The earliest, the most complete, and the most remarkable, is
that which still exists, but in a most ruined condition, in the
upper church of Assisi, in twenty-eight compartments.

About 1445.   The series by Ghirlandajo, in the Trinità at Florence, which
is extremely fine and dramatic, was painted for Francesco
Sassetti, in the chapel of his patron saint.

A third series I must mention,—the exquisite sculpture
round the pulpit in the church of Santa Croce, executed by
About 1450.   Benedetto da Maiano in the style of Ghiberti's Gates of the
Baptistery, at Florence; and, as it seemed to me, when I had
the opportunity of comparing them on the spot, hardly less
beautiful, expressive, and elaborate. These are the most interesting examples I have seen.

We will now pass in review the whole of the subjects contained in the upper church of Assisi, comprising all the incidents
I have found represented as a series in other places, and many
which are not to be met with elsewhere, or which exist only as
separate subjects: assembled here, they form the pictured
chronicle of his life. The brotherhood of St. Francis, though
vowed to poverty, had been enormously enriched by the
offerings of the charitable and devout. Within fifty years
after the death of their patriarch, one of the grandest churches
in Italy had risen over his remains, and their hospitals and
missions had extended to every part of the then known world.

---

[1] According to Vasari, Cimabue, when called to Assisi about 1265, painted in
the lower church the life of St. Francis. This would, of course, be the *earliest*
on record : it has utterly perished.

In the next century, these munificent mendicants seemed to have thought that they could not better employ their surplus wealth than by doing honour to that '*glorioso poverel di Dio*' whose name they bore. As on a former occasion they had summoned Cimabue, they now called to their aid Giotto, the greatest painter of the time. Whether Giotto painted the whole series of subjects round the nave of the upper church has been doubted, and with reason. That he painted a great part of them, seems to be pretty well ascertained: but I will not now go into this question, which is one of pure antiquarian criticism. Our attention at present must be fixed upon the subjects themselves, as illustrating the actions and miracles of the great patriarch. A reference to the previous sketch of his life will sufficiently interpret most of these, and to the others I will add some notes of explanation.

I have marked with an asterisk those which have been engraved in Ottley's ' Specimens of the Early Florentine School.'

1. When St. Francis was still in his father's house, and in bondage to the world, a half-witted simpleton, meeting him in the market-place of Assisi, took off his own garment, and spread it on the ground for him to walk over, prophesying that he was worthy of all honour, as one destined to greatness, and to the veneration of the faithful throughout the universe.[1]

2. St. Francis gives his cloak to the poor officer. The scene is represented in the valley which lies below Assisi, and St. Francis is on horseback. (In any other locality this might be mistaken for St. Martin.)

3. The dream of St. Francis, already related. Here our Saviour stands beside the bed, pointing to the heaps of armour prepared for the warriors of Christ.

4. St. Francis, kneeling before the crucifix in the Church of San Damiano, receives the miraculous communication.

5. St. Francis and his father, Pietro Bernardone, renounce each other in the Piazza of Assisi. Francis throws off his garments, and receives from the bishop a cloak wherewith to cover him.

---

[1] ' Here,' says Lord Lindsay, ' we find the oriental veneration for fatuity on the very threshold of the story.' His description of these frescoes in the *Sketches of Christian Art* is admirably written, and the most accurate and detailed I have met with. I have not only borrowed largely from him, but in many places have given his words—abbreviating where I found it impossible to be either more exact or more elegant, and adding here and there from my own notes made on the spot.

6. The vision of Pope Innocent III. 'This is a very beautiful fresco: the head of St. Francis looking up to heaven as if for aid, while he sustains the falling Church, is extremely expressive; and so is that of one of the attendants at the Pope's bedside, who has dropped his head on his arm, as overcome with sleep.'

7. Pope Honorius III. confirms the rule of the Franciscan Order.

8. St. Francis in the chariot of fire. On a certain night he had gone apart from his brethren to pray; but at midnight, when some were awake and others sleeping, a fiery chariot was seen to enter by the door of the house, and drive thrice round the court. A globe, bright and dazzling as the sun at noon-day, rested upon it, which they knew to be the spirit of St. Francis, present with them, but parted from his body.

Stirling's
Artists of
Spain, p.335.

This was one of the subjects painted by Murillo for the Capuchins at Seville, and seems to have much perplexed commentators.

9. The seats prepared in heaven for St. Francis and his Order. A large throne, and two small ones on each side of it, appear above. A monk kneels on one side; an angel, floating in the air, points to St. Francis prostrate before an altar.

10. St. Francis exorcising Arezzo. The city of Arezzo was then distracted by factions; and the saint, on approaching, beheld a company of demons dancing in the air above the walls, these being the evil spirits who stirred up men's minds to strife. Thereupon he sent his companion Silvester to command them in his name to depart. Silvester obeyed, crying with a loud voice, 'In the name of the omnipotent God, and by command of his servant Francis, go out hence, every one of you!' And immediately the demons dispersed, and the city returned to peace and propriety. In the fresco, St. Francis kneels in prayer, while Silvester stands before the city in a noble attitude of command.

11. St. Francis before the Soldan. This legend has been already related. Of this subject, the fresco by Ghirlandajo is particularly fine; and the bas-relief by Benedetto da Maiano, most beautiful.

12. St. Francis lifted from the earth in an ecstasy of devotion.

13. St. Francis exhibits to his congregation a tableau or theatrical representation of the Nativity of our Saviour.

This is curious, as being the earliest instance of those exhibitions still so common in Italy about Christmas-time, and for which the Franciscan communities are still pre-eminent.

14. St. Francis and his companions, in journeying over a desert mountain in the heat of summer, are exhausted by fatigue and thirst. The saint, through his prayers, causes the living stream to flow from the rock.

This fresco is remarkable in the history of Art, as containing the earliest successful attempt to express an action taken from common life. It is that of the thirsty man, bending over the fountain to drink; known as *l'Assetato* (the thirsty man), and deservedly praised by Vasari and by Lanzi. It is engraved in D'Agincourt.

Hist. de
l'Art par les
Monumens.

15. St. Francis preaching to the birds. ' Drawing nigh to Bevagno, he came to a certain place where birds of different kinds were gathered together; whom seeing, the man of God ran hastily to the spot, and, saluting them as if they had been his fellows in reason (while they all turned and bent their heads in attentive expectation), he admonished them, saying, "Brother birds, greatly are ye bound to praise the Creator, who clotheth you with feathers, and giveth you wings to fly with, and a purer air to breathe, and who careth for you, who have so little care for yourselves." Whilst he thus spake, the little birds, marvellously commoved, began to spread their wings, stretch forth their necks, and open their beaks, attentively gazing upon him ; and he, glowing in the spirit, passed through the midst of them, and even touched them with his robe ; yet not one stirred from his place until the man of God gave them leave ; when, with his blessing, and at the sign of the cross, they all flew away. These things saw his companions, who waited for him on the road ; to whom returning, the simple and pure-minded man began greatly to blame himself for having never hitherto preached to the birds.'

The illustration is a sketch from a small picture, now in the Louvre, quite similar in treatment, and probably a copy of the fresco by one of Giotto's scholars.

And here we must pause for a moment. The last subject will probably excite a smile, but that smile ought to be a serious smile,—not a sneer; and I cannot pass it over without remark.

Among the legends of St. Francis, some of the most interesting are those which place him in relation with the lower animals. He looked upon all beings as existing by and through God, and as having a portion of that divine principle by which he himself existed. He was accustomed to call all living things his brothers and sisters. In the enthusiasm of his charity he interpreted literally the text, ' Go ye into all the world, and preach the gospel to every *creature.*' He appears to have thought that all sentient beings had a share in the divine mission of Christ; and since a part of that divine mission was to enlarge the sphere of our human sympathies, till they embrace *all* our fellow-creatures, it should seem that the more the tender spirit of Christianity is understood and diffused, the more will the lower creation be elevated through our own more elevated intelligence and refined sympathies. Dr. Arnold says, in a striking passage of one of his letters, that ' the destinies of the brute creation appeared to him a mystery which he could not

51   St Francis preaching to the Birds.

approach without awe.' St. Francis, in his gentle and tender
enthusiasm, solved that mystery—at least to himself—by admitting animals within the pale of Christian sympathy. I shall
give a few of these legends here as the best commentary on the
subjects above described. It is recorded that when he walked
in the fields the sheep and the lambs thronged around him, hares
and rabbits nestled in his bosom; but of all living creatures he
seems to have loved especially birds of every kind, as being the
most unearthly in their nature : and among birds he loved best
the dove. ' One day he met, in his road, a young man on his
way to Siena to sell some doves, which he had caught in a
snare; and Francis said to him, " Oh, good young man ! these
are the birds to whom the Scripture compares those who are
pure and faithful before God ; do not kill them, I beseech
thee, but give them rather to me ; " and when they were given
to him, he put them in his bosom and carried them to his con-

vent at Ravacciano, where he made for them nests, and fed them every day, until they became so tame as to eat from his hand: and the young man had also his recompense; for he became a friar, and lived a holy life from that day forth.'—St. Francis had also a great tenderness for larks, and often pointed out to his disciples the lark mounting to 'heaven's gate,' and singing praises to the Creator, as a proper emblem of Christian aspiration. 'A lark brought her brood of nestlings to his cell, to be fed from his hand; he saw that the strongest of these nestlings tyrannised over the others, pecking at them and taking more than his due share of the food; whereupon the good saint rebuked the creature, saying, "Thou unjust and insatiable! thou shalt die miserably, and the greediest animals shall refuse to eat thy flesh." And so it happened, for the creature drowned itself through its impetuosity in drinking, and when it was thrown to the cats they would not touch it.'—' On his return from Syria, in passing through the Venetian Lagune, vast numbers of birds were singing, and he said to his companion, "Our sisters the birds are praising their Creator; let us sing with them,"—and he began the sacred service. But the warbling of the birds interrupted them; therefore St. Francis said to them, "Be silent till we also have praised God," and they ceased their song, and did not resume it till he had given them permission.'—' On another occasion, preaching at Alviano, he could not make himself heard for the chirping of the swallows which were at that time building their nests: pausing, therefore, in his sermon, he said, " My sisters, you have talked enough: it is time that I should have my turn. Be silent, and listen to the word of God!" and they were silent immediately.'—' On another occasion, as he was sitting with his disciple Leo, he felt himself penetrated with joy and consolation by the song of the nightingale, and he desired his friend Leo to raise his voice and sing the praises of God in company with the bird. But Leo excused himself by reason of his bad voice; upon which Francis himself began to sing, and when he stopped, the nightingale took up the strain, and thus they sang alternately until the night was far advanced, and Francis was obliged to

stop, for his voice failed. Then he confessed that the little
bird had vanquished him; he called it to him, thanked it for
its song, and gave it the remainder of his bread; and having
bestowed his blessing upon it, the creature flew away.'

Here we have a version of the antique legend of the Thes-
salian Shepherd and the Nightingale: but there the nightingale is vanquished and dies; here the lesson of humility is
given to the man. Mark the distinction between the classic
and the Christian sentiment!

'A grasshopper was wont to sit and sing on a fig-tree near
the cell of the man of God, and oftentimes by her singing she
excited him also to sing the praises of the Creator; and one
day he called her to him, and she flew upon his hand, and
Francis said to her, "Sing, my sister, and praise the Lord
thy Creator." So she began her song immediately, nor ceased
till at the father's command she flew back to her own place;
and she remained eight days there, coming and singing at
his behest. At length the man of God said to his disciples,
"Let us dismiss our sister! enough, that she has cheered us
with her song, and excited us to the praise of God these eight
days." So, being permitted, she immediately flew away, and
was seen no more.'

When he found worms or insects in his road, he was careful
not to tread upon them; 'he stepped aside, and bid the reptile
live.' He would even remove them from the pathway, lest
they should be crushed by others.

One day, in passing through a meadow, he saluted the flocks
which were grazing there, and he perceived a poor little lamb
which was feeding all alone in the midst of a flock of goats;
he was moved with pity, and he said, 'Thus did our mild
Saviour stand alone in the midst of the Jews and the Pharisees.'
He would have bought this sheep, but he had nothing in the
world but his tunic; however, a charitable man passing by,
and seeing his grief, bought the lamb and gave it to him.
When he was at Rome in 1222, he had with him a pet
lamb, which accompanied him everywhere; and in pictures of
St. Francis a lamb is frequently introduced, which may either
signify his meekness and purity of mind, or it may represent

this very lamb, ' which lay in his bosom, and was to him as a daughter.'

We now return to Giotto's frescoes :—

*16. The death of the young Count of Celano. St. Francis being invited to dine with a devout and charitable noble, before sitting down to table, privately warned him that his end drew near, and exhorted him to confess his sins, for that God had given him this opportunity of making his peace in recompense of his hospitality towards the poor of Christ. The young count obeyed, confessed himself, set his house in order, and then took his place at the entertainment ; but, before it was over, sank down and expired on the spot.

17. St. Francis preaching before the pope and cardinals, all seated in appropriate attitudes, under a magnificent Gothic Loggia.

This fresco and similar subjects are to be referred, I believe, to the following passage in his life. Francis hesitated long between the contemplative and the active religious life. He and his disciples were men quite unlearned. He wished to persuade others to follow, like himself, the way of salvation ; but he knew not how to set about it. He consulted his brethren what he should do. ' " God," said he, " has given me the gift of prayers, but not the gift of words ; yet as the Son of Man, when he was upon earth, not only redeemed men by his blood, but instructed them by his words, ought we not to follow his divine example ? " And, in his great humility, he requested not only of his brethren, but also of Clara and her sisterhood, that they would pray for him that a sign might be given what he should do. The answer was to all the same—" Go, preach the Gospel to every creature." And, when he preached, such eloquence was given to him from above, that none could resist his words, and the most learned theologians remained silent and astonished in his presence.'

A particular sermon, which he preached at Rome before Honorius III., may also be alluded to.

St. Francis, in the Rule given to his brotherhood, prescribed short sermons,—' because those of our Saviour were short ;' and as we are not the more heard above, so neither are we the more listened to below, for ' our much speaking.'

*18. When St. Antony of Padua was preaching at a general chapter of the Order, held at Arles in 1224, St. Francis appeared in the midst of them, his arms extended in the form of a cross.

19. St. Francis receiving the stigmata, as already described.

20. The death of St. Francis in the midst of his friars ; angels bear his soul into heaven.

21. The dying friar. Lying at that time on his deathbed, he beheld the spirit of St. Francis rising into heaven, and, springing forward, he cried, ' Tarry, father ! I come with thee,' and fell back dead.

22. St. Francis being laid upon his bier, the people of Assisi were admitted to see and kiss the stigmata. One Jerome, sceptical like St. Thomas, would see and touch before he believed: he is here represented kneeling and touching the side, 'the dead brow frowning with anguish.'

*23. The Lament at San Damiano. The body of St. Francis being carried to Assisi, the bearers halt before the porch of the church, and are received by St. Clara and her nuns: St. Clara leans over, embracing the body; another nun kisses his hand.

24. This compartment is in a ruined state.

*25. The vision of Pope Gregory IX. This pope, before he consented to canonise St. Francis, had some doubts of the celestial infliction of the stigmata. St. Francis appeared to him in a vision, reproved his unbelief, opened his robe, and, exposing the wound in his side, filled a vial with the blood which flowed from it, and gave it to the pope, who, on waking, found it in his hand.

*26. A certain man who had been mortally wounded by robbers, and given over by his physician, invoked St. Francis, who appears, attended by two angels, and heals him.

*27. A certain woman of Monte Marino, near Benevento, having died unshriven, her spirit was permitted, through the intercession of St. Francis, to return and reanimate the body, while she confessed and received absolution. The woman sits up in bed; an angel hovers above, awaiting the final release of the soul, while a horrible little demon, disappointed, flies away.

28. St. Francis the vindicator of innocence. A certain bishop had been falsely accused of heresy. The bishop's cathedral is seen on the left, the prison to the right; in the midst he is kneeling; a priest behind holds the crosier of which he has been deprived. The jailor steps forward with manacles, and St. Francis in his habit is seen floating above in the sky, and interceding for his votary.

Florence.
S. Trinità.

The series by Ghirlandajo in the Sassetti chapel consists of six subjects only:—

1. A famous Florentine legend, not to be found at Assisi. A child of the Spini family fell from the window of the Palazzo Spini, and was killed on the spot. While they are carrying the child to the grave, the parents invoke St. Francis, who appears visibly, and restores him to life.

2. St. Francis renounces the inheritance of his father.

3. He stands before Pope Honorius III., to whom he presents the roses which sprang from his blood.

4. He receives the stigmata.

5. St. Francis before the Soldan. He offers to walk through the fire to prove the truth of his mission.

6. Called ' The death of St. Francis,' but more properly ' The incredulity of Jerome.' The saint lies extended on a bier, surrounded by his brethren; a bishop, with spectacles on his nose, is reciting the service for the dead; a friar, in front (most admirably painted), kisses the hand of the saint; conspicuous in the group behind, Jerome stoops over, and places his hand on the wounded side. In compartments to the right and left kneel the votaries, Francesco Sassetti, and his wife Madonna Nera. This, even in its ruined condition, is one of the finest and most solemnly dramatic pictures in the world.

These frescoes are engraved in Lasinio's ' Early Florentine Masters.'

The series of bas-reliefs by Benedetto da Maiano consists of five subjects :— *Fl. Santa Croce.*

1. St. Francis receives the stigmata. 2. He receives from Honorius III. the confirmation of his Order. 3. He appears before the Soldan. 4. The incredulity of Jerome. 5. The martyrdom of the five Franciscan missionaries, as already related.
This series was engraved by the younger Lasinio, and published in 1823.

In all these instances the subjects form what may be properly termed an *historical* series. There is, however, an example of a pictured life of St. Francis which must be taken altogether in a mystical sense. I have spoken of the veneration entertained for him by his followers. They very early compared his actions and character with those of the Redeemer; and, with a daring fanaticism—for which I can hardly find a name—seemed almost to consider their seraphic patriarch less as an imitator and follower of Christ, than as a being endued himself with a divine nature; in short— for it amounted to that—as a reappearance, a sort of *avatar* of the Spirit of Christ again visiting this earth; or as the Second Angel of the Revelation, to whom it was given to set a seal on the elect. A memorial of this extravagant enthusiasm still exists in a set of twenty-six small pictures, painted by Giotto for the friars of the Santa Croce at Florence. It was the custom in the rich convents to have the presses and chests which contained the sacred vestments and *Fl. Acad. and Berlin Gal.*

utensils ornamented with carvings or pictures of religious subjects. These twenty-six pictures adorned the doors of the presses in the sacristy of the church of Santa Croce, and present the parellel (already received and accredited, not invented by the painter) between the life of our Saviour and that of St. Francis. The subjects have an ideal and mystical, rather than a literal, reference to each other. For some excellent remarks on this curious series, I must refer to the notes appended by Sir Charles Eastlake to Kugler's Handbook.

It remains to notice a few separate subjects which relate to St. Francis, and are not usually met with.

Nicholas V. (in 1449) descends into the tomb of St. Francis at Assisi, which had never been opened since his death. He *Louvre.* finds the body entire and standing upright; kneeling, he lifts the robe to examine the traces of the stigmata; attendants and monks with torches stand around; as in a picture by Lahire, in the Caravaggio style, and most striking for effect.—Another picture of the same scene, a most extraordinary and crowded composition, is engraved in the ' Dusseldorf Gallery.'[1]

A certain poor man was cast into prison by an inexorable creditor; he besought mercy in the name of the holy St. Francis; it was refused; but St. Francis himself appeared, *At Cagli.* broke his fetters, opened the doors of his dungeon, and set *Capella Tiranni.* him free. There is a picture of this subject by Giovanni Santi, the father of Raphael. St. Peter, the patron saint of prisoners, stands near with his keys; an angel attending on St. Francis is supposed to be the portrait of Raphael when a boy. I saw a drawing from this fresco at Alton Towers, differing in some respects from the minute description given by Passavant.

I am far from supposing that we have exhausted the

---

[1] This is a mere legend. The tomb in the hollow rock was opened Dec. 26, 1818, by order of Pius VII., when the skeleton was found recumbent and entire; it was left untouched, and the tomb reverently closed Jan. 1, 1819.

variety of illustration connected with the pictured life of St.
Francis, but I must stop; I must not be tempted beyond the
limits of my subject; I must forbear to give words to all the
reflections, all the comparisons between the past and the
present, which have arisen in my own mind while writing
the foregoing pages, and which will, I trust, suggest themselves to the thoughtful reader. I have heard it said that
the representations of this most popular of all the monastic
saints, and of the wild and often revolting legends which
relate to him, weary and disgust by their endless repetition.
They must do so if regarded as mere pictures; for there are
few out of the vast number which are really good; and the
finer they are, the more painful;—too often, at least, it is so.
Their effect depends, however, on the amount of faith or of
wise thoughtfulness, not less than on the taste, of the observer.
I have said enough to show what sad, what thrilling, what
solemn interest lies in the most beautiful and most ancient of
these pictured monuments; what associations of terror and
pity may be excited by some of the meanest. Many of the
subjects and groups I have slightly touched upon will be
better understood as we proceed to review the companions
and followers of St. Francis, who are supposed to share
his beatitude in heaven, and upon whom Art has bestowed on
earth a glory hardly less than his own.

St. Clara. (Perugino.)

St. Clara.

Lat. Sancta Clara.   *Ital.* Santa Chiara.   *Fr.* Sainte Claire.
August 11, 1253.

'Clara claris præclara meritis magnæ in cœlo claritate gloriæ ac in terra miraculorum sublimium clare claret.'

St. Clara, from some inevitable association of ideas, always comes before us as the very ideal of a ' Grey Sister,' ' sedate and sweet ; ' or of a beautiful saintly abbess, ' sober, steadfast, and demure ; ' and her fame and popularity as a patroness have rendered her musical and significant name popular from one end of Europe to the other, but more especially in Spain. Her story is so eminently picturesque, that we have reason to regret that as a picturesque subject so little use has been made of it.

Clara d'Assisi was the daughter of Favorino Sciffo, a noble knight; her mother's name was Ortolana. She was the eldest of their children; and her uncommon beauty, and the great wealth of her parents, exposed her to many temptations and many offers of marriage. But she had heard of those who were seeking the crown of salvation through the thorny paths of mortification and prayer; and her heart burned within her to follow their example. While yet in the first bloom of maidenhood, she had devoted herself in secret to a religious life; but her parents daily urged her to marry; and after a time, being distracted through the conflict within her own soul, she repaired to St. Francis and entreated his counsel. He, believing that the way he had chosen for himself was the true way to salvation, advised her at once to renounce the world; and he appointed the following Palm Sunday as the day on which she should come to him and make her profession.

On that day, according to the Catholic custom, Clara, arrayed in her most sumptuous apparel, accompanied her mother Ortolana, and her sister Agnes, and the rest of her family, to church; and when all the others approached the altar to receive the palm-branch with which to join the procession, she alone remained kneeling afar off—not lifting her eyes, through a sense of her own unworthiness; which when the bishop beheld, touched by her maidenly humility and bashfulness, he descended the steps of the altar, and himself placed the palm-branch in her hand. That same evening, being still arrayed in her festal garments, she threw a veil over her head and escaped from the city; and hurrying down the steep ascent on foot, she arrived breathless at the door of the chapel of the Porzioncula, where St. Francis dwelt with his then small brotherhood. When she craved admittance for a 'poor penitent,' they met her with lighted tapers, and conducted her, singing hymns of praise, to the altar of the Virgin. Then she put off her splendid attire, and St. Francis with his own hands cut off her luxuriant golden tresses, and he threw over her his own penitential habit, and she became his daughter and disciple. ' Dispose of me!' she said, kneeling at his feet; 'I am yours; for, having consecrated my will to God, it is no longer my own!' He desired her to take refuge in the convent of San Paolo, whither her father and her kinsmen pursued her, and endeavoured to force her away; but she clung to the altar, calling on God to help and strengthen her; and they were compelled to desist. Soon afterwards, her younger sister Agnes, inspired by her example, fled from her home—joined her in the convent—and solemnly renounced the world at the age of fourteen: other ladies of high rank in the city of Assisi, among whom were three of the noble house of Ubaldini, united themselves to the two sisters; and at length their mother, Ortolana—perhaps because she could not endure separation from her children: and from this time the Order of the 'Poor Clares' dates its commencement. The Rule was as austere as that of St. Francis. The habit was a gown of grey wool girded with knotted cord; on the head they wore a white coif, and over it, when they went abroad, a black veil. They went barefoot or sandalled; their bed was the hard earth; abstinence and silence were strictly ordained, more especially silence: but voluntary poverty, the grand distinction of the whole Franciscan Order, was what St. Clara most insisted on; and when, on the death of her father, she inherited great wealth, she distributed the whole of her patrimony to the hospitals and the poor, reserving nothing for herself nor for her sisterhood. They were to exist literally upon charity: when nothing was given to them, they fasted. Clara herself set an example of humility by washing the feet of the lay sisters when they returned from begging, and meekly serving them at table. The extreme austerity of her life wasted her health; but even when she had lost the use of her limbs, she sat up in bed and spun flax of marvellous fineness.

At this time the Emperor Frederic ravaged the shores of the Adriatic; and he had in his army a band of infidel Saracens, to whom he had granted the fortress of Nocera, since called from them *Nocera-dei-Mori;* and they sallied from this place of strength, and plundered the towns and villages of the valley of Spoleto, ' and made the inhabitants drink to the dregs of the chalice of wrath and cruelty.' One day they advanced nearly to the gates of Assisi, and attacked the convent of San Damiano. The nuns, seized with terror and despair, rushed to the bedside of their ' Mother,' Clara, and cowered around her like frightened doves when the hawk has stooped upon their dovecot. But Clara, then suffering from a grievous malady, and long bedridden, immediately arose, full of holy faith: took from the altar the Pix of ivory and silver which contained the Host, placed it on the threshold, and, kneeling down in front of her sisterhood, began to sing in a clear voice, ' *Thou hast rebuked the heathen, thou hast destroyed the wicked, thou hast put out their name for ever and ever!* ' whereupon the barbarians, seized with a sudden panic, threw down their arms and fled.

And the fame of this great and miraculous deliverance was spread far and wide; so that the people thronged from all the neighbouring cities to obtain the prayers and intercession of Clara. Pope Innocent IV. visited her in person, solemnly confirmed the Rule of her Order, and before her death she had the satisfaction of seeing it received throughout Christendom, while many princesses and ladies of the noblest houses had assumed the penitential cord of the Third Order of her community.

At the age of sixty, after years of acute bodily suffering, but always faithful and fervent in spirit, she expired in a kind of trance, or rapturous vision, believing herself called by heavenly voices to exchange her earthly penance for ' a crown of rejoicing.'

Her sister Agnes, who had been sent to Florence as Superior of a convent there, came to attend her on her deathbed, and succeeded her as second abbess.

After the death of St. Clara, the sisterhood, for greater safety, removed from San Damiano to San Giorgio, within the walls of Assisi, and carried with them her sacred remains. This church, now Santa Chiara di Assisi, has become the chief church of her Order.

N N

She was canonised in 1256.   She had bequeathed to her
sisterhood, in the most solemn terms, 'the inheritance of
poverty and humility;' but within the next half-century the
Clares, like the Franciscans, were released, as a body, from
their vow of poverty.   Their houses subsequently became the
favourite asylum for oppressed and sorrowing, parentless,
husbandless, homeless women of all classes.

The eloquent author of a recent Life of St. Francis styles
St. Clara 'the disobedient Clara,' and indicates some alarm
lest young ladies of our own time should incline to imitate
her disobedience, renounce their parents, and take to mortification, almsgiving, and maiden meditation, when they *ought*
to be thinking rather of balls and matrimony.

Now the idea that Heaven is best propitiated by the renunciation of all earthly duties and affections, is not peculiar to
the period in which Clara lived; nor should she be stigmatised
as disobedient because she chose what she considered the
better part,—the higher obedience.   The mistake lies in supposing that the affections and duties of this world can ever be
safely trampled under our feet, or accounted as snares, rather
than as means through which God leads us to himself.   Yet
it is a mistake too common to be justly made a reproach
against this self-denying enthusiastic woman of the thirteenth
century; who, moreover, in ignorance of the spirit of Christ's
doctrine, might easily shelter herself under the letter;—' If
any man come to me, and *hate* not his father and mother, and
wife and children, and brethren and sisters, yea, and his own
life also, he cannot be my disciple.'

' Madam,' said an English traveller to the abbess of a
foreign convent, 'you are here, not from the love of virtue,
but from the fear of vice.'   Is not this principle the basis of
all female education to the present hour?   Is not fear of evil,
rather than faith in good, inculcated by precept, by example,
by all pressure from without, leaving us unsustained from
within?—without guide as to the relative value of our duties,
until we are made to believe that God's earth and God's
heaven are necessarily open to each other?   A woman thus

timid in conscience, thus unstable in faith, untaught to reason, with feelings suppressed, rather than controlled and regulated,—whither shall she carry her perplexed life?— where lay down the burden of her responsibility? May she not be forgiven, if, like Clara, she yield up her responsibility to her Maker into other hands, and 'lay down her life in order that she may find it?'

But we must return from this moral digression to the effigies of St. Clara.

From early times she has been considered as a type of religious feeling, a personification of female piety; and I have seen figures which, no doubt, were intended to represent St. Clara in her personal character, as saint, mistaken for allegorical figures of religion.

When she bears the palm (as in this effigy, after the fine intarsiatura in the choir of San Francesco di Assisi), it is not

as martyr. It is the palm of victory over suffering, persecution, and temptation.   Or it may represent here the palm
branch which was taken from the altar and placed in her
hand.

In the very ancient portrait in her
church at Assisi, which bears the date
of 1281, and the name of Martin IV.,
pope, she carries a cross.—I give a
sketch made on the spot.

She also bears the lily ; and is distinguished from the numerous female
saints who bear the same emblem by
her grey habit, and the cord of St.
Francis, which stamp her identity at
once.

In devotional pictures she is generally young, beautiful, and with a
peculiar expression of soft resignation.   She wears the habit of her
Order, the grey tunic, the knotted
girdle, and the black veil. Her *proper*
attribute is the Pix containing the
Host, in allusion to the miraculous
dispersion of the Saracens ; the figure
after Perugino (51), sketched in the
little lonely church called *San Cosi-
mato*, which belongs to the Poor Clares,
is an example.

Rome.

St. Clara.
(Portrait at Assisi.)

Sometimes she is kneeling before
the Virgin, or our Saviour ; and presenting the Pix.

As the *Madre Serafica*, foundress and superior of the first
community of Franciscan nuns, she stands with her book and
her crosier.   In the Madonna pictures, painted for her Order,
she usually stands on one side of the throne of the Virgin,
and St. Francis on the other.   In a picture by Moretto, she
is grouped with St. Catherine, the two together symbolising
wisdom and piety ; and when grouped with Mary Magdalene,
they are symbols of penitence and piety.

Bassano.
Vienna Gal.

Pictures from her history, those at least which I have met with, are confined to three subjects :—

1. She makes her profession by night at the feet of St. Francis; as in a picture by Zurbaran.

Aguado Gal.

2. She opposes the Saracens. This is the great event of her life, and is often represented. I remember a picture in the Bologna Gallery, in which the Saracens, terrible bearded barbarians, are tumbling backwards over each other from their scaling ladders, while St. Clara, carrying the Host, and attended by her sisterhood, calmly stands above.

Lucio Massart.

3. The most beautiful picture of St. Clara I have ever seen represents the death of the saint, or rather the vision which preceded her death; it was painted by Murillo, for his friends the Franciscans of Seville,—' and thence *stolen* by Soult.' I saw it some years ago in the Aguado Gallery. St. Clara lies on her couch, her heavenly face lighted up with an ecstatic expression. Weeping nuns and friars stand around;—she sees them not,—her eyes are fixed on the glorious procession which approaches her bed: first, our Saviour, leading his Virgin-mother; they are followed by a company of virgin-martyrs, headed by St. Catherine, all wearing their crowns and bearing their palms, as though they had come to summon her to their paradise of bliss. Nothing can be imagined more beautiful, bright, and elysian than these figures, or more divine with faith and transport than the head of St. Clara. I do not know who is now the enviable possessor of this lovely picture. There is a small poor sketch of the subject in the Louvre, there called a Murillo.

A series of pictures from her life usually begins with her profession by night at the feet of St. Francis, but I have never seen it treated with that picturesque feeling and effect of which it is susceptible. The walls of her lonely, venerable old church at Assisi are covered with a complete series of ancient frescoes, attributed to Giottino, but in a most ruined state, having been whitewashed over. I could just make out a few of the subjects where an attempt had been recently made to clean them. 1. She receives the palm branch before the

altar; 2. she flies from her father's house; 3. she kneels before
St. Francis, and receives the habit from his hands; 4. she dies
in presence of the Divine personages and the virgin-martyrs,
as in Murillo's picture; 5. she is carried to the tomb,—among
the attendants is seen Cardinal Bonaventura.

In the vault over the choir the paintings are less injured,
and must have been exquisitely beautiful. There are four
compartments: 1. The Madonna and Child enthroned; beside
them St. Clara standing; and around, angels bearing censers,
flowers, and palms. 2. St. Catherine and St. Margaret. 3.
St. Agnes, and Agnes, the sister of St. Clara, as a nun. 4.
St. Christina and St. Cecilia. I do not know whether any
copies or engravings exist of these lovely figures.

The church, as I remember, had a cold, forsaken, melancholy air. Very different was the impression made by the
church of San Francesco, which we entered at the moment
when it was crowded with worshippers, and the sounds of a
magnificent organ, swelled by human voices, rolled through
the dimly lighted vaults,—dim, yet glorious; covered, wherever the eye could penetrate, with groups from sacred story;
with endless variety of ornament—with colour, with life, with
beauty!

St. Antony of Padua.

Lat. Sanctus Antonius Thaumaturgus. *Ital.* Sant' Antonio di Padova, In
Santo. *Sp.* San Antonio de Padua, Sol brillante de la Iglesia, Lustre
de la Religion Serafica, Gloria de Portugal, Honor de España, Tesorero
de Italia, Terror del Infierno, Martillo Fuerte de la Heresia, entre los
Santos por excelencia, el Milagrero. June 13, 1231.

Habit. Grey in the earliest pictures, afterwards dark brown, with the
hood and cord of St. Francis.
Attributes. The book and lily; a flame of fire in his hand, or in his
breast. The infant Christ in his arms, or on his book. A mule kneeling.

Even in the lifetime of St. Francis, arose one who imbibed
his spirit and carried out his views, and whose popularity in

religious Art is next to his own. St. Antony of Padua was
a Portuguese by birth; and at the time that the remains of
the five friars who had suffered martyrdom at Morocco were
brought to Lisbon, he was so touched by the recital of their
sufferings, that he took the habit of St. Francis, and devoted
himself to the life of a missionary, with a fixed determination
to obtain the crown of martyrdom in the cause of Christ.
For this purpose he set off for Morocco to convert the Moors,
but God had disposed of him otherwise, for, having landed
in Africa, he was seized with a lingering illness, which
paralysed all his efforts, and obliged him to re-embark for
Europe. Contrary, or, as they may be called, favourable
winds, drove him to the coast of Italy, and he arrived at
Assisi at the very moment when St. Francis was holding the
first General Chapter of his Order. St. Francis was soon
aware of the value of such a coadjutor, and, feeling the want
of a man of science and learning in his community, encouraged
him to devote himself to his studies. Antony did so, and
taught divinity with great distinction in the universities of
Bologna, Toulouse, Paris, and Padua; but at length he forsook all other employments, renounced the honours of the
schools, and devoted himself wholly as a preacher among the
people. To an easy, graceful carriage, a benign countenance,
and a flow of most persuasive eloquence, he added advantages
not yet displayed by any of the Franciscan teachers—great
skill in argument, and an intimate acquaintance with the
learning of the theological schools.

I will not now dwell upon the miracles which the enthusiasm
of his followers afterwards imputed to him. There can be no
doubt that he exercised, in his lifetime, as a missionary
preacher, a most salutary and humanising influence. Italy
was at that time distracted by intestine wars, and oppressed
by a tyranny so monstrous, that, if it were but possible, we
should, for the honour of humanity, take refuge in unbelief.
The excesses and barbarities of the later Roman emperors
seemed to be outdone by some of the petty sovereigns of
Northern Italy. Antony, wherever he came, preached peace,
but, to use his own words, it 'was the peace of justice, and

the peace of liberty.' The generous boldness with which he rebuked the insane cruelties of Eccellino, seeking him in his own palace to denounce him as 'intolerable before God and man,' ought to cover him with eternal honour. Everywhere he pleaded the cause of the poor, and the crowds who assembled to hear him being greater than could be contained in any church, he generally preached in the open air. Like St. Francis, he was a man of a poetical imagination, and a tender heart, overflowing with the love of nature, and particularly of the lower creatures, appealing to them often as examples to his audience. The whiteness and gentleness of the swans, the mutual charity of the storks, the purity and fragrance of the flowers of the field,—these he dwelt on often with delight; and as St. Francis was said to have preached to the fowls of the air, so St. Antony is said to have preached to the fishes of the sea. The plain fact seems to have been, that in preaching to some obstinate unbelievers he was heard to say that he might as well preach to the fishes, for they would more readily listen to him ; but the legend relates the story thus :— ' St. Antony being come to the city of Rimini, where were many heretics and unbelievers, he preached to them repentance and a new life ; but they stopped their ears, and refused to listen to him. Whereupon he repaired to the sea-shore, and, stretching forth his hand, he said, " Hear me, ye fishes, for these unbelievers refuse to listen! " and, truly, it was a marvellous thing to see how an infinite number of fishes, great and little, lifted their heads above water, and listened attentively to the sermon of the saint ! ' The other miracles related of St. Antony I pass over here: it will be sufficient to describe the pictures in which they are represented. After an active ministry of ten years, he died, worn out by fatigues and austerities, in his thirty-sixth year, reciting his favourite hymn to the Virgin,—' O gloriosa Domina ! ' The brotherhood desired to keep his death a secret, that they might bury him in their church, fearing that the citizens of Padua would appropriate the remains; but the very children of the city, being divinely instigated thereto, ran about the streets crying with a loud voice, ' *Il Santo è morto ! il Santo è morto !* ' whence it has been the custom in

Padua, from that time even to this day, to style St. Antony
IL SANTO, without adding his name.

Within a year after his death he was canonised by
Pope Gregory IX., and the citizens of Padua decreed that
a church should be erected to him at the public expense.
Niccola Pisano planned and commenced this magnificent
edifice in 1237, but it was not brought to its present form
for two centuries later. 'The exterior,' with its extraordinary
spires and its eight domes, has somewhat the appearance of
a mosque. Within, the lofty polygonal apsis with its elongated
pointed arches, and the rich Gothic screens which surround
the choir, testify to the partiality of the Franciscans for the
Gothic style, which, in Italy, they seem to have considered
as more peculiarly their own.' v. Murray's Handbook.

The chapel which contains the shrine of the saint was
begun in 1500 by Giovanni Minello, and Antonio his son;
continued by Sansovino, and completed by Falconetto in
1553. It is one mass of ornament, splendid with marble
and alabaster sculpture, bronzes, and gold and silver lamps,
—the very luxury of devotion.

There is not in all Italy a church more rich in monuments
of ancient and modern art than this of Sant' Antonio. Among
the most curious of these monuments must be reckoned the
earliest known effigy of St. Antony, and which appears to
have been followed in all the best representations of him.
He is a young man, with a mild, melancholy countenance, no
beard, wearing the habit and cord of St. Francis, the right
hand extended in benediction, the Gospel in the left; a
votary kneels on each side. In the devotional figures his
most usual attributes are the lily and the crucifix; the lily
being sometimes twined round the crucifix. In pictures of the
Siena school he holds a flame of fire in his hand, as emblem
of his ardent piety; as in this sketch from a picture in the
Academy of Siena. A very common representation is that
of St. Antony caressing the Infant Christ, who is seen
standing upon his book: or he holds the divine Infant in his
arms. In such representations we must be careful to distinguish him from St. Francis. p. 280.

O O

It is related that on one occasion, as he was expounding to his hearers the mystery of the Incarnation, the form of the Infant Christ descended and stood upon his book. This is called 'the Vision of St. Antony of Padua,' and is a very frequent subject.

The miracles and incidents of the life of St. Antony, either treated as a series or as separate pictures, generally find a place in every Franciscan church or convent. The most celebrated series which occurs in painting is that which was executed by Titian and Campagnola in a building near his church at Padua, called the 'Scuola del Santo,' a kind of chapter-house belonging to the convent. There is another example

S. Petronio.

at Bologna. The most celebrated instance in sculpture is the fine series of basso-relievos on the walls of the chapel which

Padua.
S. Antonio.

contains his shrine. In these, and in every other instance I can remember, the subjects selected are the same. The miracles attributed to St. Antony are all of a homely and

65   St. Antony.

prosaic character when they are not manifestly absurd ; the influence he exercised in the domestic and social relations of life seems to have suggested most of these legends :—

1. The saint, after laying aside the Augustine habit, receives the Franciscan habit at Coimbra in Portugal. On this occasion he dropped his baptismal name of Ferdinand, and took that of Antony, the patron of the convent at Coimbra.

2. A certain noble lady, dwelling in Padua, was the wife of a valiant officer ; and not less remarkable for her beauty and modesty, than for her particular devotion to the saint. Her husband, wrought upon by some malignant slanderer, stabbed his innocent wife in a transport of jealousy, and then rushed from his house in an agony of despair and remorse ; but meeting St. Antony, he was induced to return home, where he found his

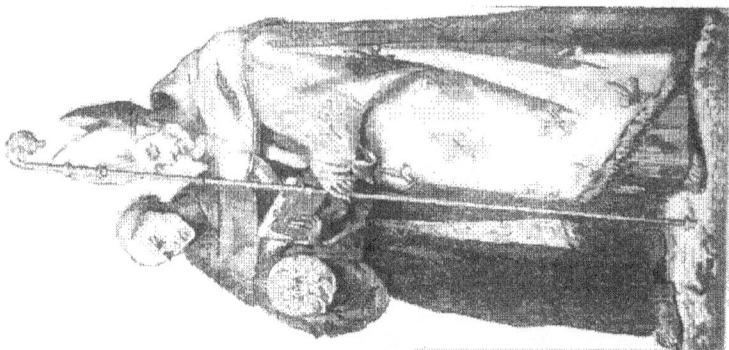

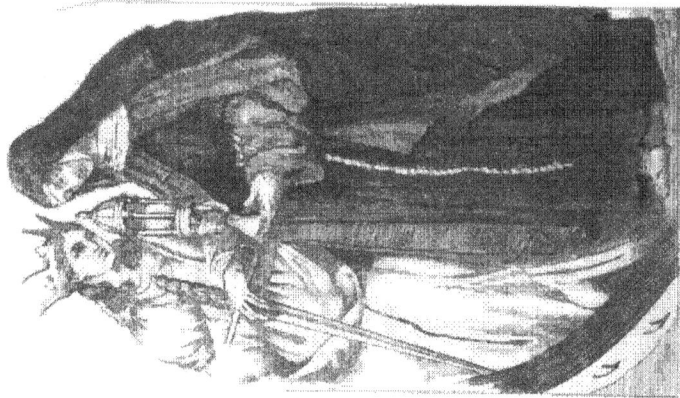

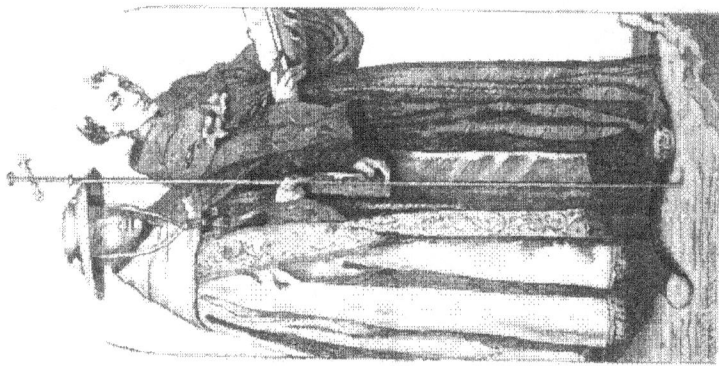

Th. Zimmerman fecit.

to any of the above examples.   It originally formed part of the predella of
an altarpiece in Santa Croce.   The group of listening women ranged in
front is exquisite for simplicity, grace, and devout faith in the power of the
saint.   Mr. Rogers has the original drawing.

A Miracle of St. Antony of Padua.   (Pesellino.).

'7. There was a certain youth of Padua named Leonardo, who came to
make confession to the saint, and revealed to him, with many tears, that in
a fit of anger he had kicked his mother.   The saint, unable to restrain his
horror and indignation at such an unnatural crime, exclaimed 'that the
foot that had so offended deserved to be cut off!'   The young man, rushing
from the confessional in despair, seized an axe and cut off his foot.   A
spectator ran to inform the saint, who hastened to the youth, and by his
prayers healed the severed limb.

The bas-relief is by Tullio Lombardi.   The fresco by Titian.   In both
the mother is interceding for her guilty son.   There is another example by
Trevisani.

Dresden Gal.
772

8. There was a certain Alcardino, a soldier by profession, who, as it
should seem, was little better than an atheist, for he absolutely refused to
believe in the miracles of the saint ; and when the children ran about the
streets, crying out ' Il Santo è morto,' he only shrugged his shoulders.   ' I
will believe,' he said, 'in all these wonders if the glass cup which I hold
in my hand be not broken ;' and he at the same time flung it from the
balcony where he stood, upon the marble pavement below.   The slab of

marble was broken by the collision ; the glass remained uninjured ;—a
miracle that must have sufficed to convince the most obstinate heretic in
the world : accordingly, we are assured that Alcardino was ever after a
reverent believer in the power of Sant' Antonio.

The bas-relief is by Gian-Maria di Padova. The fresco by one of Titian's
scholars.

9. A nobleman of Ferrara, the husband of a beautiful and virtuous wife,
had been induced to believe her unfaithful, and treated her with extreme
harshness. The lady brought forth a son, which the husband refused to
consider as his own offspring, and the unhappy mother, well nigh in
despair, entreated the interference of Sant' Antonio. The saint repaired
to the house, and desired that the child might be brought to him in
presence of the father. He then desired that the infant should be
unswathed, and commanded him to declare who was his real father, upon
which the child, stretching out his little hands, pronounced his name.
Then Saint Antony placed the child in the arms of the father, at tho
same time reciting the words of the psalm, ' Out of the mouths of babes
and sucklings,' &c.

The bas-relief is by Antonio Lombardi. The fresco, by far the best of
all those in the Scuola, is by Titian ; the heads very fine and expressive,
and the story admirably told.

10. The legend of the mule is one of the most popular of the miracles of
St. Antony, and is generally found in the Franciscan churches. It occurs
three or four times in the church at Padua. A certain heretic called Bovidilla entertained doubts of the real presence in the sacrament, and, after a
long argument with the saint, required a miracle in proof of this favourite
dogma of the Roman Catholic Church. St. Antony, who was about to
carry the Host in procession, encountered the mule of Bovidilla, which fell
down on its knees at the command of the saint, and, although its heretic
master endeavoured to tempt it aside by a sieve full of oats, remained
kneeling till the Host had passed.

The bronze bas-relief in the Chapel of the Sacrament is by Donatello. Padua.
The fresco is attributed to Campagnola. The same subject was painted
by Van Dyck for the Recollets at Malines.

11. St. Antony rebukes the tyrant Eccellino, who humbles himself
before him. The fresco is in the Scuola, and this is the only example I
have seen of an incident which is worth all the miracles together.

12. Luca Belludi, after the death of St. Antony, while weeping before
the altar, and deploring the sufferings of Padua under the horrible tyranny
of Eccellino, is comforted by a vision of the saint, who foretells the death
of the tyrant. This subject is in the Scuola. The chapel in which this

revelation is said to have occurred is the chapel of St. Philip and St.
James, called also the *Capella Belludi*, and celebrated for the ancient

Legend. Art,
i. 221.
frescoes to which I have already referred ; and I may add, that the figure
of a warrior on horseback in the Crucifixion of St. Philip is, according to

Lord
Lindsay.
an ancient tradition, the portrait of Eccellino.   The tomb of Luca Belludi
is of late date, about 1791.

13. Thirty-two years after the death of St. Antony, his remains were
transported to the church erected to his honour. On this occasion the
tomb being opened in the presence of Cardinal Bonaventura and Jacopo di
Carrara, prince of Padua, the tongue of the saint was found entire. This
scene has been painted in fresco by Contarini.

Artists of
Spain, p. 841.
Perhaps the finest work ever executed in honour of St.
Antony of Padua is the great picture by Murillo in the
cathedral at Seville. 'Kneeling near a table, the shaven
brown-frocked saint is surprised by a visit from the Infant
Jesus, a charming naked Babe, who descends in a golden flood
of glory, walking the bright air as if it were the earth, while
around him floats and hovers a company of cherubs, most of
them children, forming a rich garland of graceful forms and
lovely faces.   Gazing up in rapture at this dazzling vision,
St. Antony kneels with arms outstretched to receive the
approaching Saviour.   On a table is a vase containing white
lilies, the proper attribute of the saint, painted with such
Zeuxis-like skill, that birds wandering among the aisles have
been seen attempting to perch on it and peck the flowers.'
The figures are larger than life.

St. Antony with the Infant Saviour in his arms or standing
on his book, has been a favourite subject with the Spanish
painters.   Murillo—who, it must be remembered, was particularly patronised by the Capuchins of Seville—has painted
it nine times with variations : one of these is in the possession of Mr. Munro ; another, very beautiful, in the Berlin
Gallery.

Alton
Towers.
In the collection of Lord Shrewsbury there is a remarkable
picture of this subject attributed to that extraordinary man
Alonzo Cano.   St. Antony sustains in his arms the Infant
Christ, whom the Virgin, above, appears to have just relin-

quished, and holds her veil extended as if to resume her
Divine Child. The head of St. Antony is rather vulgar, but
most expressive; the Child most admirably painted, looking
up, as if half-frightened, to his mother. This is one of the
finest pictures of the Spanish school now in England, but it
is too dramatic in the sentiment and treatment to be considered as a religious picture.

57   St Antony of Padua with the Infant Christ. (L. Caracci.)

28   St Bonaventura.   (Raphael.)

St. Bonaventura.

The Seraphic Doctor.   Cardinal, and Bishop of Albano.   July 14, 1274.

CARDINAL BONAVENTURA, styled the *Seraphic Doctor*, was not only the pride and boast of the Seraphic Order, but is regarded as one of the great luminaries of the Roman Catholic Church.   He was born at Bagnarea in Tuscany, in the year 1221, and baptized by the name of Giovanni Fidanga.   In his infancy he had a dangerous illness, in which his life was despaired of.   His mother, in the extremity of her grief, laid her child at the feet of St. Francis, beseeching him to intercede with his prayers for the life of her son: the child recovered.   It is related, that when St. Francis saw him he exclaimed, ' O buona ventura! ' and hence the mother, in a transport of gratitude, dedicated her child to God by the name of Bonaventura.   She brought him up in sentiments of enthusiastic piety; and while he surprised his masters by the progress he made in his studies, she taught him that all his powers, all his acquirements, and all his faculties of head and heart, were absolutely dedicated to the divine service.

In 1243, at the age of twenty-two, he took the habit of St.
Francis, and went to Paris to complete his theological studies.
Within a few years he became celebrated as one of the
greatest teachers and writers in the Church.   He was remarkable at the same time for the practice of all the virtues enjoined by his Order, preached to the people, attended the sick,
and did not shrink from the lowliest ministering to the poor.
His humility was so great that he scarcely dared to present
himself to receive the Sacrament, deeming himself unworthy,
and, according to the legend, in recompense of his humility
the Host was presented to him by the hand of an angel.

While at Paris he was greatly honoured by Louis IX. (St.
Louis), and consulted by him on many occasions. In the year
1256 he was chosen General of the Franciscan Order at the
age of thirty-five. At that time the community was distracted
by dissensions between those of the friars who insisted upon the
inflexible severity of the original Rule, and those who wished to
introduce innovations. By his mildness and his eloquence he
succeeded in restoring harmony. Pope Clement IV., in 1265,
appointed him Archbishop of York; Bonaventura declined the
honour, and continued to teach and preach in his own country.
A few years afterwards, Gregory X. raised him to the dignity
of cardinal, and Bishop of Albano, and sent two nuncios to
meet him on the road with the ensigns of his new dignity.
They found him in the garden of a little convent of his Order,
near Florence, at that moment engaged in washing the plate
from which he had just dined: he desired them to hang the
cardinal's hat on the bough of a tree till he could take it v. woodcut
in his hands. Hence, in pictures of him, the cardinal's hat 64, p. 327.
is often seen hanging on the bough of a tree. At the great
Council held in the city of Lyons in 1274, for the purpose of
reconciling the Greek and Latin Churches, St. Bonaventura
was one of the most distinguished of the ecclesiastics who
were present, and the first who harangued the assembly. He
appears to have acted as the pope's secretary. The fatigues
which he underwent during this Council put an end to his
life: before it was dissolved, he was seized with a fever, of
which he died at the age of fifty-three, and was buried at

P P

Lyons in the church of the Franciscans; but during the wars
of the League the Huguenots plundered his shrine and threw
his ashes into the river Soane. He was canonised by Sixtus
IV. (himself a Franciscan) in the year 1482.

In devotional pictures painted for the Franciscans, Bonaventura is the frequent *pendant* of St. Francis or St. Clara.
In every picture I have seen he is beardless, and his face,
though often worn and meagre with fasting and contemplation,
is not marked by the lines of age.[1] He is sometimes represented wearing the cope over the grey habit of his Order,
with the mitre on his head as Bishop of Albano, and the
cardinal's hat lying at his feet or suspended on the branch of
a tree behind him. Sometimes he wears the simple Franciscan
habit, and carries the Pix or the sacramental cup in his hand,
or it is borne by an angel; and, occasionally, we find him in
the full costume of a cardinal (the crimson robes and the
crimson hat), with a book in his hand, significant of his
great learning. When grouped with St. Francis—the
superior saint—he is, in every instance I can remember, a
simple Franciscan friar, distinguished by the cardinal's hat
at his feet, or the sacramental cup in his hand, or the angel
presenting the Host. In the great picture by Crivelli, the
Host, or sacramental wafer, is seen above his head, as if
descending from heaven.

Coll. of Lord Ward.

[1] The figure of one of the Doctors of the Church in the 'Cappella di S. Lorenzo,'
in the Vatican, painted by Angelico for Nicholas V.,—a beautiful, simple, majestic
figure, with an aged bald head and very long parted beard, the cardinal's hat at
his feet,—represents, I think, St. Jerome, one of the 'Four great Latin Fathers,'
long established as of primary importance in the system of ecclesiastical decoration prevalent from the thirteenth to the sixteenth century. The figure is certainly
inscribed *St. Bonaventura;* but my impression, when I saw these frescoes and
examined them with a good glass, was, that the letters underneath are comparatively modern. We find in their proper places the other three doctors, St. Augustine, St. Ambrose, and St. Gregory: there was no reason for substituting
St. Bonaventura for the greatest of all, St. Jerome; besides that, Bonaventura
died at the age of fifty-three, is uniformly beardless, and ought to wear the
Franciscan habit and cord, which distinguish him from St. Jerome. This figure
has lately been engraved in an exquisite style by Mr. Gruner for the Arundel
Society; and I suggest these considerations, because it seems of some consequence
that the proper traditional type of a saint so important as Bonaventura should
not be liable to misconception.

According to a Spanish legend, St. Bonaventura, after his death, returned to the earth for three days to complete his great work, the Life of St. Francis. He is thus represented in a very extraordinary picture attributed to Murillo; he is seated Louvre. Sp. Gal. in a chair, wearing his doctor's cap and gown, with a pen in his hand, and a most ghastly, lifeless expression of countenance. Mr. Stirling doubts the authenticity of this picture, but it is very striking.

'St. Bonaventura receiving the Sacrament from the hand of an Angel' was painted by Van Dyck for the Franciscans at Antwerp. It has been coarsely engraved.

ST. BERNARDINO OF SIENA, FOUNDER OF THE OBSERVANTS.

May 20, 1444.

THIS saint was born at Massa, a little town in the Sienese territory, in 1380. He was of the noble family of Albizeschi; and, after his mother's death, was educated by his aunt, Diana degli Albizeschi, to whom he appears to have owed the development of his talents, as well as that extreme purity of mind and manners which distinguished his youthful years. He was extremely beautiful and graceful in person; but so modest, and, at the same time, so dignified, that his presence alone was a restraint on the libertine conversation of his companions,—as the mere appearance of the youthful Cato overawed the profligate Romans in the midst of one of their festivals.

At the age of seventeen he entered a confraternity devoted to the care of the poor and to the sick in the hospitals. Soon afterwards a pestilence broke out at Siena, which carried off a great number of the inhabitants, and, amongst the rest, many of the ministering priests, as well as the physicians, fell victims to the pestilence. Bernardino, assisted by twelve young men like himself, undertook the whole care of the plague hospital, and for four months attended night and day:

during this time it pleased God to preserve him from the contagion, but his fatigues brought on a delicacy of health from which he never recovered.

At the age of twenty-three he took the habit of St. Francis, and became one of the most celebrated and eloquent preachers of his Order. His ministry was not confined to his own country; he preached from one end of Italy to the other, and published a great number of sermons and treatises of piety, which have a high reputation in his own Church. Of the wonderful success of his preaching, many striking anecdotes are related. His hearers were not only for the moment affected and melted into tears, but in many instances a permanent regeneration of heart and life seemed to have taken place through his influence. Those who had defrauded made restitution; those who owed money hastened to pay their debts; those who had committed injustice were eager to repair it. Enemies were seen to embrace each other in his presence; gamblers flung away their cards; the women cut off their hair, and threw down their jewels at his feet: wherever he came, he preached peace; and the cities of Tuscany, then distracted by factions, were by his exhortations reconciled and tranquillised, at least for a time. Above all, he set himself to heal, as far as he could, the mutual fury of the Guelphs and Ghibelines, who, at that period, were tearing Italy to pieces.

He steadily refused to accept of any ecclesiastical honours; the bishopric of Siena, that of Ferrara, and that of Urbino, were offered to him in vain.

Philip Visconti, duke of Milan, one of the tyrants of that day, took offence at certain things that he had spoken in his sermons against the oppressions which he exercised. The duke threatened him; and, finding this in vain, he thought to soften him by the present of a hundred gold ducats, which he sent to him in a silver dish. The saint of course declined the present, but as the messengers insisted, and averred that they dared not take it back, he took it from their hands, and, desiring them to follow him, he repaired to the public prison and laid out the whole in releasing the poor debtors.

He was the founder of a reformed Order of Franciscans.

styled in Italy *Osservanti*, in France *Pères ou Frères de l'Observance*, because they *observed* the original Rule as laid down by St. Francis, went barefoot, and professed absolute poverty. This Order became very popular.

The health of St. Bernardino, always delicate, suffered from the fatigues of his mission and the severe abstinence to which he had condemned himself. While preaching in the kingdom of Naples, he sank under his exertions; being taken ill at Aquila, in the Abruzzi, he there expired, and there his remains are preserved in the church of San Francesco, within a shrine of silver. He was canonised by Pope Nicholas V. in 1450: and there are few saints in the calendar who have merited that honour so well;—none better, perhaps, than this exemplary and excellent friar. He is venerated throughout the whole of Italy, but more particularly in his native place, Siena.

It is related of San Bernardino, that when preaching he was accustomed to hold in his hand a tablet, on which was carved, within a circle of golden rays, the name of Jesus. A certain man, who had gained his living by the manufacture of cards and dice, went to him, and represented to him that, in consequence of the reformation of manners, gambling had gone out of fashion, and he was reduced to beggary. The saint desired him to exercise his ingenuity in carving tablets of the same kind as that which he held in his hand, and to sell them to the people. A peculiar sanctity was soon attached to these memorials; the desire to possess them became general; and the man, who by the manu-

59   St. Bernardino.

facture of gaming-cards could scarcely keep himself above
want, by the fabrication of these tablets realised a fortune.
Hence in the devotional figures of St. Bernardino he is usually
holding one of these tablets, the Ⅰ.Ⅾ.Ⓢ. encircled with rays,
in his hand.

Another attribute is the *Monte-di-Pietà*, a little green hill
composed of three mounds, and on the top either a cross, or
a standard on which is the figure of the dead Saviour, usually
called in Italy a *Pietà*.   St.
Bernardino is said to have
been the founder of the charitable institutions still called
in France *Monts-de-Piété*,
originally for the purpose
of lending to the very poor
small sums on trifling
pledges—what we should
now call a loan society—
and which in their com-
mencement were purely disinterested and beneficial. In
every city which he visited
as a preacher, he founded a
Monte-di-pietà; and before
his death, these institutions
had spread all over Italy
and through a great part of
France.[1]

60   St. Bernardino.

---

[1] Although the figures holding the *Monte-di-Pietà* are, in Italian prints and
pictures, styled 'San Bernardino da Siena,' there is reason to presume that the
honour is at least shared by another worthy of the same Order, ' Il Beato Bernardino da Feltri,' a celebrated preacher at the end of the fifteenth century. Mention
is made of his preaching against the Jews and usurers, on the miseries of the poor,
and on the necessity of having a *Monte-di-Pietà* at Florence, in a sermon delivered
in the church of Santa Croce in the year 1488. Of the extent to which usury was
carried in those times, and of the barbarous treatment of the poorer class of
debtors, we read in most of the contemporary authors; and it appears that the
Franciscan friars, especially the two Bernardinos, and a certain Fra Marco di
Ravenna (commemorated in a very rare and curious print called ' The Seven Works
of Mercy,' v. *Bartsch,* xiii. p. 88), were instrumental in remedying these evils.

The best devotional figures of St. Bernardino have a general resemblance to each other, which shows them to have been painted from some known original; probably the contemporary picture by Pietro di Giovanni. He is always beardless; his *Acad. Siena.* figure tall, slender, and emaciated; his features delicate and regular, but haggard and worn; his countenance mild and melancholy: he carries in his hand either the tablet with the name of Jesus, which is the common attribute; or the Monte-di-Pietà.

St. Bernardino. From the bas-relief by A. della Robbia.

In sculpture, the most beautiful representation of St. Bernardino is that of Agostino della Robbia, a colossal figure in high relief on the façade of the chapel of the *Confraternità di San Bernardino* at Perugia. Around him is a glory of eight angels, who are sounding his praise on various instruments of music; and the rest of the façade is covered with elaborate small bas-reliefs from his life and miracles.

In the separate subjects from his life which are to be met with in the Franciscan churches, he is represented preaching to a numerous audience, who listen with eager upturned faces; as in a fine old fresco in the San Francesco at Perugia: or he is restoring a young girl to life who had choked herself by swallowing a bone; as in a picture *'Storia della Pittura.'* by Pesellino, engraved in Rossini's work.

The best series of pictures from his life is in his chapel in

But unless we could ascertain the date of the first Monte-di-Pietà in Italy, it would not be easy to determine to which Bernardino the honour (and the effigy) properly belongs.

the Ara-Celi at Rome, painted by Bernardino Pinturicchio, who has put forth his best powers to do honour to his patron saint :—

1. St. Bernardino assumes the Franciscan habit. 2. He preaches, standing on a little green hillock : the attitude and expression admirable; they are those of a preacher, not an orator. 3. He beholds the crucified Saviour in a vision. 4. He is seen, studying the Scriptures in the solitude of Colombiere, near Siena. 5. He dies, and is laid on his bier; the sick, the maimed, the blind, gather around it to be healed by touching his remains; a mother lays down her dead child, and seems to appeal to the dead saint to restore it. 6. His glorification : he appears in Paradise, standing between St. Louis of Toulouse and St. Antony of Padua.

A very remarkable series is that by Pesellino, which I recollect to have seen with interest in the sacristy of San Francesco at Perugia; but had not time to make a note of the separate subjects, eight in number.

There is a picture by Ludovico Caracci, of St. Bernardino, ' *che mostra ai Soldati la Città di Carpi, chi miracolosamente non la viddero.*' I have not found this legend in any life of St. Bernardino to which I have had access.

Mo<!ena Ga
Malvasia,
· Felsina
Pittrice.'

ST. ELIZABETH OF HUNGARY.

LANDGRAVINE OF THURINGIA.

Lat. Sancta Elisabetha Mater Pauperum. *Ital.* Santa Elisabeta di Un-
gheria. *Fr.* Madame Saincte Elisabeth. La chère Sainte Elisabeth.
Sp. Santa Isabel. *Ger.* Die Heilige Elizabeth von Ungarn (or, vou
Hessen). Die liebe Frau Elizabeth. Nov. 19, 1231.

Ave gemma speciosa !
Mulierum sydus, rosa !
Ex regali stirpe nata,
Nunc in cœlis coronata ;
Mundo licet viro data
Christo tamen desponsata.
Utriusque sponsalia,
Simul servans illibata ;
Saram sequens fide pia,
Et Rebeccam prudentia,
O dilecta ! O beata !
Nostra esto advocata,
Elisabeth egregia !

(*From an old German Breviary,
printed at Nuremberg,* 1515.)

As St. Clara was the traditional type of female piety, her contemporary, St. Elizabeth, became the traditional type of female
charity. Of all the glorified—victims must I call them? or
martyrs ?—of that terrible but poetical fanaticism of the
thirteenth century, she was one of the most remarkable ; and
of the sacred legends of the Middle Ages, hers is one of the
most interesting and most instructive. I call it a *legend,*
because, though in all the material facts perfectly authentic,
and, indeed, forming a part of the history of her country,
there is in it just that sprinkling of the marvellous and the
fanciful which has served to idealise her character and convert
into a poem the story of her life.

That short sad life, crowded as it was outwardly with striking

Q Q

contrasts and vicissitudes of fortune, was yet more full—filled even to overflowing—with unseen, untold joys and sorrows; with pangs and struggles, such as then haunted the unreasoning minds of women, distracted between their earthly duties and affections, and their heavenward aspirations,—as if this world were not God's world and his care, no less than that other world!   The story of St. Elizabeth, and those graceful effigies which place her before us, offering up her roses, or with her fair crowned head bending over some ghastly personification of pain and misery, will be regarded with different feelings according to the point from which they are viewed. For some will think more of the glory of the saint; others, more of the trials of the woman : some will look upon her with reverence and devotion, as blessed in her charities, and not less blessed in her self-sacrifice ; others, with a sad heart-moving pity, as bewildered in her conscience and mistaken in her faith:—but none, I think, whatever be their opinions, can read the chronicle of her life without emotion.[1]

In the year 1207, Andreas II. was King of Hungary; and Herman, of poetical renown, the patron of the Minnesingers, was Landgrave of Thuringia, and held his court in the castle of the Wartburg.

In that year the Queen of Hungary brought forth a daughter, whose birth was announced by many blessings to her country and her kindred ; for the wars which had distracted Hungary ceased, and peace and good-will reigned, at least for a time; the harvests had never been so abundant, crime, injustice, and violence had never been so unfrequent, as in that fortunate year.   Even in her cradle the young Elizabeth showed sufficiently that she was the especial favourite of Heaven.   She was never known to weep from childish petulance ; the first words she distinctly uttered were those of prayer ; at three years old

---

[1] The authorities followed in the life of St. Elizabeth are Count Montalembert's *Histoire de S. Élisabeth de Hongrie, Duchesse de Thuringe,* third edition, and the notes to Mr Kingsley's beautiful drama, *'The Saint's Tragedy.'* Both cite the original and often contemporary documents.   The common legendaries, recounting merely her charities and her miracles, were here almost useless.

she was known to give away her toys, and take off her rich
dresses to bestow them on the poor; and all the land rejoiced
in her early wisdom, goodness, and radiant beauty.

These things being told to Herman of Thuringia by the
poets and wise men who visited his court, he was filled with
wonder, and exclaimed, ' Would to God that this fair child
might become the wife of my son!' and thereupon he resolved
to send an embassy to the King of Hungary, to ask the young
princess in marriage for his son, Prince Louis. He selected
as his messengers the Count Reinhard of Muhlberg, Walther
de Varila, his seneschal, and the noble widow, Bertha of
Beindeleben, attended by a train of knights and ladies, bearing rich presents. They were hospitably and favourably
received by the King of Hungary and his queen Gertrude,
and returned to Wartburg with the little princess, who was
then four years old. The king, her father, bestowed on her a
cradle and a bath, each of pure silver and of wondrous workmanship; and silken robes curiously embroidered with gold,
and twelve noble maidens to attend upon her. He also loaded
the ambassadors with gifts. He sent to the landgrave and
his wife Sophia magnificent presents—stuffs, and jewels, and
horses richly caparisoned, and many precious things which he
had obtained through his intercourse with Constantinople and
the East, the like of which had never before been seen in
Western Germany; and it is recorded that, whereas the
ambassadors had set off on their mission with two baggage-
waggons, they returned with thirteen.

When the princess Elizabeth arrived at the castle of the
Wartburg at Eisenach, she was received with infinite rejoicings, and the next day she was solemnly betrothed to the
young Prince Louis; and the two children being laid in the
same cradle, they smiled and stretched out their little arms to
each other, which thing pleased the landgrave Herman and
the landgravine Sophia; and all the ladies, knights, and
minstrels who were present regarded it as an omen of a blessed
and happy marriage.

From this time the children were not separated; they grew
up together, and every day they loved each other more and

more. They called each other by the tender and familiar names
of brother and sister; but Louis knew perfectly the difference
between his relationship with Elizabeth and with his own sister
Agnes, and he very soon perceived that his Elizabeth was quite
unlike all the other children in the court, and exercised over
them some extraordinary ascendancy : all her infant thoughts
seemed centred in heavenly things; her very sports were
heavenly, as though the angels were her playmates; but
charity, and compassion for the suffering poor, formed, so to
speak, the staple of her life. Everything that was given to
her she gave away; and she collected what remained from
the table, and saved from her own repasts every scrap of food,
which she carried in a basket to the poor of Eisenach, the
children of the poor being more especially her care.

As long as her noble father-in-law the landgrave Herman
was alive, no one dared to oppose the young Elizabeth in her
exercises either of devotion or charity, though both had excited
some feelings of disapprobation and jealousy in the court; even
her betrothed husband Louis, influenced by those around him,
began to regard her as one destined to be the bride of Heaven
rather than his own. When she was about nine years old,
and Louis about sixteen, the landgrave died; and Elizabeth,
having lost in him her father and protector, became, with all
her saintly gifts and graces, a forlorn stranger in her adopted
home. Louis had succeeded his father, but remained under
the tutelage of his mother. The landgravine, Sophia, dis-
liked the retiring character of her daughter-in-law; the
princess Agnes openly derided her; and the other ladies of
the court treated her with neglect.

On the occasion of some great religious festival, the landgravine carried the two young princesses to the church of
St. Catherine at Eisenach. They were attired, according to
the custom of the time, in their habits of ceremony, wearing
long embroidered mantles, their hair cast loose over their
shoulders; golden coronets on their heads, and bracelets on
their arms. On entering the church they knelt down before
the crucifix; Elizabeth, on raising her eyes to the image of
the dying Saviour, was struck with an irresistible reverence,

and instinctively took off her golden crown, placing it at the foot of the cross. She then meekly continued her prayer. The landgravine whispered bitter reproaches, and ordered her to replace her crown. Elizabeth, weeping, replied, 'Dear lady mother, reproach me not! Here I behold the merciful Jesus, who died for me, wearing his crown of thorns; how can I wear in his presence this crown of gold and gems? *my* crown is a mockery of *His!*' Then, covering her face with her long mantle, she held her peace, and continued to pray fervently. Her mother and sister, seeing the eyes of the people fixed on them, were obliged also to take off their crowns and cover their faces; 'which they misliked greatly,' adds the chronicle. They were more angry than ever with Elizabeth; and the whole court, perceiving her disgrace, failed not to treat her with contumely, and to jeer at what they called her pretended piety; so that her life was made bitter to her, even in her young days. She endured all with unvarying gentleness. The hardest trial of her patience was when the princess Agnes was wont to tell her, in a mocking tone, that 'her brother Louis would never marry such a *Beguine,* but would send her back to Hungary to her father.' This also Elizabeth bore in silence: she would go to her chamber and weep awhile; then, drying her tears, she would take up her alms-basket, and go to visit the poor children of whom she had made friends and companions; and in teaching them and caressing them she found comfort.

All this time Louis was observing her and watching her deportment under the contemptuous treatment of his mother and sister, and of those who thought to do them a pleasure by studiously neglecting or publicly insulting the object of their scorn. He did not openly show her any attention; he had some doubts whether she was not too far above him in her austere yet gentle piety. But often when she suffered from the contumely of others, he would secretly comfort her with kindest words, and dry up her tears. And when he returned home after an absence, he was accustomed to bring her some little gift which he had purchased for her, either a rosary of coral, or a little silver crucifix, or a chain, or a golden pin, or a purse, or a knife. And when she ran out to meet him joyfully, he would take her in his arms, and kiss her right heartily. And thus she grew up to maidenhood, looking to him, and only to him, for all her earthly comfort; trusting and loving him next to her Heavenly Father, to whom she prayed hourly for his well-being, and that his heart might not be turned away from her, for she knew that every earthly influence was employed to make him false to her and to his early vows.

It happened, on one occasion, that Louis went on a long hunting excursion with some neighbouring princes, and was so much occupied by his guests, that, when he returned, he brought not his accustomed gift, nor did he salute her as usual. The courtiers, and those who were the enemies of Elizabeth, marked this well; she saw their cruel joy, and her heart sank with apprehension. She had hitherto kept silence, but now, in the bitterness of her grief, she threw herself on her old friend, Walther de Varila, who had brought her an infant from Hungary, who had often nursed her in his arms, and who loved her as his own child. A few days afterwards, as he attended the landgrave to the chase, he took the opportunity to ask him what were his intentions with regard to the Lady Elizabeth; 'For,' said he, 'it is thought by many that you love her not, and that you will send her back to her father.' On hearing these words, Louis, who had been lying on the ground to rest, started to his feet, and, throwing his hand towards the lofty Inselberg which rose before them, 'Seest thou,' he said, 'yon high mountain? If it were all of pure gold from the base to the summit, and if it were offered to me in exchange for my Elizabeth, I would not give her for it!— no—I love her better than all the world! I love only her! and I will have my Elizabeth!' ('Ich will mein Elsbeth haben!') Then Walther, right joyful, said, 'My sovereign lord, may I tell her this?' and Louis answered, 'Yea, tell her this, that I love only her in the world!' Then from the purse which hung at his belt he drew forth a little silver mirror, curiously wrought, surmounted with an image of our Saviour. 'Give her this,' he added, 'as a pledge of my truth.'

When they returned, Walther hastened to seek Elizabeth, and gave her the loving message and the gift. And she smiled an angel smile, and kissed the mirror reverently, and saluted the image of Christ, and thanked him for all his mercies, but most of all for that he had kept true and tender towards her the heart of her betrothed husband; and, having done this, she put the mirror in her bosom, next to her heart.

About a year afterwards, their marriage was formally solemnised with great feasts and rejoicings which lasted three days.

Louis was at this time in his twentieth year. He was tall and well-made, with a ruddy complexion, fair hair, which he wore long in the German fashion, blue eyes, remarkable for their serene and mild expression, and a noble ample brow. He was of a princely temper, resolute, yet somewhat bashful, 'and in his words was modest as a maid.' He was never known to be unfaithful to his Elizabeth, from the hour in which they had been laid together in her cradle to the hour of his death.

Elizabeth was not quite fifteen. Her beauty was still immature; but, from its peculiar character, she appeared older than she really was. She had the beauty of her race and country, a tall slender figure, a clear brown complexion, large dark eyes, and hair as black as night; her eyes, above all, were celebrated by her contemporaries,—'they were eyes which glowed with an inward light of love and charity, and were often moistened with tears.'

She lived with her husband in the tenderest union, but carried into her married life the austere piety which had distinguished her from infancy; and the more she loved her husband, the more she feared herself. By the side of her innocent happiness 'a gulf still threatening to devour her opened wide,'—a gulf of sin—misery—death; death to both, if they stood in the way of each other's salvation.

She therefore redoubled her secret penances; rose in the night, and left her couch to pray, kneeling on the bare cold earth. She wore hair-cloth next her tender skin, and would sometimes scourge herself, and cause her ladies to scourge her.

Louis sometimes remonstrated, but in general he submitted, from some secret persuasion that himself and his people were to benefit by the prayers and the sanctity of his wife. Meantime she was cheerful and loving towards him, dressed to please him, and would often ride to the chase with him. When he was absent she put on the dress of a widow and wore it till his return, when she would again array herself in her royal mantle and meet him with a joyful smile, taking him in her arms as he dismounted from his horse, and greeting him with a wifely tenderness.

She had for her spiritual director a certain priest named Conrad of Marbourg, a man of a stern character, who, after a time, through her excitable mind and sensitive conscience and gentle womanly affections, ruled her, not merely with a rod of iron, but a scourge of fire.

Conrad had denounced as unpleasing to God certain imposts which were laid on the people for the express purpose of furnishing the royal table. And he commanded Elizabeth not to eat of any food served up at table, except of such as had been justly paid for, or produced from the private and hereditary estates of her husband. Not always able to distinguish between the permitted meats and drinks and those interdicted by her confessor, Elizabeth would sit at her own royal banquets abstinent whilst others feasted, and content herself with a crust of bread and a cup of water. On one occasion Louis took the cup out of her hand, and, putting it to his lips, it appeared to him that he tasted wine of such a divine flavour that he had never tasted any like it. He called to the cup-bearer, and asked him of what vintage was this extraordinary wine? The cup-bearer, astonished, replied, that he had poured water into the cup of the landgravine. Louis held his peace, for he had long believed that his wife was served by the angels; and some other circumstances which occurred during their married life, convinced him that she was under the especial favour and protection of Heaven.

One day that he entertained several of the neighbouring

princes, he desired of Elizabeth that she would appear in the presence of his guests as became his wife and the lady of his love. She, always obedient, called her maids around her, and arrayed herself in her royal robes, her tunic of green and golden tissue, her tiara of jewels confining her long dark tresses, and over her shoulders her embroidered mantle lined with ermine. Thus sumptuously attired, she was about to cross one of the courts of the castle which led to the apartment of her husband, perhaps with some secret thought that he would approve of the charms she had adorned for his sake, when she beheld prostrate on the pavement a wretched beggar, almost naked, and shivering with cold, hunger, and disease. He implored her charity; she told him she could not then minister to him, and was about to pass on, but he, sustaining his trembling limbs on his staff, dragged himself after her, and implored her that she would not leave him to die, but that, for the sake of Christ our Redeemer and the holy John the Baptist, she would have pity upon him. Now Elizabeth had never in her life refused what was asked from her in the name, either of the Saviour, or of St. John the Baptist, who was her patron saint and protector. She paused; and, from a divine impulse of mingled piety and charity, she took off her royal mantle and threw it over his shoulders. Then she retreated to her chamber, not knowing how she should excuse herself to her husband. At that moment the landgrave came to seek her; and she, throwing herself into his arms, confessed what she had done. While he stood irresolute whether to admire or upbraid her, her maiden Guta entered the chamber, having the mantle on her arm. ' Madam,' said she, ' in passing through the wardrobe I saw the mantle hanging in its place: why has your Highness disarrayed yourself? ' And she hastened to clasp it again on her shoulders.

Then her husband led her forth, both their hearts filled with unspeakable gratitude and wonder. And when Elizabeth appeared before the guests, they arose, and stood amazed at her beauty, which had never appeared so dazzling; for a glory more than human seemed to play round her form, and the jewels on her mantle sparkled with a celestial light.

' And who,' says the legend, ' can doubt that the beggar was our Lord himself, who had desired to prove the virtue of his servant, and who had replaced the mantle by the hand of one of his blessed angels?'

On another occasion, when Elizabeth was ministering to her poor at Eisenach, she found a sick child cast out from among the others, because he was a leper, and so loathsome in his misery that none would touch him, or even go nigh to him; but Elizabeth, moved with compassion, took him in her arms, carried him up the steep ascent to the castle, and while her attendants fled at the spectacle, and her mother-in-law Sophia loaded her with reproaches, she laid the sufferer in her own bed. Her husband was then absent, but shortly afterwards his horn was heard to sound at the gate. Then his mother Sophia ran out to meet him, saying, ' My son, come hither! see with whom thy wife shares her bed!'—and she led him up to the chamber, telling him what had happened. This time, Louis was filled with impatience and disgust; he rushed to the bed and snatched away the coverlid; ' but behold, instead of the leper, there lay a radiant infant with the features of the new-born in Bethlehem; and while they stood amazed, the vision smiled, and vanished from their sight.'

Sacred and Legend. Art, i. 305; ii. 851, 393. (We have here the beautiful legendary parable, so often repeated in the lives of the saints; for example, in those of St. Gregory, St. Martin, St. Julian, and others; and which doubtless originated either in the words of our Saviour,— Matt. xxv. ' Inasmuch as ye have done it to the least of these my brethren, ye have done it unto me;' or in the text of St. Paul, Heb. xiii. 2. —' Be not forgetful to entertain strangers, for thereby some have entertained angels unawares.')

Elizabeth, in the absence of her husband, daily visited the poor who dwelt in the suburbs of Eisenach, and in the huts of the neighbouring valleys. One day, during a severe winter, she left her castle with a single attendant, carrying in the skirts of her robe a supply of bread, meat, and eggs, for a certain poor family; and, as she was descending the frozen and slippery path, her husband, returning from the chase, met her bending

under the weight of her charitable burden. 'What dost thou
here, my Elizabeth?' he said; 'let us see what thou art
carrying away?' and she, confused and blushing to be so
discovered, pressed her mantle to her bosom; but he insisted,
and, opening her robe, he beheld only red and white roses,
more beautiful and fragrant than any that grow on this earth,
even at summer-tide, and it was now the depth of winter!
Then he was about to embrace his wife, but looking in her
face, he was overawed by a supernatural glory which seemed
to emanate from every feature, and he dared not touch her;
he bade her go on her way, and fulfil her mission; but taking
from her lap one of the roses of Paradise, he put it in his
bosom, and continued to ascend the mountain slowly, with
his head declined, and pondering these things in his heart.[1]

In the year 1226, the landgrave Louis accompanied his
liege lord, the Emperor Frederick II., into Italy.

In the same year, a terrible famine afflicted all Germany;
but the country of Thuringia suffered more than any other.
Elizabeth distributed to the poor all the corn in the royal
granaries. Every day a certain quantity of bread was baked,
and she herself served it out to the people, who thronged
around the gates of the castle, sometimes to the number of
nine hundred; uniting prudence with charity, she so arranged
that each person had his just share, and so husbanded her
resources that they lasted through the summer; and when
harvest time came round again, she sent them into the fields
provided with scythes and sickles, and to every man she gave
a shirt and a pair of new shoes. But, as was usual, the
famine had been succeeded by a great plague and mortality,
and the indefatigable and inexhaustible charity of Elizabeth

---

[1] There are several different versions of this beautiful and celebrated
legend. Sometimes the incident occurs before her marriage, and then it is
her father-in-law, Herman, who discovers the roses: sometimes it is placed in the
period of her widowhood, and then it is her cruel brother-in-law, Henry. I have
given the most *accredited* version, that which is adopted by Count Montalembert,
who must henceforth be considered as the first authority in all that concerns
the legend of Elizabeth. See, in his Life of her, the chapter '*De la grande
charité de la chère Sainte Elisabeth, et de son amour pour la pauvreté.*' Third
edition, p. 50.

was again at hand. In the city of Eisenach, at the foot of the Wartburg, she founded an hospital of twenty beds for poor women only; and another, called the Hospital of St. Anne, in which all the sick and poor who presented themselves were received; and Elizabeth herself went from one to the other, ministering to the wretched inmates with a cheerful countenance, although the sights of misery and disease were often so painful and so disgusting that the ladies who attended upon her turned away their heads, and murmured and complained of the task assigned to them.

She also founded an hospital especially for poor children. As I have already said, children were at all times the objects of her maternal benevolence. It is related by an eye-witness, that 'whenever she appeared among them, they gathered round her, crying "Mutter! Mutter!" clinging to her robe and kissing her hands. She, mother-like, spoke to them tenderly, washed and dressed their ulcerated limbs, and even brought them little toys and gifts to amuse them.' In these charities she not only exhausted the treasury, but she sold her own robes and jewels, and pledged the jewels of the state. When the landgrave returned, the officers and councillors went out to meet him, and fearing his displeasure, they began to complain of the manner in which Elizabeth, in their despite, had lavished the public treasures. But Louis would not listen to them; he cut them short, repeating, 'How is my dear wife? how are my children? are they well? Let her give what she will, so long as she leaves me my castles of Eisenach, Wartburg, and Naumburg!' Then he hurried to the gates, and Elizabeth met him with her children, and threw herself into his arms and kissed him a thousand times, and said to him tenderly, 'See! I have given to the Lord what is his, and he has preserved to us what is thine and mine!'

In the following year, all Europe was arming for the third Crusade; and his liege lord Frederick II., having assumed the cross, summoned Louis to join his banner. No help! Louis must go where duty called him; and he took the cross, with many other princes and nobles, from the hands of Conrad, bishop of Hildesheim. Returning thence to his castle of

Wartburg, and thinking on all the sorrow it would cause his Elizabeth, he took off his cross and put it into his purse to hide it until he should have prepared her for their parting: but many days passed away, and he had not courage to tell her what was at his heart.

One evening, while they sat together in her bower, she asked him for alms for her poor; and, as he resisted, she playfully unbuckled his purse, and put her hand into it, and drew forth the cross. Too well she knew that sign! the truth burst upon her at once, and she swooned at his feet. On recovering her senses she wept much, and said, 'O my brother! if it be not against God's will, stay with me!' And he answered with tears, 'Dear sister! I have made a vow to God; I must go!' Then she said, 'Let it be as God willeth: I will stay behind and pray for thee.' So Louis departed in the summer of that year; and Elizabeth went with him two days' journey before she had the strength to say farewell. Then they parted with tears and many embracings; and her ladies and her knights brought her back half dead to the Wartburg; while Louis with his knights pursued their journey. Among these was Count Louis of Gleichen, whose monument may still be seen in the Cathedral of Erfurt, lying between his two wives. The landgrave pursued his journey happily towards Palestine, until he came to Otranto in Calabria; there he was seized with a fever, and died in the arms of the Patriarch of Jerusalem. He commanded his knights and counts who stood round his bed that they should carry his body to his native country, and defend his Elizabeth and his children—with their life-blood, if need were—from all wrong and oppression.

Now, after the departure of her husband, Elizabeth had brought forth her youngest daughter, and, occupied with the care of her children and the care of her poor, had resolved to wait in patience the return of him who was never more to return. When the evil tidings arrived, she swooned away with grief; and if God, the Father of the widow and the orphan, had not sustained her, she had surely died.

Louis had two brothers, Henry and Conrad. The eldest of

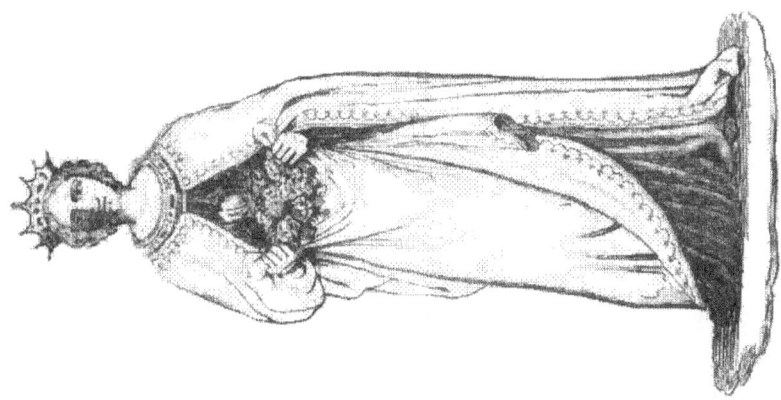

St Elizabeth of Hungary.

for her support. She spun wool, and as her poor fingers became weaker and weaker, and she earned less and less, her clothes became ragged, and she mended them with shreds of any colour, picked up here and there, so that her appearance excited the derision of the people, and the very children—those children whom she had so tended and cherished—pursued her in the streets as a mad woman! All these humiliations, and more and worse, she endured with an humble and resigned spirit, and the pious looked upon her as a second St. Clara.

But even into her poor retreat the wicked world pursued her. It was reported—but only in distant parts, where she was not known—that she was living with the priest Conrad in an unholy union ; and her old friend, Walther de Varila, thought it right to visit her and to warn her of these reports. She made no answer, but, sadly shaking her head, she bared her shoulders and showed them lacerated by the penitential scourge inflicted by her harsh director. So Walther de Varila said on more, but sorrowfully went his way.

After this visit Conrad dismissed her two women, who till now had served her faithfully, and placed round her person creatures of his own, who made her drink to the very dregs the cup of humiliation. True, it was said that she was comforted by celestial visitants; that the angels, and the blessed Virgin herself, deigned to hold converse with her; but not the less did the poor visionary, or favoured saint, gradually fade away, till, laid upon her last bed, she turned her face to the wall and began to sing hymns with a most sweet voice; when her strength failed, she uttered the words ' Silence !' and so died. The legend adds, that angels bore her spirit into heaven; and, as they ascended through the night, they were heard from afar chanting the response ' *Regnum mundi contempsi.*' She had just completed her twenty-fourth year, and had survived her husband three years and a half.

No sooner had Elizabeth breathed her last breath than the people surrounded her couch, tore away her robe, cut off her hair,—even mutilated her remains for relics. She was buried amid miracles and lamentations, and four years after her death she was canonised by Gregory IX.

In the same year was founded the Church of St. Elizabeth at Marbourg. It was completed in forty-eight years, and her shrine there was enriched by the offerings of all Germany. The church is one of the finest specimens of pure early Gothic, and in perfect preservation. The richly ornamented chapel of St. Elizabeth is in the transept,—the stone steps around it worn hollow by the knees of pilgrims. The shrine of St. Thomas of Canterbury was not more venerated and visited in England than the shrine of St. Elizabeth in Germany. This shrine is still preserved in the sacristy, but merely as a curiosity ; for at the time of the Reformation it was violated, with circumstances of great and brutal levity, by her own descendant, Philip, landgrave of Hesse, styled in history 'the Magnanimous,' and her remains were dispersed no one knows how or whither.

The Castle of Wartburg, once the home of Elizabeth, is now almost a ruin. The chamber she inhabited is still carefully perserved, not because it was *hers*, but because it was Luther's. Here he found a refuge from the vengeance of priests and princes ; here he completed his translation of the Bible ; here, as he himself relates, he contended bodily with the demons who came to interrupt his work ; and here they still show the stain on the wall from the inkstand which he flung at the head of Satan ;—looking on which, we may the more easily forgive the sick fancies and soul tortures of that gentlest and loveliest of all saints, Elizabeth.

I remember climbing the rocky bypath to the summit of the Wartburg, the path where Elizabeth was encountered with her lapful of roses ; and I cannot help thinking, that to have performed that feat twice a day, required indeed all the aspiring fervour of the saint, as well as the tender enthusiasm of the woman young and light in spirit and in limb. Poor Elizabeth ! Her memory stil lives in the traditions of the people, and in the names given to many of the localities near Eisenach and Marbourg ; they still cultivate roses round the vicinity of the steep and stony Wartburg : I recollect seeing the little cemetery which lies near the base of the mountain, all one blush of roses;—you could not see the tombstones for the rose-bushes, nor the graves for the rose-leaves heaped on them.

And so much for the history of Elizabeth of Hungary; which having read and considered, we now turn to the effigies which exist of her.

She ought, of course, to be always represented as young and beautiful, but some of the German artists have overlooked the historical description of her person, and converted the dark-eyed, dark-haired Hungarian beauty into the national blonde. They have also given her the features of a matron of mature and even venerable age; and it is curious that this mistake is not made in the Italian pictures. Her proper attribute is the lapful of roses, which should be red and white, the roses of Paradise (*love* and *purity*,—like those which crown St. Cecilia). She sometimes wears the attire of a sovereign princess, sometimes the veil of a widow, and sometimes the habit and cord of a Franciscan nun; in general a cripple or beggar is prostrate at her feet, and the diseased cripple has sometimes the lineaments of a child. Where three crowns are introduced, they represent her sanctity as virgin, as wife, and as widow.

I will give some examples:—

1. The statue in the Cathedral at Marbourg is perhaps the most ancient. She stands, as patroness of the church, a grand dignified figure, with ample massive drapery falling round her form; a crown on her head; in one hand she holds the church (according to custom), the other hand is broken off;—it was probably extended in benediction: at her feet is the figure of a cripple.

2. A colossal figure on one of the windows of the Cathedral of Cologne, north of the nave.

3. She stands in a niche, holding up a basket of roses,—no Basle Musée. crown, long *golden* hair flowing over her robe of crimson and ermine.

4. She stands, holding up with both hands the folds of her F. Angelico. robe, filled with roses.

5. A most beautiful figure in a Coronation of the Virgin; S. Botticelli

S 3

she is looking up with a soft devout expression, her lap full of roses, and the three crowns embroidered on the front of her tunic.

Paolo
Morando.
Verona. B.
Bernardino.

6. She stands in the dress of a nun, veiled; a rosary in her hand, and the roses in her lap; —one of a group of Franciscan saints in an altarpiece of the glorified Madonna. I give a slight sketch of this figure from the original picture. It was impossible to render the expression in the head, which is wonderfully beautiful and sweet, and quite justifies the eloquent praise of Vasari.[1]

Holbein.
Munich Gal.

7. She stands in royal attire, ministering to some diseased beggars who kneel at her feet, the leprous boy being conspicuous among them.

Boisserée
Gal.

8. She stands, veiled as a widow, giving a vest to a kneeling beggar. As is usual with ancient votive pictures, the saint is colossal, the beggar diminutive.

9. St. Elizabeth spinning with five of her maids in a print by Hans Burgmair.

62   St. Elizabeth.   (Paolo Morando.)

Of the subjects taken from her life, the most ancient, I presume, are the sculptures over the altar of her chapel in the

[1] ' Santa Elisabetta, che è bellissima figura, con aria ridente e volto grazioso, e con il grembo pieno di rose ; e pare che gioisca veggendo per miracolo di Deo che il pane, che ella stessa, gran signora, portava ai poveri, fosse convertito in rose, in segno che era accetta a Dio quella sua umile carità.'— Vasari, i. 659. Fl. edit. The other saints in this fine picture are St. Francis, St. Antony of Padua, St. Louis King, St. Louis of Toulouse, St. Bonaventura, St. Ives of Bretagne, and St. Eleazar of Sabran.

Cathedral at Marbourg. They are carved in wood, in very high relief, and in the pure German religious style, somewhat like that of Albert Dürer, but certainly more ancient. In the centre is the death of St. Elizabeth. Seven figures of priests and attendants surround her bed; the most conspicuous and authoritative of these, which I presume to represent her confessor, Conrad, has the head broken off, and is the only figure mutilated. On one side, she is carried to the tomb; on the other, is the exaltation of her relics after her canonisation in presence of the Emperor Frederick.

On the doors which close in this sculpture are painted several subjects from her life; among them the following:—

1. She gives her royal mantle to the beggar. 2. The miracle of the poor leper laid in her bed. 3. The parting of Elizabeth and her husband. 4. She is expelled from her castle of the Wartburg.

But the most celebrated picture from the life of St. Elizabeth is that which Murillo painted for the Church of the Caritad at Seville, one of the series of pictures illustrating ' the works of charity.' It is thus described by Mr. Stirling:—

'The composition consists of nine figures assembled in one of the halls of her hospital. In the centre stands "the king's daughter of Hungary," arrayed in the dark robe and white head-gear of a nun, surmounted by a small coronet; she is engaged in washing, at a silver basin, the scald head of a beggar-boy, which, being painted with revolting adherence to nature, has obtained for the picture its Spanish name *el Tiñoso.* Two of her ladies, bearing a silver ewer and a tray with cups and a napkin, stand at her right hand, and from behind peers a spectacled dueña; to her left hand there is a second boy, likewise a tiñoso, removing with great caution, and a wry face, the plaister which covers his head, a cripple resting on his crutches, and an old woman seated on the steps of the dais. More in the foreground, to the right of the group, a half-naked beggar, with his head bound up, leisurely removes the bandage from an ulcer on his leg, painted with a reality so curious and so disgusting, that the eye is both arrested and sickened. In the distance, through a window or opening, is seen a group of poor people seated at table, waited on by their gentle hostess. In this picture, although it has suffered somewhat from rash restoration, the management of the composition and the lights, the brilliancy of the colouring, and the manual skill of the execution, are above all praise. Some objection may, perhaps, be made to the exhibition of so much that is sickening in the details. But this, while it is justified by the legend, also

Artists of Spain, p. 862.

heightens the moral effect of the picture. The disgust felt by the spectator is evidently shared by the attendant ladies ; yet the high-born dame continues her self-imposed task, her pale and pensive countenance betraying no inward repugnance, and her dainty fingers shrinking from no service that can alleviate human misery, and exemplify her devotion to her Master. The old hag, whose brown scraggy neck and lean arms enhance by contrast the delicate beauty of the saint, alone seems to have leisure or inclination to repay her with a look of grateful admiration. The distant alcove in which the table is spread, with its arches and Doric pillars, forms a graceful background, displaying the purity of Murillo's architectural taste.'

Among the *pictures* of this ' chère Sainte Elisabeth,' I am tempted to include one in verse, which, in its vivid graphic power and truth of detail, may be compared to Murillo. In the ERLINDE of Wolf von Goethe (the accomplished grandson of the great poet) a laughing dame ridicules the saintly charity of Elizabeth and the austerity of her court, where to cook for the sick and to serve beggars was the vocation !

> Für Kranke kochen und für Bettler sparen,
> Wird dort verlangt.

Another lady, who had formerly attended on Elizabeth, thus replies :—

> Deride not thou that saintly name ! I see
> That mild face now, as she so cheerfully
> Trod the rough path that down the Wartburg goes
> To where the hospital she founded rose,
> We, stumbling on, drawing our robes aside,
> Impatient at the stones that round us lay,—
> She, floating on down the steep mountain-side,
> Spite of the rugged path and toilsome way ;—
> Then, like a hive, the hospital began
> To stir, and send forth greetings glad and loud ;
> The sickly children tottering towards her ran,
> And from the windows look'd a sick and aged crowd.
>
> But the poor cripple (ofttimes scorn'd and vex'd),
> The idiots by their painful lot perplex'd,—
> These, who found scoffs and shame their bitter part,
> Were still the dearest to her pious heart :
> They hung upon her robe with joyous cries,
> And gazed with love into her loving eyes.

The sick and dying when she strove to cheer,
Through the long room the cry rose—'Here! oh, here!'
With tender care their wounds she drest,
And laid the suffering to rest :
With softest words she calm'd th' impatient mood ;
And if the handmaids who around her stood
Sought in her ministry to share,
The sick would suffer only *her* sweet care,
And her fair hands were kiss'd, her name was blest !

Deep in my heart these pious deeds I kept,
Nor could I rest to see her stand,
Drest in coarse serge—of gold and gem bereft—
Near the rich jewell'd ladies of the land.
Oft would I throw my splendid robes aside,
And often to the wretched serfs would go
(Near Eisenach, where she sometimes would abide)
And give, like her, gold to relieve their woe.
But as she did—how vainly have I tried,
Life, love, and joy renouncing, all to bring
Unto our Lord as the best offering ![1]

---

[1] 'Erlinde,' ersten Abtheilung, p. 25.

Die heil'ge Frau verspotte nicht!
Ich sehe noch ihr mildes Angesicht,
Wenn sie den Pfad, der sich von Wartburg windet,
Zum Hospitale stieg, das sie gegründet.
Wenn wir voll Ungeduld die Röcke rappten,
Bald hierhin und bald dorthin tappten,
Schien sie des rauhen Weges trotz zu schweben,
Und wie in einem Bienenhaus,
Begann es im Spital zu leben.
Die kranken Kinder stolperten belebt heraus ;
Am Fenster zeigten sich die alten Schwachen.
Die Krüppelein, die and're oft belachen,
Die blöden Sinnes, oft verspottet und betrübt,
Sie hat die fromme Frau am innigsten geliebt.
Sie hingen sich mit starrem Blick an ihr Gewand,
Mit off'nem Munde lachend, an sie fest gebannt.
Und trat sie ein, wo schwere Sieche lagen,
Da ging es an ein Rufen, an ein Fragen.
„Zu mir"—„Zu mir," so scholl es durch den Saal;
Die eklen Schaden ohne Zahl
Verband sie, bettete die Kranken ;

July 8, 1336. ST. ELIZABETH OF PORTUGAL, another queenly saint who wears the Franciscan habit, was the grand-niece of St. Elizabeth of Hungary, and daughter of Peter III. king of Aragon. She was married young to Dionysius, king of Portugal, a wise, just, and fortunate prince as regarded his people; faithless, profligate, and cruel in his conjugal and domestic relations. Elizabeth, after a long and unhappy marriage, was left a widow in 1325, and died in 1336 at the age of sixty-five. Having been canonised late by Urban VIII (in 1625), she does not appear in early pictures; and, as I think, only in Spanish and Portuguese Art, for I can recollect no instance in Italian or German pictures. She is represented, like Elizabeth of Hungary, in the habit of a Franciscan nun, or a widow's hood and veil, over which she wears the royal crown: she is usually dispensing alms, and distinguished from the *other* St. Elizabeth by her venerable age, or, by having the arms of Portugal or Aragon placed in some part

Artists of
Spain, p.999. of the picture. Mr. Stirling mentions 'a fine composition from her exemplary life,' by Carreño de Miranda, but not the

---

Die Zornigen, mit unnennbarer Huld,
Ermahnte sie zu freundlicher Gebuld.
Das war ein Handküssen, Segnen, Danken.
Und wollt' auch eine Magd sich überwinden,
Doch ließ von ihr kein Kranker sich verbinden.
Es mußt' im Innern mich erfassen
Tief solche Frömmigkeit.
Mir wollt' es keine Ruhe lassen,
Wenn sie im groben Kleid
Bei stolz geputzten Frauen stand.
Oft warf ich ab das Prunkgewand.
Zur letzten Hütte bin ich hingeeilt,
Wenn sie in Eisenach verweilt;
Den kleinen Schatz trieb es mich, hinzugeben,
Wie sie, den Schwachen Trost zu bringen;
Doch nimmer wollt' es mir gelingen,
Dem Herrn, mein ganzes Thun und Leben
Entsagend als ein Opfer darzubringen.

For the translation of this beautiful and animated picture I am indebted to the daughter of Barry Cornwall.

scene or subject chosen. Pictures of this sainted queen, so very rarely met with, ought to excite some interest and attention. She is remarkable for three things, besides the usual amount of prayers, penances, miracles, and charities which go to the making of a saint:—for forty years of unfailing patience under a wifely martyrdom almost intolerable;—for having been on every occasion the peacemaker and reconciling angel between her faithless but accomplished husband and his undutiful son, when she might easily have avenged her wrongs, and fomented discord, by the assertion of her own rights; this procured her in Spain the charming title of *Sant' Isabel de Paz;*—last, and not least, she is the original and historical heroine of Schiller's ' Fridolin,' though in the ballad and in Retzsch's designs the scene is transferred to Germany, and Elizabeth becomes ' Die Gräfin von Savern.' I have never met with this beautiful well-known legend with reference to Elizabeth queen of Portugal, to whom it rightfully belongs. It is mentioned by all her biographers, not even excepting the ' *Biographie Universelle.*' [1]

ST. LOUIS OF FRANCE.

Lat. Sanctus Ludovicus Rex. *Ital.* San Luigi, Rè di Francia. August 25, 1270.

THE life of Louis IX. as king of France does not properly belong to our subject, and may easily be referred to in the usual histories and biographies. On his merits as a glorified saint rest his claims to a place in sacred Art; and on these I must dwell briefly, for the reasons given already in speaking of the canonised kings and princes of the Benedictine Order. The

---

[1] In the French catalogue of the Royal Gallery at Naples, there is a picture with this title :—' *François Albano.*—Miracle de S. Rose. Un homme assiste à l'office divin dans une chapelle dédiée à S. Rose, pendant que son ennemi court vers l'endroit où il avait placé ses braves, pour voir si sa vengeance était accomplie ; mais ceux-ci s'étant mépris le brûlent dans le même four qu'ils avaient préparé pour le dévot.' I do not remember the picture, but, from the above ill-written, almost unintelligible description, I can just surmise that it refers to this legend.

Franciscans claim St. Louis, and commemorate him in their pictures and churches, because, according to their annalists, he put on the habit of the 'Third Order of Penitence' before he embarked on his first crusade, and died in the cowl and cord of St. Francis.

St. Louis was born at Poissy in 1215. His father, Louis VIIL, and his mother, Blanche of Castile, are the Louis and Blanche who figure in Shakspeare's 'King John.' During his minority his mother governed France with admirable discretion, and it is recorded that till his twelfth year he had no other instructor.

There is a very pretty story of Blanche of Castile, which may fitly find a place here. I have never met with any representation of it, but it would certainly form a most graceful subject.

One day, as Queen Blanche sat in her banquet-hall in great state, she marked among the pages of honour standing around one whom she had not seen before. Now it was the custom in those days for the sons of princes to be brought up in the courts of sovereigns, and to serve as pages before they could aspire to the honour of knighthood. Queen Blanche then, observing this youth, and admiring his noble mien, and his long fair hair, which, being parted on his brow, hung down over his shoulders, she asked who he was, and they told her that it was Prince Herman, the son of the sainted Elizabeth of Hungary. On hearing this, Queen Blanche rose from her seat, and, going towards the youth, she stood and gazed upon him for a few moments with earnest attention. Then she said, 'Fair youth, thou hadst a blessed mother; where did she kiss thee?' The youth, blushing, replied by placing his finger on his forehead between his eyes. Whereupon the queen reverently pressed her lips to that spot, and, looking up to heaven, breathed a '*Sancta Elisabeth, Patrona nostra dulcissima, ora pro nobis !* '

This incident appears to me very graceful and picturesque in itself, and, besides its connection with the history of 'la chère Sainte Elisabeth,' it exhibits the character and turn of mind of her who formed the character of St. Louis.

I have a great admiration for St. Louis, and never could look on the effigies which represent him in his sacred character without a deep and solemn interest. There is not a more striking example of the manner in which the religious enthusiasm of the time reacted on minds of the highest natural endowments, called to the highest duties. The talents and virtues of Louis have never been disputed, even by those who sneered at his fanaticism. Voltaire, not much given to eulogising kings, and still less saints, sums up his character by saying, ' Il n'est guère donné à l'homme de pousser la vertu plus loin!' Gibbon allows that he united the virtues of a king, a hero, and a man. A monument of his love for his people, and of his wisdom as sovereign and legislator, exists in his code of laws known as ' the Ordinances of St. Louis,' which became as dear to the French as the laws of Edward the Confessor had been to the Anglo-Saxon race. He showed the possibility of combining, as a religious king, qualities which a Machiavelli or a Bolingbroke would have held to be incompatible;—the most tender humanity, unblemished truth, inflexible justice, and generous consideration for the rights of other princes,—infidels excepted,—with personal intrepidity, with all the arts of policy, with the most determined vindication of his own power. He was feared and respected by other nations, who made him the umpire in their disputes: he was adored by his subjects. His chivalrous gallantry, his respect for women, his fidelity to his wife, his obedience to his noble-minded mother, his tenderness for his numerous children, complete a portrait which surely justifies the words of Voltaire: ' Il n'est guère donné à l'homme de pousser la vertu plus loin!'

The strongest contrast that could be placed before the fancy would be the characters of Louis IX. and Louis XI. It would be a question, perhaps, whether the piety of the first, or the odious tyranny of the latter, caused on the whole the greatest amount of individual misery; but we look to the motives of the two men, and to the end of time we shall continue to revere the one and to abhor the other. True, both were superstitious; but what a difference between the superstition of

T T

Louis XI. on his knees before 'Our Lady of Clery,' and the superstition of Louis IX. walking bareheaded with the crown of thorns in his hand, and moistening it with devout tears!

In the thirteenth century two passions were uppermost in the minds of Christian men,—the passion for relics, and the passion for crusading.

When the Emperor Baldwin II. came to beg aid from Louis, he secured his good-will at once by offering to surrender the 'holy crown of thorns,' which for several centuries had been preserved at Constantinople, and had been pledged to the Venetians for a large sum of money. Of all the relics then believed in, credible or incredible, this, next to the 'True Cross,' was the most precious and venerable in the eyes of Christians. Louis redeemed the pledge; granted to Baldwin succours in men and money, and then, considering himself enriched by the exchange, he brought the Crown of Thorns to Paris, carrying it himself from Sens, barefoot and bareheaded; having been so thrice happy as to obtain also a small piece of the True Cross, he built in honour of these treasures the chapel since called *La Sainte Chapelle*, one of the most perfect and exquisite monuments of the artistic skill of the Middle Ages.

Paris.

In the year 1247 Louis was seized with a dangerous malady; his life was despaired of, but, after lying for some hours insensible in a kind of trance, he revived, and the first words he uttered were, 'La Lumière de l'Orient s'est répandue du haut du ciel sur moi par la grâce du Seigneur, et m'a rappelé d'entre les morts!' He then called for the Archbishop of Paris, and desired to receive from his hands the cross of a crusader. In spite of the grief of his wife, the remonstrances of his mother, the warnings of his prelates and of his wisest counsellors, he persisted in his resolve; and the Archbishop of Paris, with tears and audible sobs, affixed the cross to his dress. In the next year, as soon as his health would permit, and accompanied by his wife, his brothers, and the flower of his nobility, he embarked for Egypt, with a fleet of eighteen hundred sail, and an army of fifty thousand men.

I need not dwell on the horrors and disasters of that campaign. The result was, that, after seeing one of his brothers and most of his followers perish,—after slaughter, famine, pestilence, and, worse than all, their own vices and excesses, had conspired to ruin his army,—Louis was taken prisoner, Throughout these reverses, amid these indescribable horrors, when the ' Greek fire ' fell among his maddened troops, no doubt entered the mind of Louis that he was right in the sight of God. If not destined to conquer, he believed himself called to martyrdom : he regarded as martyrs those of his people who perished round him : his faith, his patience, his devout reliance on the goodness of his cause, his tender care for his followers, with whom or for whom he every hour hazarded his life, never wavered for one moment. He was ransomed at length, and passed from Egypt to Palestine, where he spent three years. He then returned to France. He reigned for sixteen years wisely and well, recruited his finances, enlarged the bounds of his kingdom, saw a new generation of warriors spring up around him, and then, never having laid aside the cross, he set forth on a second crusade. A wild hope of baptizing the King of Tunis induced him to land in Africa ; his troops again perished of some terrible malady caused by the climate, and Louis himself, after dictating to his son Philip some of the wisest precepts that ever fell from the lips of a sovereign, expired in his tent, laid on ashes as a penitent, and wearing, as the Franciscans assert, the humble habit of their Order.

He was canonised by Boniface VIII. in 1297, twenty-seven years after his death. Part of his body was carried by Charles of Anjou to his capital, Palermo, and deposited in the magnificent church of Moureale : the rest was enshrined at St. Denis. His remains and his shrine were destroyed and desecrated in the first French Revolution.

The devotional figures of St. Louis represent him with his proper attribute, the crown of thorns, which he reverently holds in one hand ; his sword in the other, and the crown and sceptre of royalty at his feet: when painted for the Franciscans in the grey habit and cord of the Tiers-Ordre, they are careful to place his diadem on his head. In the French type, of course the best authority, he is beardless; but the Italian and Spanish painters sometimes give him a long beard, as in a little figure by Raphael, in the collection of Lord Ward.

Florence. S. Croce.   In an ancient fresco of the Crucifixion, St. Louis stands on one side of the cross, wearing the Franciscan habit, and crowned.

Le Brun.   'St. Louis praying for the city of Paris,' which is seen below. He is attended by two angels, one of whom bears the crown of thorns, the other a nail from the cross.

C. Coello. Madrid Gal.   St. Louis in a Holy Family: his sword in one hand, the crown of thorns in the other; his crown and sceptre at his feet. On the other side St. Elizabeth offers a basket of roses to the Infant Saviour.

63   St. Louis.
(Ancient French stained glass.)

The most ancient series from his life is that which was painted on the windows of his chapel at St. Denis.

1. He departs on his first crusade, inscribed, 'Louis s'en va sur mer.'

2. Being in prison in Egypt, a monk consoles him.

3. He instructs his children, three of whom are at his feet.

4. 'Il se fait donner la discipline.' He is scourged by two monks.

5. He is collecting relics, which he is putting into a bag.

6. He places a poor leper in his own bed.

7. His death. His soul is carried by angels into heaven.

8. Miracles performed by him after his death.

These curious specimens of Art are engraved in Le Noir's 'Musée des Monumens Français.'

I have also met with the following historical subjects:—

St. Louis bestows on Bartolomeo of Braganza a piece of the

true cross, and a thorn from the crown of thorns. Queen Parma.
Margaret and several attendants are grouped around them. Church of San Luigi.

St Louis sends missionaries to the East: in a bas-relief. Paris. Invalides.

He was, as we have seen, a great collector of relics. In the
Trinità at Florence there is a picture which represents him
receiving with great reverence the hand of St. John Gualberto,
presented by Benizio, abbot of Vallombrosa.

St. Isabella of France was the sister of St. Louis. She, as
well as her brother, was educated by their admirable and energetic mother, Blanche of Castile. She expended her dowry in August 31
founding the celebrated convent of Longchamps, which she
dedicated to the 'Humility of the Blessed Virgin.' Before the
Revolution this was a rich nunnery of ' Poor Clares.' Isabella
was canonised by Pope Leo X. at the request of the nuns of
Longchamps ; and, as long as that convent existed, her festival
was celebrated there with great magnificence.

Pictures of St. Isabella are to be found in the churches in
Paris, but all are works of modern Art. She is usually represented in the habit of a Franciscan nun, and in the act of
distributing alms or food to the poor.

The best picture of her which I can remember is a graceful
figure by Philip de Champagne in the church of St.-Paul et
St.-Louis.

St. Louis of Toulouse.

Ital. San Ludovico Vescovo. August 19, 1297.

Louis of Anjou was the nephew of St. Louis, king of France,
and son of Charles of Anjou, king of Naples and Sicily. His
mother, Maria of Hungary, who had the direction of his education in childhood, brought him up in habits of piety and

self-denial. 'It is no hardship,' she said, 'for a Christian to practise, for the sake of virtue, that severe sobriety which the Lacedæmonians and other warlike nations exacted from their children for the attainment of martial strength and hardihood.'

It happened that, when Louis was only fourteen, his father was taken prisoner by the King of Aragon; and was obliged to deliver up his three sons, with several of his nobles, as hostages. Louis spent several years in captivity. The inhumanity exercised towards himself and the other hostages, according to the barbarous customs of that period, broke altogether a spirit naturally gentle and contemplative. A sense of the instability of human greatness caused a feeling of disgust against the world, and an indifference to the rank to which he was born. On regaining his liberty in 1294, he yielded all his rights to the kingdom of Naples to his brother Robert, divested himself wholly of all his princely and secular dignities, and received the tonsure and the habit of St. Francis at the age of twenty-two. Soon afterwards, Pope Boniface nominated him Bishop of Toulouse. He travelled, to take possession of his bishopric, barefoot, and in his friar's habit; and, during the short remainder of his life, endeared himself to his people by the practice of every virtue. Travelling into Provence in the discharge of his charitable duties, he came to his father's castle of Brignolles, where he first saw the light, and died there in his twenty-fourth year. He was canonised in 1317 by Pope John XXII., and his body, which was first deposited with the Franciscans at Marseilles, was afterwards carried away by Alphonso of Aragon, and enshrined at Valencia.

Louis, bishop of Toulouse, is in general represented as youthful, beardless, and with a mild expression; wearing his episcopal robes over his Franciscan habit. His cope is sometimes richly embroidered with golden fleurs-de-lis upon a blue ground, or the fleur-de-lis is introduced as an ornament on some part of his dress: or a crown and sceptre lie at his feet, alluding to his rejected kingdom of Naples. He wears the mitre as bishop, or he carries it in his hand, or it is borne by an angel.

In the altarpieces of the Franciscan convents and churches he is often grouped with the other saints of his Order; as in a beautiful picture by Moretto, in which he stands with San Bernardino: in another by Cosimo Roselli, a Coronation of the Virgin, in which he stands with St. Bonaventura. I give a sketch of this group.

Milan. Brera.

Louvre. No. 1204. See p. 289.

64   St. Louis and St. Bonaventura. (Cosimo Roselli.)

St. Louis is also conspicuous in a large picture by Carlo Crivelli, formerly in the Brera, and certainly painted as an altarpiece for one of the great Franciscan churches in the north

Gallery of Lord Ward.

of Italy. In the centre is the Virgin enthroned: on her knee the Infant Christ, from whom St. Peter, kneeling reverently, receives the mystical keys; an altogether poetical version of the subject, as I have already observed. On one side is a martyr-bishop, no otherwise distinguished than by his palm;[1] behind him St. Bernardino of Siena, with the standard as preacher. On the other side stands St. Louis of Toulouse; behind him St. Bonaventura with the sacramental cup, while the Host is suspended from heaven above his head. St. Francis and St. Augustine, as the two patriarchs of the Order, look out from behind the throne.

Sacred and
Legend. Art,
i. 174.

I have never met with any pictures from his life. 'The Death of St. Louis of Toulouse,' by B. Bonfigli, is engraved by Rossini; the subject appears to me rather doubtful.

Rossini.
Storia della
Pittura,
t. 52.

Having been, perhaps, diffuse in my account of the eight principal Franciscan saints, because of their universality and the interest and beauty of the works of Art in which they appear, I shall deal more briefly with the others, who are rarely met with, and are for the most part confined to particular countries and localities.

Feb. 22,
1297.

ST. MARGARET, styled OF CORTONA, from the name of the city which was the scene of her penitence and of her death, was a native of Alviano, near Chiusi, in Tuscany. She lost her mother in early infancy, and, being driven from home by a 'father cruel, and a step-dame false,' she took to evil courses, and led for nine or ten years an abandoned life in her native place. One of her lovers was a gentleman of Montepulciano. After paying her a visit, he was waylaid and assassinated by robbers. A little dog which had accompanied him returned to

------

[1] There is reason to suppose that the picture was painted at Ascoli, in the March of Ancona (v. *l'Ape Italiana*, vol. iv.) In that case the bishop represented is probably Sant' Emigio (*Lat.* Emygdius), the first bishop and patron of the city of Ascoli, and martyred about the year 308.

his mistress, and pulling her by the gown, and whining in a most lamentable manner, endeavoured to induce her to follow. She, after a time, surprised at the absence of her lover, went forth, and, guided by the dog, she found his body hidden under some bushes, covered with wounds, and in a horrible state of decay. Appalled by the spectacle, and seized with compunction, she returned a weeping penitent to the house of her father; but as she knelt upon the threshold, he, being instigated by the stepmother, closed the door against her: whereupon she took refuge in a neighbouring vineyard, and sat down. While thus forsaken by all human help, all human pity, a tempting demon whispered that it would be better for her to return to her former way of life, than remain there and die. But she prayed most earnestly that in this strait God would not abandon her, but be to her father, mother, lover, protector, lord, all that she had lost. She did not pray in vain, for it was miraculously revealed to her, that her prayer was accepted; that she should repair to Cortona, and to the convent of Franciscans there: which she did, and, entering the church barefoot, with a rope round her neck, she cast herself down before the altar, and entreated to be admitted as a penitent into the Order. But such had been her evil life, and such her bad reputation, that the brotherhood refused to admit her till she had given proofs of her sincere repentance, and of such humility, charity, and purity of life as changed their distrust into admiration. She took the habit of the Third Order of St. Francis in 1272. It is related, that as she knelt one day before the image of the crucified Redeemer, he bent his head in compassion and forgiveness. She was regarded from that time with a religious reverence by the people of Cortona; and became the local Magdalene.

There are few pictures of this interesting saint, who is little known out of Tuscany. She is usually represented as young and beautiful; veiled; not always in the grey habit proper to a professed Franciscan nun, but in a dress chequered like a plaid (the coarse woollen manufacture of the country), and a cloak thrown over it; with the cord as girdle, showing that she was a member of the *Third Order*. A little dog, gene-

U U

rally a spaniel, is at her feet; this is her proper attribute. The dog is with propriety omitted in the finest devotional effigy I can refer to: in the Assumption of the Virgin, painted by Andrea del Sarto for the Duomo at Cortona, where St. Margaret is kneeling in front of the Twelve Apostles, and looking up.

Pitti Pal.

Pitti Pal.

In a picture by Lanfranco she is sustained in the arms of angels; here the dog is not omitted.

Her beautiful church, and the adjoining convent with its cypress-grove, crown the highest point of the hill on which stands Cortona, girt with its Cyclopean walls, older than those of Troy; and as we toil up the stony winding path, we pause at every opening to look down upon the lake of Thrasymene,—over the battle-field where the Roman legions encountered the forces of Hannibal, and left the plain strewn with their dead and the rivulets running with their blood. From these terrible and magnificent associations, we turn, at length, to enter the church of the lowly Penitent, where the first thing that strikes us is her statue in white marble, stand-ing out of the shadowy gloom, cold, calm, and pale, her dog crouching at her feet. Her shrine, in which she lies beneath the high altar, is faced with silver in very modern taste. The ancient tomb, which contained her remains before she was canonised, is now preserved in a small chapel adjoining the church. It is placed over a door. She lies extended under a double Gothic arch, the canopy over her head sustained by lovely angels; her face is beautiful; the attitude particularly simple and graceful, and the drapery so disposed as to show that, beneath its folds, her hands are clasped in prayer. The lower part of the tomb is adorned with four bas-reliefs. On one side she takes the penitential habit; on the other she dies, and her spirit is borne into heaven. The two central compart-ments struck me as beautifully significant and appropriate with reference to the history of the saint:—1. The Magdalene anointing the feet of our Saviour, expressing the pardoning grace which had redeemed her; 2. The Raising of Lazarus, expressing her hopes of resurrection. The whole exceedingly beautiful, and in the finest taste of the best time of Gothic Art,—about the end of the thirteenth century.

In the portico of the same church is a quaint old fresco, representing St. Margaret at the moment she discovers the body of her lover.

When Pietro di Cortona was ennobled by his native city, he testified his gratitude by presenting a crown of gold to the shrine of St. Margaret, of whom he painted several pictures.

There is a very beautiful drawing by this master in the Goethe collection at Weimar, representing St. Margaret of Cortona at the foot of the Crucifix; and so expressive, that I have thought it might have suggested to Goethe the scene of the penitence of Margaret in the ' Faust.'

ST. IVES OF BRETAGNE, whose proper style is ' Saint Yves- Helori, Avocat des Pauvres,' is claimed by the Franciscans on rather uncertain grounds. They assert that he took the habit of the Third Order of this community at Quimper in 1283. This being denied, or at least doubted, by the Jesuit authorities, it has followed that in pictures painted for the Franciscan churches, he wears the knotted cord, and in those painted for the Jesuits it is omitted. But wherever we find him,—in church, chapel, or gallery,—we may be sure that the effigy was painted for, or dedicated by, one of the legal profession.

Ital. Sant' Ivo. May 19,1303.

This famous saint—of whom it was wickedly said that the lawyers had chosen him for their *patron*, but not their *pattern* —was born in 1253. He was descended from a noble family in Bretagne. His mother, Aza du Plessis, attended carefully to his early education ; from her he derived his habits of truth, his love of justice, his enthusiastic piety. When quite a child he was heard to declare he would be a saint,—just as a lively boy of our own times announces his intention to be admiral or lord chancellor ;—and in this saintly ambition his mother encouraged him.

At the age of fourteen he was sent to Paris, to study jurisprudence, and afterwards to Orleans, where he made himself master of civil and canon law. But, true to his first vocation, he lived in these cities the life of an anchorite, and the hours not

devoted to study were given to religious meditation, and to the
most active charity. On his return to his own country his
parents wished him to marry, but he had already made a secret
vow of celibacy, to which he adhered during the rest of his life.

About this time he studied theology under a learned Franciscan friar, and henceforth he made the Holy Scriptures his
guide and interpreter in his legal knowledge. When he was
about thirty, the Bishop of Treguier appointed him Judge
Advocate of his diocese. In this office his profound knowledge
of law, his piety, and his charity were equally conspicuous. He
pleaded gratuitously the cause of the widows and orphans: and
when adverse parties were brought before him, he exhorted
them, in the most moving language, to be reconciled as Christians,
and often settled their differences without the intervention of
the law. After some years spent in the exercise of every virtue,
he entered the priesthood. On the eve of his ordination, he
went to the hospital where he had been accustomed to minister
to the poor and sick, and, taking off his legal habiliments, his
furred gown, his tippet, his bonnet, and his boots, he distributed them to four poor old men. He retired thence bareheaded
and barefoot. He afterwards united his duties of pastor with
those of advocate of the poor; still using his legal knowledge
to defend the cause of the destitute and the oppressed, and
leading the life of an apostle and minister of religion, while
conducting the most complicated legal affairs of the diocese.
His health sank under his official labours and his religious
austerities, and he died, at the age of fifty, in the year 1303.

His countrymen of Bretagne, who idolised him while living,
regarded him as a saint when dead; and Jean de Montfort, Duke
of Bretagne, went himself to Avignon, then the seat of the
popes, to solicit his canonisation. It was granted by Clement
VI. in 1347. Since then, St. Ives has been honoured as the
patron saint of lawyers, not merely in Basse-Bretagne, but all
over Europe. Through the intercourse between our southern
shores and those of Brittany, St. Ives was very early introduced
into England, and by our forefathers held in great reverence.

Pictures of this good saint are not common, but they are very
peculiar and interesting, and easily recognised. He has no

especial attribute, but is always represented in his legal attire, as Judge, or as Doctor of Laws, holding a paper in his hand: sometimes his furred robe is girded with the Franciscan cord. In a picture by Empoli, he is seated on a throne, wearing the lawyer's bonnet, the glory round his head; before his throne stand various persons of all classes, rich and poor, widows and orphans, to whom he is dispensing justice. The costume is not that of the thirteenth, but the seventeenth century. In a picture by De Klerck, he rejects a bribe. In a picture by Rubens, he stands as patron saint, attired as ' Docteur en Droit: ' a widow and an orphan are kneeling at his feet. In another picture by Empoli he is kneeling, and St. Luke presents him to the Virgin and Child, who are seen above.

Florence Gal.

Brussels.

Louvain.

Louvre.

The Franciscans are rich in princely saints; besides those already mentioned, we have another in St. Elzear or Eleazar, Count of Sabran in 1300. He had, like most other saints, a wise and pious mother, who loved him infinitely, but prayed in his infancy that he might be taken away from her then, rather than live to be unacceptable to his Maker. He was married young to Delphine, heiress of Glendenes, with whom he lived in the strictest continence and harmony, and both were equally remarkable for their enthusiastic piety and devotion. ' Let none imagine,' says the writer of his life, ' that true devotion consists in spending all our time in prayer, or falling into a slothful and faithless neglect of our temporal concerns. It is a solid virtue to be able to do the business we undertake well and truly.' The piety of Eleazar rendered him more honest, prudent, and dexterous in the management of temporal affairs, public and private, valiant in war, active and prudent in peace, and diligent in the care of his household. His wife Delphine emulated him in every virtue; both enrolled themselves in the Third Order of St. Francis, and after the death of Eleazar, at the age of twenty-eight, Delphine, after residing for some years with her friend Sancha, Queen of Naples (widow of Robert of Anjou, who was the brother of St. Louis of Toulouse), withdrew to complete seclusion, and died very old about 1369.

St. Eleazar and St. Delphine appear in the Franciscan pictures, generally together. They are richly dressed, and St. Eleazar is distinguished by holding in his hand a bundle of papers, from which seals are depending, in allusion to the following beautiful incident. After his father's death, while looking over his papers, he discovered certain letters containing the most false and bitter calumnies against himself, even urging his father to disinherit him, as unfit to reign, &c. He was urged to avenge himself on the traitor; but, instead of doing so, he sent for him, burned the letters in his presence, forgave him, and dismissed him with kind words and gifts, so that he converted a secret enemy into an open, true, and devoted friend. In the picture of Morando, already mentioned, St. Eleazar appears without his wife, holding the sealed papers in his hand.

May 8, 1261. The ST. ROSA DI VITERBO, who figures in that city, and in the churches on the road between Monte Pulciano and Rome, with her grey tunic, her knotted girdle, and her chaplet of roses, was not a professed nun, but a member of the Third Order of St. Francis. She lived in the thirteenth century, and was conspicuous for her charity, her austerity, her eloquence, and the moral influence she exercised over the people of Viterbo. Living, she was their benefactress, and has since been exalted as their patroness in heaven. Besides the local effigies, which are numerous, I remember her in a beautiful Florence Acad. picture by Fra Paolino da Pistoia (a scholar of Fra Bartolomeo), an 'Assumption of the Virgin,' in which she figures below with St. Francis and St. Ursula.

Artists of Spain, p. 821. 'Santa Rosa di Viterbo haranguing an audience,' is the subject of a picture by Sebastian Gomez.

We must be careful to distinguish St. Rosa di Viterbo, the Franciscan nun, from St. Rosa di Lima, the Dominican nun.

April 2, 1508. ST. FRANCIS DE PAULA, founder of the reformed Franciscan Order of the Minimes, was born at Paola, a little city in

Calabria, on the road between Naples and Reggio. His parents, who were poor and virtuous, had from his earliest infancy dedicated him to a religious life. He accompanied them on a pilgrimage to the shrine of his patron saint, St. Francis of Assisi; on his return home he withdrew to a solitary cavern near Reggio, and turned hermit at the age of fifteen.

After a while the fame of his sanctity caused others to join him; the people of the neighbourhood built for them cells and a chapel, and from this time (1436) dates the institution of the Minimes, or Hermits of St. Francis. They followed the Franciscan rule with additional austerities, keeping Lent all the year round.

Francis de Paula took for the motto of his brotherhood the word *Charity*, because the members professed intimate love and union not only towards each other, but to *all* mankind; and they were to be styled Minimes, as being not only *less*, but the *least* of all in the Church of God.

The fame of his sanctity and of many miraculous cures per-formed for the sick, at length reached the ears of Louis XI. of France, who was then dying in his castle of Plessis-le-Tours, like an old wolf in his den. He sent to desire the presence of the man of God (for so he termed him), promising him great privileges for his Order, and princely recompence, if he would visit him. Francis, who thought that this desire to see him proceeded more from a wish to prolong life than to prepare for death, declined the invitation. Louis then addressed himself to Sixtus IV., and, by the command of the pontiff, Francis repaired to Tours.

When he arrived at Amboise he was met by the dauphin and by the greatest lords of the court,—honoured, says Philippe de Comines, '*comme s'il eut été le Pape.*' On his arriving at the castle of Plessis, Louis fell prostrate at his feet, and entreated of him to obtain from Heaven the prolongation of his life. The good simple friar displayed on this occasion more good sense and dignity, as well as more virtue, than the king, descended from a line of kings: he rebuked Louis, told him that life and death were in the hands of God, and that no

hope remained for him but in submission to the divine will ;
he then performed for him the last offices of religion.   After
the death of Louis, Charles VIII. and Louis XII. detained
the good saint almost continually in France, and near the
court, where he had great influence.   The courtiers called him,
in derision, ' le Bonhomme ; ' but the people gave that title to
him and to his Order in a different spirit, and the ' Bons-
hommes ' became very popular in France.

St. Francis de Paula died at Plessis-le-Tours in 1507.   Louise
d'Angoulême, the mother of Francis I., prepared his winding-
sheet with her own hands, and he was canonised by Leo X. in
1519.   In 1562 the Huguenots rifled his tomb, and burned his
remains, using for that purpose
the wood of a large crucifix
which they had hewed to pieces.
This circumstance, at once a
desecration and a consecration,
rather increased his popularity
with the opposite party.   There
was no saint whose effigy was so
commonly met with in France
—*was*, for since the Revolution
' nous avons changé tout cela.'

Of course there are no very
early pictures of St. Francis de
Paula.   The best are Spanish,
and the best of these by Murillo,
who painted him for his beloved
Capuchins at least six times.
This characteristic sketch is from
one of his pictures.

St. Francis de Paula.

The saint is here represented as a very old man with a long
grey beard.   He wears a dark brown tunic, and the cord of
St. Francis.   The peculiarity of the habit, and that which
distinguishes the Minimes from the Cordeliers, consists in
the short scapulary hanging down in front a little below the
girdle, and rounded off at the ends, to the back of which is
sewed a small round hood (not pointed behind like that of

the Capuchins), frequently drawn over the head. In pictures
the word ' Charitas ' is generally introduced : sometimes it is
displayed in a glory above, sometimes it is written on a scroll
carried by an angel.

There is a picture by Lavinia Fontana representing Louise, Bologna Gal
Duchesse d'Angoulême, attended by four ladies of honour,
kneeling at the feet of St. Francis de Paula, to whom she
presents her infant son, afterwards Francis I. The heads in
this picture, as might be expected from Lavinia Fontana,
one of the best portrait-painters of her time, have all the
spirited and life-like treatment of portraiture. The whole
picture is beautifully painted—in some parts equal to Guido.

It is related in the legendary life of this saint, that when
he was about to cross the strait from Reggio to Messina, and
the mariners refused to convey him, he spread his mantle on
the waves, stepped upon it, accompanied by two lay brothers,
and thus they were borne over the sea, till they landed safely
at Messina. This, as I have already observed, is a legend
common to many saints, from whom St. Francis de Paula is
distinguished by his dress, as described, and by his *two* companions. There is a fine picture of this subject in the Louvre,
in which the calm trust of the saint and his companions, and Sp. Gal
the astonishment of the Sicilian peasants, who behold their
approach to the shore, are very well expressed.

A large and fine picture by Solimene exhibits St. Francis Dresden Gal
de Paula kneeling, and commending to the care of the Ma- No. 954.
donna and Infant Saviour a beautiful little boy about three
years old, who is presented by his guardian Angel. The
Divine Child, with a most sweet and gracious expression,
stretches out his hand to receive his little votary, whom I
suppose to be the god-son of the saint, Francis I. *Kings*, not
children, figure in the legend of St. Francis de Paula.

For this saint Charles VIII. founded and endowed the
Church of the Trinità-de'-Monti, at Rome.

x x

ST. JUAN DE DIOS was the founder of the Hospitallers, or
Brothers of Charity; he is the subject of one of Murillo's
finest pictures, and his story is very interesting.

He was born in Portugal, at Monte-Mayor, in the diocese of
Evora, in the year 1495. His parents were poor, and unable to
do anything for his education, but his mother brought him up
in habits of obedience and piety. It happened that, when he
was about nine years old, a certain priest, travelling in those
parts, came to their door and asked hospitality. He was kindly
received, and lodged for some time in their house. This man
had been a great traveller, and had passed through many
vicissitudes of fortune. His conversation awakened in the child
that love of adventure which distinguished him for so many
years of his life. He ran away from his father's cottage in
company with this priest, who, after seducing him from his
home, abandoned him on the road to Madrid, and left him at
a little village near Oropesa, in Castile.

The boy, thus forsaken, hired himself to a shepherd, in
whose service he remained some years; he then enlisted in
the army, served in the wars between Charles V. and Francis
I., and became a brave, reckless, profligate soldier of fortune.
Once or twice the impressions of piety, early infused into his
mind by his good mother, were revived through the reverses
he met with. He was wounded almost to death on one occasion : and on another, having been placed as sentinel over some
booty taken from the enemy, which, in one of his reveries he
suffered to be carried off, his commanding officer ordered him
to be hanged upon the spot; the rope was already round
his neck, when another officer of high rank, passing by,
was touched with compassion, and interfered to save his life,
but only on condition that he should immediately quit the
camp; Juan returned to his old master at Oropesa, and
resided with him some years; but his restless spirit again
drove him forth into the world, and he joined the levies which
the Count d'Oropesa had raised for the war in Hungary.
He remained in the army till the troops were sent back to
Spain and disbanded; then, after paying his devotions at
the shrine of Compostella, he returned to his native

village of Monte-Mayor. Here he learned that, in consequence of his flight, his mother and his father had both died of grief. Remorse took such possession of his mind as to shake his reason. He regarded himself as a parricide. He determined that the rest of his life should be one long expiation of his filial ingratitude and disobedience. Not knowing for the present how to gain a living, he hired himself as shepherd to a rich widow, Doña Leonora de Zuniga, who had a large farm near the city of Seville. In this situation he gave himself up to prayer and to meditation on his past life. The vices, the misery, the suffering of every kind which he had witnessed, had left a deep impression upon a character which appears to have been singularly endowed by nature, and perpetually at strife with the circumstances of his position. He contrasted the treatment of the miserable poor with that of the horses in Count d'Oropesa's stable; even the sheep of his flock were better cared for, he thought, than multitudes of wretched souls for whom Christ had died. These reflections pressed upon him until at length he quitted the service of his mistress, and repaired to Morocco with the intention of ministering to the captives amongst the Moors; he even aspired to the glory of martyrdom. Being come to Gibraltar, he found there a Portuguese nobleman, who, with his wife and four daughters, had been banished to Ceuta, on the opposite coast of Africa: he thought he could not do better than engage in the service of this unfortunate family. At Ceuta they were all reduced to the greatest misery by poverty and sickness; the daughters sold their clothes and ornaments; the unhappy father was overwhelmed with despair. Juan, after having sold the little he possessed, hired himself out as a labourer, and supported the whole family, for some time, by his daily labour. He ceased not his charitable cares till they had found relief elsewhere; then, relinquishing, as too presumptuous, his hope of martyrdom, he returned to Spain, and lived for some time by selling religious books and images of saints, devoting himself meanwhile to the ministry of the wretched and the poor. He had a vision at this time, in which he fancied he beheld a radiant child holding in his hand a pomegranate (*pomo-de-Granada*), and the child said to him, ' Go, thou shalt bear the cross in Granada.' He repaired, therefore, to Granada, where the people were celebrating the festival of Saint Sebastian. The crowd was unusually great because of the presence of a famous preacher, who made such an impression on Juan's already excited mind, that, in the midst of the church, he burst into shrieks and lamentations: then rushing through the streets with cries of ' mercy! mercy!' he cast himself upon the stones. The people seized him and carried him to a madhouse, where, in his paroxysms of violence, they adopted the only remedy ever thought of in those times, —they scourged him every day till the blood flowed from his wounds. The preacher whose sermon had reduced him to this condition came to see him, and, struck with pity, perhaps with remorse, applied himself to heal this perturbed spirit; his gentle voice restored the patient to calmness, and he was liberated.

From this time forth, persisting in his vocation, he dedicated himself to the service of the sick and the poor. He began by bringing first one, then another, to his own little home, a deserted shed, so small it scarcely held two or three persons: when it was full he laid himself down on the outside. By degrees the number increased; a few charitable people united themselves with him, and thus began the first Hospital of the Order of Charity. He was accustomed to dedicate the whole day to the ministry of his sick poor; and towards the night he went forth for the purpose of seeking out the deserted wretches, whom he frequently carried on his back to the refuge he had prepared for them. He worked for them, he begged for them. The eloquence of his appeals was almost irresistible, so that those whom he protected wanted for nothing. He contrived a large building, in which to receive in the winter-time poor houseless travellers who were passing through the city: it was circular, with a great fire in the midst, and sometimes contained not fewer than two hundred destitute wretches.

It does not appear to me that Juan de Dios ever entertained the idea of founding a religious Order and placing himself at the head of it. He formed no plan of conduct. He drew up no rules for himself or others. He did his work of charity with a singleness of mind and purpose, a passionate, concentrated devotion, which looked not to the right nor to the left, nor even forward; he saw nothing but the misery immediately before him; he heard nothing but the cry for help—he craved nothing but the means to afford it. Thus passed ten years of his life, without a thought of himself; and when he died, exhausted in body, but still fervent and energetic in mind, he, unconsciously as it seemed, bequeathed to Christendom one of the noblest of all its religious institutions.

Under how many different names and forms has the little hospital of Juan de Dios been reproduced throughout Christian Europe, Catholic and Protestant! Our houses of refuge, our asylums for the destitute; the brotherhood of the ' Caritad ' in Spain, that of the ' Misericordia ' in Italy, the 'Maisons de Charité' in France, the 'Barmherzigen Brüder' in Germany —all these sprang out of the little hospital of this poor, low-born, unlearned, half-crazed Juan de Dios! I wonder if those who go to visit the glories of the Alhambra, and dream of the grandeur of the Moors, ever think of *him*.

Juan de Dios died at Granada in 1550. He was beatified by Urban VIII., and canonised by Alexander VIII. in 1690. In France he was honoured as ' le bien-heureux Jean de Dieu, Père des Pauvres.'

There are few good pictures of this saint, but many hundreds of bad ones. Formerly every hospital, ' della Misericordia,' and every ' Maison de Charité,' contained his effigy in some form or other. In general, he is represented wearing the dark-brown tunic, hood, and large falling cape of the Capuchins : he has a long beard, and holds in his hand a pomegranate (*Pomode-Granada*), surmounted by a cross, a poor beggar kneeling at his feet. He is thus represented in the colossal statue of white marble which stands in St. Peter's. Pictures of him often exhibit in the background the interior of an hospital, with rows of beds.

The only representation of this good saint which can rank high as a work of Art is a famous picture by Murillo, painted for the Church of the ' Caritad ' at Seville. In a dark stormy night, Juan is seen staggering—almost sinking—under the weight of a poor dying wretch, whom he is carrying to his hospital. An angel sustains him on his way. ' The dark form of the burden, and the sober grey frock of the bearer, are dimly seen in the darkness, through which the glorious countenance of the seraph, and his rich yellow drapery, tell like a burst of sunshine.' Mr. Ford says of this picture, ' equal to Rembrandt in powerful effect of light and shade.' I have heard others say, that in power of another kind, appealing irresistibly to the heart, it also excels; they could not look up to it without being moved to tears. The companion picture was the ' St. Elizabeth ' already described. The latter, rescued from the Louvre, was on its way to Seville, to be restored to the church whence it had been stolen; but, detained by Government officials, it now hangs on the walls of the Academy at Madrid, ' and no pale Sister of Charity, on her way to her labours of love in the hospital, implores the protection, or is cheered by the example, of the gentle St. Elizabeth.' It is some comfort that ' The Charity of San Juan de Dios ' remains in its original situation.

We do not in this country decorate hospitals and asylums with pictures—unless, perhaps, ostentatious portraits of Lord Mayors, donors, and titled governors; otherwise I would recommend as a subject, ' Dr. Johnson carrying home, in his arms, the wretched woman he had found senseless in the street : '—even though it might not equal in power Murillo or Rembrandt, the sentiment and the purpose would be sufficient to consecrate it.

Artists of
Spain, p.860

May 8, 1587.

St. Felix de Cantalicio is chiefly remarkable for having been the first saint of the Order of the Capuchins, and figures only in the convents of that Order. He was born at Citta Ducale, in Umbria, in the year 1513, of very poor parents. He betook himself to a Capuchin convent, and was at first received as a lay brother; but afterwards took the habit, and was sent to the Capuccini at Rome; here he passed forty-five years of his life in the daily mission of begging for his convent. It was his task to provide the bread and the wine, and it was observed that there had never been known, either before or after, such an abundance of these provisions as during his time. His prayers and penances, his submission and charity, were the admiration of his own community, and at length of all Rome. He died in the year 1587. The Capuchins were extremely anxious to have him canonised, and the usual miracles were not wanting as proofs of his beatitude; but it was not till the year 1625 that Urban VIII., at the urgent entreaty of his brother, Cardinal Barberini, who had himself been a Capuchin, consented to give him a place in the Calendar of Saints.

At this time the Italian schools of painting were on the

St. Felix de Cantalicio.

decline and the Spanish schools rising into pre-eminence.
The Superior of the Capuchins at Seville was amongst the
early patrons of Murillo. The result has been, that it would
be difficult to find in Italy a good picture of this saint, while
there are several of extraordinary beauty in the Spanish
schools. He is represented in the habit of his Order, the
dark-brown tunic, large peaked hood hanging down behind,
hempen girdle, and wooden sandals: his proper attribute,
which distinguishes him from other saints of the Order, is the
beggar's wallet, with two ends like a purse, slung over his
shoulder to contain the alms begged for his convent.

It is related of him, that, going out one stormy night to beg
for the poor brethren of his convent, he met the vision of a
child, radiant with beneficence and beauty, who offered him
alms in the shape of a loaf of bread, and then, giving him his
benediction, vanished from his sight. This legend is frequently met with in the pictures of the Spanish school.

S. Didacus,
S. Didace,
or Frèr
Jacques.
Nov. 13,
1463.

St. Diego d'Alcala was another Capuchin saint canonised,
as it seems to me, from very unworthy motives, in times when
the title of saint was bestowed with a shocking and presumptuous levity, as if it were a mere decoration at the button-hole;
and an official place in heaven given away like a place at
court, or sold ' for a consideration.'

Of this Diego d'Alcala there is not much to be said. He
was a lay brother in a Capuchin convent at Alcala about 1463;
and—as far as I can understand, after wading with much
pain and disgust through a very lying and, what is worse,
vulgar and unmeaning legend—he seems to have been an
ignorant simple creature; not answerable, *he*, poor man! for
the palpable and interested inventions of his brotherhood. He
was canonised by Sixtus V. (himself a Franciscan), at the
request of Philip II. It appears that the Infant Don Carlos
(for whom romance and tragedy have done what Sixtus did
for San Diego,—bestowed on him a sort of poetical canonisation or apotheosis) had been cured of a grievous wound through
the intercession of this Diego, whom the friars at Alcala had

exalted as a mirror of sanctity; and Philip, from *gratitude*, say the same authors, rested not till he had obtained from Pope Sixtus his formal canonisation: the bull was published in 1588.

Eleven or twelve years after the canonisation of San Diego, a certain Spanish gentleman residing at Rome, Don Enrico Herrera, dedicated, in the Church of San Giacomo degli Spagnuoli, a chapel to his honour, and engaged Annibal Caracci to adorn it with the history of the saint.

This was just after Annibal had finished the frescoes in the Farnese Palace. Worn out by his work, and broken in spirit by the treatment he had met with, he retired to a little lodging, near the Quattro Fontane, and had resolved to undertake nothing more, for some time at least. The offer of two thousand crowns, and the persuasions of his scholar Albano, induced him to yield: he was, however, so ill, that it was with difficulty he could rouse himself to make the necessary drawings and sketches for the work. Albano nursed him with the tenderness and solicitude of a son; aided him, cheered him; ran backward and forwards from the Quattro Fontane to the chapel of San Giacomo; and painted several of the frescoes with great pains and diligence, as his work was to pass for that of his master;—Annibal every now and then rising from his sick-bed to retouch or finish the work begun by his affectionate pupil. When the chapel was completed, Don Enrico refused to pay, alleging that, according to the agreement, Annibal was to have executed the work with his own hand; and was about to cite the painter before a tribunal. Meantime the applause excited by the frescoes began to mollify Enrico; and it was represented to him, that, as the whole work was executed after the designs and under the direction of Annibal, it might properly be said to be his. Don Enrico, therefore, after some murmuring, withdrew his projects of litigation, and consented to pay the 1600 crowns, the other 400 having been paid in advance. And now began between the two painters a contest of a far different kind. Annibal insisted on giving 1200 crowns to Albano, and keeping only 400 for himself, which he said overpaid him for the little he had executed, and a few sorry drawings (*miseri disegni*) not worth the money.

Y Y

Albano, not to be outdone in generosity, absolutely refused to take anything; saying, that he was only his master's *creatura* and disciple, working under his orders, and profiting by his instructions. At length they agreed to submit to the arbitration of Herrera, who decided that the 1600 crowns should be equally divided between them: even then it was with the greatest difficulty that Annibal could be persuaded to receive his share; and, when he did, it was with a certain air of timidity and bashfulness,—*mostrando in certo modo temersene e vergognarsene.*

Soon afterwards poor Annibal died, the figure of San Diego over the altar being one of his last works. Albano, I need hardly say, became subsequently one of the most famous painters of the Bologna school.

I have given this charming anecdote, as related by Malvasia, because it is in such delightful contrast with the stories of the mutual jealousies, poisonings, and stabbings, which disgraced that period of Italian Art.

With regard to the frescoes, they were taken from the walls when the Church of San Giacomo was destroyed a few years ago, and transferred to canvas. I saw them in this state when at Rome in 1846. They comprise the following subjects:—

1. San Diego takes the Franciscan habit. 2. A mother shut her child in an oven, and lighted a fire under by mistake: the saint, in. pity to the mother, takes out the child uninjured. 3. Travelling with another lay-brother, and being ready to perish with hunger by the way, an angel spreads for them a repast of bread and wine. 4. He restores sight to a blind boy, by touching his eyes with oil from a lamp suspended before an altar of the Madonna. (This was in some respects imitated, but far surpassed, by Domenichino, in his fresco of the Epileptic Boy.) 5. San Diego, being the porter, or, as some say, the cook of his convent, is detected by the guardian giving away bread to the poor, and, on opening his tunic, finds his loaves converted into roses: (an impertinent version of the beautiful legend of St. Elizabeth.)

There were some others, but I do not well remember what they were. The whole series was engraved at the time by Guilain.

I will mention one or two other pictures of this saint.

By Murillo. 1. San Diego, bearing a cross upon his shoulders, holds up his tunic full of roses. 2. He kneels, in the act of blessing a copper pot of broth. 3. San Diego, while cooking for the brotherhood, is rapt in ecstasy, and raised above the earth, while angels are performing his task of boiling and frying below. Three ecclesiastics entering on the left, regard this miracle with devout admiration. 4. San Diego stands fixed in devotion before a cross. Behind Diego, and observing him, is seen the Cardinal Archbishop of Pampeluna with several friars; the consummate vulgarity of the head of Diego, with the expression of earnest yet stupid devotion, as fine as possible—as fine in its way, perhaps, as the San Juan de Dios. But now I have done with San Diego d'Alcalà.

Sold from the Soult Gal. May 20, 1852.

Aguado Gal.

We must be careful not to confound St. Francis de Paula with ST. VINCENT DE PAULE, who wears the habit of a Cordelier, and not of a Minime. He also was very popular in France. Those who have been at Paris will remember the familiar effigies of this amiable saint, with his foundling baby in his arms or lying at his feet. He was the first institutor of hospitals for deserted children (that is to say, the first in France: there had existed one at Florence from the thirteenth century), and the founder of the Sisters of Charity. He was born in 1576 at Puy, in Gascony, not far from the foot of the Pyrenees. His parents were small farmers, and he began life as his father's shepherd. The contemplative sweetness and piety of his disposition, something which distinguished him from the peasants around, induced his father to send him for education to a convent of Cordeliers; and he assumed the habit of the Franciscan Order at the age of twenty. The next ten years were spent as a theological student and a tutor, and his life would probably have passed in the quiet routine of conventual duties if a strange accident had not opened to him a far wider career. He had occasion to go to Marseilles to transact some affairs, and, returning by sea, the small bark was attacked midway in the Gulf of Lyons by some African

July 19, 166

pirates; and Vincent de Paule, with others on board, was carried to Tunis, and there sold for a slave.

Vincent spent two years in captivity, passing from the hand of one master to that of another. The last to whom he was sold was a renegado, whose wife took pity on him. She would occasionally visit him when he was digging in their field, and would speak kindly words to him. One day she desired him to sing to her. He, remembering his sacred profession, and at the same time thinking on his home and country, burst into tears, and when he found voice he began to sing, '*By the waters of Babylon we sat down and wept,*' and then, as if taking heart, he ended with the triumphant strain of the '*Salve Regina.*' Either by his songs or his preaching this woman was turned to the true faith. She converted the husband, and they all escaped together and landed at Aigues-mortes. Vincent, having placed his converts in a religious house, repaired to Rome, whence he was despatched by Paul V. on some ecclesiastical business to Paris: he arrived there in 1609. From this period may be dated his long apostleship, of which I can give only a short abstract. His compassion had been strongly excited by the condition of the wretched galley-slaves at Marseilles. He himself had tasted of chains and slavery; he himself knew what it was to be sick and neglected and friendless. He began by visiting the prisons where criminals were confined before they were sent off to the galleys; he beheld, to use his own expressions, ' des malheureux renfermés dans de profondes et obscures cavernes, mangés de vermines, atténués de langueur et de pauvreté, et entièrement négligés pour le corps et pour l'âme.' The good man was thrown into great perplexity; for on the one hand he could not reconcile such a state of things with the religion of Christ, which it was his profession to uphold and to preach, and on the other hand he could not contravene the laws of justice. He knew not how to deal with ruffians so abased, who began by responding to his efforts for their good, only by outrage and blasphemy; and he was himself poor and penniless, a mendicant friar. Yet this precursor of Howard the Good did not lose courage; he preached to them, comforted them, begged for their maintenance. His next efforts were for the wretched girls abandoned in the streets of Paris, many of whom he reclaimed, and established the hospital of 'La Madeleine' to receive them. A few years afterwards he instituted the Order of the Sisters of Charity, an order of nuns 'qui n'ont point de monastères, que les maisons des malades, pour cellules qu'une chambre de louage, pour chapelle que l'église de leur paroisse, pour cloître que les rues de la ville et les salles des hôpitaux, pour clôture que l'obéissance, pour grille que la crainte de Dieu, et pour voile qu'une sainte et exacte modestie, et cependant elles se préservent de la contagion du vice, elles font germer partout sur leurs pas la vertu.' This beautiful description is applicable to this day ;—to this day the institution remains one of those of which Christendom has most reason to be proud. The rules and regulations which Vincent de Paule drew up for this new Order were admirable, and within a few years afterwards he had the satisfaction to see these congregations of charity spring up in all the cities of France.

One of the most singular things in the history of this saint is his intercourse with the haughty Richelieu, with whom he remained on terms of friendship till the death of the cardinal in 1642. The following year he was called from the bedsides of the galley-slaves, and the sick in the hospital, to attend Louis XIII. in his last moments. In 1648 he instituted the hospital for foundlings : he had been accustomed to pick up the poor children out of the street, and carry them home either to his charitable Sisters or some of the ladies of rank who aided him in his good works ; but these wretched orphans accumulated on his hands, and at length he succeeded in founding 'la Maison des Enfans trouvés,' which he placed under the superintendence of the Sisters of Charity.

When the wars of the 'Fronde' broke out, he was everywhere found ministering to the sufferers and preaching peace.

Amongst the charitable projects of Vincent de Paule was one to assist the Catholics of Ireland, then horribly oppressed ; and he carried his enthusiasm so far as to forget his peaceful and sacred profession, and endeavoured to persuade Richelieu to send troops into that country, offering to raise a hundred thousand crowns towards their pay. Richelieu contented himself with smiling at the request; perhaps also gave him a hint to be content with looking after his Sisters of Charity, instead of meddling with the angry politics of the time.

The enthusiastic admiration with which this excellent man was regarded throughout the country was honourable to the people who had given him, by common consent, the name of 'l'Intendant de la Providence, et Père des Pauvres.' He died at St. Lazare, in 1660, in his eighty-fourth year, and was canonised by Pope Clement XII. in 1747.

In 1844.

The effigies of St. Vincent de Paule which meet us in the churches of Paris, and more particularly in the magnificent church lately dedicated to him, represent him in his Franciscan habit, generally with a new-born infant in his arms, and a Sister of Charity kneeling at his feet. We have, fortunately, authentic portraits of the man; and it is a pleasure to feel that the benevolent features, the bright clear eye, the broad forehead, and the silver hair and beard, fill up the outline suggested by the imagination.

Over the entrance of his church at Paris is a fine circular window of stained glass, representing St. Vincent surrounded by the Sisters of Charity.

Oct. 19.

St. Peter of Alcantara, one of the latest of the canonised Franciscans, was born at Alcantara in Estramadura, in 1499, and, after a long life of sanctification, died in 1562 ; he was canonised by Clement IX., 1669. Of this friar we have the oft-repeated legend of walking on the water, through trust in Munich Gal. God. About the time he was canonised, Claudio Coello painted an exceedingly fine picture of this subject. The saint appears walking on the sea, with a terrified lay brother at his side : pointing up to heaven, he calmly bids him trust, like Peter, in divine aid. The picture is life-size, and struck me as admirably fine—dramatic, without exaggeration. I give a sketch from it. Another beautiful picture of this saint, by Murillo,

67   St. Peter of Alcantara walking on the Sea.

was in the Aguado Gallery; it represents him kneeling at his devotions, and the Holy Dove hovering over his head.

ST. JOHN CAPISTRANO is only met with in late pictures. At the time that all Europe was thrown into consternation by the capture of Constantinople by the Turks, the popes, Eugenius IV., Nicholas V., and Pius II., endeavoured to set on foot a crusade for the defence of Christendom, and sent forth this eloquent and enthusiastic friar to preach through Europe.

At the siege of Belgrade, where Mahomet was repulsed by the brave Hungarians under John Corvinus, the Franciscan preacher was everywhere seen with his crucifix in his hand, encouraging the troops, and even leading them on against the

infidels. He died the same year, and was canonised by
Alexander VIII. in 1690, a few years after the deliverance
of Vienna from the Turks in 1683, and in commemoration of
that event.

The proper attribute of this saint is the crucifix, or the
standard with the cross. In the little Franciscan Predella (an
early work of Raphael, in the gallery of Lord Ward), the figure
with the standard is styled, in the account of the picture, 'San
Giovanni Capistrano;' but having been painted before his
canonisation, it represents, I think, St. Antony of Padua. A
colossal statute of St. John Capistrano stands on the exterior
of the cathedral at Vienna, a very appropriate situation: he
has a standard in one hand, a cross in the other, and tramples
a turbaned Turk under his feet.

March 30.   ST. PETER REGALATO of Valladolid is another Franciscan
saint, who appears in the late Italian and Spanish pictures
painted for the Order. He was remarkable only for the
extreme sanctity of his life and his ' sublime gift of prayer.'
He died at Aquileria, in the province of Osma, in Spain, in
1456, and was canonised by Benedict XIV. in 1746.

March 9,   Before concluding these notices of the Franciscan worthies
1463.   connected with Art, I must mention ST. CATHERINE OF
BOLOGNA, called also *Santa Caterina de' Vigri ;* for, although
one of the latest who were formally canonised, she had been
venerated previously in her own city for nearly two centuries
under the title of LA SANTA.

She was of a noble family, and early placed in the court of
Ferrara as maid of honour to the Princess Margaret d'Este.[1]
After the marriage of the princess, from motives and feelings

---

[1] Nicholas III. of Ferrara had, by his second wife, Parisina (the heroine of
Lord Byron's poem), two daughters, twins,—Lucia and Ginevra. The Princess
Margaret mentioned here must have been his eldest natural daughter of that
name, who married, in 1427, Galeotti Roberto Malatesta, Lord of Rimini, '*e
colla sua ambizione, fece esercitar tanta pazienza al marito che diventò santo.*' Who
knows but that this lady, who converted her husband into a saint by trying his
patience, may by a similar process have assisted in the beatification of her maid
of honour ?

which are not clearly explained, she entered a convent of Poor Clares, where she became distinguished not only for the sanctity and humility of her life, which raised her to the rank of abbess at an early age, but also for a talent for painting. Several specimens of her art are preserved, it is said, in the churches and convents at Bologna. I have seen but one—the figure of St. Ursula, which has been inserted in the first series of this work. It is painted in distemper on panel; the face mild and sweet, but, from the quantity of gilding and retouching, it is difficult to judge of the original style and execution of the picture. ^{v. Legend of St. Ursula.}

In a small chapel in her convent at Bologna they still preserve and exhibit to strangers the black and shrivelled remains of Santa Caterina de' Vigri, dressed out sumptuously in brocade, gold, and jewels. And in the Academy is a picture by Morina, in which she stands with St. Stephen and St. Lawrence, wearing her Franciscan habit and veiled. Her proper attributes would be, perhaps, her palette and pencils; but I have never seen her so represented. ^{Bologna Acad.}

68   Angel, from the Chapel of San Bernardino. (Agostino della Robbia.)

Z Z

60   St. Dominick.

THE DOMINICANS.

ST. DOMINICK and the worthies of his Order are glorious in the history of Art.   They are conspicuous in some of the grandest works which have been consecrated to sacred purposes since the revival of painting and sculpture.   The cause is not to be attributed to their popularity, which never seems to have equalled that of St. Francis and his followers ; nor to their greater riches and munificence as patrons;—but to their pre-eminence as artists. They produced from their own community two of the most excelling painters who have drawn their inspiration from religious influences—Angelico da Fiesole, and Bartolomeo della Porta. Of these two celebrated friars I have already spoken in their relation to the general history and progress of Art. I should call them emphatically *religious* painters, in contradistinction to the mere *church* painters. It is true that, as Dominicans, they worked for the glorification of their own Order, and the decoration of their own churches and convents; no doubt they had a share of that *esprit de corps* which characterised more or less all the religious communities, and most especially the Dominicans: but had they worked with no higher aim, from no purer inspiration, their pictures would not have remained to this day the delight and wonder of the world,—could not have the power even now to seize on our sympathies, to influence us through our best feelings. They do so still, because, however differing in other respects, they were in this alike,—that each was deeply impressed with the sanctity of his vocation; and did in heart and soul, and in devout faith and earnestness, dedicate himself to the service of God and the teaching of men: and as it was said of Angelico that every picture he painted was 'an act of prayer,' through which his own pure spirit held communion with a better and a purer world, so it might be said of Bartolomeo, with his bolder genius and more ample means, that every picture he painted was as an anthem of praise sung to the pealing organ, and lifting up soul and sense at once, like a divine strain of harmony.

Neither of them worked for money, though even in their lifetime the sale of their works enriched their convents: nor for fame;—that 'infirmity of noble minds' had not penetrated into their cells, whatever other infirmities might be there. Even the exaltation of their community was present in their minds as a secondary, not as a primary, object. The result has been, that the Dominicans, at all times less popular as an Order, and as subjects less poetical and interesting, than the Franciscans, are important in their relation to Art through the consummate beauty of some of the works in which they are represented. No pictures painted for the Franciscans, however curious and instructive as specimens, however finished as performances, can be compared with those which these inspired Dominican painters executed for the convents of their Order at Florence, Rome, and elsewhere.

The habit I have already described. We find in reference to it the usual legend, that the form and colour were dictated by the Blessed Virgin herself in a vision to one of the brethren, a monk of Orleans. It is white and black; the *white* denoting purity of life; the *black*, mortification and penance. Hence, when the Dominicans are figured as dogs (*Domini Canes*), a common allegory, they are always white with patches of black. In the famous and otherwise very remarkable fresco of the 'Church Militant,' painted by Simone Memmi in the chapel 'degli Spagnuoli,' we see five or six of 'these dogs of the Lord,' engaged in worrying the heretics, who figure as wolves; while two others guard the flock of the faithful, figured as sheep peacefully feeding at the foot of the pope's throne, and within the shadow of the Church. A particular description of the other parts of this elaborate composition may be found in Kugler.

Florence.
b. Maria
Novella.

Handbook
of Painting
in Italy.

There are four principal saints who are of universal celebrity, and are to be found in all the Dominican edifices :—

St. Dominick, as patriarch and founder of the Order.

St. Peter Martyr, distinguished by the gash in his head. In early pictures usually the companion or pendant of St. Dominick.

St. Thomas Aquinas, the *Angelic Doctor*, who, in the Dominican pictures, takes the same rank which St. Bonaventura occupies in the Franciscan pictures; he represents the learning of the Order.

These three appear in the ancient works of Art, and in the pictures of Angelico.

St. Catherine of Siena, the great female saint of the Dominican Order, does not appear in any pictures painted before the latter half of the fifteenth century. Fra Bartolomeo is, I think, the first painter of any note who has treated her as a devotional subject.

In later pictures we find—St. Antonino, the good Archbishop of Florence.

St. Raymond.

St. Vincent Ferraris.

And, confined almost wholly to Spanish Art,—

St. Peter Gonsalez.

St. Rosa de Lima.

St. Louis Beltran.

Pope Pius V., a Dominican, was canonised in 1712 by Clement XI. I have never met with him in pictures as *Saint Pius*, though such may exist; and probably, as the canonisation took place just at the worst period of the decline of Art, they are worthless.

Of all these, only the first four are of any great interest and importance as subjects of Art.

All the later Dominican saints have been canonised for the wonders they performed as preachers and missionaries, for the numbers converted from sin, from heresy, or from paganism by their all-persuasive eloquence, and yet more by their all-convincing miracles. The Spanish Dominicans were particularly remarkable for their 'signs and wonders,' their autos-da-fé, and their triumphs over the Moors and Jews. I think it unnecessary to give any specimens of their oratory. The most admired sermons of St. Vincent, into which I have looked cursorily, reminded me, in the peculiar fervour of their style, of sermons I had heard in the tabernacles and camp-meetings in America. Yet some of the apologues invented by the Dominican preachers are extremely ingenious, picturesque, and significant; and they are otherwise remarkable for one pervading characteristic,—the exaltation of their own Order, the advancement of their own objects, rather than the enforcement of any general religious or moral truths. Here is a specimen, not unworthy of John Bunyan —if John had been a Dominican friar instead of a Puritan tinker:—

'A certain scholar in the University of Bologna, of no good repute, either for his morals or his manners, found himself once (it might have been in a dream) in a certain meadow not far from the city, and there came on a   Legenda Aurea.

terrible storm ; and he fled for refuge until he came to a house, where,
finding the door shut, he knocked and entreated shelter. And a voice
from within answered, "I am Justice; I dwell here, and this house is mine ;
but as thou art not just, thou canst not enter in." The young man turned
away sorrowfully, and proceeding further, the rain and the storm beating
upon him, he came to another house ; and again he knocked and entreated
shelter : and a voice from within replied, "I am Truth ; I dwell here, and
this house is mine ; but as thou lovest not truth, thou canst not enter here."
And further on he came to another house, and again besought to enter ;
and a voice from within said, "I am Peace ; I dwell here, and this house is
mine ; but as there is no peace for the wicked and those who fear not God,
thou canst not enter here." Then he went on further, being much afflicted
and mortified, and he came to another door, and knocked timidly, and a
voice from within answered, "I am Mercy ; I dwell here, and this house is
mine ; and if thou wouldst escape from this fearful tempest, repair quickly
to the dwelling of the brethren of St. Dominick ; that is the only asylum for
those who are truly penitent." And the scholar failed not to do as this
vision had commanded. He took the habit of the Order, and lived henceforth an example of every virtue.'

The following legend is more daringly significant, and,
besides being repeated in various forms, has been represented
in Art :—

'St. Dominick, being at Rome, had a vision in which he beheld Christ,
who was sitting in judgment, and held in his hand three sharp arrows which
were the arrows of the divine wrath ; and his Mother hastened and threw
herself at his feet, and said, "What wouldst thou do, O my Son ?" and he
replied, "The world is so corrupt with pride, luxury, and avarice, that I am
come to destroy it." Then the Blessed Virgin wept in supplication before
him, and she said, "O my Son, have pity upon mankind !" and he replied,
"Seest thou not to what a pitch they have carried their iniquity ?" and she
said, "O my Son, restrain thy wrath, and be patient for a while, for I have
here a faithful servant and champion, who shall traverse the whole earth
and subdue it to thy dominion, and to him I will join another who shall
fight valiantly in thy cause." And Christ replied—"Be it so !" Then the
Virgin placed before him St. Dominick and St. Francis ; and our Lord,
looking upon them, relented from his wrath.'

There are many old prints, perhaps also pictures, which appear
to be founded on this legend ; St. Dominick or St. Francis, or
both, are either prostrate on the earth, or covering it with the
skirts of their habits or mantles, while Christ (the *Saviour !*)
appears above as the stern avenger, armed to punish or destroy,
with the Virgin-mother interceding at his feet.

Rubens has been severely censured for a profane picture of this kind, in which St. Francis figures as the redeeming angel, shielding the earth with his extended robe. But Rubens did not invent the subject, nor did St. Francis; it originated, I presume, from this characteristic vision of St. Dominick,—of which we are now to speak.

70   St. Dominick.

St. Dominick.

Lat. Sanctus Dominicus, Pater Ordinis Prædicatorum. *Ital.* San Domenico. San Domenico Calaroga. *Fr.* Saint Dominique, Fondateur des Frères Prêcheurs. *Sp.* San Domingo. August 4, 1221.

In the days when Alexander III. was pope, and Frederic Bar- A.D. 1160. barossa emperor of Germany, Don Alphonso IX. then reigning in Castile, Dominick was born at Calaruga, in the diocese of Osma, in the kingdom of Castile. His father was of the illustrious family of Guzman. His mother, Joanna d'Aza, was also of noble birth. His appearance in the world was attended by the usual miracles. Before he was born, his mother

dreamed that she had brought forth a black and white dog
carrying in his mouth a lighted torch.   When his godmother
held him in her arms at the font, she beheld a star of wonderful splendour descend from heaven and settle on his brow.
Both these portents clearly denoted that the saint was destined
to be a light to the universe.   Moreover, such was his early
predilection for a life of penance, that when he was only six
or seven years old he would get out of his bed to lie on the
cold earth.   His parents sent him to study theology in the
University of Valencia, and he assumed the habit of a canon
of St. Augustine at a very early age.   Many stories are related of his youthful piety, his self-inflicted austerities, and
his charity.   One day he met a poor woman weeping bitterly ;
and when he inquired the cause, she told him that her only
brother, her sole stay and support in the world, had been
carried into captivity by the Moors.   Dominick could not
ransom her brother ; he had given away all his money, and
even sold his books to relieve the poor; but he offered all
he could,—he offered up himself to be exchanged as a slave in
place of her brother.   The woman, astonished at such a
proposal, fell upon her knees before him.   She refused his
offer, but she spread the fame of the young priest far and
wide.

Dominick was about thirty when he accompanied Diego,
bishop of Osma, on a mission to France.   Diego was sent there
by King Alphonso, to negotiate a marriage between his son,
Prince Ferdinand, and the daughter and heiress of the Count
de la Marche.   They had to pass through Languedoc, where, at
that time, the opinions of the Albigenses were in the ascendant,
and Dominick was scandalised by these heretical 'reveries.'
Their host at Toulouse being of this persuasion, Dominick spent
the whole night in preaching to him and his family.   Such was
the effect of his arguments, that the next morning they made
a public recantation.   This incident fixed the vocation of the
future saint, and suggested the first idea of a community of
preachers for the conversion of heretics.

The marriage being happily arranged, Dominick soon
afterwards made a second journey to France with his bishop,

accompanying the ambassadors who were to conduct the young princess to Spain. They arrived just in time to see her carried to her grave; and the sudden shock appears to have left a deep and dark impression on the mind of Dominick. If ever he had indulged in views and hopes of high ecclesiastical preferment, to which his noble birth, his learning, his already high reputation appeared to open the way, such promptings of an ambitious and energetic spirit were from this time extinguished, or rather concentrated into a flame of religious zeal.

On a journey which he made to Rome in 1207, he obtained the pope's permission to preach in the Vaudois to the Albigenses. At that time the whole of the South of France was distracted by the feuds between the Catholics and the heretics. As yet, however, there was no open war, and the pope was satisfied with sending missionaries into Languedoc. Dominick, armed with the papal brief, hastened thither; he drew up a short exposition of faith, and with this in his hand he undertook to dispute against the leaders of the Albigenses. On one occasion, finding them deaf to his arguments, he threw his book into the flames, and, wonderful to relate! it leaped three times from the fire, and remained uninjured,—while the books which contained the doctrines of the heretics were utterly consumed! By this extraordinary miracle many were convinced; but others, through some strange blindness, refused to believe either in Dominick or his miracles.

Then began that terrible civil and religious war, unexampled in the annals of Europe for its ferocity.

What share Dominick may have had in arming the crusade against the miserable Albigenses is not ascertained. His defenders allege that he was struck with horror by the excesses of barbarity then committed in the name and under the banners of the religion of Christ. They assert positively that Dominick himself never delivered over the heretics to the secular power, and refused to use any weapons against them but those of argument and persuasion. But it remains an historical fact, that at the battle of Muret, where twenty thousand of the Albigenses were massacred by the troops of

Simon de Montfort, Dominick was kneeling on an eminence—
some say in a neighbouring chapel—with his crucifix in his
hand, praying that the Church might prevail: he has been
compared to Moses holding up the rod of the Lord while the
captains of Israel slew their enemies with the edge of the sword,
'sparing not the women nor the little ones.' That Dominick,
however mistaken, was as perfectly convinced as ever Moses was
of the righteousness of his cause and of the divine protection,
I see no room to doubt: the man was a fanatic, not a hypocrite.

About this time he united with himself several ecclesiastics,
who went about barefoot in the habit of penitents, exhorting
the people to conform to the Church   The institution of the
Order of St. Dominick sprang out of this association of
preachers, but it was not united under an especial rule, nor
confirmed, till some years later,—by Pope Honorius in 1216.

It was during his sojourn in Languedoc that St. Dominick
instituted the ROSARY.   The use of a chaplet of beads, as a
memento of the number of prayers recited, is of Eastern origin,
and dates from the time of the Egyptian Anchorites.   Beads
were also used by the Benedictines, and are to this day in use
among the Mahommedan devotees.   Dominick invented a
novel arrangement of the chaplet, and dedicated it to the
honour and glory of the Blessed Virgin, for whom he entertained a most especial veneration.   A complete rosary consists
of fifteen large and one hundred and fifty small beads; the
former representing the number of *Pater-nosters*, the latter the
number of *Ave-Marias*.   In the legends of the Madonna I
shall have much to say of the artistic treatment of the 'mysteries
of the rosary:' meantime, with reference to St. Dominick, it
will be sufficient to observe that the rosary was received with
the utmost enthusiasm, and by this simple expedient Dominick
did more to excite the devotion of the lower orders, especially
of the women, and made more converts, than by all his ortho-
doxy, learning, arguments, and eloquence.

In 1218, St. Dominick having been charged by the pope
with the care of reforming the female convents at Rome,
persuaded them to accept of a new Rule which he drew up
for them: and thus was instituted the Order of the Dominican

Nuns. The institution of the 'Third Order of Penitence' followed soon after, but it never was so popular as the Third Order of St. Francis.

From this time we find Dominick busily employed in all the principal cities of Europe, founding convents. He was in Spain in the beginning of 1219 ; afterwards at Paris, where, by permission of Blanche of Castile, mother of St. Louis, he founded the magnificent convent of his Order in the Rue St. Jacques, from which the Dominicans in France obtained the general name of Jacobins. At Paris, meeting Alexander II., king of Scotland, he at the earnest request of that prince sent some of his brotherhood into Scotland, whence they spread over the rest of Great Britain.

From Paris he returned to Italy, and took up his residence in the principal convent of his Order at Bologna, making occasional journeys to superintend the more distant communities. Wherever he travelled he fulfilled what he had adopted as the primary duty of his institution. He preached wherever he stopped, though it were only to repose for an hour: everywhere his sermons were listened to with eagerness. When at Bologna he preached not only every day, but several times in the day, to different congregations. Fatigue, excitement, and the extreme heat of the season, brought on a raging fever, of which he died in that city on the 6th of August, 1221. He was buried in a modest tomb in a small chapel belonging to his Order ; but on his canonisation by Gregory IX., in 1233, his remains were translated to the splendid shrine in which they now repose.

The adornment of the ' Arca di San Domenico '—for so this wonderful tomb is styled in Italy—was begun as early as 1225, when Niccolò Pisano was summoned to Bologna to design the new church of the Dominicans, and the model of the shrine which was to be placed within it. The upper range of bas-reliefs, containing scenes from the life of the saint, by Niccolò and his School, dates from 1225 to about 1300. The lower range, by Alfonso Lombardi, was added about 1525, in a richer, less refined, but still most admirable style.

Bologna

We come now to the various representations of this famous saint; and, first, it will be interesting to compare the innumerable effigies which exist of him with the description of his person left by a contemporary, Suor Cecilia, one of his Roman disciples. The accuracy of the portrait has been generally admitted:—

'In stature he was of moderate size; his features regular and handsome; his complexion fair, with a slight colour in his cheek; his hair and beard inclining to red, and in general he kept his beard close shaven. His eyes were blue, brilliant, and penetrating; his hands were long, and remarkable for their beauty; the tones of his voice sweet, and at the same time powerful and sonorous. He was always placid, and even cheerful, except when moved to compassion.' The writer adds, that 'those who looked on him earnestly were aware of a certain radiance on his brow; a kind of light almost supernatural.' It is possible that the attribute of the star placed on his brow or over his head may be derived from this traditional portrait, and, as in other instances, the legend of the godmother and the star afterwards invented to account for it.

The devotional figures of St. Dominick always represent him in his proper habit,—the white tunic, white scapulary, and long black cloak with a hood. In one hand he bears the lily; in the other a book. A star is on his forehead, or just above his head. The dog with the flaming torch in its mouth is the attribute peculiar to him. Every one who has been at Florence will remember his statue, with the dog at his side, over the portal of the Convent of St. Mark. But in pictures the dog is frequently omitted, whereas the lily and the star have become almost indispensable.

It is related in one of the Dominican legends, that a true portrait of St. Dominick was brought down from heaven by St. Catherine and Mary Magdalene, and presented to a convent of Dominican nuns. From this original (some ancient picture, probably, by Angelico, for the formal simplicity of the *pose* is very like him), Carlo Dolce painted the figure I have placed at p. 354.

St. Dominick. (Lucas v. Leyden.)

The head of St. Dominick at the beginning of this chapter is from Angelico's 'Coronation of the Virgin,' in the Louvre. There is, certainly, nothing of the inquisitor or the persecutor in this placid and rather self-complacent head; rather, I should say, some indication of that self-indulgence with which the heretics reproached this austere saint. In other heads by Angelico we have an expression of calm, resolute will, which is probably very characteristic; as in the standing figure in an altarpiece now in the Pitti Palace, and many others. In the pictures by Fra Bartolomeo, St. Dominick has rather a mild full face. In no good picture that I have seen is the expression given to St. Dominick severe, or even ascetic. In the Spanish pictures the head is often coarse, with a black beard and tonsure; altogether false in character and person.

A very ancient and interesting figure of St. Dominick, formerly in the church of St. Catherine of Siena at Pisa, is now in the Academy there. It was painted for a certain ' Signore di Casa Cascia,' by Francesco Traini. The character of the head agrees exactly with the portrait drawn by Suor Cecilia. '*Il volto trà il severo e il piacevole; i capelli rossiccii, tagliati a guisa di corona; barba rasa.*' He holds a lily in his right hand, in the left an open book on which is inscribed, ' *Venite, filii, audite me, timorem Domini docebo vos.*' The hands very small and slender. Around this figure are eight small subjects from his life.

Besides the devotional figures, in which he stands alone, or grouped with St. Peter Martyr or St. Catherine of Siena near the throne of the Virgin, there are some representations of St. Dominick which are partly devotional, partly mystical, with a touch of the dramatic. For example, where he stands in a commanding attitude, holding the keys of St. Peter, as in a fresco in the S. Maria-sopra-Minerva; or where the Infant Christ delivers to him the keys in presence of other saints, as in the altarpiece of Orcagna in the Strozzi Chapel; and in the innumerable pictures which relate to the institution of the rosary, which, as a subject of Art, first became popular after the victory of Lepanto in 1571. Gregory XIII. instituted the Festival of the Rosary to be held in everlasting commemoration of that triumph over the infidels. From this period we find perpetual Madonnas ' del Rosario;' and St. Dominick receiving the rosary from the hand of the Virgin, or distributing rosaries, became a common subject in the Dominican churches.

The most famous example is by Domenichino, a large, splendid picture; but the intention of the artist in some of the groups does not seem clear. The Madonna del Rosario is seated above in glory; in her lap the Divine Infant; both scatter roses on the earth from a vase sustained by three lovely cherubs. At the feet of the Virgin kneels St. Dominick, holding in one hand the rosary; with the other he points to

Roma.

Florence.

Bologna
Acad.

the Virgin, indicating by what means she is to be propitiated.
Angels holding the symbols of the ' Mysteries of the Rosary '
(the joys and sorrows of the Virgin) surround the celestial personages.　On the earth, below, are various groups, expressing
the ages, conditions, calamities, and necessities of human life:
—lovely children playing with a crown; virgins attacked by
a fierce warrior, representing oppressed maidenhood; a man
and his consort, representing the pains and cares of marriage,
&c.　And all these with rosaries in their hands are supposed
to obtain aid, ' *per intercessione dell' sacratissimo Rosario.*'　I
confess that this interpretation appeared to me quite unsatisfactory when I looked at the picture, which, however, is one
blaze of beauty in form, expression, and transcendent colouring.—'*Mai si videro puttini e più cari e amorosi; mai ver-
ginelle più vaghe e spiritose; mai uomini più fieri, più gravi,
più maestosi!*'　I remember once hearing a Polish lady recite
some verses in her native language, with the sweetest voice,
the most varied emphasis, the most graceful gestures imagi-
nable; and the feeling with which I looked and listened,—at
once baffled, puzzled, and enchanted,—was like the feeling
with which I contemplated this masterpiece of Domenichino.

(margin: Malvasia, Felsina Pittrice.)

(margin: Malvasia.)

A series of subjects, more or less numerous, from the life of
St. Dominick, may commonly be met with in the Dominican
edifices.

The most memorable examples are:—

1. The bas-reliefs on the four sides of his tomb or shrine,
by Niccolò Pisano and Alfonso Lombardi.　*(margin: Bologna.)*

2. The set of six small and most beautiful compositions by
Angelico, on the predella of the ' Coronation of the Virgin.'　*(margin: Louvre.)*

3. The set of eight subjects round the figure by Traini,
already mentioned.　*(margin: Pisa.)*

I shall here enumerate, in their order, all the scenes and
incidents I have found represented, either as a series or separately:—

1. The dream of the mother of St. Dominick.　Giovanna d'Aza is asleep
on her couch, and before her appears the dog holding the torch.　In front,
two women are occupied washing and swaddling the infant saint.

2. The dream of Pope Innocent III. (exactly similar to his vision of St. Francis). He dreams that the Church is falling to ruin, and that Dominick sustains it.

3. When St. Dominick was at Rome, praying in the Church of St. Peter that the grace of God might be upon his newly-founded Order, he beheld in a vision the blessed apostles, Peter and Paul. Peter presented to him a staff, and Paul a volume of the Gospel, and they said to him, 'Go, preach the Word of God, for he hath chosen thee for that ministry.' Of this subject, the bas-relief by Niccolò Pisano is as fine as possible. I give a sketch of the principal group.

72   St. Dominick receives from St. Peter and St. Paul the commission to preach.
(Niccolò Pisano.)

4. The burning of the heretical books. The book of St. Dominick is seen leaping from the fire. In the picture by Angelico, the Albigenses are dressed as Turks; the good painter could form no other idea of heretics and infidels. The grand dramatic fresco by Lionello Spada, in the chapel at Bologna, should be compared, or rather contrasted, with the simple elegance of Angelico.

5. On Ash Wednesday in 1218, the abbess and some of her nuns went to

the new monastery of St. Sixtus at Rome, to take possession of it; and, being in the chapter-house with St. Dominick and Cardinal Stephano di Fossa-Nova, suddenly there came in one, tearing his hair, and making great outcries, for the young Lord Napoleon, nephew of the cardinal, had been thrown from his horse and killed on the spot. The cardinal fell speechless into the arms of St. Dominick, and the women and others who were present were filled with grief and horror. They brought the body of the youth into the chapter-house, and laid it before the altar; and Dominick, having prayed, turned to the body of the young man, saying, '*O adolescens Napoleo! in nomine Domini nostri J. C. tibi dico surge!*' and thereupon he arose sound and whole, to the unspeakable wonder of all present.

This is a subject frequently repeated. The bas-relief by Niccolò, the little picture by Angelico, and the fresco by Mastelletta, should be compared. In the first two, the saint and the dead youth fix the attention; in the last, it is the *furibondo cavallo* which makes us start.

6. The supper of St. Dominick. 'It happened that when he was residing with forty of his friars in the convent of St. Sabina at Rome, the brothers who had been sent to beg for provisions had returned with a very small quantity of bread, and they knew not what they should do, for night was at hand, and they had not eaten all day. Then St. Dominick ordered that they should seat themselves in the refectory, and, taking his place at the head of the table, he pronounced the usual blessing: and behold! two beautiful youths clad in white and shining garments appeared amongst them; one carried a basket of bread, and the other a pitcher of wine, which they distributed to the brethren: then they disappeared, and no one knew how they had come in, nor how they had gone out. And the brethren sat in amazement; but St. Dominick stretched forth his hand, and said calmly, "My children, eat what God hath sent you:" and it was truly celestial food, such as they had never tasted before nor since.'

The treatment of this subject in the little picture by Angelico is perfectly exquisite. The friars, with their hoods drawn over their heads, are seated at a long table; in the centre is St. Dominick, with his hands joined in prayer. In front, two beautiful ethereal angels seem to glide along, distributing from the folds of their drapery the 'bread from paradise.'

7. The English pilgrims. When Simon de Montfort besieged Toulouse, forty pilgrims on their way from England to Compostella, not choosing to enter the heretical city, got into a little boat to cross the Garonne. The boat is overset by a storm, but the pilgrims are saved by the prayers of St. Dominick.

This subject is often mistaken; I have seen it called, in Italian, '*La Burrasca del Mare.*' In the series by Traini it is extremely fine; some of the pilgrims are struggling in the water; others, in a transport of gratitude, are kissing the hands and garments of the saint.

8. He restores to life a dead child. The great fresco of this subject in the chapel 'dell' Arca' at Bologna is by Tiarini, and a perfect masterpiece in the scenic and dramatic style; so admirably *got up*, that we feel as if

3 B

assisting, in the French sense of the word, in a side-box of a theatre. To understand the scene, we must remember that St. Dominick, being invited to the funeral banquet, ordered the viands to be removed, and the child to be placed on the table instead ; the father, with outstretched arms, about to throw himself at the feet of the saint,—the mother, with her eyes fixed on her reviving child, seeming only to live in his returning life,—are as fine and as animated as possible. It is Rubens, with Italian grace and Venetian colour.

9. 'Pope Honorius III. confirms the Order of St. Dominick,' often met with in the Dominican convents. There is a fine large picture of this subject in the sacristy of *St. John and St. Paul* at Venice, painted by Tintoretto with his usual vigour. The small sketch is, I think, in the Collection of the Duke of Sutherland.

10. St. Dominick, in the excess of his charity and devotion, was accustomed, while preaching in Languedoc, to scourge himself three times a day ;—once for his own sins ; once for the sins of others ; and once for the benefit of souls in purgatory. There is a small, but very striking, picture of this subject by Carlo Dolce. Dominick, with bared shoulders, kneels in a cavern ; the scourge in his hand ; on one side, the souls of sinners liberated by his prayers, are ascending from the flames of purgatory ; far in the background is seen the death of Peter Martyr.

F Pitti.

11. The death of the saint. In the early pictures of this subject we often find inscribed the words of St. Dominick, 'Caritatem habete ; humilitatem servate, paupertatem voluntariam possidete.'

12. Fra Guala, prior of a convent at Brescia, has a vision, in which he beholds two ladders let down from heaven by the Saviour and the Virgin. On these two angels ascend, bearing between them a throne, on which the soul of St Dominick is withdrawn into paradise.

13. The solemn translation of the body of St. Dominick to the chapel of San Domenico in Bologna ; in the series by Traini.

14. The apotheosis of the saint. He is welcomed into heaven by our Saviour, the Virgin, and a choir of rejoicing angels, who hymn his praise. Painted by Guido with admirable effect on the dome of the chapel at Bologna.

We must now turn from St. Dominick to his far more stern disciple--

St. Peter Martyr.

St. Peter the Dominican. *Ital.* San Pietro (or San Pier) Martire. *Fr.* Saint Pierre le Dominicain, Martyr. April 28, 1252.

THIS saint, with whom the title of Martyr has passed by general consent into a surname, is, next to their great patriarch, the glory of the Dominican Order. There are few pictures dedicated in their churches in which we do not find him conspicuous, with his dark physiognomy and his bleeding head.

He was born at Verona about the year 1205. His parents and relatives belonged to the heretical sect of the *Cathari*, prevalent at that time in the North of Italy. Peter, however, was sent to a Catholic school, where he learned the creed according to the Catholic form, and for repeating it was beaten on his return home. St. Dominick, when preaching at Verona, found in this young man an apt disciple, and prevailed on him to take the Dominican habit at the age of fifteen. He became subsequently an influential preacher, and remarkable for the intolerant zeal and unrelenting cruelty with which he pursued those heretics with whom he had formerly been connected. For these services to the Church he was appointed Inquisitor-General by Pope Honorius III. At length two noblemen of the Venetian states whom he had delivered up to the secular authorities, and who had suffered imprisonment and confiscation of property, resolved on taking a summary and sanguinary vengeance. They hired assassins to waylay Peter on his return from Como to Milan, and posted them at the entrance of a wood through which he was obliged to pass, attended by a lay brother. On his appearance, one of the assassins rushed upon him and struck him down by a blow from an axe; they then pursued and stabbed his companion: returning, they found that Peter had made an effort to rise on his knees, and was reciting the Apostles' Creed, or, as others relate, was in the act of writing it on the ground with his blood. He had traced the word ' *Credo*,' when the assassins coming up completed their work by piercing him through with a sword. He was canonised in 1253 by Innocent IV. ; and his shrine in the Sant' Eustorgio at Milan, by Balduccio of Pisa, is one of the most important works of the fourteenth century.

In spite of his celebrity in Art, his fame, and his sanctity, the whole story and character of this man are painful to contemplate. It appears that in his lifetime he was not beloved by his own brotherhood, and his severe persecuting spirit made him generally detested. Yet, since his death, the influence of the Dominican Order has rendered him one of the most popular saints in Italy. There is not a Dominican church in Romagna, Tuscany, Bologna, or the Milanese, which does not contain effigies of him; and, in general, pictures of the scene of his martyrdom abound.

In the devotional figures he wears the habit of his Order, and carries the palm as martyr, and the crucifix as preacher; the palm, if not in his hand, is placed at his feet. He is otherwise distinguished from St. Dominick by his black beard and tonsure, St. Dominick being of a fair and delicate complexion; but his peculiar attribute—where he stands as martyr—is the gash in his head with the blood trickling from it;—or the sabre or axe struck into his head, as in this figure from a picture in the Brera;—or he is pierced through with a sword, which is less usual.

73　St. Peter Martyr.
(Cima da Conegliano.)

I will now mention a few examples :—

Milan Gal.　　1. By Guercino :—St. Peter M., kneeling with the sabre at his feet.

2. By Bevilacqua:—He presents a votary to the Madonna: Milan Gal.
on the other side is Job, the patriarch of patience, holding a
scroll on which is inscribed, ' Eruet Te de Morte et Bello de
Manu Gladii.'

3. By Angelico:—He stands on one side of the throne of Fl. Gal.
the Madonna pierced through with a sword, with a keen,
ascetic, rather than stern and resolute, expression.

The finest, the most characteristic, head of St. Peter P. Pitti.
Martyr I have ever seen is in a group by Andrea del Sarto,
where he stands opposite to St. Augustine, '*in aria e in attc
fieramente terribile,*' as Vasari most truly describes him; and
never, certainly, were fervour, energy, indomitable resolution,
more perfectly expressed. I have mentioned in another place P. 234.
the significant grouping of the personages in this wonderful
picture.

The assassination—or, as it is styled, the ' martyrdom '—of
St. Peter occurs very frequently, and seldom varies in the
general points of treatment. The two assassins, the principal
of whom is called in the legend Carino; the saint felled to the
earth, his head wounded and bleeding, his hand attempting to
trace the word ' Credo; '—these, with the forest background,
constitute the elements of the composition.

We have an example of the proper Italian treatment in a
small picture, by Giorgione, in our National Gallery, which
is extremely animated and picturesque. But the most renowned of all, and among the most celebrated pictures in
the world, is the ' San Pietro Martire' of Titian; painted as
an altarpiece for the chapel of the saint, in the church of SS.
Giovanni e Paolo (which the Venetians abbreviate and har-
monise into SAN ZANIPOLO), belonging to the Dominicans. Venice
The dramatic effect of this picture is beyond all praise; the
death-like pallor in the face of San Pietro, the extremity
of cowardice and terror in that of his flying companion,
the ferocity of the murderers, the gloomy forest, the trees
bending and waving in the tempest, and the break of calm
blue sky high above, from which the two cherubim issue with
their palms, render this the most perfect *scenic* picture in the
world.

It is a mistake to represent St. Peter Martyr assassinated on the steps of an altar or within a church, as in some Spanish pictures.

I must mention another most interesting work which relates to St. Peter Martyr. Fra Bartolomeo has introduced him into most of the large pictures painted for his Order, and has given him the usual type of head; but in *one* picture he has represented him with the features of his friend Jerome Savonarola, that eloquent friar who denounced with earnest and religious zeal the profane taste which even then had begun to infect the productions of Art, and ended by entirely depraving both Art and artists. After the horrible fate of Savonarola, strangled and then burned in the great square at Florence, in 1498, Bartolomeo, who had been his disciple, shut himself up in his cell in San Marco, and did not for four years resume his pencil. He afterwards painted this head of his friend, in the character of Peter Martyr, with a deep gash in his scull, and the blood trickling from it, probably to indicate his veneration for a man who had been his

74   Jerome Savonarola
in the character of St. Peter Martyr.

spiritual director, and who by his disciples was regarded as a martyr; and if ever the Dominicans regain their former influence, who knows but that we may have this resolute adversary of the popes and princes of his time canonised as another 'St. Jerome'?

ST. THOMAS AQUINAS.

Ital. San Tomaso di Aquino, Dottore Angelico.　March 7, 1274.

ST. THOMAS AQUINAS, as a theologian one of the great lights
of the Roman Catholic Church, was of the illustrious family
of the Counts of Aquino, in Calabria. His grandfather had
married the sister of the Emperor Frederic I. : he was, consequently, grand-nephew of that prince, and kinsman to the
emperors Henry VI. and Frederic II. His father Landolfo,
Count of Aquino, was also Lord of Loretto and Belcastro, and
at this latter place St. Thomas was born in the year 1226.
He was remarkable in his infancy for the extreme sweetness
and serenity of his temper, a virtue which, in the midst of the
polemical disputes in which he was afterwards engaged, never
forsook him. He was first sent to the Benedictine school at
Monte Casino, but when he was ten years old his masters
found they could teach him no more. When at home, the
magnificence in which his father lived excited rather his
humility than his pride : always gentle, thoughtful, habitually
silent, piety with him seemed a true vocation. The Countess
Theodora, his mother, apprehensive of the dangers to which
her son would be exposed in a public school, was desirous that
he should have a tutor at home : to this his father would not
consent, but sent him to finish his studies at the University of
Naples. Here, though surrounded by temptations, the warnings and advice of his mother so far acted as a safeguard, that
his modesty and piety were not less remarkable than his
assiduity in his studies. At the age of seveneten he received
the habit of St. Dominick in the convent of the Order at
Naples. The Countess Theodora hastened thither to prevent
his taking the final vows : feeling that he could not resist her
tenderness, he took flight, and, on his way to Paris, was waylaid near Acquapendente, by his two brothers Landolfo and
Rinaldo, officers in the emperor's army. They tore his friar's
habit from his back, seized upon him, and carried him to their
father's castle of Rocca-Secca. There his mother came to him,

and in vain supplicated him to change his resolution. She ordered him to be confined and guarded from all communication with others ; no one was suffered to see him but his two sisters, who were directed to use their utmost persuasions to turn him from his purpose. The result was precisely what one might have foretold ; he converted his two sisters, and they assisted him to escape. He was let down from a window of the castle in a basket. Some of the Dominican brethren were waiting below to receive him, and in the following year he pronounced his final vows.

Notwithstanding his profound learning, the humility with which he concealed his acquirements, and the stolid tranquillity of his deportment, procured him the surname of *Bos*, or the Ox. One instance of his humility is at once amusing and edifying. On a certain day, when it was his turn to read aloud in the refectory, the superior, through inadvertence or ignorance, corrected him, and made him read the word with a false quantity. Though aware of the mistake, he immediately obeyed. Being told that he had done wrong to yield, knowing himself in the right, he replied, ' The pronunciation of a word is of little importance, but humility and obedience are of the greatest.'

From this time till his death, he continued to rise in reputation as the greatest theological writer and teacher of his time. Pope Clement IV. offered to make him an archbishop, but he constantly refused all ecclesiastical preferment. In 1274 he was sent on a mission to Naples, and was taken ill on the road, at Fossa-Nova, where was a famous abbey of the Cistercians. Here he remained for some weeks unable to continue his journey, and spent his last hours in dictating a commentary on the Song of Solomon. When they brought him the Sacrament, he desired to be taken from his bed and laid upon ashes strewn upon the floor. Thus he died, in the fiftieth year of his age, and was canonised by John XXII. in 1323.

St. Thomas Aquinas represents the learning, as St. Peter Martyr represents the sanctity, of the Dominicans. Effigies of him are frequent in pictures and in prints, and the best of them bear a general resemblance, showing them to have been derived from a common original. The face is broad and rather heavy; the brow fine and ample; the expression mild and thoughtful. His attributes are—1. a book, or several books; 2. the pen or ink-horn; 3. on his breast a sun, within which is sometimes a human eye, to express his far-seeing wisdom; 4. the sacramental cup, because he composed the Office of the Sacrament still in use. He is often intently writing, or looking up at the holy Dove hovering above him, the emblem of inspiration: he is then distinguished from other doctors and teachers, who have the same attributes, by his Dominican habit.

The most ancient and most remarkable pictures of St. Thomas Aquinas have been evidently intended to express his great learning and his authority as a doctor of the Church. I will mention five of these, all celebrated in Art:—

1. By Francesco Traini, of Pisa. St. Thomas Aquinas, of colossal size, is enthroned in the centre of the picture. He holds an open book, and several books lie open on his knees: rays of light proceed from him in every direction; on the right hand stands Plato, holding open his Timeus; on the left Aristotle, holding open his Ethics; Moses, St. Paul, and the four Evangelists, are seen above, each with his book; and over all, Christ appears in a glory: from him proceed the rays of light which fall on the Evangelists, thence on the head of St. Thomas, and emanate from him through the universe. Under his feet lie prostrate the three arch-heretics, Arius, Sabellius, and the Arabian Averrhoes, with their books torn. In the lower part of the picture is seen a crowd of ecclesiastics looking up to the saint; among them, Pope Urban VI., inscribed *Urbanus Sex Pisanus*, who was living when the picture was painted, about 1380. It is still preserved with great care in the Church of Sa. Caterina, at Pisa. A figure by Benozzo Gozzoli, now in the Louvre, is so like this of Traini, that it should seem to be a copy or imitation of it, made when he was at Pisa in 1443.

2. By Taddeo Gaddi, in the large fresco in S. Maria Novella. Florence. St. Thomas is seated on a magnificent throne, over which hover

3 c

75   St. Thomas Aquinas.   (Benozzo Gozzoli.)

seven angels carrying the symbols of the theological virtues.
On his right hand sit Peter, Paul, Moses, David, and Solomon;
on the left the four Evangelists.   Crouching under his feet
are the three great heretics, Arius, Averrhoes, and Sabellius.
In a row beneath, and enthroned under beautiful Gothic
niches, are fourteen female figures, representing the Arts and
Sciences; and at their feet are seated fourteen figures of great
theological and scientific writers.

Rome.   3. By Filippino Lippi, in the S. Maria-sopra-Minerva; a
large elaborate fresco, similar to the preceding in the leading
allegory, but the whole treated in a more modern style.   St.
Thomas is enthroned on high, under a canopy of rich classic
architecture; under his feet are the arch-heretics, and on each
side stand the theological virtues.   In front of the picture
are assembled those renowned polemical writers, disputants,
and scholars, who are supposed to have waited on his teaching, and profited by his words.

4. St. Thomas is kneeling before a crucifix. From the mouth of the crucified Saviour proceed the words, 'Bene scripsisti de me, Thomas; quam mercedem accipies?' (Thou hast written well of me, Thomas; what recompense dost thou desire?) The saint replies, 'Non aliam nisi te, Domine!' (Thyself only, O Lord!) 'A companion of St. Thomas, hear- Vasari. ing the crucifix thus speaking, stands utterly confounded and almost beside himself.' This refers to a celebrated vision, related by his biographers (not by himself), in which a celestial voice thus spoke to him. The same subject was painted by Francesco Vanni in the Church of San Romano at Pisa.

5. By Zurbaran, his masterpiece, the 'San Tomas' now in the Museum at Seville. This famous picture was painted for the Dominican college of that city. Not having seen it, I insert Mr. Stirling's description :—

'It is divided into three parts, and the figures are somewhat larger than life. Aloft, in the opening heavens, appear the Blessed Trinity, the Virgin, St. Paul and St. Dominick, and the angelic doctor St. Thomas Aquinas ascending to join their glorious company ; lower down, in middle air, sit the four Doctors of the Church, grand and venerable figures, on cloudy thrones ; and on the ground kneel, on the right hand, the Archbishop Diego de Deza, founder of the college, and on the left the Emperor Charles V., attended by a train of ecclesiastics. The head of St. Thomas is said to be a portrait of Don Augustine de Escobar, prebendary of Seville ; and, from the close adherence to Titian's pictures observable in the grave countenance of the imperial adorer, it is reasonable to suppose that in the other historical personages the likeness has been preserved wherever it was practicable. The dark mild face immediately behind Charles is traditionally held to be the portrait of Zurbaran himself. In spite of its blemishes as a composition, —which are perhaps chargeable less against the painter than against his Dominican patrons of the college ; and in spite of a certain harshness of outline,—this picture is one of the grandest of altarpieces. The colouring throughout is rich and effective, and worthy of the school of Roelas ; the heads are all of them admirable studies ; the draperies of the doctors and ecclesiastics are magnificent in breadth and amplitude of fold ; the imperial mantle is painted with Venetian splendour ; and the street view, receding in the centre of the canvas, is admirable for its atmospheric depth and distance.'

On a certain occasion, when St. Thomas was returning by sea from Rome to Paris, 'a violent storm terrified the crew and the passengers; the saint only was without fear, and continued in tranquil prayer till the storm had ceased.' I suppose this to be the subject of a picture in *St. Thomas d'Aquin* at Paris, painted by Scheffer.

I must mention two other learned personages who have been represented, though very rarely, in Art, and who may be considered in connection with St. Thomas Aquinas.

ALBERTUS MAGNUS, a Dominican, and a famous teacher of theology, was the master of St. Thomas. He is sometimes called in Italy *Sant' Alberto Magno*, and is painted as the pendant to St. Thomas Aquinas in two pictures, by Angelico da Fiesole, now in the Academy at Florence (Nos. 14 and 20).

Of DUNS SCOTUS, the Franciscan, the rival and adversary of St. Thomas in theological disputation, there is a fine and striking picture at Hampton Court; it belonged to James II., and is attributed to Ribera, by whom it was probably painted for a Franciscan convent. I shall have more to say of this celebrated friar in reference to the legends of the Virgin, as he was one of the earliest defenders of the *Immaculate Conception*. The disputes between him and St. Thomas gave rise to the two parties called *Thomists* and *Scotists*, now forgotten.

Dante has placed S. Thomas Aquinas and S. Albertus Magnus as companions in paradise :—

> ' Questi che m' è a destra più vicino
> Frate e maestro fummi ; ed esso Alberto
> È di Cologna, ed io Tomas d' Aquino.'

In the Collection of Mr. Rogers there is a fine old head of St. Thomas Aquinas, with his book, pen, and ink-horn. It is in the manner of Ghirlandajo.

ST. CATHERINE OF SIENA.

Lat. Sancta Catherina Senese, Virgo admirabilis, et gloriosa Sponsa Christi. *Ital.* Santa Caterina di Siena. La Santissima Vergine Senese. *At Siena,* La Santa. April 30, 1380.

WHAT St. Clara is for the Franciscans, St. Catherine of Siena is for the Dominicans,—the type of female sanctity and self-denial, according to the Rule of her Order.

She is represented, in many beautiful and valuable pictures, alone, or grouped with St. Dominick or St. Peter Martyr, or with her namesake St. Catherine of Alexandria, as types respectively of wisdom and sanctity. At Siena, where she figures as protectress of the city, she is often grouped with the other patrons, St. Ansano and St. Bernardino the Franciscan. It is from the painters of that peculiar and beautiful school of Art which flourished at Siena that we are to look for the finest and most characteristic effigies of St. Catherine as their native saint and patroness. Some very singular representations from the legends of her life and from her ecstatic visions, which, critically, do not rank high as works of Art, derive a strong, an almost painful, interest from the *facts* of her history, from her high endowments, from her real and passionate enthusiasm —her too real agonies and errors, and from the important part which she played in the most troubled and eventful times of Italian story. Whether we regard her under the moral and religious, or the poetical and picturesque aspect, Catherine of Siena is certainly one of the most interesting of the female saints who figure in Art.

The city of Siena, as those who have not seen may read, is situated on the highest point of one of those lofty eminences which rise up from the barren hilly district to the south of Tuscany. The country, as we approach it, has the appearance of a great volcanic sea, consolidated even while the waves were heaving. The Campagna of Rome, in its melancholy yet glorious solitude, is all poetry and beauty compared to the dreary monotony of the hilly waste which surrounds Siena. But the city itself, rising with its ample walls and towers, is wonderfully striking. It is built on very unequal ground. You look down into peopled ravines—you gaze up at palace-crowned heights; and every now and then you come on wide vacant spaces of greensward and trees, between the inhabited part of the city and the massive walls, and heaps of ruined buildings showing the former size and splendour of the city, when it could send out a hundred thousand fighting men from its twenty-four gates.

Between two high ridges,—one crowned by the beautiful cathedral barred with white and black marble, the other by the convent of St. Dominick,—sinks a deep ravine, to which you descend precipitately by narrow lanes; and at the bottom of this ravine there is a famous fountain—the Fonte-Branda (or Blanda). It is called a fountain, but is rather a gigantic well or tank; a wide flight of steps leads down to a great Gothic hall, open on one side, into which pour the gathered streamlets of the surrounding hills, pure, limpid, abundant.

This ancient fountain was famous for the coldness and Inferno, c. 80. affluence of its waters in the days of Dante. Adam of Brescia, the hypocrite and coiner, when tormented in fire, says, that ' to behold his enemies in the same plight would be to him sweeter and more refreshing than the waters of Branda to his burning tongue : '

'Per Fonte-Branda non darei la vista :'

—a horrid association of ideas which, with those who have seen the fountain itself, is merged in a never-forgotten picture of gay and busy life, and sunshine and sparkling waters. Around the margin of this cool, capacious, shadowy well, congregate men, women, and children in every variety of costume, with merry voices—merry, not musical:—and cattle and beasts of burden, with their tinkling bells. From time immemorial the Fonte-Branda has been the favourite resort of the gossips and loungers of the city. The dwellings of dyers, wool-combers, bleachers, and fullers, and all other trades requiring an abundant supply of water, are collected in the neighbourhood of this fountain; and on the declivity of the hill stands an oratory, once the dwelling of St. Catherine of Siena. From it we look up to the convent and church of St. Dominick, the scene of many passages in her story, which is thus related:—

In the year 1347 there dwelt in the city of Siena a certain Giacomo Benincasa, who was a dyer by trade, and for his station a rich and prosperous man; for those were the palmy days of Siena, when as a free republic she equalled Florence in arts and arms, and almost rivalled her in the production of the fine woollen fabrics, which are still the staple manufacture of the place. Benincasa and his wife Lapla dwelt, as I have said, not far from the Fonte-Branda; and they had many children, of whom the youngest and the most beloved was named Catherine. She was so fair, so gay, so graceful in her infancy, that the neighbours called her Euphrosyne; but they also remarked that she was unlike her young companions; and as she grew up, she became a strange, solitary, visionary child, to whom an unseen world had revealed itself in such forms as the pictures and effigies in the richly adorned churches had rendered familiar to her eye and her fancy.

One evening Catherine, being then about seven years old, was returning with her elder brother, Stefano, from the house of her married sister, Bonaventura, and they sat down to rest upon the hill which is above the Fonte-Branda; and as Catherine looked up to the Campanile of St. Dominick, it appeared to her that the heavens were opened, and that she beheld Christ sitting on a throne, and beside him stood St. Peter, St. Paul, and St. John the Evangelist. While she gazed upon this vision, lost in ecstasy, her brother stretched forth his hand and shook her, to recall her to herself. She turned to him,—but when she looked up again, the heavens had closed, and the wondrous vision was shut from her sight; —she threw herself on the ground and wept bitterly.

But the glory which had been revealed to her dwelt upon her memory. She wandered alone away from her playmates; she became silent and very thoughtful. She remembered the story—she had seen the pictures—of her holy patroness and namesake, Catherine of Alexandria; and she prayed to the

Virgin Mary that she would be pleased to bestow her Divine
Son upon her also, and that he should be her chosen bridegroom.   The most Blessed Virgin heard and granted her
prayer, and from this time forth did Catherine secretly
dedicate herself to a life of perpetual chastity, being then
only eight years old.

76   Vision of St. Catherine of Siena. (Vanni.)

Her mother and her father were good and pious both, but
they understood not what was passing in the mind of their
child.   Her love of solitude, her vigils and her dreams, her
fastings and penances, seemed to them foolishness.   Her
mother rebuked her; and her father, as she grew up fair and
beautiful to look upon, wished her to marry like her sisters ;
but Catherine rejected all suitors; she asked only to dwell
with him whom, in her heart, she had espoused: she regarded
herself as one consecrated and set apart, and her days were
passed in solitude, or before the altar in prayer.   Her parents
were excited to anger by her disobedience; she was no longer
their well-beloved child ; they dismissed the woman servant,

and laid all the household duties, even the meanest and most
toilsome, on Catherine. Moreover, they treated her harshly,
and her brothers and sisters mocked her. But Catherine
thought in her heart, ' Were not the saints thus afflicted ? did
not the martyrs of old suffer far more and worse?' and she
endured all unrepining; she performed submissively and
diligently whatever duties were required of her : but she lived
almost without food and sleep; and, to discourage her earthly
suitors, she became negligent in her attire, and cut off her
long and beautiful tresses, offering them up at the foot of the
altar. Her mother and her sister Bonaventura spoke hard
words to her; they again pressed her to accept a husband
approved by her father, but she refused. Shortly afterwards
Bonaventura died in childbirth, which Catherine knew was a
judgment upon her for her wicked advice ; nevertheless, she
prayed so earnestly that her sister might be delivered from
purgatory, that her prayer was granted, and it was revealed to
her that the soul of Bonaventura was translated into paradise.

But, for all this, her parents still urged her with offers of
marriage; until one day, as Benincasa entered his daughter's
chamber, or cell, he found her kneeling in prayer, and on
her head sat a snow-white dove. She appeared unconscious
of its presence. Then the good man trembled within himself,
and he feared lest in opposing her vocation he might offend
against the Holy Spirit, who thus, in visible form, attended
and protected her. So, from this time forth, he resolved to
say no more, and left Catherine free to follow the promptings
of her own heart. She went up to the convent of St. Dominick, humbly entreated admission, and was received as a
Penitent of the Third Order. She never inhabited the
convent as a professed and secluded nun; but she vowed
herself to an absolute silence for three years, slept on a deal
board with a log for a pillow, and shut herself up in the little
chamber or garret she had appropriated in her father's house,
ascending at early dawn, or coming night, the steep path
which led to the summit of the hill, to perform her devotions
in the convent church, afterwards the scene of her miraculous
visions.

3 D

But in her vocation Catherine did not find that peace which she had looked for. The story relates that the arch-enemy of man rendered her task of self-denial as difficult as possible; that he laid in her path horrible snares;—tortured her, tempted her with foulest images and fancies and suggestions, just as he had tempted the holy hermit St. Antony in the days of old. In these visitations, as it is recorded, Catherine did not argue with her spiritual deceiver; she knew from experience that the father of lies could argue better than she could,—that argument, indeed, was one of his most efficient weapons. She prayed, she fasted, she scourged herself at the foot of the altar till the blood flowed down from her shoulders; and she called on Christ, her affianced bridegroom, to help her. He came, he comforted her with his *visible* presence. When at midnight she arose and went into the church to compose her soul by prayer, he appeared before her, walked up and down the cold pavement with her, talked to her with ineffable graciousness and sweetness:—thus she herself related, and some believed; but others, wicked and doubting minds, refused to believe, and there were times when she distrusted herself and the goodness of God towards her:—'If these mysterious graces vouchsafed to her should be after all but delusions, but snares, of the enemy!' For a time she laid aside her strict austerities and her recluse life, and devoted herself to the most active charity. She visited the poor around, she nursed the sick; but, through the ill offices of Satan, she was tried and tempted sorely, even through her charitable self-devotion.

There was a poor woman, a neighbour, whose bosom was half eaten away by a cancer, and whom few could venture to approach. Catherine, overcoming the strong repugnance of her nature to such an office, ministered to her, sometimes in the cold winter night carrying the wood on her back to make a fire; and, although the woman proved ungrateful, and even spiteful towards her, forsook her not till death had released her. There was another woman who was a leper, and, as such, was banished beyond the walls of the city. Catherine sought her out and brought her home, gave up her bed to her, tended her, and nursed her, and in consequence was herself infected by leprosy in her hands. Now this woman also proved ill-conditioned and thankless, and peevishly exacted as her right what was bestowed in Christian charity. But Catherine endured everything from her with unwearied patience; and when at length the woman died, and there was no other to undertake the perilous and disgusting office, she washed her, laid her out, and buried her with her own hands, which, from being diseased, were from that moment miraculously healed.

Another time, as she was wending her way through the city on some compassionate errand, she saw two robbers carried forth to the place of execution without the walls, and they filled the air with imprecations and cries of despair, rejecting the offices of religion, while the multitude followed after them with curses. And Catherine was moved with a deep and holy compassion; for these men, thus hurried along to a shameful, cruel, merited death, were they not still her brethren in Christ? So she stopped the car and demanded to be placed by their side; and so tender and so persuasive were the words she spoke, that their hard hearts were melted; they confessed their sins and the justice of their sentence, and died repentant and reconciled.

Catherine, that her virtue and her sanctity might be fully manifested, was persecuted and vilified by certain envious and idle nuns of the convent of St. Dominick, among whom a sister, Palmerina, was especially malignant; and these insisted that her visions were merely dreams, and that all her charitable actions proceeded from vainglory. She laid her wrongs, weeping, at the feet of Christ. He appeared to her bearing in one hand a crown of gold and jewels, in the other a crown of thorns, and bade her choose between them; she took from his hand the crown of thorns and placed it on her own head, pressing it down hastily, and with such force that the thorns penetrated to her brain, and she cried out with the agony. Palmerino afterwards repented, and, falling at the feet of Catherine, begged her forgiveness, which was immediately granted.

Catherine would often pray in the words of Scripture for a
new heart: whereupon, as it is related, our Saviour appeared
to her in a vision, took her heart from her bosom, and replaced
it with his own : and there remained a wound or scar on her
left side from that time.

Many other marvellous gifts and graces were vouchsafed to
her, but these I forbear to relate, for the greatest of all remains
to be recorded.

When Catherine was at Pisa, she was praying at early
dawn in the chapel of St. Christina, before a crucifix venerable
for its sanctity; and while she prayed, being absorbed in
rapturous devotion, she was transfixed, that is, received the
stigmata, as St. Francis had done before; which miracle, notwithstanding her endeavour to conceal it, was attested by
many who knew her, both in her lifetime and after her death.[1]

The conversion, through her prayers or her eloquence, of many
wicked and unjust persons to a new life, the revelations with
which she was favoured, her rigorous self-denial, and her extraordinary virtues, spread the fame of Catherine through all the
cities of Tuscany, and even as far as Milan and Naples. At this
time (about 1376) the Florentines, having rebelled against the
Holy See, were excommunicated by the pope, Gregory XL
They would have braved his displeasure but that it reacted on
their commercial relations with other countries, with France
more particularly; and they wished for a reconciliation. They
chose for their ambassadress and mediator Catherine of Siena.

She set out, therefore, for Avignon, where the popes then
resided, and, being received by the papal court with all respect
and deference, she conducted the negotiation with so much
discretion that the pope constituted her arbitress, and left
her to dictate the terms of peace between himself and the
turbulent Florentines. But on her return to Florence she
found the whole city in a state of tumult, and when she would

---

[1] The crucifix commemorated in this legend is a painting on panel by Giunta
Pisano (about 1260). It was afterwards removed from Pisa by a special decree
of the pope, and placed in the oratory of St. Catherine at Siena, where I saw it
in 1347.

have harangued the populace, they not only refused to listen
to her, but obliged her to take refuge in a convent of her
Order, where she remained concealed till the sedition was put
down.   Catherine, and others too, believed that much of the
misery and misrule which then afflicted Italy arose from the
absence of the Roman pontiffs from their own capital.   She
used all her influence with the pope to induce him to return to
Rome, and once more fix the seat of government in the Lateran;
and it is related that her urgent and persuasive letters, at this
time addressed to the pope and the cardinals, decided their
wavering resolution.   The pope left Avignon in September
1376; Catherine met him on the way, attended on him when
he made his public entry into Rome; and when, in his alarm
at the consequences of the step he had taken, the Holy Father
was about to return to Avignon, she persuaded him to remain.
He died the following year. 'The Great Schism of the West'
followed; and Christendom beheld two infallible popes, supported by two factions arrayed against each other.   Catherine
took the part of the Italian pope, Urban VI., and showed, in
advocating his cause, more capacity, good sense, and honesty
of purpose, than the most favourable of his biographers ever
discovered in the character and conduct of that violent and
imbecile pontiff.   He appointed her his ambassadress to the
court of Joanna II. of Naples, and she at once accepted the
mission; but those who were to accompany her refused to
undertake a journey so beset with dangers, and, after various
delays, the project was abandoned.   Pity that the world was
not edified by the spectacle of Catherine of Siena, the visionary
ascetic nun, playing the part of plenipotentiary in the most
licentious court of Europe, and brought face to face with such
a woman as the second Joanna of Naples !

In the midst of these political and religious dissensions
Catherine became sick to death, and after a period of grievous
bodily suffering, still full of enthusiastic faith, she expired,
being then thirty-three years old.   In her last moments, and
while the weeping enthusiasts who surrounded her bed were
eagerly gathering and recording her dying words as heavenly
oracles, she was heard to murmur—'No! no! no!—not vain-

glory !—not vainglory !—but the glory of God !'—as if she
were answering some accuser within;—as if to the half-alarmed
conscience there had been a revelation of some merely human
purposes and feelings lurking behind the ostensible sanctity.
But who can know this truly ?—and it is fair to add, that the
words have been differently interpreted, indeed in quite an
opposite sense, as expressing an *assertion*, not a *doubt*.

Among the devout admirers of Catherine during her lifetime was the painter Andrea Vanni. He belonged to a family
of artists, the first of whom, his grandfather, flourished in the
beginning of the fourteenth century ; the last, Raffaello Vanni,
died towards the end of the seventeenth. The family was
noble ; and it appears that Andrea, besides being the best
painter of his time, was Capitano del Popolo, and sent as
ambassador from the republic of Siena to the pope, and afterwards to Naples, where, during his embassy, he painted several
pictures ; hence he has been styled by Lanzi the Rubens of his
age. St. Catherine appears to have regarded him with maternal
tenderness. Among her letters are three addressed to him
during his political life, containing excellent advice with
respect to the affairs intrusted to him, as well as his own moral
and religious conduct. These letters bear as superscription
on the outside, ' *A Maestro Andrea di Vanni, Dipintore ;* '
and begin, ' *Carissimo Figliuolo in Christo.*' In one of them
she points out the means of obtaining an influence over the
minds of those around him, and then adds, ' *Ma non veggo il
modo che noi potessimo ben reggere altrui se prima non reg-
ghiamo noi medesimi.*' (I do not see how we are to govern
others unless we first learn to govern ourselves.) Among
the works of Andrea in his native city, was a head of Christ,
said to have been painted under the immediate instruction of
St. Catherine, representing the Saviour as she had, in her
visions, beheld him. Unhappily, this has perished : it would
certainly have been a most curious document, and would
have thrown much light on Catherine's own mind and
character. Equally, however, in importance and interest, is
the authentic effigy of his sainted friend and patroness which

Vanni has left us. This portrait was painted originally on
the wall of the Church of San Domenico, in that part of the
nave which was the scene of Catherine's devotions and mystic

visions, and which has since
been divided off and en-
closed as a place of peculiar
sanctity. The fresco, now
over a small altar, has long
been covered with glass and
carefully preserved, and is
in all respects most striking and lifelike. I give a
sketch from it, in which the
general character of the
head is tolerably preserved ;
but it would be difficult to
transfer, even to a finished
copy, its peculiar beauty.
It is a spare, worn, but
elegant face, with small regular features. Her black
mantle is drawn round her ;
she holds her spotless lily
in one hand, the other is
presented to a kneeling nun,
who seems about to press it
reverentially to her lips ;
this figure has been called
a votary, but I think it may represent the repentance and
pardon of her enemy Palmerina.

77   St. Catherine of Siena.

In the single devotional figures, so commonly met with in
the Dominican churches, St. Catherine is distinguished by
the habit of the Order and the stigmata ; these together fix
the identity at once. It is true that one of the earliest of her
biographers, the good St. Antonino of Florence, who was
born seven or eight years after her death, asserts distinctly
that the stigmata were not impressed visibly on her body, but

on her *soul:* and about a century later, the Franciscans petitioned Pope Sixtus IV. that Catherine of Siena might not be represented in a manner which placed her on an equality with their own great saint and patriarch. Sixtus, who before his elevation had been a Franciscan friar, issued a decree, that in the effigies of St. Catherine the stigmata should thenceforth be omitted. This mandate may have been in some instances, and at the time, obeyed; but I cannot, on recollection, name a single picture in which it has not been disregarded.

The lily is an attribute scarcely ever omitted; and she also (but rarely) bears the palm,—not as martyr, but expressing her victory over temptation and suffering. The book so often placed in her hand represents the writings she left behind her. The crown of thorns is also given to her, in reference to the legend already related.

I will now give a few examples:—

D Museum.

1. In a rare Sienese print of the fifteenth century. She stands with a hideous demon prostrate under her feet: in one hand the lily and the palm; in the other a church, which may represent the Church, of which she was styled the defender, in its general sense, or a particular church dedicated to her.

2. She stands holding her lily; probably one of the first pictures of her in her character of saint, painted for the Dominicans at Perugia.[1]

3. She stands with Mary Magdalene 'rapt in spirit,' and looking up at a vision of the Virgin and Saviour: by Fra Bartolomeo, in the Church of San Romano at Lucca,—as fine

Vasari.

as possible. Vasari says, ' *è una figura, della quale, in quel grado, non si può far meglio.*'

4. She stands holding a cross and a book. A beautiful figure by Ghirlandajo.

5. She stands holding her book and lily. Statue in white marble by Attichiati.

---

[1] This elegant figure, which is engraved in Rossini's *Storia della Pittura* (vol. i.), is not by Bufalmacco, to whom it is attributed, nor in his style. Bufalmacco painted about 1350-60; Catherine died in 1380, and was not canonised till a century afterwards.

6. She kneels with St. Dominick before the throne of the Madonna; the lily at her feet. The Infant Saviour is turned towards her, and with one hand he crowns her with thorns, with the other he presents the rosary. This small but most beautiful altarpiece was painted by Sasso Ferrato

78   St. Dominick and St. Catherine of Siena. (Sasso Ferrato.)

for the Santa-Sabina, on the Aventine, the first church of the Dominicans at Rome. I give a slight sketch of the composition of this picture — the masterpiece of the

3 E

painter, with all his usual elegance, and without his usual insipidity.

7. She kneels, and our Saviour, a majestic figure standing, places on her head the crown of thorns; behind St. Catherine are Mary Magdalene, St. Raphael with Tobit, St. Peter, St. Paul, and St. Philip the apostle. A magnificent group, painted by F. Bissolo.

8. She receives the stigmata, fainting in a trance before the crucifix, and sustained in the arms of two sisters of her Order. The fresco in her chapel, by Razzi, is justly cele-

79   St. Catherine of Siena, fainting. (Razzi.)

brated, and I give a sketch merely to show the arrangement. Here St. Catherine and her companions wear the white tunic and scapulary, without the black mantle—an omission favourable to the general effect of the colour, which is at once most delicate, rich, and harmonious: and the beauty of the faces, the expression of tender anxiety and reverence in the nuns, the divine languor on the pallid features of St. Catherine, render this fresco one of the marvels of Art.

As a subject, St. Catherine fainting before the crucifix is of very frequent occurrence, but generally she is sustained in the arms of angels, as in the picture by Raffaello Vanni, and in another by Tiarini, or, while she sleeps or swoons, angels hover round her.

The Sposalizio of St. Catherine of Siena is variously represented, and often in a manner which makes it difficult to distinguish her from St. Catherine of Alexandria, except by the habit and the veil.

The earliest and finest example is perhaps the beautiful altarpiece by Fra Bartolomeo, painted for his Convent of St. Mark at Florence, but, since the time of Francis I., one of the ornaments of the Louvre. The Virgin sits enthroned holding her Divine Son; before her kneels St. Catherine, receiving from the Infant Christ the mystic ring. On one side of the throne stand St. Peter, St. Bartholomew, and St. Vincent Ferraris; on the other, St. Francis and St. Dominick are embracing each other. This is one of the pictures seen and admired by Raphael when he visited Fra Bartolomeo at Florence between 1505 and 1507, and which first roused his attention and emulation with regard to colour.

Historical subjects relative to St. Catherine are rarely met with out of their native city; all those of which I have preserved memoranda exist in the churches and oratories at Siena.

In her chapel in the San Domenico, besides the beautiful fresco by Razzi, already described, we have on one side the scene with the robbers, by the same painter; on the other the healing of a demoniac, by Francesco Vanni.

In her oratory (formerly the *Bottega di Tintoria* of her father) is the cure of a sick man, who at her command rises from his bed; by Pacchiarotti: and by Salimbeni, the scene in which she harangues the revolted Florentines. St. Catherine

before Gregory XI. at Avignon, pleading the cause of the
Florentines,—and her return to Florence,—are by Sebastian
Folli, a late Sienese painter; and by Pacchiarotti, the finest
of all,—the pilgrimage of St. Catherine to visit the tomb of
St. Agnes of Montepulciano. This St. Agnes was a Dominican
nun, who, uniting great intelligence and activity of mind
with superior sanctity, was elected abbess of her convent at
the age of fifteen, and died about 1317. Although held in
great veneration by the people in the south of Tuscany, she
was not formally canonised till 1604; consequently we see
few pictures of her, and those of a very late date, and confined
to the locality. But to return to St. Catherine. She was
among those who, through respect and devotion, visited the
tomb of Agnes, accompanied by two of her nieces, who on
that occasion took the veil: the fresco is magnificent, and
contains heads which for depth and beauty of expression have
been compared to Raphael.

Siena.

The library of the Duomo is decorated with a series of ten
large frescoes representing the principal events in the life of
Pius II., painted by Pinturicchio with the assistance of Raphael.
The last of these is the ceremony of the Canonisation of Catherine
of Siena, performed by Pius II. with great solemnity in 1461.
The body of the saint, exhumed for the purpose, lies extended
before the pope; a lily is placed in her hand; several cardinals
and a crowd of assistants, bearing tapers, stand around.

In the year 1648, a special office was appointed in honour of
St. Catherine of Siena by Urban VIII., in which it was said
that Catherine was descended from the same family as the
Borghesi;—she who was only the daughter of a dyer! That
noble house, greatly scandalised by such an imputation, made a
Baillet. Vies formal complaint to the papal court:—' C'était injurieusement
des Saints.
faire passer leur maison pour roturière et plébéienne, et laisser
également à leurs descendants un affront éternel dans toute la
Chrétienté ; '—and they insisted on having these obnoxious
passages expunged from the Ritual. There cannot be a stronger
proof of the change which had taken place in point of religious
feeling between the fourteenth and the seventeenth century.

Gregory XI., the friend of St. Catherine, lies buried in the Rome. Church of St. Francesca Romana. Over his tomb is a very fine bas-relief representing his solemn entry into Rome, on the occasion of the return of the papal court from Avignon. Catherine of Siena is seen conspicuous in the assemblage of cardinals, prelates, and princes, who form the triumphant procession.

ST. ANTONINO, ARCHBISHOP OF FLORENCE.

May 10, 1461.

THE story of this good saint is connected in a very interesting manner with the history of Art.

He was born at Florence, of noble parents, about the year 1384. While yet in his childhood the singular gravity of his demeanour, his dislike to all childish sports, and the enthusiasm and fervour with which he was seen to pray for hours before a crucifix of particular sanctity,—then, and I believe now, in the Or-san-Michele,—caused his parents to regard Florence. him as one set apart for the service of God. At the age of fifteen he presented himself at the door of the Dominican convent at Fiesole, and humbly desired to be admitted as a novice. The prior, astonished at the request from one so young, and struck by his diminutive person and delicate appearance, deemed him hardly fit to undertake the duties and austerities imposed on the Order, but would not harshly refuse him. 'What hast thou studied, my son?' he asked, benignly; the boy replied modestly that he had studied the Humanities and the Canon Law. 'Well,' replied the prior, somewhat incredulous, 'return to thy father's house, my son; and when thou hast got by heart the Libro del Decreto, return hither, and thou shalt have thy wish,'—and so with good words dismissed him, not thinking, perhaps, to see him again. Antonino, though not gifted with any extraordinary talents, had an indomitable will, and was not to be frightened, by tasks or tests of any kind, from a resolution over which he had brooded

from infancy.   He turned away from the gate of the convent,
and sought his home.   At the end of a year he appeared again
before the prior :—'Reverend father, I have learned the book
of Decrees by heart; will you now admit me?'   The good
prior, recovering from his astonishment, put him to the proof,
found that he could repeat the whole book as if he held it in
his hand, and therefore, seeing clearly that it was the will of
God that it should be so, he admitted him into the brotherhood,
and sent him to Cortona to study during the year of his novi-

A.D. 1405. ciate.   At the end of that period, he returned to Fiesole and
pronounced his vows, being then sixteen.   The remainder of
his life showed that his had been a true vocation.   Lowly,
charitable, and studious, he was above all remarkable for the
gentle but irresistible power he exercised over others, and
which arose not so much from any idea entertained of his
superior talents and judgment as from confidence in the simplicity of his pure, unworldy mind and in his perfect truth.

Now, in the same convent at Fiesole where Antonino
made his profession, there dwelt a young friar about the same
age as himself, whose name was Fra Giovanni, and who was
yet more favoured by Heaven ; for to him, in addition to the
virtues of humility, charity, and piety, was vouchsafed the
gift of surpassing genius.   He was a painter: early in life
he had dedicated himself and his beautiful art to the service of
God and of His most blessed saints; and, that he might be
worthy of his high and holy vocation, he sought to keep himself unspotted from the world, for he was accustomed to say,
that 'those who work for Christ must dwell in Christ.'   Ever
before he commenced a picture which was to be consecrated
to the honour of God, he prepared himself with fervent prayer
and meditation, and then he began, in humble trust that it
would be put into his mind what he ought to delineate; and
he would never change or deviate from the first idea, for, as

Vasari. he said, '*that* was the will of God' (*così fusse la volontà di
Dio*); and this he said, not in presumption, but in faith and
simplicity of heart.   So he passed his life in imagining those
visions of beatitude which descended on his fancy, sent indeed
by no fabled Muse, but even by that Spirit 'that doth prefer

before all temples the upright heart and pure;' and surely never before or since was earthly material worked up into soul, nor earthly forms refined into spirit, as under the hand of this most pious and most excellent painter. He became sublime by the force of his own goodness and humility. It was as if paradise had opened upon him, a paradise of rest and joy, of purity and love, where no trouble, no guile, no change could enter; and if, as it has been said, his celestial creations seem to want power, not the less do we feel that they need it not,—that before these ethereal beings power itself would be powerless: such are his angels, resistless in their soft serenity; such his virgins, pure from all earthly stain; such his redeemed spirits, gliding into paradise; such his sainted martyrs and confessors, absorbed in devout rapture. Well has he been named IL BEATO and ANGELICO, whose life was 'participate with angels' even in this world!

Now this most excellent and favoured Giovanni, and the good and gentle-hearted Antonino, dwelling together in their youth within the narrow precincts of their convent, came to know and to love each other well. And no doubt the contemplative and studious mind of Antonino nourished with spiritual learning the genius of the painter, while the realisation of his own teaching grew up before him in hues and forms more definite than words and more harmonious than music; and when in after years they parted, and Antonino was sent by his superiors to various convents, to restore by his mild influence relaxed discipline,—and Angelico by the same authority to various churches and convents at Florence, Cortona, Arezzo, Orvieto, to adorn them with his divine skill,—the two friends never forgot each other.

Many years passed away, in which each fulfilled his vocation, walking humbly before God; when at length the fame of Angelico having gone forth through all Italy, the pope called him to Rome to paint for him there a chapel of wondrous beauty, with the pictured actions and sufferings of those two blessed martyrs, St. Stephen and St. Laurence, whose remains repose together without the walls of Rome; and while Angelico was at his work, the pope took pleasure in looking on and conversing with him, and was filled with reverence for his pure and holy life, and for his wisdom, which, indeed, was not of this world.

At this period the Archbishop of Florence died, and the pope was much troubled to fill his place, for the times were perilous, and the Florentines were disaffected to the Church.

One day conversing with Angelico, and more than ever struck with his simplicity, his wisdom, and his goodness, he offered him the dignity of archbishop; and great was the surprise of the Holy Father when the painter entreated that he would choose another, being himself addicted to his art, and not fit to guide or instruct or govern men; adding that he knew of one far more worthy than himself, one of his own brotherhood, a man who feared God and loved the poor,—learned, discreet, and faithful; and he named the Frate Antonino, who was then acting in Naples as Vicar-General. When the pope heard that name, it was as if a sudden light broke through the trouble and darkness of his mind; he wondered that he had not thought of him before, as he was precisely the man best fitted for the office. Antonino therefore was appointed Archbishop of Florence, to the great joy of the Florentines, for he was their countryman, and already beloved and honoured for the sanctity and humility of his life; when raised to his new dignity he became the model of a wise and good prelate, maintaining peace among his people, and distinguished not only by his charity but his justice and his firmness.

He died in 1459 at the age of seventy, having held the dignity of archbishop thirteen years, and was buried in the Convent of St. Mark. Adrian VI. canonised him, and the bull was published in 1523.

There are, of course, no effigies of St. Antonino in his character of saint earlier than this date, and, except at Florence, I do not recollect meeting with any. As, however, he is the only distinguished canonised prelate of the Order, it may be presumed that an episcopal saint introduced into the Dominican pictures, and not accompanied by any particular attribute, represents St. Antonino. He is always exhibited as archbishop. This sketch is from a characteristic full-length

80 St. Antonino of Florence.
(Ghirlandajo.)

figure the size of life, by Domenico Ghirlandajo. Here he wears the pallium as archbishop over his Dominican habit. In his splendid chapel in the San Marco at Florence, dedicated by the Salviati, is his statue in white marble, by John of Bologna. The frescoes on each side represent the ceremonies which took place on his canonisation. In the first, he is lying in state in the church, surrounded by five cardinals and nineteen bishops; in the second, he is borne to his resting-place in the chapel, in a procession of prelates, princes, and magistrates. As these frescoes contain portraits from the life of the most distinguished Florentines then living, they About 1490. have become invaluable as documents, and are, besides, admirably painted by Passignano in his best manner—that is to say, very like Paul Veronese.

There is also a well-known figure of St. Antonino, one of the first objects we meet when entering the Duomo of Florence by the principal door. He is seated on a throne, attired in his episcopal robes, and in the act of blessing the people.

One among the legendary stories of St. Antonino is frequently represented. During a terrible pestilence and famine which afflicted Florence in his time, there were two blind men, who were beggars by profession, and who had amassed in their vocation many hundred crowns; yet, in this season of affliction they not only withheld their hoards, but presented themselves among those who sought aid from public charity. The moment Antonino fixed his eyes on them, the true state of the case was by a miracle made known to him. Severely did he then rebuke those selfish hypocrites, took from them their hidden wealth, which he sent to the hospital,

3 F

and, though he maintained them generously during the rest of their lives, he made them perform strict penance for their former sinful and unfeeling avarice.

St. Raymond de Peñaforte, who figures chiefly in Spanish Art, was of an illustrious family of Barcelona, nearly allied to the kings of Aragon. He was born at his father's castle at Peñaforte in Catalonia, in 1175; entered the Church early, and became a perfect model to the clergy by his zeal, devotion, and boundless liberality to the poor, whom he called his creditors. He assumed the habit of the Order of St. Dominick a few months after the death of its founder, and devoted himself to the duties it enjoined—those of preaching, instructing the poor, and converting sinners and heretics. Late in life he was elected the third General of his Order. It is said of him, by way of eulogy, that being commissioned by the pope's legate to preach a holy war against the Moors, this servant of God acquitted himself with so much prudence, zeal, and charity, that he sowed the seeds of the overthrow and total expulsion of these infidels in Spain. He died at Barcelona in the year 1275, in the hundredth year of his age, and was canonised by Pope Clement VIII. in 1601. His miracles, performed before and after his death, filled fifteen folio pages.

The most celebrated of these, and one which is frequently represented in pictures, being authenticated by the bull of his canonisation, is thus related:—He was confessor to Don James, king of Aragon, called El Conquistador, a warlike and accomplished prince after the fashion of princes—that is, he was inclined to serve God and obey his confessor in all things that did not interfere with his policy or his pleasures. He had, in fact, but one fault; he was attached to a certain beauty of his court from whom Raymond in vain endeavoured to detach him. When the king summoned his confessor to attend him to Majorca, the saint refused unless the lady were left behind: the king affected to yield—but soon after their arrival in Majorca, Raymond discovered that the lady was also there in the disguise of a page: he remonstrated; the king grew

angry; Raymond intimated his resolution to withdraw to
Spain; the king forbade any vessel to leave the port, and made
it death to any person to convey him from the island.   The
result is thus gravely related: ' St. Raymond, full of confidence in God, said to his companion, "An earthly king has
deprived us of the means of escape, but a heavenly King will
supply them !"—then, walking up to a rock which projected
into the sea, he spread his cloak on the waters, and, setting
his staff upright, and tying one corner to it for a sail, he made
the sign of the cross and boldly embarked in this new kind of
vessel.   He was wafted over the surface of the ocean with
such rapidity that in six hours he reached Barcelona.'   This
stupendous miracle *might* perhaps have been doubted if five
hundred credible witnesses had not seen the saint land on the
quay at Barcelona, take up his cloak, which was not even
wetted by the waves, throw it round him, and retire modestly
to his cell, more like a humble penitent than one in whose
favour Heaven had so wonderfully wrought.   It is pleasant to
know that Don Jayme afterwards repented, and governed his
kingdom (and his conduct) by the advice of Raymond till the
death of the saint.

Devotional effigies of St. Raymond are found in the Dominican churches and convents, and are in general productions
of the Spanish and Bologna schools about the period of his
canonisation (1601).   He wears the habit of his Order; in
the background, the sea, over which he is gliding on his black
mantle.   The representation of the miracle as an historical
subject is frequent: the best is that of Ludovico Caracci in
the San Domenico at Bologna;   it exhibits the saint kneeling
on his black mantle, looking up to heaven with a devout
and confiding expression, and thus borne over the waves.
Sir Edmund Head, in the 'Handbook of the Spanish and
French Schools,' mentions a series of six pictures from the
life of Raymond painted by Pacheco for the *Merced* at Seville
—but does not say what are the subjects chosen.
It appears to me that there is some confusion here, and also
in Mr. Stirling's 'Artists of Spain' (p. 318), between this

St. Raymond of Peñaforte, the Dominican, and St. Raymond Nonnatus of the Order of Mercy, who died in 1240, after having been created a cardinal by Gregory IX.

April 5, 1419. Another Spanish Dominican who figures in Art is St. VINCENT FERRARIS. He was born at Valencia in Spain, in 1357, of virtuous and religious parents, who stinted themselves of necessary things to provide for his education and that of his brother Boniface. He took the habit of the Order of St. Dominick in his eighteenth year; and became one of the greatest preachers and missionaries of that Order. There was scarce a province or a town in Europe that he did not visit; he preached in France, Italy, Spain, and, by the express invitation of Henry IV., in England.

From the descriptions we have of this saint, it appears that he produced his effect by appealing to the passions and feelings of his congregation. The ordinary subjects of his sermons were sin, death, the judgments of God, hell, and eternity; delivered, says his eulogist, with so much energy, that he filled the most insensible with terror. Like another Boanerges, he preached in a voice of thunder; his hearers often fainted away, and he was obliged to pause till the tears, sobs, and sighs of his congregation had a little subsided; he possessed himself what has been called an extraordinary gift of tears; and, take him altogether, this saint appears to me a Roman Catholic Whitfield. It is said that he performed many miracles, and that preaching in his own tongue he was understood by men of different nations; Greeks, Germans, Sardinians, Hungarians, and others, declared that they understood every word he uttered, though he preached in Latin, or in the Spanish dialect as spoken at Valencia. The last two years of his life were spent in Brittany and Normandy, then desolated by the English invasion; there he was seized with his last illness, and died at Vannes, at the age of 62. Jeanne de France, Duchess of Brittany, washed his body and prepared it for the grave with her own hands. He was canonised by Calixtus III. in 1455.

The proper attribute of this saint is the crucifix, held aloft in his hand as preacher and missionary. In allusion to the fervour and inspiration which characterised his discourses, he is sometimes represented with wings to his shoulders; likening him, in his character of a preacher of the Gospel, to the Evangelists, being, like them, a messenger of good tidings: but I am not sure that this attribute has been sanctioned by ecclesiastical authority; and, at all events, these large emblematical wings, in conjunction with the Dominican habit, have a strange uncouth effect.

The finest existing picture of him is that of Fra Bartolomeo, painted for his convent of San Marco at Florence; it represents the saint addressing his congregation from the pulpit, one hand extended in exhortation, the other pointing to heaven. There can be no doubt that the head was painted from some known portrait; and the impressive fervour of the countenance and manner must have been characteristic, as well as the features. It is, in fact, as fine as possible in its way. Here he has no wings; but in the picture by Murillo, painted a hundred and fifty years later, and which I saw in the Aguado Gallery some years ago, he has the large symbolical wings. I do not know where this picture now is.

Fl. Acad.

St. HYACINTH, though an early saint, is found only in very late pictures.

*San Giacinto.
August 15,
1257.*

At the time that St. Dominick was at Rome, in 1218, Ivo, bishop of Cracow, and chancellor of Poland, arrived there on a mission from his government to the Holy See. In his train were his two nephews, Hyacinth and Ceslas. Ivo, moved by the preaching of St. Dominick, and the success which attended his mission, requested of him to send some of the brethren of his Order to preach the Gospel in his distant and half barbarous diocese. Dominick excused himself, having otherwise disposed of all his disciples. This circumstance made a deep impression upon Hyacinth, the eldest of the bishop's nephews, of whom we are now to speak. He was born of the noble family of the Aldrovanski, one of the most illustrious in Silesia, had recently completed his studies at Bologna, and was distinguished by his virtues, talents, piety, and modesty, and by the prudence and capacity with which he managed the secular affairs of life without allowing them to interfere with his religious duties.   He was struck by the preaching of St. Dominick, and by the recollection of the barbarism, the heathenism, the ignorance which prevailed in many parts of his native country; he offered himself as a missionary, and, with his cousin Ceslas, he took the habit of the Order of St. Dominick, and pronounced his vows in the Church of St. Sabina at Rome in 1218.

The event showed that it was in no transient fit of enthusiasm that he took this resolution.   From that time he devoted himself to the preaching of the Gospel in the wild, unsettled countries of the north; he penetrated to the shores of the Black Sea, he preached amongst the Tartars, the Russians, the Sclavonians; thence travelling towards the north, he preached amongst the Danes, the Swedes, the Norwegians, and in other countries round the Baltic: it is said that he left no region unvisited, from the borders of Scotland to China.   If we consider in what a condition these countries still were in the thirteenth century, his missionary services can only be compared to some which have distinguished these later days.

Hyacinth had to traverse uninhabited wilds, uncleared forests still infested with wild beasts, hordes of barbarians to whom the voice of the Gospel had never reached;—on foot, without arms, and thinly clad, without money, without an interpreter, often without a guide, and trusting only in the cause of truth and in Divine Providence.   Thus forty years of his life were spent.   Worn out by fatigue, he had merely strength to return to his cell in the monastery of his Order which he had founded at Cracow, and died there on the 15th of August 1257.   He was canonised by Clement VIII., more than three hundred years after his death, in 1594.   Anne of Austria, wife of Louis XIII., carried into France her hereditary veneration for St. Hyacinth.   At her request, Ladislaus, king of Poland, sent her some relics of the saint, which she placed in the Dominican convent at Paris, and he became an object of the popular veneration. This, I presume, is the reason why so many pictures of St. Hyacinth are found in the churches of Paris even to this day.

The effigies of St. Hyacinth represent him in the habit of his Order, bearing the crucifix as preacher, and frequently the pyx containing the Host (Le Sant Ciboire). It is related of him that when his convent at Kiov in Russia was sacked by the Tartars he escaped, carrying with him the pyx and the image of the Virgin, which he had snatched up from the altar. On arriving at the banks of the Dniester, he found it swollen to a raging torrent; the barbarians were behind him, and, resolved that the sacred objects he bore should not fall into the hands of the pagans, after recommending himself to Heaven he flung himself into the stream : the waters miraculously sustained him, and he walked over their surface as if it had been dry land. This is the incident of his life which is usually represented in his pictures, and great care must be taken not to confound him with St. Raymond.

Another of his miracles was the resuscitation of a drowned youth, who had remained lifeless for twenty-four hours.

All the pictures I have met with of this saint have been painted since the date of his canonisation, and are found in the Dominican convents :—

By Leandro Bassano : St. Hyacinth passing the river Dniester with the Ciborio and the image of the Virgin. *Louvre.*

By L. Caracci : the apparition of the Virgin and Child to St. Hyacinth. An angel holds a tablet on which are inscribed the words which the Virgin addresses to him—' Be at peace, O Hyacinth ! for thy prayers are agreeable to my Son, and all that thou shalt ask of him through me shall be granted.' Painted for the Capella Turini in Bologna, but carried off by the French and never restored. There is an interesting account of this picture in Malvasia. When Guido first saw it he stood silent, and then exclaimed ' that it was enough to make a painter despair and throw away his pencils ! ' How *Felsina Pittrice, vol. i. p. 292 edit. 1841.*

different from the modest Correggio's '*anch' io sono pittore !* '
The sight of excellence makes the *vain* man—not the great
man—despair.

By Malosso of Cremona : St. Hyacinth preaches to a
multitude, and converts the heathen by curing the bite of a
scorpion which lies at his feet. Painted for the Church of the
Dominicans at Cremona.

By Brizzio : St Hyacinth restores a drowned youth (*l'Anne-
gato*). A very fine dramatic picture, in the Church of St.
Dominick at Bologna.

In the modern decorations of ' Notre Dame de Lorette ' at
Paris, we find in two large frescoes the two famous miracles
of St. Hyacinth. The first represents the restoration of the
drowned youth : in the other he is on the point of crossing
the Dniester.

Oct. 9, 1181. ST. LOUIS BELTRAN, or BERTRAND, a native of Valencia,
and a celebrated Dominican preacher and missionary in the
sixteenth century. He believed himself called by God to
spread the light of the Gospel through the New World, and
embarked for Peru, where he spent several years. It was
not, says his biographer, from the blindness of the heathens,
but from the cruelty, avarice, and profligacy of the Christians,
that he encountered the greatest obstacles to his success.
After a vain attempt to remedy these disorders, he returned
to Spain, died at Valencia, and was canonised by Clement X.
in 1671. He was a friend of St. Theresa, and seems to have
been a sincere and energetic man as well as an exemplary
priest.

Pictures of this saint abound in the Dominican churches in
Spain, and particularly in the Valencian school. I do not
know that he is distinguished by any particular attribute ; he
would wear, of course, the habit of his Order, and carry the
crucifix as preacher ; Peruvian scenery or Peruvian converts
in the background would fix the identity.

In the year 1647 (the year in which he was declared a Beato) the plague broke out at Valencia, and the painter Espinosa placed himself and his family under the guardian-ship of San Louis Beltran, who preserved, by his interces-sion, the whole family. Espinosa, in gratitude, vowed to his protector a series of pictures, which he placed, in 1655, in the chapel of the saint in the convent of San Domingo at Valencia. They are said to be in 'a masterly style;' but the subjects are not mentioned.

There is a picture of him in the Church of S. Maria-sopra-Minerva at Rome, under his Italian appellation, San Ludovico Bertrando.

<hr />

SANTA ROSA DI LIMA, I believe the only canonised female saint of the New World, was born at Lima in Peru, in 1586. 'This flower of sanctity, whose fragrance has filled the whole Christian world, is the patroness of America, the St. Theresa of Transatlantic Spain.' She was distinguished, in the first place, by her austerities. 'Her usual food was an herb bitter as wormwood. When compelled by her mother to wear a wreath of roses, she so adjusted it on her brow that it became a crown of thorns. Rejecting a host of suitors, she destroyed the lovely complexion to which she owed her name, by an application of pepper and quicklime. But she was also a noble example of filial devotion, and maintained her once wealthy parents, fallen on evil days, by the labour of her hands.' All day she toiled in a garden, and at night she worked with her needle. She took the habit of the Third Order of St. Dominick, and died in 1617. She was canonised by Clement X. According to the Peruvian legend, the pope, when entreated to canonise her, absolutely refused, exclaim-ing, '*India y santa! asi como llueven rosas;*' (India and saint! as likely as that it should rain roses!) whereupon a miraculous shower of roses began to fall in the Vatican, and ceased not till the incredulous pontiff acknowledged himself convinced.

The best pictures of this saint are by the late Spanish

[margin: Aug 30, 1617.]

[margin: Stirling's 'Artists of Spain,' p. 1008.]

3 G

painters. One by Murillo, which has been engraved, represents her crowned with thorns, and holding in her hand full-blown roses, on which rests the figure of the Infant Saviour.

A large picture of St. Rosa di Lima, with the Infant Saviour, on which is inscribed the name of Murillo, is in the collection of Mr. Bankes, at Kingston Hall, Dorset.

With this Transatlantic saint we conclude the notices of the Dominican Order, as illustrated in Art.

THE CARMELITES.

Ital. I Carmini.   *Fr.* Les Carmes.

NEITHER as an Order, nor individually, are the Carmelites interesting or important in their relation to Art.

They pretend, as I have already observed, to a very high antiquity, claiming as patriarch and founder the prophet Elijah, 'who dwelt solitary in the midst of Carmel; he gave example to many devout Anchorites, of whom an uninterrupted succession from the days of Elijah inhabited Mount Carmel, and early embraced the Christian faith; and this community of the Hermits of Mount Carmel continued till the thirteenth century. They built a monastery near the fountain of Helias (Elijah), and an oratory dedicated to the Virgin, thence called 'Our Lady of Mount Carmel:' but, as yet, they had no written Rule; wherefore, by the advice of one of their number, Berthold by name, they desired of Albert, patriarch of Jerusalem, that he would give them a Rule of discipline. He prescribed to them a form taken from the Rule of St. Basil, but more severe; and a parti-coloured mantle of white and red stripes,—for such, according to an ancient tradition, was the miracle-working mantle of Elijah the prophet, the mantle famed in Holy Writ. When, however, the Carmelites arrived in the west, and Pope Honorius III. was induced to confirm the Rule of the Order, he altered the colour of the mantle, and appointed that it should be white, and worn over a dark-brown tunic. Hence, in England, the Carmelites were called *White Friars.* They were introduced into this country direct from Palestine, by Sir John de Vesci on his return from the Holy Wars. He settled them near his castle at Alnwick, and they became subsequently more numerous and popular here than in any other country of Europe before the time of St. Theresa. The third General of their Order was an English Carmelite, St. Simon Stock, who introduced an alteration in the habit,— the scapulary, the long narrow strip of cloth hanging down to

[marginal notes: Baillet. Butler. Dugdale. 'La Madonna del Carmine.' Dugdale. Helyot.]

the feet, of the same colour as the tunic: this, in pictures, distinguishes the Carmelites from the Premonstratensians, who also wear the brown tunic and white cloak, but no scapulary.

The Carmelites chose for the protectress of their Order the Virgin Mary; and Honorius III. commanded that they should be styled 'The Family of the Most Blessed Virgin.' Hence, in all the convents of the Carmelites, the Virgin, under her title of the '*Madonna del Carmine*,' holds such a conspicuous place. She is frequently exhibited standing with her white mantle outspread, while her 'Family'—the friars and nuns of the Order—are gathered beneath its protecting folds; and among them St. Albert as bishop, St. Angelus the martyr, and, in late pictures, St. Theresa of Spain, are generally distinguished above the rest.

The rosary, having been instituted in especial honour of the Virgin, also found favour with the Carmelites, and sometimes the Virgin is represented as presenting a rosary to a Carmelite saint.

Next in importance to the Virgin, we find, in the Carmelite churches, Elijah the prophet as patriarch of the Order, or the Scriptural stories of his life. He is fed by ravens in the wilderness; or he is sacrificing on Mount Carmel before the priests of Baal; or he is carried up to heaven in the chariot of fire. Thus a whole series of subjects from the life of Elijah decorates the cloisters of the Carmini at Florence; and on entering the Carmini at Venice, the first objects which strike us are the statues, in white marble, of Elijah and Elisha.

Next after the Virgin and Elijah, we shall generally find conspicuous—

April 8, 1214.   St. ALBERT, bishop of Vercelli, and patriarch of Jerusalem, regarded by historians as the real founder of the Carmelite Order. He wears the episcopal robes, and carries the palm as martyr; for it is recorded in his Life, that being summoned from Palestine by Innocent III. to attend a council in the

Lateran, as he was preparing to embark he was assassinated at Acre by a wretch whom he had reproved for his crimes.[1]

In the cathedral at Cremona they preserve a singular ancient vessel ornamented at the four corners with winged monsters, and apparently of the ninth or tenth century, in which, according to tradition, St. Albert kneaded bread for the poor.

St. ANGELUS the Carmelite, bearing the palm as martyr, is found in late pictures only. According to the apocryphal legend, this St. Angelus came from the East about the year 1217, landed in Sicily, and preached at Palermo and Messina. He was assassinated by a certain Count Berenger, a powerful lord of that country, who for several years had lived openly in unhallowed union with his own sister. St. Angelo rebuked him severely, as John the Baptist had formerly rebuked Herod, and found the same recompence. By command of Berenger he was hung upon a tree and shot with arrows: at least his martyrdom is thus represented in a disagreeable picture by Ludovico Caracci, where St. Angelo is hanging from a tree with his white and brown habit fluttering against the blue sky;—the city of Palermo, very like the city of Bologna, being seen in the background.

May 5, 1220. Saint Anga, Angelo, or Angiolino.

Another picture by the same painter represents the supposed meeting of St. Angelo, St. Francis, and St. Dominick; or, as it is expressed in Italian, '*San Francesco e San Domenico, che complimentano affettuosamente con Sant' Angelo Carmelitano.*'

Both these pictures were painted for the Carmelites at Bologna, and are in the Academy there.[2]

---

[1] We must not confound St. Albert *the Carmelite* with St. Albert *Cardinal* and Bishop of Liege. It is this last St. Albert who, as patron saint of the Archduke Albert, figures in Rubens' fine picture of St. Ildefonso; but, except in this single instance, I have not met with him. He may probably be found in Flemish prints of the seventeenth century, as a compliment to the archduke, whose wife, the celebrated Clara-Eugenia, made St. Clara fashionable in her time.

[2] They were formerly styled subjects from the life of San Pier Toma, another Carmelite friar, who lived in the fourteenth century, who was not a martyr, and was never formally canonised. He was, however, a real personage, while the very existence of St. Angelo has been called in question.

I have seen prints and pictures of St. Angelo in which red and white roses are falling from his mouth, symbols of his eloquence; and I remember one in which two graceful angels are picking up the roses as they fall.

In the year 1668 the learned authors of the *Acta Sanctorum* (known as the Bollandists) not only threw discredit on the whole legend of St. Angelo, but treated as chimerical the supposed origin and high antiquity of the Carmelites as an Order. Thereupon arose a most bitter contest. The Carmelites were loud and angry in refutation and expostulation. From the time of St. Theresa they had had so much influence in Spain, that they procured the condemnation of the obnoxious volumes by the Spanish Inquisition. The Bollandists, who belonged to the Society of Jesuits, appealed to the pope against this judgment; and the dispute ran so high between the Carmelites and Jesuits, and caused such general scandal, that Innocent XII. published a brief, commanding the two parties to keep silence on the subject from that time, for ever.

It was during this contest, that is, about the middle of the seventeenth century, that we find the churches of the Carmelites filled with pictures, in general very bad ones, which were intended as an assertion of their claims to superior sanctity as well as superior antiquity:—pictures of Elijah, as their patriarch; of St. Albert, as their lawgiver; of St. Angelo, as their martyr; of St. Simon Stock, receiving the scapulary from the hands of the Virgin; and particularly of their great saint, the '*Serafica Madre Teresa*, of whom we are now to speak.

C1   St. Theresa.

St. Theresa.

Ital. Santa Teresa, Fondatrice dei Scalzi. *Fr.* Sainte Thérèse de Jésus des Carmes-Déchaussés. *Sp.* La Nuestra Serafica Madre Santa Teresa de Gesù. Patroness of Spain. Oct. 17, 1582.

> 'Scarce has she learnt to lisp the name
> Of martyr, yet she thinks it shame
> Life should so long play with that breath
> Which, spent, could buy so brave a death.
> She never undertook to show
> What death with love should have to doe ;
> Yet, tho' she cannot tell you why,
> She can love, and she can die ;
> And has a heart dares hope to prove
> How much less strong is death than love !'

(From *Crashaw's Hymn* 'in memory of the virtuous and learned ladye
Madre de Teresa, that sought an early martyrdom.')

St. Theresa, even setting aside her character as saint and patroness, was an extraordinary woman,—without doubt the most extraordinary woman of her age and country ; which,

perhaps, is not saying much, as that country was Spain, and
she lived in the sixteenth century. But she would have been
a remarkable woman in any age and country. Under no
circumstances could her path through life have been the
highway of commonplace mediocrity; under no circumstances
could the stream of her existence have held its course
untroubled; for nature had given her great gifts, large
faculties of all kinds for good and evil, a fervid temperament,
a most poetical and 'shaping power' of imagination, a strong
will, singular eloquence, an extraordinary power over the
minds and feelings of others,—genius, in short, with all its
terrible and glorious privileges. Yet what was she to do with
these energies—this genius? In Spain, in the sixteenth
century, what working sphere existed for such a spirit lodged
Handbook
of Spain. in a woman's form? Mr. Ford calls her 'a love-sick nun;'
in some respects the epithet may be deserved,—but there have
been, I am afraid, some thousands of love-sick nuns; there
have been few women like St. Theresa. It is impossible to
consider in a just and philosophic spirit either her character
or her history without feeling that what was strong, and
beautiful, and true, and earnest, and holy, was in herself; and
what was morbid, miserable, and mistaken, was the result of
the influences around her.

Theresa d'Avila was born at Avila in Castile, on the 28th
of March 1515, one of twelve children. Her father, Don
Alphonso Sanchez de Cepeda, was a nobleman of distinguished
character, exceedingly pious. Her mother, Beatrix, appears to
have been in all respects an admirable woman; her only fault
was, that she was a little too much given to reading romances
and books of chivalry. Between the piety of the father and
the romance of her mother was the character of Theresa formed
in her childhood, and these early impressions influenced her
through life. Amongst her brothers was one whom she distinguished by particular affection: she tells us that they read
together the lives of the saints and the holy martyrs, until
they were filled with the most passionate desire of obtaining
for themselves the crown of martyrdom; and when they

were children of eight or nine years old, they set off on a
begging expedition into the country of the Moors, in hopes of
being taken by the infidels and sacrificed for their faith. She
adds that, when she and her little brother were studying the
lives of the saints, what most impressed their minds was, to
read, at every page, that the penalties of the damned are to
be for ever, and the glory of the blessed also for ever.
They tried to conceive the idea of eternity, and they repeated,
looking in each other's faces, awe-struck, 'What! for ever!
for ever!' and the idea filled them both with a vague terror.
As they had been disappointed in their hope of obtaining
martyrdom amongst the Moors, they resolved to turn hermits;
but in this also they were prevented. However, she tells us
that she gave all her pocket-money in alms; and if she played
with other children of her age, they were always nuns and
friars, walking in mimic processions, and singing hymns.
Theresa lost her mother at the age of twelve, a loss to her
irreparable: what her destinies might have been, had this
parent lived, it is in vain to speculate. The few years which
follow, exhibit her as passing from one extreme to another.
The love of pleasure, the love of dress, self-love, and the pride
of position, the desire to be loved, to be admired—all the
passions and feelings, in short, natural to a young girl of her
age, endowed with very extraordinary faculties of all kinds,
made her impatient of restraint. The influence of some
worldly-minded relations, and, above all, the increasing taste
for poetry and romance, conspired to diminish in her mind the
pious influences which had been sown there in her early youth.
In fact, at the age of sixteen, there seems to have remained no
settled principle in her mind but that thoroughly feminine
principle of womanly dignity. Her father, however, seems to
have been aware of the dangers to which she was exposed, and
placed her in a convent, with orders that she should be kept
for a time in strict seclusion.

In a girl of a different character this would have been a
perilous experiment. With Theresa, her enthusiastic and
ardent nature took at once the turn towards religion. Something whispered to her that she could be safe nowhere but

within the walls of a cloister : she abhorred the idea of a marriage which had been proposed to her, but she equally abhorred
the idea of seclusion. In the midst of these internal struggles
she fell dangerously ill. A feeling of the vanity and insecurity
of all earthly things grew upon her mind ; and after another
struggle, which ended in another fit of illness, she took to
reading the epistles of St. Jerome, and this decided her vocation. She obtained the permission of her father to take the
vows ; but, passionate in all her affections, the separation
from her family had nearly cost her her life. She was twenty
when she entered the convent of the Carmelites at Avila.
After she had pronounced her vows, her mind became more
settled ; not, however, her health, which for many years seems
to have been in a most precarious state. She tells us that she
passed nearly twenty years without feeling that repose for
which she had hoped when she sacrificed the world. She
draws a striking picture of her condition at this time. ' On
one side I was called as it were by God, on the other side I
was tempted by regrets for the world. I wished to combine
my aspirations towards heaven with my earthly sympathies,
and I found that this was impossible; I fell,—I rose, but it
was only to fall again ; I had neither the calm satisfaction of
a soul reconciled with God, nor could I taste those pleasures
which were offered by the world. I tried to think, and could
not think ; disgust and weariness of life seized upon me ; and
in the midst of pious meditations and prayers, nay, in the
midst of the services of the church, I was impatient till the bell
rang and relieved me from duties to which I could give but half
my heart. But at length God took pity upon me : I read the
Confessions of St. Augustine ; I saw how he had been tempted,
how he had been tried, and at length how he had conquered.'
This seems to have been the turning-point in her life. She threw
herself with more confidence upon the resources of prayer, and
at length her enthusiastic and restless spirit found peace. When
her mind was too distracted or too weak for the exaltation of
religious thought, instead of tormenting herself with vain
reproach and penance, she sought and found relief and a fresh
excitement to piety in the practice of works of charity : she

laboured with her hands; she tried to fix her thoughts upon
others; and nothing is more striking in the history of this
remarkable woman than the real piety, simplicity, modesty,
and good sense, which every now and then break forth in the
midst of her visionary excitement, her egotism, her pretensions
to superior sanctity and peculiar revelations from heaven :—
the first were native to her character, the latter fostered and
flattered by the ecclesiastics around her.

It was in the year 1561 that she conceived the idea of
reforming the Order of the Carmelites, into which several
disorders had crept.   Most of the nuns in her monastery
entered into her views: many of the inhabitants of her native
town, over whom she had gradually acquired a strong influence, assisted her with money.   In 1562 she laid the foundation of the new monastery at Avila.   She dedicated it to St.
Joseph, the spouse of the Virgin, to whom she had early vowed
a particular devotion, and whom she had chosen for her patron
saint.   It is perhaps for this reason, as well as in his relation
to the Virgin, that we find St. Joseph a popular subject in the
Carmelite churches, and particularly in those dedicated to St.
Theresa.   She had many difficulties, many obstacles, to con-
tend with.   She entered the little convent she had been enabled
to build with eight nuns only; but in the course of twenty
years she had not only reformed the female members of her
Order, but had introduced more strict obligations into the
convents of the men.   It was her principle that the convents
of the Carmelites under her new Rule should either have no
worldly possessions whatever, and literally exist upon the
charity of others, or that they should be so endowed as not
to require any external aid.   This was a principle from which
her spiritual directors obliged her to depart: such, however,
was her success, that at the period of her death she had
already founded seventeen convents for women and fifteen
for men.   During the later years of her life, her enthusiastic
and energetic mind found ample occupation.   She was continually travelling from one convent to another, called from
province to province, to promulgate her new regulations for
the government of her Order.   She had to endure much

opposition and persecution from the friars; and a schism took place which obliged Gregory XV. to interfere and to divide the Carmelites into two different congregations, placing Theresa at the head of that styled the 'Barefooted Carmelites:' in Italy, *Scalzi*, the unshod; and sometimes *Padri Teresiani*.

Besides compiling exhortations and treatises for the use of her nuns, she wrote, at the express command of her spiritual directors, a history of her own life; and left behind her some mystical compositions, singularly poetical and eloquent, even judging from the French translation. Crashawe thus alludes to her writings—

> ' Oh 'tis not Spanish, but 'tis Heaven she speaks ! '

Sometimes, indeed, the language has the orientalism of the Canticles; and in this instance, as in others, may it not be possible that fervour of temperament was mistaken for spiritual aspiration? Theresa, in the midst of all her terrors of sin, could find nothing worse to say of Satan himself than ' Poor wretch! he loves not !' and her idea of hell was that of a place whence love is banished. It appears to me that she was right in both instances: is not *hate*, as a state of being, another word for *hell?* and does not the incapacity of love, with conscious intellect, stamp the arch-fiend? But I am writing a book on Art, not on morals or religion; else there would be something more to be said of the works of Theresa. To return, therefore, to my subject, and conclude the life of our saint. She had never, since the terrible maladies of her youth, entirely recovered the use of her limbs, and increasing years brought increasing infirmities. In 1582 she was seized with her last illness, in the palace of the Duchess of Alva. She refused, however, to remain there, and was carried back to her convent of San José. She died a few days afterwards, repeating the verse of the Miserere, ' *A broken and a contrite heart, O Lord, Thou wilt not despise !* ' She was canonised in 1621 by Gregory XV., and was declared by Philip III. the second patron saint of the Spanish monarchy after Santiago; a decree solemnly confirmed by the Spanish Cortes in 1812.

Her shrine is at Avila, in the church of her convent. 'Her statue sanctifies the portal. The chapel is a very holy place, and frequented by pilgrims—in smaller numbers, however, than heretofore. The nuns never presume to sit on the seats of the choir, but only on the steps, because the former were occupied by the angels whenever St. Theresa attended mass.' (I must observe that the angels are *always* supposed to assist invisibly at mass.)

There is so much in St. Theresa's life and character eminently picturesque, that I must regret that, as a subject of Art, she has been—not neglected, but, in all senses of the word, ill-treated.

The authentic portraits of her which exist in Spain, and which were all taken in later years of her life, after she had become celebrated, and also corpulent and infirm, represent her person large, and her features heavy,—in some pictures even coarse. In the devotional figures she is generally kneeling at prayer, while an angel hovers near, piercing her heart with a flame-tipped arrow, to express the fervour of divine love with which she was animated. I give a sketch from a Spanish picture just to show the *materialism* of the conception. All the Spanish pictures of her sin in this respect; but the grossest example—the most offensive—is the marble group of Bernini, in the Santa Maria della Vittoria at Rome. The head of St. Theresa is that of a languishing nymph; the angel is a sort of Eros; the whole has been significantly described as a '*parody* of Divine love.' The vehicle, white marble,—its place in a Christian church,—enhance all its vileness. The least destructive, the least prudish in matters of Art, would here willingly throw the first stone.

Other representations of St. Theresa exhibit her looking up in rapture at the Holy Dove, which expresses the claim to direct inspiration made for her—never by her. And sometimes she holds a heart with the name of Jesus, the I.H.S., engraved on it; as in this figure (83), by Bramantino, which, like all the other Italian figures of St. Theresa, is wholly uncharacteristic.

82   St. Theresa.   (From a Spanish picture formerly in the Louvre.)

'An excellent work of Ribalta adorns the saloon of
the Valencian Academy of San Carlos.   It represents
St. Theresa seated at table and writing from the dictation

of the Holy Spirit, hovering at her ear in the likeness of a snow-white dove : her countenánce beaming with heavenly light.'

The finest picture I have seen of St. Theresa, is by Rubens, painted for the 'Petits Carmes' at Antwerp, and now in the Musée of that city. It represents the saint pleading at the feet of the Saviour in behalf of sinners in purgatory. In the Rubens-religious style, in colour, and character, and life, this picture is as fine as possible; and it must accomplish its purpose in point of expression, for, as I well recollect, I could not look on it without emotion. The annexed etching will give some faint idea of its beauty as a composition. Rubens, who had been in Spain, has here given a real and characteristic portrait of the saint. The features are large and heavy, yet bright with enthusiastic adoration and benignity.

Another picture by the same painter represents St. Theresa in her cell, enraptured by an apparition of the Saviour; an angel behind him bears the fire-tipped arrow of divine love. This, I believe, is one of the few pictures of Rubens never engraved.

83   St. Theresa. (Italian.)

By Massarotti :—St. Theresa intercedes for the city of Cremona, when besieged by the French.

By Guercino :—St. Theresa with her patron saint, Joseph. Another, in which our Saviour reveals to her the glory of Paradise. Another, in which the Virgin presents to her the Milan Gal. rosary. Another, in which St. Theresa receives the habit from the hand of the Blessed Virgin, in presence of her patron St. Joseph, St. Albert, and St. Juan de la Cruz : painted for the Carmelite nuns at Messina.

Attributed to Alonzo Cano :—A St. Theresa, crowned with thorns and holding in her hands the instruments of the Passion. Another, in which she ministers to a sick child. Both pictures too poor and bad for Alonzo Cano; the heads, however, are characteristic.

In a small picture in the possession of Mr. Ford, St. Theresa is kneeling on one knee, sustaining on the other an open book, in which she is about to write; an ink-horn and a distaff lie at her feet; above, the Holy Dove is seen descending from the skies. On a prie-dieu behind are the words, ' *Misericordiam Domini æternam cantabo.*'

There are some pictures of her in the magnificent church of the Scalzi at Venice, but none good.

The fame and the effigies of St. Theresa have been extended to the East. Miss Martineau found a figure of her in the convent of her Order on Mount Carmel ; and I extract the beautiful and animated account of this picture, as equally characteristic of the writer and the subject :—

'The church of the convent is handsome ; and it contains a picture worth noting,—the portrait of St. Theresa, whom I agree with Bossuet in thinking one of the most interesting of the saints of his Church. The bringing together of remote thoughts in travel is as remarkable to the individual, as the bringing together of remote personages in the action of human life. How I used to dwell on the image of St. Theresa in my childhood, and long, in an ignorant sympathy with her, to be a nun ! And then, as I grew wiser, I became ashamed of her desire for martyrdom, as I should have been of any folly in a sister, and kept my fondness for her to myself. But all the while that was the Theresa of Spain ;—now wandering among the Moors in search of martyrdom, and now shutting herself up in her hermitage in her father's garden at Avila. It had never occurred to me that I should come upon her traces at Mount Carmel. But here she was, worshipped as the Reformatrix of her Order. It was she who made the Carmelites barefooted : *i.e.*, sandaled, instead of shod. It was she who dismissed all the indulgences which had crept in among her Order ; and she obtained, by her earnestness, such power over the baser parts of human nature in those she had to deal with, as to reform the Carmelite Order altogether : witness, before her death, the foundation of thirty convents, wherein her rule was to be practised in all its severity. Martyrdom by the Moors was not good enough for her : it would have been the mere gratifi-

cation of a selfish craving for spiritual safety.   She did much more for God
and man by living to the age of sixty-seven, and bringing back the true spirit
into the corrupted body of her Order.   There she is,—the woman of genius
and determination,—looking at us from out of her stiff head-gear,—as true
a queen on this mountain-throne as any empress who ever wore a crown!'
—*Eastern Life*, voL iii. p. 235.

In companionship with St. Theresa we find her friend SAN ^{December}
JUAN DE LA CRUZ, a Spanish Carmelite, whom she had united ^{14, 1591.}
with herself as coadjutor in her plans of reform.   He was the
first barefooted Carmelite, and famous for his terrible penances and mortifications.   He is often represented in pictures
with St. Theresa, kneeling before the throne of the Virgin.
He died in 1591, and was canonised by Clement X. in 1675.
Mr. Stirling mentions a series of fifty-eight plates on the
history of St. Juan de la Cruz, 'a holy man who was frequently favoured with interviews with our Saviour, and who
on one of these occasions made an uncouth sketch of the
divine apparition, which was long preserved as a relique in
the Convent of the Incarnation at Avila.'

A fine picture by Murillo, in the gallery of the King of
Holland, represents San Juan de la Cruz in his Carmelite
habit, kneeling before an altar, on which lie a crucifix and
some lilies; four vellum folios, lettered with the titles of his
works, are on the ground at his feet.

ST. ANDREA CORSINI, though he lived in the fourteenth ^{Feb. 4, 1373}
century, was not canonised till the middle of the seventeenth,
some years later than St. Theresa.

He was born in 1302, one of the noble family of Corsini at
Florence, and, until his sixteenth year, was wild, disobedient,
and addicted to vicious company, so that his parents were
well-nigh in despair.   One day, his mother, in a passion of
grief and tears, exclaimed, 'Thou art the wolf whom I saw in
my dream!'   The youth, startled by this apostrophe, looked
at her, and she continued, fixing her eyes upon him—'Before thou wert born I dreamed I had given birth to a wolf,
but I saw that wolf enter in at the open door of a church,
and behold he was changed into a lamb!'   He heard

3 I

her in silence.   The next day, passing by the Church of the
Carmelites, an irresistible impulse induced him to enter; and,
kneeling down before the altar of the Virgin, he poured out
his soul in penitence and prayer.   So complete was the change
in his mind and disposition, that he refused to return to the
house of his parents, and became a Carmelite friar at the age
of seventeen.   From this time to the age of seventy he lived
an example of humility and piety, and died Bishop of Fiesole
in 1373.   He was so much venerated by the Florentines, that
they attributed to his especial intercession and protection
their victory over Niccolò Picinino, in the battle of Anghiari
in 1440.   He was canonised by Urban VIII. in 1629.

Soon after his canonisation, Guido painted for the Corsini
family the beautiful picture which is now at Bologna.   It
represents St. Andrea as Bishop of Fiesole, standing and
looking up to heaven with the finest expression it is possible
to conceive: in one hand he holds the pastoral staff; in the
left, which is gloved, he holds the Scriptures.   Another picture, painted for the Corsini family at Rome, represents St.
Andrea kneeling, and surrounded by a choir of angels.

His sumptuous chapel in the Carmini at ˙Florence is
adorned with bas-reliefs from his life, in white marble.   The
one on the left represents his first celebration of mass; in his
great humility he avoided the festive and triumphant prepara-
tions made by his family to solemnise the occasion, and withdrew to a little chapel at some distance from the city, where,
instead of the usual cortege of prelates, priests, and singers,
the Virgin herself and a choir of angels assisted in the celebration.   On the other side is the victory of the Florentines
at Anghiari; the saint appears hovering above, with his
pastoral staff in one hand, and a sword in the other.   In the
bas-relief over the altar, he is carried up to heaven by angels.
Guercino painted him for the Carmini at Brescia; and in general he may be found in the Carmelite churches, always attired
as bishop; but the pictures are of a late date, and not good.
The palm distinguishes St. Albert from St. Andrea Corsini.

May 25,
1607.   SANTA MARIA MADDALENA DE' PAZZI was another Floren-

tine saint of this Order, one of the noble family of the Pazzi, of whom nothing is recorded but her extreme sanctity and humility, and the temptations and tribulations of her solitude. She was beatified by Urban VIII. in 1626, and canonised by Alexander VIII. in 1670. There is a church at Florence bearing her name.

The pictures in her honour are, of course, of the latest Italian school. The best of these, by Luca Giordano, represents the mystic Sposalizia, always the chief incident in the life of a sainted nun. Here an angel gives her away, and presents her hand to the Saviour; another angel holds the lily, emblem of the purity of these espousals.

I cannot quit the subject of the Carmelites, in their connection with Art, without mentioning one of their Order, conspicuous as a favourite theme for painters and poets,—the Sœur Louise de la Miséricorde, who, when she lived in the world and for the world, was the Duchesse de la Vallière. She was never canonised, therefore the pictures of her in her Carmelite dress do not properly belong to sacred Art; but if sorrow and suffering and a true repentance,—if the lasting influence of her example and undying interest and celebrity of her story,—could be regarded as a species of canonisation, she might well claim a place among the martyrs as well as among the saints. She entered the Carmelite Order in the year 1674, at the age of thirty. The picture of 'Mary Magdalene renouncing the world,' which Le Brun painted by her command as an altarpiece for the convent in which she made her profession, has been considered as a portrait of her; but I believe there is no foundation for the traditional interest given to this picture, and to the still more famous print of Edelinck, the masterpiece of the engraver. The fine penitent Magdalene in the Munich Gallery, a head in profile, is more likely to be the portrait of La Vallière so often alluded to by writers on her life and that of Le Brun. Pictures and prints of the 'Sœur Louise de la Miséricorde,' in her Carmelite habit, were once very popular: there is a very good one in the British Museum.

The Jesuits.

CONFINING myself within the limits of my subject, I have but little to say of the Jesuits in their relation to sacred Art.

It seems to me, looking on them from this point of view, a misfortune to them that their rise as a religious community, and the period of their greatest influence, should have been coeval with the decline and absolute depravation of the Fine Arts. It was also a misfortune to Art and artists, that there was nothing in the spirit of the Order which conduced to their regeneration. There was no want of means, no want of munificence. Wealth incalculable was lavished on the embellishment of their sumptuous churches. Decorations of gold and silver, of alabaster and lapis-lazuli, of rare and precious marbles,—light, brilliance, colour,—all was combined that could render the temples, built under the Jesuit auspices, imposing and dazzling to the vulgar eye. The immediate end was gained; the transient effect was produced; but, in absolutely ignoring the higher powers and neglecting the more lasting effects in Art, they have lost—at least they have failed to gain—some incalculable advantage, which might have been theirs, in addition to others of which they well knew how to avail themselves.[1]

If the Jesuits were not wholly insensible to the ancient influences of Art as a vehicle of instruction, they yet showed

---

[1] In the first edition of this volume, the Jesuits were represented as having neglected the capabilities of Art as a means of *instruction*. This, on further consideration, must be retracted; for certainly, as a means of education, and for their own religious views and political purposes, the arts were, by this sagacious and powerful Order, largely employed. The innumerable engravings and illustrated books of the lives of the Saviour, the Virgin Mary, and the saints, some in a very cheap, and almost all in an attractive form, which inundated the Low Countries and Germany during the seventeenth century, were issued mostly under the direction and at the expense of the Jesuits. They were also the chief patrons —crowned heads excepted—of Rubens and Van Dyck.

themselves incapable of arresting—they even did much in assisting—the downward tendencies of the later schools. Some two or three pictures painted for the Order are really fine in their way; some may be valuable as documents; none are in any degree allied to the poetry of Art. And this was, perhaps, not to be imputed to them as a reproach : we are not to infer that the Jesuits, as a body, were answerable for the decline of Art in the seventeenth century: it had begun a hundred years before the canonisation of their great saint ; a hundred years before their gorgeous churches arose—monuments of those worldly tendencies in Art, which, if they did not cause, they, at least, did not cure. Nor, amid the many distinguished and enlightened men,—men of science, classical scholars, antiquarians, astronomers, mathematicians,—which their Order sent forth to every region of the world, can I recollect the name of a single artist, unless it be Father Pozzi, renowned for his skill in perspective, and who used his skill less as an artist than as a conjuror, to produce such illusions as make the vulgar stare; —to make the impalpable to the grasp appear as palpable to the vision; the near seem distant; the distant, near; the unreal, real ; to cheat the eye; to dazzle the sense;—all this has Father Pozzi most cunningly achieved in the Gesù and the Sant' Ignazio at Rome; but nothing more, and nothing better, than this. I was angry with him; I wearied of his mock altarpieces and his wonderful roofs which pretended to be no roofs at all. Scenic tricks and deceptions in Art should be kept for the theatre. It appeared to me nothing less than profane to introduce *shams* into the Temples of God !

Certainly it cannot be said of the principal saints of the Jesuits that they deserved this fantastic treatment. Their Ignatius Loyola, their Francis Xavier, their Francis Borgia, are among the most interesting, as well as the most extraordinary, men the world has seen. Nothing can be conceived more picturesque, as well as instructive, than their lives and characters: nothing finer as subjects of Art;—but Art has done little or nothing for them, therefore I am here constrained to say but little of them.

In pictures the Jesuits are not easily distinguished. They

wear the black frock buttoned up to the throat; but the
painters of the seventeenth century, avoiding the mass of black,
and the meagre formal lines, have generally given to the Jesuit
saints, those at least who were ordained priests, the dress of
priests or canons,—the albe or the chasuble, and, where the
head is covered, the square black cap.   In Spain and Italy they
now wear a large black hat turned up at each side,—such as
Don Basilio wears in the opera; but such hats I have never
seen in sacred pictures.   By an express clause in their regulations, the Jesuits were permitted to assume the dress in use in
the country they inhabited, whenever they deemed it expedient.

July 31,
1556.
ST. IGNATIUS LOYOLA, the founder of the Jesuits, was born
in his father's castle of Loyola, in the year 1491, of a race so
noble that its head was always summoned to do homage to the
throne by a special writ.   He began life as page in the court
of Ferdinand the Catholic, and afterwards entered the army,
in which he was distinguished for his romantic bravery and his
love of pleasure.   His career, under ordinary circumstances,
would probably have been that of the cavaliers of his time, who
sought distinction in court and camp; but it was suddenly
arrested.   At the siege of Pampeluna, in 1521, he was wounded
in both legs by a cannon-ball.   Dreading the disfigurement
of his handsome person, he caused his wounds to be twice reopened and a protruding bone sawed off, at the hazard of his
life; but the intense agony, though borne with unshrinking
courage, was borne in vain—he was maimed for life.

In the long confinement consequent on his sufferings, he
called for his favourite books of romance and poetry, but none
were at the moment to be found; they brought him the Life
of Christ and the Lives of the Saints.   A change came over
his mind: he rose from his sick couch another man.   The
'lady' to whom he henceforth devoted himself was to be
'neither countess nor duchess, but one of far nobler state,'—
the Holy Virgin, Mother of the Saviour; and the wars in
which he was to fight were to be waged against the spiritual
foes of God, whose soldier he was henceforth to be.

As soon as he was sufficiently recovered he made a pilgrimage to Our Lady of Montserrat, and hung up his sword and lance before her altar. He then repaired to Manresa. Here he gave himself up for a time to the most terrible penances for his past sins, and was thrown into such a state of horror and doubt that more than once he was tempted to put an end to his miserable existence. He escaped from these snares. He beheld visions, in which he was assured of his salvation; in which the mysteries of faith were revealed to him : he saw that which he had formerly only believed. For him what need was there to study, or to consult the Scriptures, for testimony to those divine truths which were made known to him by immediate intercourse with another world? He set off for Jerusalem with the intention of fixing his residence in the holy city ; but this was not permitted, and he returned to Spain. Here he was opposed in his spiritual views by those who condemned him for his former life and his total want of theological learning. He could not obtain the privilege of teaching till he had gone through a course of study of four years' duration. He submitted; he had to begin with the rudiments, to sit on the same form with boys studying grammar—to undergo whatever we can conceive of most irksome to a man of his age and disposition. After conquering the first difficulties he repaired to Paris. Here he met with five companions, who were persuaded to enter into his views : Faber, a Savoyard of mean extraction, but full of talent and enthusiasm; Francis Xavier, a Spaniard of a noble family, handsome in person, and singularly accomplished; the other three were also Spaniards, then studying philosophy at Paris, —Salmeron, Laynez, and Bobadilla. These, with four others, under the direction and influence of Ignatius, formed themselves into a community. They bound themselves by the usual vows of poverty, chastity, and obedience; and they were to take besides a vow of especial obedience to the head of the Church for the time being, devoting themselves without condition or remuneration to do his pleasure, and go to any part of the world to which he should see fit to send them.

Ignatius repaired to Rome, and spent three years there before he could obtain the confirmation of his Institute.   It was at length granted by Paul III.   The essential duties of the new Order were to be three:—preaching in the first place ; secondly, the guidance of souls through confession ; and thirdly, the education of the young.   As Ignatius carried into his community the ideas and habits of a soldier, so the first virtue inculcated was the soldier's virtue, absolute unhesitating obedience ; and he called his society the ' Company of Jesus,' just as a company of soldiers is called by the name of its captain.

He died first General of his Order in 1556, and was canonised by Gregory XV. in 1622.

When once we have seen a head of St. Ignatius Loyola in a print or a picture, we can never afterwards mistake it.   The type does not vary, and has never been idealised.   It does not appear that any portrait of him was painted during his life, although they show such a picture in the Casa Professa at Rome.   Impressions in wax were taken from his features after death ; and from these, assisted by the directions of Father Ribadeneira, Sanchez Coello painted a head which afterwards served as a model.   In its general character, this head is familiar to us in Art: a square, high, powerful brow ; a melancholy and determined, rather than stern, countenance ; short black hair, bald on the temples, very little beard, and a slight black moustache.   ' So majestic,' says his biographer, ' was the aspect of Loyola, that, during the sixteenth century, few, if any, of the books of his Order appeared without the impress of that imperial countenance.'

Artists of Spain, p. 239.

Essays in Eccles. Biog. vol i.

Of the figure painted by Rubens for the Jesuits at Antwerp, and now at Warwick Castle, I give a sketch here. The head in the original is wonderfully fine, and quite true to the Spanish type: he wears the chasuble as priest, and his hand is on an open book, on which are inscribed the first words of his Rule,—*Ad majorem Dei gloriam.*   The square black cap hangs behind him.   The chasuble is splendid,—of a deep scarlet embroidered with gold.

84　　　　St. Ignatius Loyola.　(Rubens.)

In general, Ignatius is distinguished by the IHS, the mono-
gram of the Order,—sometimes in a glory in the sky above,
sometimes on a tablet borne by angels. The heart crowned
with thorns, the *Sacré Cœur*, is also an attribute; it is the
crest or *device* of the Order.

The subjects taken from his life have not been, as far as I
know or can learn, the most striking and picturesque incidents
of that wonderful life :—not Ignatius studying on his sick bed ;
—nor Ignatius performing his midnight watch in the chapel
of Our Lady, hanging up his lance before her altar, and
dedicating himself to her service ;—nor the solemn vows in the
chapel at Montmartre ;—nor the prayer at Jerusalem ;—nor

3 K

even his death scene. These *may* exist, but neither in prints nor in pictures have I met with them. The favourite subjects have been his miracles, his visions, or his penances.

After his penances in the cavern at Manresa, he began his vocation of saint in the usual manner, by healing the sick, and casting out demons. The particular time and locality chosen Vienna Gal. by Rubens for his splendid picture of 'the miracles of St. Ignatius' I cannot fix; but it must have been a later period, for Ignatius is here dressed as an ordained priest, and stands on the steps of an altar, which could not have occurred before 1540. One hand rests on the altar; the other is raised as in command. Near him stand his nine companions, Pierre Faber, Francisco Xavier, Iago Laynez, Alfonso Salmeron, Nicolas Bobadilla, Simon Rodriguez, Claude le Jay, Jean Codur, and Pasquier Brouet. These formed the first Society; all became historically memorable, and the heads here are so fine, so diversified, and have so much the air of portraits, that I think it probable Rubens had authority for each of them— (I speak, of course, of the picture, and not of the print, which, though fine, is in this respect defective). The principal group at the foot of the altar consists of a demoniac woman, with her relatives, among whom the son and the daughter of the afflicted creature are admirable: another demoniac, who has broken his bonds, lies raging and struggling on the ground. On the right, a young mother presents her sick child: another points out the saint to her two children; over the head of the saint are angels, who seem to chase away the hideous demons, disappearing in the distance. All the figures are life-size, and the execution, in the manner of Rubens, is as fine as possible.

'The Vision of St. Ignatius' represents the miraculous comfort afforded to him when on his way to Rome. Having gone aside into a little chapel to pray, leaving Laynez and his companions on the outside, he beheld the form of our Saviour, bearing his cross, who, standing before him, pronounced the words, '*Ego vobis Romæ propitius ero.*' There is another vision of St. Ignatius, which I have seen represented, in which our Saviour commands him to give to his new community the divine name. An angel generally holds a tablet, on which are the words ' *In hoc vocabitur tibi nomen.*' Both these subjects I have seen in the Jesuit churches.

' Loyola haunted by demons in his sleep,' is a fine sketch by Rubens.

The statue of St. Ignatius, cast in silver from the model by Pierre le Gros (in his usual bad taste), the glory round the head being of precious stones, was formerly in the Church of the Gesù at Rome, but disappeared soon after the suppression of the Order in 1773. An imitation of it now stands in the same place.

Prints of St. Ignatius are without number. I believe that the foregoing legend will sufficiently explain them.

ST. FRANCIS XAVIER, the Patron Saint and Apostle of the Indies, was born in 1505. He, also, was of a most illustrious Dec. 3, 1552. family, and first saw the light in his father's castle among the Pyrenees. He was sent to study philosophy and theology at Paris. Here, in the college of St. Barbara, he became the friend and associate of Loyola. It appears from his story that he did not at once yield up his heart and soul to the guidance and grasp of the stronger spirit. Learned himself, a teacher in the chair of philosophy, gay, ardent, and in the prime of life, he struggled for a while, but his subjugation was afterwards only the more complete. He took the vow of obedience; and when John III, King of Portugal, sent a mission to plant the Christian religion in the East, where the Portuguese were at one time what the Spaniards had become in the West, lords of a territory of which the boundaries were unknown, Francis Xavier was selected by his spiritual guide, Ignatius, as leader of the small band of missionaries who sailed for Goa: and, adds his biographer, a happier selection could not have been. ' Never was a summons to toil, to suffering, and to death, so joyously received. In the visions of the night,

he had often groaned beneath the incumbent weight of a wild
Indian, of ebon hue, and gigantic stature, seated on his
shoulders.   In those dreams he had often traversed tem-
pestuous seas, enduring shipwreck, famine, and persecution in
their most ghastly forms; and, as each peril was encountered,
his panting soul invoked yet more abundant opportunity of
making such glorious sacrifices for the conversion of mankind.   And now, when the clearer sense and the approaching
accomplishment of those dark intimations were disclosed to
him, passionate sobs attested the rapture which his tongue was
unable to speak.   He fell on his knees before Ignatius, kissed
the feet of the holy father, repaired his tattered cassock, and,
with no other provision than his breviary, left Rome on the
15th of March 1540, for Lisbon, his destined port of em-
barkation for the East.'[1]

The rest of his life was wholly spent in India, principally
in Japan and on the coasts of Travancore and Malabar.   By
such a spirit as his we can conceive that toils and fatigues,
chains and dungeons, would be encountered with unfailing
courage ; and death, which would have been to him a glorious
martyrdom, met not only with courage, but exultation.   But
ruffian vices, abject filth, the society of the most depraved and
most sordid of mankind,—for such were the soldiery and the
traders of Portugal, who were the companions of his voyages
from coast to coast,—these must in truth have been hard to
bear, these must have tried him sorely.   Yet in the midst of
these he writes of his *happiness*, as if it were too great; as if
it were beyond what ought to be the lot of mortals !   He
never quailed under obstacles ; never hesitated when called
upon : his cheerfulness equalled his devotion and his charity.
' Whatever may have been the fate of Xavier's missions or
the cause of their decay, it is nothing more than wanton
scepticism to doubt that, in his own lifetime, the apparent
results were such as to justify the most sanguine of his

---

[1] Essays in Ecclesiastical Biography.   My brief sketch of the Jesuit saints
is taken principally from these volumes ; from Baillet; and from Ribadeneira,
himself one of the early Jesuits, and for some time confessor to St. Francis
Borgia.

anticipations. Near Cape Comorin he appointed thirty different teachers, who, under himself, were to preside over the same number of Christian churches; many an humble cottage there was surmounted by a crucifix, the mark of its consecration to public worship; and many a rude countenance reflected the sorrows and the hopes which they had been taught to associate with that sacred emblem.'

It was the happiness of Xavier, that he died in the full belief of the good he had done, and of the unspeakable, the everlasting benefits which, in conferring merely the rite of baptism, he had obtained for hundreds of thousands of human souls, thereby saved from perdition.

He died in an attempt to reach China. Its jealous coasts were so guarded, that it was only by bribing a mercenary Chinese trader that he obtained the boon of being carried thither and left in the night-time on the shore, or concealed till he could travel to the city of Canton. He had reached the little island of Sancian, where the Portuguese had a factory; there he was abandoned by his guide and his interpreter, and, being seized with fever, he first took refuge on board a crowded hospital-ship, among the sick sailors and soldiers: growing rapidly worse, he entreated to be taken on shore; they took him out of the vessel, and laid him on the sands, where he remained for many hours, exposed to the extremes of heat and cold—the burning sun, the icy night-blast—and none were there to help or to soothe his last moments. A Portuguese, at length moved with a tardy compassion, laid him under a rude shelter; and here he breathed his last breath, regretting, Baillet. it is said, that he should die a natural death, instead of suffering a glorious martyrdom; but afterwards, repenting of this regret, he resigned himself to believe that all was good which was in accordance with the will of his Divine Master. He died in his forty-sixth year.

His body was buried in a little sand-hill near the shore; a cross still marks the spot. His remains were afterwards disinterred, and carried first to Malacca and then to Goa, where, soon after his beatification by Paul III., a magnificent church

was built in his honour.   He was formally canonised by
Gregory XV., in 1622, in the same year with St. Ignatius,
and the bull was published by Urban VIII. in 1623.

In the figures of St. Francis Xavier which are to be seen
very commonly in the Jesuit churches and in the prints published by his Order, he is represented in the habit of a priest,
wearing the surplice over a black frock: he is tall and robust,
generally bareheaded, and with a short, full, black beard; he
holds aloft the crucifix or presses it with uplifted eyes to his
bosom or bears the lily in his hand.

It does not appear that St. Francis Xavier arrogated to
himself the power of working miracles, but many were imputed
to him by his biographers.   In Japan he is said to have
imitated Moses in the wonders he performed: and it is also
said that the Bonzes of Japan emulated these, just as the
magicians of Egypt, with their vain enchantments, counter-
feited the miracles of Moses and Aaron.

The extreme puerility of some of these legends of St.
Francis Xavier contrasts very painfully with the truly Christian heroism of this extraordinary man, and with the real
majesty of his actions and his character.   His life was so
wonderful, so varied, that it needed no embellishment from
vulgar inventions; yet these have not been spared.   It is
with some regret I refer to them, but, as I am writing of
legendary Art, I must mention those which I have seen represented.

In Japan he healed the sick, cast out devils, and raised the
dead to life; and it is particularly recorded that at Cangoxima
he restored to life a beautiful girl.   His miracles are combined into one grand dramatic scene in the fine picture
painted by Rubens as a companion to the ' St. Ignatius '
already described.

Here St. Francis Xavier is standing on a kind of raised
pedestal or platform, from which he has been preaching to the
people : he wears his black habit and mantle ; the right hand
extended, the left pointed upwards.   Behind him, a novice of

the Order carries the book of the Gospel; in front is a man
raised from the dead; near whom is a group of three women,
one of whom removes the linen from his face, the others look
up to the saint, their features beaming with faith and gratitude.
Behind these is a group of a Japanese rising from his bier;
a negro removes the grave-clothes; a Portuguese officer, in
complete armour, looks up at the resuscitated man with amazement. A blind man is groping his way to the feet of the saint.
A lame man and several others complete the assemblage in
the foreground. In the background is a temple of classical
(not Indian) architecture, and a hideous idol tumbling from
its altar. The Virgin (or *Religion*) appears in the opening
heavens holding the sacramental cup; angels bearing the cross
seem floating downwards in a stream of light. There are
altogether more than thirty figures; and in vigour and harmony
of colour, in character, in dramatic movement, this is even a
more wonderful picture than its companion. Rubens painted
the two with his own hand. He received from the Jesuit
fathers one hundred florins a day while he worked upon them,
and they were suspended in their great church at Antwerp on
the festival in honour of the canonisation of St. Francis
Xavier in 1623. On the suppression of the Jesuit Order,
Maria Theresa sent the painter Rosa to purchase them for
her gallery, and paid for each picture 18,000 florins—about
£2000. They have since adorned the gallery of the Belvedere
at Vienna.

We have the 'miracles of St. Francis Xavier' by Poussin,
treated in his usual classical style, which, in this instance,
spoils and weakens the truth of the representation. The
Japanese look like Athenians, and the Bonzes might figure as
high priests of Cybele.

It is related that when Xavier was on his voyage to India he
preached and catechised every day, so that the vessel in which
he sailed was metamorphosed from a floating inferno, into a
community of orderly and religious men. Like the Vicar of
Wakefield in his prison, he converted his own miseries and

privations into a means of solacing the wretched, and awakening the most depraved and evil-minded to better hopes and
feelings. But the legend spoils this beautiful and faithful
picture of a true devotedness. It tells us that one day, as
Xavier was preaching to the sailors and passengers, his crucifix
fell into the sea, and was miraculously restored at his earnest
prayer, for a craw-fish or lobster appeared on the surface of
the waters bearing the crucifix in its claws. I have seen this
legend painted in the Jesuit churches, and well remember the
pulpit of a little chapel in the Tyrol, dedicated to St. Francis
Xavier, on the top of which was a carving of a lobster holding
the cross or crucifix in its claws. It is also related that St.
Francis multiplied the fishes in the net of a poor fisherman.
This also I have seen represented, and at first I supposed it to
allude to *the* miraculous draught of fishes, but it was explained
by this legend.

There is a picture in the Fitzwilliam Museum at Cambridge,
which represents a vision of St. Francis Xavier. It is by one
of the Caracci.

St. Francis Xavier preaching to the Pagans in the East, is
a very common subject. So is the death of the saint, of which
I remember two good pictures : one by Carlo Maratta, in the
Gesù ; and another, remarkable for the pathos and the beauty
of the treatment, by Gianbattista Gauli, in the Church of the
Jesuit novices at Rome.

S. Andrea-
in-Monte-
Cavallo.

A picture by Seghers, which I only know from the engraving of Bolswert, represents St. Francis Xavier, in his
sleepless nights, comforted by a vision of the Blessed Virgin,
surrounded by a glory of angels.

I have seen a picture entitled ' St. Francis Xavier baptising a Queen of India,' which probably refers to the baptism
of the Queen of Saxuma in Japan : she was converted by
the beauty of a picture, which Xavier had shown her, of
the Madonna and the Infant Christ ; 'but,' adds the faithful historian, ' her conversion was merely superficial.' The
Japanese queen contemplating with reverence and admiration
the image of the Virgin-mother would be a most picturesque
subject.

On the whole, I have never seen a picture of St. Francis Xavier which I could consider worthy either of him, or of the rich capabilities of character and scenery with which he is associated.[1]

The third great saint of the Jesuit community is ST. FRANCIS BORGIA. His family was at once most illustrious and most infamous. On one side he was nearly allied to the Emperor Charles V.; on the other he was of the same race as Alexander VI. and Cæsar Borgia. Hereditary duke of Gandia, a grandee of Spain, distinguished in his youth and manhood as courtier, soldier, statesman; a happy husband, a happy father,—nothing that this world could offer of greatness or prosperity seemed wanting to crown his felicity, if this world could have sufficed for him. But what was the world of this enthusiastic, contemplative, tender, poetical nature? It was the Spanish court in the sixteenth century; it was a subserviency to forms from which there could have been but two means of escape,—that personal emancipation which his position rendered impossible, or the exchange of the earthly for the spiritual—I will not say bondage, but—obedience. The manner in which this was brought about strikes us like a *coup de théâtre*, but has all the authority of a fact, and all the solemnity of a sermon.

Several events of Borgia's young life had fostered in his mind a deep religious feeling, 'a melancholy fear subdued by faith.' The death of the poet Garcilasso de la Vega, his dear and intimate friend; some dangerous maladies from which he had with difficulty recovered,—had predisposed him to set but little value upon life, although his love for his beautiful consort Eleonora de Castro, a numerous family of hopeful children, and the high employments to which he was called

---

[1] For an account of the miracles of St. Francis Xavier performed in Japan, see the Life of the saint by the Père Bouhours, translated by Dryden, 1688.

3 L

by his sovereign, had filled that life full of affections and
duties.   He was in his twenty-ninth year when the Empress
Isabella, the first wife of Charles V., died in the bloom of her
youth and beauty, and at a moment when her husband was
celebrating his most brilliant triumphs.   Borgia as her master
of horse, and his wife Eleonora as her first lady of honour,
were bound to attend the funeral cavalcade from Madrid to
Granada, where Isabella was to be laid in the Capilla de los
Reyes.   The court ceremonial also required that, at the moment
when the body was lowered into the tomb, the duke should
raise the lid of the coffin, uncover the face, and swear to the
identity of the royal remains committed to his charge.   He
did so—he lifted the winding-sheet, he beheld the face of the
beautiful and benign empress who had been his friend not
less than his sovereign lady.   It was a revelation of unspeakable horror, a sight the fancy dare not attempt to realise.   He
took the required oath; but, in the same hour, made a solemn
vow to renounce the service of the earthly and the perishable
for the service of the heavenly and imperishable ;—to bend
no more to mortal man, but only to the unchangeable, eternal
God.

Yet this vow could not be at once fulfilled.   The idea of
throwing off his allegiance, of forsaking his Eleonora, or withdrawing her from the world and from her children, never
entered his mind; and in the meantime the Emperor appointed him viceroy of Catalonia.   He repaired to his government; give himself up to active duties; attended to the
administration of justice ; cleared the country of robbers ;
encouraged agriculture; founded schools.   At Barcelona,
while occupied with plans for the education of the people,
he became acquainted with one of the Jesuit Society, then
in its infancy—Father Aroas.   Pleased with his intelligence
and with the grand and comprehensive plan of education
conceived as the basis of the new community, he entered into
correspondence with Loyola, and thenceforth became but
as an instrument in the hands of that wonderful man.   The
death of his wife, by which he was at first struck down by
grief, emancipated him from the dearest of his earthly ties ;

but his long-considered resolve to quit the world was executed at last with a deliberation and solemnity worthy of himself. He spent six years in settling his affairs and providing for the welfare of his children; then, bidding a last farewell to every worldly care and domestic affection, he departed for Rome to place himself and every faculty of his being at the feet of St. Ignatius. That sagacious chief sent him to preach in Spain and Portugal; calculating, perhaps, on the effect to be produced on the popular mind by seeing the grandee of Spain, the favourite and minister of an emperor, metamorphosed into the humble Father Francis. It was in this character that he visited his cousin Charles V. soon after his abdication. What a conference must that have been!

In 1555, Father Francis was elected the third General of his Society, and filled the office for seven years. Returning to Italy after an absence, he was taken ill at Ferrara, and just lived to reach Rome, where he died, spent with fatigues. He was at first buried in the Gesù at Rome, near his predecessors, Loyola and Laynez; but, by order of his grandson, the Cardinal Duke of Lerma (the famous minister of Philip III.), his remains were exhumed, and borne in state to Madrid, where they now lie. To the last he had firmly refused to lend the sanction of his name and co-operation to the Inquisition; to the last he was busied with the great scheme of education devised by Loyola, but perfected by himself. He was beatified by Pope Urban VIII. in 1624, but not canonised till 1716.

Such is the mere outline of the history of this interesting and admirable man;—a life so rich in picturesque incident, that we should wonder at the little use which has been made of it by the artists of his own country, did we not know to what a depth of degradation they had fallen at the time he took rank as a canonised saint; and it is in his saintly character only,—as the Jesuit preacher, not as the cavalier,—that he is generally represented. With regard to the proper character of head, we must remember that no *authentic* portrait remains of St. Francis Borgia. He absolutely refused, when

General of the Order, to allow any picture to be painted of
him. When he was seized with his last illness, he again
refused; and when, in spite of this refusal, in his dying
moments a painter was introduced into his room, he testified
his disgust by signs and gestures, and turned his face to the
wall. Those heads I have seen of him, particularly one
engraved for the Jesuit Society by Wierx, represent a narrow,
meagre face, weak in the expression, with a long aquiline
nose: altogether such a face as we do not like to associate
with the character of Francis Borgia. The picture by Velasquez, in the Duke of Sutherland's Gallery, I suppose to
have been painted about the period of his beatification. It
represents him on his arrival at Rome at the moment he is
about to renounce the world; he appears to have just dismounted from his horse, and, with only two gentlemen in his
train, is received at the door of the Jesuit College by Ignatius
Loyola, and three others of the Society, one of whom is probably intended to represent Laynez. The picture is deeply
interesting, but, considering the fame and acknowledged
powers of the painter, and the singular capabilities of the subject in expression, form, and colour, I confess it disappointed
me: it ought to be one to command—to rivet—the attention;
whereas it is flat and sombre in effect, and not very significant
in point of character.

Goya painted a series of pictures from the life of St. Francis
Borgia, which are now in the cathedral at Valencia. They
must be bad and unworthy of the subject, for Goya was a
caricaturist and satirist by profession, and never painted a
tolerable sacred picture in his life.

St. Francis Xavier baptising in Japan, with St. Francis
Borgia kneeling in the foreground, is the subject of a large
picture by Luca Giordano, painted at Naples for the church
of San Francesco Saverio,—it is said in three days,—thus
justifying his nickname of *Luca-Fa-Presto*. There are many
other pictures of St. Francis Borgia, unhappily not worth
mentioning, being generally commonplace; with the exception, however, of a very striking Spanish print, which I remember to have seen I know not where;—Borgia in his

Jesuit habit, with a fine melancholy face, holds in his hand
a skull crowned with a diadem, in allusion to the Empress
Isabella.

ST. STANISLAS KOTZKA, the son of a Polish nobleman and   Nov. 13,
senator, was among the first fruits of the Jesuit teaching, and   15:9.
distinguished for his youthful piety. He was educated till he
was fourteen, chiefly by his mother, studied afterwards at
Vienna, and entered the Jesuit community through the
influence of St. Francis Borgia. He did not, however, live to
complete his noviciate, dying at Rome at the age of seventeen.
The sanctity and purity of his young life had excited deep
interest and admiration, and he was canonised by Benedict
XIII. in 1727.

It is related that when he fell sick at Vienna, in the house
of a Protestant, an angel brought to him the Eucharist;
hence he is often represented lying on a couch with an angel
at his side. Prints and pictures of this youthful saint are
often met with. He is, or was, regarded as joint patron of
Poland with the young St. Casimir, and like him bears the
lily as his attribute.

In a picture by Pomerancia, he is represented caressing, and
caressed by, the Infant Christ.

One of the finest works of Carlo Maratta is the St. Stanislas,
over one of the altars in the Sant'-Andrea-in-Monte-Cavallo.   Rome.
It represents the young saint kneeling before a benign and
beautiful Madonna. In another part of the same church is a
statue of St. Stanislas by Pierre le Gros, once celebrated and
admired as a wonder of Art: the drapery is of black marble,
the head, hands, and feet of white marble; and he lies on a
couch of *giallo-antico*. Nothing can be worse in point of
taste; nothing more beautiful than the workmanship and the
expression of the head.

ST. LOUIS GONZAGA, eldest son and heir of Ferdinand   or St. Aloy-
Gonzaga, Marchese di Castiglione, was born in 1568. His   June 21,
mother, who watched over his education in his infant years,   1591.

had instilled into his mind early feelings of piety. The religious movement of the age, the influence of St. Charles Borromeo and of the first Jesuit fathers, no doubt combined with the impressions of his childhood and gave shape and consistency to the native bias of his mind. With some difficulty he obtained his father's consent to resign his heritage to a younger brother, and entered the Society of Jesus before he was eighteen. He continued his studies under the direction of his superiors, distinguished himself by his talent and his enthusiastic piety, and died in consequence of a fever caught in attending the sick during the ravages of an epidemic at Rome in the summer of 1591. He was in his twenty-third year. He was beatified by Gregory XV. in 1621, and canonised by Benedict XIII. in 1726. He is represented in the black frock of his Order, with a young, mild, and beautiful face, and holding a lily in his hand. The bas-relief in white marble, by the French sculptor Pierre le Gros, over the altar of the chapel of St. Louis in the ' Sant' Ignazio ' at Rome, is perhaps the best devotional representation of this young saint: he is ascending into heaven, borne by angels. It is, however, in the mean fantastic taste of the time.

There is a striking picture by Pietro da Cortona, representing all the Jesuit saints combined into a *Sagra Conversazione*. On one side stands St. Ignatius holding the volume of the Rule of his Order; on the other side St. Francis Xavier, holding the lily; in front St. Francis Borgia kneels, holding a skull on a book; behind St. Ignatius stands the two young saints, St. Louis and St. Stanislas; and behind St. Francis Xavier, the missionary-martyrs of Japan, holding their palms. There is a good print after this composition in the British Museum.

Eng. Klnk-
all, 1731.

The Jesuits have no female saint.

THE ORDER OF THE VISITATION OF ST. MARY.

THIS congregation of nuns was instituted in 1610 to receive those women who, by reason of their infirmities of body or mind, their extreme poverty, previous errors of life, or a state of widowhood, were excluded from the other regular communities.

The joint founders of this modern Order were ST. FRANCIS DE SALES, bishop of Geneva, and ST. JEANNE-FRANÇOISE DE CHANTAL, two saints of great and general interest for their personal character and influence, but popular rather than important as subjects of Art.

ST. FRANCIS DE SALES, of a noble family of Savoy, was born near Annecy in 1567. His mother, who had reared him with difficulty, and loved him with inexpressible tenderness, had early dedicated him in her heart to God, and it is recorded that the first words he uttered distinctly were, '*Dieu et ma mère m'aiment bien!*' and to the last moment of his life, love, in its scriptural sense of a tender all-embracing charity, was the element in which he existed. Jan. 29, 1622.

He was Bishop of Geneva from 1602 to 1622, and most worthily discharged all the duties of his position. He is celebrated for his devotional writings, which are almost as much admired by Protestants as by Catholics for their eloquence and Christian spirit: he is yet more interesting for his benign and tolerant character; his zeal, so tempered by gentleness. The learned Cardinal du Perron, famous as a controversialist, once said, ' If you would have the heretics convinced, bring them to me; if you would have them converted, send them to the Bishop of Geneva.' The distinction here drawn, and the feeling expressed, seem to me alike honourable to the speaker.

By the *unco guid* of his own time and faith St. Francis de Sales was blamed for two things especially. In the first place, he had, in his famous book, the 'Introduction to a Devout Life,' permitted dancing as a recreation. Even his eulogists think it necessary to explain and excuse this relaxation from

strict discipline;—and a fanatic friar of his own diocese had
the insolence, after preaching against him, to burn his book
in the face of the congregation: the mild bishop did not even
remonstrate.

The second subject of reproach against him was, his too
great gentleness to sinners who came to him for comfort and
advice.   The most lost and depraved of these he would address
in words of encouragement: 'All I ask of you is, not to despair!'   To those who remonstrated against this excess of
mercy, he contented himself with replying, 'Had Saul been
rejected, should we have had St. Paul?'

This good prelate died suddenly in 1622, and was canonised
by Alexander VII. in 1665.   Bossuet, Bourdaloue, and
Fléchier *enshrined* him in their eloquent homage.

Portraits and devotional prints and pictures of St. Francis de
Sales were formerly very popular in France.   In the churches
of the convents of the Visitation, and in the churches of the
Minimes, they were commonly met with.   The Minimes have
enrolled him in their own Order, in consequence of his extreme veneration for their patriarch St. Francis de Paula; but
if he is to be included in any Order, I believe it should be
that of the Augustines, as a regular canon or priest.

He was so remarkable for the beauty of his person, and the
angelic expression of his regular and delicate features, that
painting could hardly idealise him.   He is represented in the
episcopal cope, generally bareheaded; and in prints the usual
attribute is a heart pierced and crowned with thorns, and
surmounted by a cross placed within a glory of light.

The finest devotional figure of him I have ever seen is in
the large picture by Carlo Maratta, in the Church of the
Filippini (Oratorians) at Forli.

August 21,
1641.

STE. JEANNE-FRANÇOISE DE CHANTAL, the latest of the
canonised saints who is of any general interest, was the
grandmother of Madame de Sevigné; and some people will
probably regard her as more interesting in that relationship,
than even as a canonised saint.

Mademoiselle de Fremiot, for that was her maiden and secular name, was even as a child remarkable for her religious enthusiasm. One day a Calvinist gentleman, who visited her parents, presented her with some bon-bons. She immediately flung them into the fire, saying, as she fixed her eyes upon him, ' Voilà, Monsieur, comment les hérétiques brûleront dans l'enfer ! '

She did not, however, grow up a cruel fanatic, though she remained a devout enthusiast. She married, in obedience to her parents, the Baron de Chantal; at the same time making a secret vow, that if ever she were left a widow she would retire from the world and dedicate herself to a religious life.

Her husband died when she was in her twenty-ninth year, and for the next ten years of her life she was sedulously employed in the care and education of her four children ; still preparing herself for the fulfilment of her vow.

In the year 1610 she assisted St. Francis de Sales in the institution of the Order of the Visitation. Having arranged the future destinies of her children, and married her son advantageously to Mademoiselle de Coulanges, she prepared to renounce all intercourse with the world, and to assume the direction of the new Order, as ' *la Mère Chantal.*' Her children, who seem to have loved her passionately, opposed her resolution. On the day on which she was to withdraw from her home, her son, the father of Madame de Sevigné, threw himself on the ground before the threshold of her door. She paused for a moment and burst into tears ; then, stepping over him, went on, and the sacrifice was consummated.

Before her death, Madame de Chantal counted seventy-five houses of her Order in France and Savoy ; and, from its non-exclusive spirit, this community became useful as well as popular. When St. Vincent de Paul instituted the *Hospice de la Madeleine*, as a refuge for poor erring women, he placed it under the superintendence of the Sisters of the Visitation, called in France ' *Sœurs de Sainte Marie.*'

La Mère Françoise died in 1641, and was canonised by Clement XIV. (Ganganelli) in 1769. Madame de Sevigné did not live to see her ' *sainte Grande-Maman* ' receive the

honours of beatification; but, from various passages of her
letters, she appears to have regarded her with deep veneration,
and to have cherished for her sake 'une espèce de fraternité
héréditaire avec les Sœurs de Ste. Marie, qu'elle ne manquait
point de visiter partout où elle allait.'

Long before her canonisation, pictures and prints of La
Mère de Chantal, as foundress of her community, were commonly met with: the only subject from her life represents her
receiving from the hands of St. Francis de Sales the Rule of
the Order of the Visitation.

85 A Monk received into Paradise. (From the *Paradiso* of F. Angelico da Fiesola.)

INDEX.

PRINTED BY BALLANTYNE, HANSON AND CO.
EDINBURGH AND LONDON

www.ingramcontent.com/pod-product-compliance
Lightning Source LLC
Chambersburg PA
CBHW022128020426
42334CB00015B/810